PRINCES
of PIGSKIN
A CENTURY OF KERRY FOOTBALLERS

Introduction by

CON HOULIHAN

JOE Ó MUIRCHEARTAIGH & T.J. FLYNN

The Collins Press

Published in 2007 by
The Collins Press,
West Link Park,
Doughcloyne,
Wilton,
Cork

British Library Cataloguing in Publication Data

Ó Muircheartaigh, Joe
    Princes of pigskin : a century of Kerry footballers
    1. Gaelic football - Ireland - Kerry - History
    I. Title II. Flynn, T. J.
    796.3'3

ISBN-13: 9781905172511

Typesetting and design: Stuart Coughlan @ edit+
Font: Sabon, 11.5 point

Printed in Spain

PRINCES
of PIGSKIN
A CENTURY OF KERRY FOOTBALLERS

ACKNOWLEDGEMENTS

From the start, it was a pleasure and an honour to meet and speak to so many men and women associated with the story of Kerry football. In all, we interviewed over 200 people and each added an invaluable piece to the jigsaw. Without their time and effort, this book, simply, would not have been possible.

We would particularly like to thank Ray McManus at Sportsfile, Seamus O'Reilly of *The Clare Express*, Michael Brennan and Declan Malone at *The Kerryman*, Padraig Kennelly at *Kerry's Eye* and Kieran McCarthy at *The Kingdom* for opening their photographic libraries to us.

Shelagh Honan and John Kelly also did a wonderful job in photographing many Kerry legends. Special thanks to Weeshie Fogarty of Radio Kerry. He truly went beyond the line for us at various times and we thank him sincerely for his advice and assistance.

We would like to offer a huge thanks to Micheál Cotter, Fr Tom Looney, Pádraig Murphy, J.J. Barrett, Fr Jackie McKenna, Mick Finucane, the late Declan Horgan and everybody at the Kerry Association in Dublin for providing crucial insights.

Our editor at *The Clare People*, Gerry Collison, has been patient and supportive while we've completed this project and Noel, Vinny, Colin and John of the *People* also gave great advice. The Collins Press took this book on board wholeheartedly from the beginning and provided an invaluable support system and the staff at the Kerry County Library were always accommodating and welcoming.

Some of the players we spoke with have since passed away. Martin 'Bracker' O'Regan, Ned Roche, Liam Higgins, Eddie Walsh, Tim O'Donnell, Mick Falvey, Ted O'Sullivan, Timmy Healy and Tim Kennelly. They may be gone but their stories will continue to amuse and enthrall.

Finally, Joe Ó Muircheartaigh would like to thank Fiadh, Ella and Shelagh who provided the inspiration for the project. And for their support, T.J. Flynn says a sincere 'thank you' to his family, particularly his parents Tommy and Eileen, and to Laurie for her positive presence.

I ndiaidh a chéile a thógtar na caisleáin.

A kingdom wasn't built in a day.

Ancient Irish saying

Introduction

Con Houlihan

The ancient Chinese had the most advanced computers over 5,000 years ago. They were also dab hands at minting one-liners. I like this one especially: '*A man has a public life and a private life and a secret life.*'

You may think that the public life of the GAA has been well recorded – I have my doubts. It has, but only in modern times – that means since the coming of television. Earlier generations of those who reported hurling and Gaelic football loved the Association not wisely but too well. Unpleasant truths were brushed under the green carpet. Thus the private life was little known to the public.

There was also a secret life – that wasn't revealed at all. When you delve into the origins of Gaelic football in Kerry, you find surprising facts that some people would wish unrevealed. The new game got a good start in Kerry because the ancient game of cad or caid was long popular in the county.

Caid was an uncivilised 'game' but it was better than faction fighting – because weapons weren't allowed. Caid might have lasted much longer but for the invention of pneumatic rubber. Then the more perceptive people decided that there were better ways of keeping holy the Sabbath than brawling over a bull's scrotum stuffed with straw.

Facing page:
John Egan goes for goal in the 1982 All-Ireland final against Offaly.
(The Kerryman)

Because the name is associated with a famous English school, it tends to overshadow the probability that it originated in Ireland. Certainly it was well established in Kerry before the foundation of the GAA.

I have often said in pub and in print that Michael Cusack created Gaelic football by combining what he deemed the better elements of soccer and rugby – it wasn't that simple.

On mature reflection I realise that the early form of the young game was closer to rugby and bore little relation to soccer. In P.D. Mehigan's seminal book, *Gaelic Football*, you can see this for yourself.

'Masses of men drove into each other while the fleeter of foot waited on the outskirts.' That's from a report of an early All-Ireland. Cusack seems to have introduced his innovations gradually. Historians have told us that the GAA 'swept through the country like wildfire'. That is only half true: Hurling made a slow recovery – Gaelic football proliferated.

It became popular because it was a much safer game to play than rugby and much easier for spectators to understand. Killorglin Laune Rangers was the first Kerry club to reach the All-Ireland final – it was then much like the All-Ireland Club competition today.

Laune Rangers were originally a rugby club; they went with the tide when the new game took over.

Their captain, J.P. O'Sullivan, has an interesting niche in our sporting history. He was a wealthy merchant: one of his daughters, May, eloped with a local working man and went to live in London. His name was Paddy Breen; he returned from London to play for Kerry on occasions. One of his grandsons, Gary Breen, is well known in the green shirt of The Republic. One of J.P.'s sons, Dr Eamonn, was closely associated with Kerry teams a generation ago. He wasn't a coach or a manager; he minded the squad when they trained in the Fitzgerald Stadium. He was the master in the local Mental Hospital. Caid and its offspring, rugby, helped Kerry to become prominent in Gaelic football.

There was another factor: the number of primary teachers produced by the county was far above the national average. This increased with the coming of the new State and the aim to further the Gaelic language. Most of those who played the new game in Kerry and elsewhere were town dwellers. Farmers and farm workers couldn't participate fully. Keeping holy the Sabbath didn't exclude milking the cows and saving the hay in broken weather.

When Tralee's John Mitchels brought Kerry its first All-Ireland, all but a few of the players were 'townies'. The pattern continued: very few rural workers have won All-Ireland glory because they were tied to the land. When silage and the milking machines brought freedom, the rural workers were still absent from the roll of honour. By then they were almost extinct as a class.

Kildare and Kerry are credited with playing a great part in creating Gaelic football – their encounters in the All-Ireland final of 1903 caught the public imagination as never before. They met in the town of Tipperary in the July of 1905. It ended Kerry 1-4, Kildare 1-3. It was declared a draw.

It was hardly surprising: Kerry's 'goal' was of dubious validity. It came a few minutes from the end. The ball had gone into touch in a Kerry attack – a spectator kicked it back onto the pitch. A 'goal' resulted. The umpires were in doubt. A spectator hit the green-flag man smartly over the head with a bicycle pump and put up the flag.

The Central Council sensibly ordered a replay.

Who was the hero who put the ball back into the play and who was the brave man who hit the umpire on the head? The number of claimants resembled that of most who imagined that they were in the G.P.O. in Easter Week.

Life went on. The teams met again in August in the fair city of Cork – it ended at Kerry 0-7, Kildare 1-4.

The second replay was at the same venue in October. Kerry won by three points to two. It was a tearshed for Kildare – and seemingly a watershed for the new game.

Greater days were to come for Kerry when they won glory without the help of a 'player' in his street clothes or a man wielding a bicycle pump.

Between 1924 and 1932 came the first golden era: a magic flow brought six Championships. It was a bitter and barren period in Irish life: the Civil War ended in 1923 but the malady lingered on.

We have been told so often that the GAA healed the wounds bequeathed by the conflict that we tend to believe it. That was a psychological impossibility; the Association, however, helped to varying degrees in different parts of the country. In no county was the war more obscene than in Kerry – and there the Association achieved a kind of miracle.

John Joe Sheehy had been the leader of the anti-Treaty forces in west Munster; Con Brosnan had been a captain in the Free State Army; they played together in the team of the first golden era. That team grew up together – and collapsed dramatically to Dublin in the All-Ireland final in 1934. Three barren years followed. Kerry got to the semi-final in 1937. They met Cavan. The game was deemed a classic.

It is remembered for another reason. The GAA employed a brand-new commentator, a holy priest named Canon Hamilton. He was the ultimate proof of Ernest Hemingway's one-liner: 'Enthusiasm isn't enough.'

The good man hadn't done his homework – and so you heard something like this: 'A Kerry player gets the ball and kicks it towards the Cavan goal. A Cavan man kicks it back out.' I suppose you could say that he was a loose cannon. Michael O'Hehir had a soft act to follow.

Kerry had a good run between 1937 and 1941. Galway interrupted what might have been a five-in-a-row. The All-Ireland final of 1938 could fairly be described as bizarre – twice. Galway and Kerry were tied with perhaps a minute to go. Charlie O'Sullivan sent a ball winging over the bar from about 40 yards – Kerry folk rejoiced. Alas – the celebrations were premature. Seemingly the referee had signalled for full time while the ball was in flight.

The replay provided even more food and drink for thought. Galway were a few points ahead with about five minutes to go – some joker in the crowd blew a loud blast on a whistle. Galway's followers swarmed onto the pitch. Some of the Kerry players departed to their dressing place in Barry's Hotel. It took about twenty minutes for the stewards and the referee to clear the pitch.

The referee decided that time be played out. Kerry had difficulty in fielding a full team. Eventually play was resumed. Kerry got a point but were still a goal behind when the official whistle sounded. As time went by, several Kerrymen who had watched the game in their street clothes claimed to have been among the substitutes who played in those last five minutes.

Cork broke Kerry's monopoly in Munster in 1945 and went on to win the All-Ireland. Kerry stormed back in the following year and encountered Roscommon in the final. The Connacht champions dominated the game and led by six points with about three minutes to go. Many Kerry followers were on their way to the pubs when goals by Tom O'Connor and Paddy Burke brought a melodramatic finish. Kerry won the replay handsomely. Roscommon had a great team in that era; amazingly they haven't won the All-Ireland since 1944.

Life went on. It seemed that Kerry would never again achieve the dominance of the late '20s and '30s and the period between 1937 and 1941. Those were the romantic years when Kerry couples arranged their honeymoons for late September.

In 1975 we saw Kerry's imperial ambitions revived. A brilliant victory over champions Dublin was like a declaration of intent. Dublin frustrated the revival in 1976 but the best was yet to be. A modest man from the Barony of Iveragh was to lead Kerry into greener pastures.

Few people in The Kingdom think of him by his first name: Micko is reserved for the man from the Island. It hardly bothers O'Dwyer: he has brought common sense to the status of genius.

He steered Kerry to a glorious four-in-a-row run. History beckoned. Black puddings – and even white puddings – were displayed in rings of five. Nobody would have been surprised if some young woman had announced that she was about to give birth to quadruplets.

On the momentous day we saw history loom; Kerry led Offaly by four points with six minutes to go. Matt Connor pointed two frees but Kerry looked safe. Then came an action replay of the fable about the contest to see what bird could fly the highest.

The part of the wee wren was taken in Croke Park by Seamus Darby – his late goal turned dreams to dust.

Kerry and Mick O'Dwyer recovered and achieved a three-in-a-row. Then after 1986 came a sojourn in the wilderness when Kerry folk would have been happy with one-in-a-row. At last, after it seemed that the gods of football had deserted us, Páidí Ó Sé led Kerry to the winners' enclosure.

And though our achievements since 1986 are modest, the county has produced two superstars. Maurice Fitzgerald and Seamus Moynihan would be nap selections for the Irish team of all time.

We haven't done too badly.

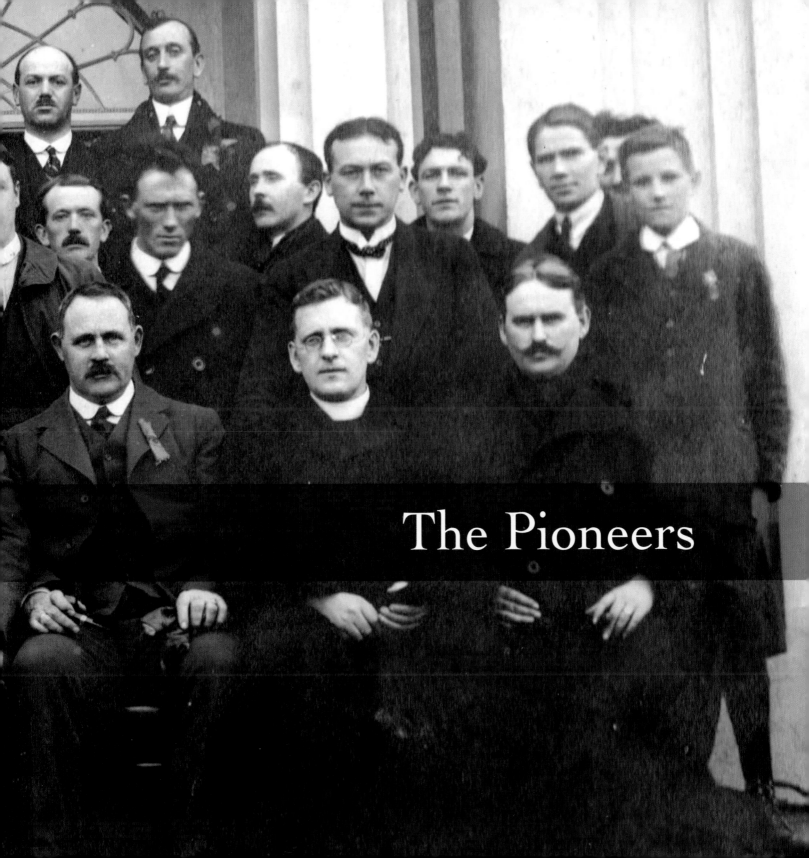

The Pioneers

Dick Fitzgerald

Fitzgerald sits at the beginning, the Statue of Liberty looking out over its people. The gateway to the new world.

Back at the turn of the twentieth century, when he was still a slip of a lad growing up on College Street, Killarney, the big story of Kerry football was a blank canvas in front of him. Dick Fitzgerald was one of the first to put his brushstrokes on it, to make a lasting impression. A pioneer, a visionary. An innovator.

He's remembered for a number of things. For rubber-stamping the green and gold as the county colours in 1913. For the sad, untimely manner of his death when, aged 46, he tragically fell from the roof of Killarney Courthouse, a 100 yards from where he was born.

He's remembered for the goals he scored and the role he played in Kerry's first five All-Ireland successes. Five titles in a career that began when Kerry was a barren county. But that's just the tip of the story.

From very early, Fitzgerald secured for himself the exciting life. He was the youngest member of Kerry's maiden 1903 All-Ireland winning team and he used the experience as a platform to propel himself.

Later, he would shape the football vista of the county. He organised games and established street leagues. Travelled to Clare and coached the county for their All-Ireland final in 1917. He delegated at Congress and refereed two All-Irelands. Fitzgerald began promoting football against a flinty background because these were tough, political times. Bullets sniped around corners. Games were suppressed by the British forces.

Around the time he was born his future club, Dr Crokes, was just off the ground and experiencing serious intimidation. The RIC was ordered to make its presence felt at club games and when club members met, it was common for the police to burst in on meetings. Outside, more RIC forces would gather, armed with batons. It was love in a cold climate.

As Fitzgerald's playing career was tapering away, his concern with politics was increasing and he became an active member in a local IRA column.

'He was involved with the "lads" for a period of time,' says Fr Tom Looney, a distant relation of Fitzgerald's. 'They'd be on the run for days, staying across on Tomies Mountain, across the Killarney lakes near O'Sullivan's Cascade. And

Previous pages:
The Kerry team at the McCarthy residence in Dunboyne, County Meath, where they stayed in the lead up to the All-Ireland final against Wexford in 1914. It was Kerry's third major final in Croke Park in two years.
(Paddy and Marie Healy)

Facing page:
Dick Fitzgerald, one of Kerry's greatest, in his own or any era.
(Seamus O'Reilly)

3

of course they'd have to get provisions over in order to survive. But it wasn't easy because every move was being watched. Paddy Dillon, my granduncle, was the Kerry goalkeeper in 1903 and he later lost an arm in an accident. He'd row a boat across the lake to where the lads were hiding out and drop them off all the provisions they needed. The RIC never suspected a thing. They thought, "What harm can a one-armed man do?"'

But Fitzgerald was eventually hauled in. After the Easter Rising of 1916 he was shipped off to Frongoch, an internment camp in north Wales once used to house German prisoners of war.

He spent the best part of a year there but it wasn't all doom and gloom and while locked up, he met an old friend – Michael Collins.

There were so many Irish interned there – hundreds – that Fitzgerald began organising games and the centrepiece was a tournament played on a county-by-county basis. A mini All-Ireland.

Kerry and Louth – two of the best teams in Ireland at the time – contested the final and Fitzgerald captained Kerry to a one-point win.

By now, he was was known as a wizard throughout the county for his football skill; his ability to swerve the ball from tight angles was his main weapon. In the 1903 All-Ireland final replay he fired over one free a few yards from the corner flag, having scored a last minute goal to draw the previous game.

In time, his face would be recognised throughout the country and word of his talent would travel over the ocean.

A fellow clubman of Fitzgerald's at Dr Crokes, Florrie O'Sullivan, had emigrated from Killarney to New York. With a huge Irish population in the cities of America's east coast, football was taking off. Trophies brought bragging rights in the tenements from Boston to Chicago and the American championship was a prized crown. Shortly after O'Sullivan touched down in his new land in 1906 he told the football fraternity of Fitzgerald and a telegram was sent to Killarney.

It asked that three men, 'Dick Fitzgerald, Paddy Dillon and another player', be sent over to the States to help New York win the championship. Money for the ship fare arrived in October and the three, Donie McCarthy making up the group, crossed the Atlantic. They spent over two months abroad, played three games and New York got return for their investment. They won the championship.

When the trio arrived back to Cobh on Christmas Eve and travelled to Killarney later that evening the whole town came out to greet them.

'It was a big deal, three fellows going to New York and coming back in a short space of time just to play football. It was unheard of at the time,' says Fr Looney. 'When they came to Killarney there was a procession through the streets for them.

Hundreds of people turned up. A pipe band welcome.'

The value of promoting the game in America opened up to Fitzgerald during this trip and he led Kerry on their first competitive journeys abroad in 1927 and 1929 – trips that would progress the legend of football in the county.

Before all this, he married Paddy Dillon's sister, Kitty, but a few years later she passed away and Fitzgerald was left broken hearted.

'At the time, Dick would have been disillusioned with politics as well and shortly after Kitty passed away, Dick was laid to rest himself,' says Fr Looney. It was late September 1930 and his death occurred on the eve of Kerry's All-Ireland final with Monaghan. It sent tremors across the country. Up to that point, he was involved as a selector for the county team and hasty arrangements were made to call off the game, but they quickly fell through.

'It was a national tragedy,' adds Fr Looney. 'Dick was a young man, an Irish hero and a footballer known all over.' The following morning, Gardiner Street church beside Croke Park was shoehorned with mourners who gathered for a special mass.

The game itself was played out with an eerie feeling. Both teams wore black armbands and after the Artane Boys Band finished the anthem, they played Chopin's 'Death March'.

When the game was done, a plan was drawn up to fund and build a monument to Fitzgerald. The public's backing shattered all expectations. A mere monument became a county-wide project and six years later, Fitzgerald Stadium was complete. A year on, it hosted the Tipperary versus Kilkenny All-Ireland hurling final.

'Kerry trainer Dr Eamonn O'Sullivan was a big believer in occupational therapy and he backed the project, so hundreds of patients at St Finian's worked on building the stadium,' continues Fr Looney. 'The main labour input came from them and it must have been a huge source of pride to see the hurling final played there in '37. Before the pitch was built it was a rolling hillside and they worked to dig that hill out for the field. But everybody got behind the project. It shows the love people had for Fitzgerald to say that the pitch was ready just six years after his death. They felt he had done a great service for Kerry. On and off the field.'

Fitzgerald put mediocrity on trial and left a legacy. In 1913 and 1914 he captained back-to-back All-Irelands – the first man to do so – and in between led Kerry to the Croke Memorial Cup.

These three victories began to cement the county's reputation. The sun was just shining on Kerry football.

TJF

Thady O'Gorman

The first All-Ireland title took longer than expected to arrive. A dozen years before Kerry's name was scratched into the record books, it looked like the door could be broken down at any moment.

Laune Rangers were progressing the case nationally, looking to bring an All-Ireland to the county. They were beaten in the final of 1892 by Dublin side Young Irelands and, a year before, the Ballyduff hurlers captured the All-Ireland title when they defeated Wexford.

A charge on Gaelic games was expected but shortly after the loss to Young Irelands things stalled. Kerry didn't reach another football final for eleven years and the hurlers fared no better.

That Laune Rangers side was led by J.P. O'Sullivan, the county's first football great, and once he had left the playing fields, his absence created a vacuum.

Still, that push for glory under O'Sullivan shone a light into the future and paved the way for one of the greatest rivalries to envelop Irish sport.

1892 was the first Kerry/Dublin All-Ireland final. It went ahead in Clonturk Park, Dublin, in front of a hostile crowd. It wasn't painted as the Culchies versus the City Slickers, like the later meetings of 1955 and 1975, but a sizzle of friction still pierced the air.

When the Laune Rangers team showed up, they were greeted by a seemingly fierce Dublin audience.

The Kerry Sentinel covered the game and gave it a noticably local colour. It said the Dublin support 'hooted and groaned the Kerrymen in the midst of play in a manner that was not alone discreditable to those guilty of it but calculated to take the spirit and heart out of the Killorglin men which they did effectually'.

It described the supporters' actions as 'an irritating and annoying exhibition of metropolitan clannishness'.

It wasn't because of the reception they received, but O'Sullivan didn't lead Kerry to glory that year. However, he did leave an invaluable legacy. His strength and ability as a forward were lauded in reports and his reputation spread and stood as a thing to be emulated – the first in a chain that would last beyond the next century, growing, evolving and expanding with the passing years.

Dick Fitzgerald, Sean Brosnan, Paddy Kennedy and Mick O'Connell. Mikey

Facing page:
An early Tralee team with O'Gorman pictured with the ball. It was the reorganisation of football in the county capital that kickstarted Kerry's emergence as a football force.
(The Kerryman)

Sheehy, Maurice Fitzgerald and Colm Cooper. All of them traceable along the chain, all emulating those that went before. J.P. O'Sullivan is the first link and as well as this gift, he also bestowed on the county a son, Eamonn, who would become involved in Kerry teams as trainer over the course of five decades.

Eamonn's scientific training methods, coupled with his psychological approach, would reap rewards for the county in years to come. As much as any one player's contribution to the county on the field, Dr Eamonn O'Sullivan's was equal off it. His philosophy and approach have been adapted by Kerry manager and Dr Crokes clubman, Pat O'Shea.

Eamonn was just a kid when Kerry would finally find success – Thady O'Gorman stepping into the captain's role once held by Eamonn's father – and finally Kerry were emerging from the wilderness. In the years leading up to the twentieth century, interest in football was beginning to taper off and newly-formed clubs were struggling to survive.

At the county convention of 1905 the chairman, Eugene O'Sullivan, tackled the issue head on. He looked for a concentrated effort and asked for clubs to work together to help the county prosper nationally.

The chairman also pleaded with clubs that were finding it difficult to survive to persevere. The clubs bought in.

In early April that year, the county began what was the 1903 All-Ireland championship – held over for two years because of delays – beating Cork in a Munster final and Mayo in the semi-final.

After more than a decade, the juggernaut was rolling again and slowly, football fever was beginning to take hold. The spark that finally lit the bonfire came with that year's All-Ireland final – which was replayed twice.

Thady played his part in catapulting Kerry to success. For years, he and his twin brother Jim were two driving forces among the Kerry forwards. When Dick Fitzgerald was added to the cocktail for the 1903 campaign, they had plenty of ammunition to blow teams out of their way.

Across Kerry, interest in the final against Kildare was picking up and when match day arrived, close to 15,000 people swarmed around the pitch in Tipperary Town. Because of a delayed train, the bulk of Kerry's support was late in arriving into Tipperary and the game was underway by the time they had their first glimpse of action.

It would have consequences on how the game was played out.

Without any stand or embankment from which to view the game, spectators lined the perimeter of the field, staying behind the playing lines as best they could. When the Kerry contingent arrived late and buoyed for action, further confusion rained down.

Spectators were buffetted and pushed, and the start of the second half was delayed because crowds flooded onto the field. When the game resumed, lines became blurred.

With ten minutes left, the crowd surged forward again and became involved in play. Hundreds stepped over the sideline as Kildare moved the ball behind the crowd.

Kerry players stopped playing, claiming the ball had gone out of play, but Kildare continued and goaled. Kerry protested but the score stood.

Two minutes remained when Dick Fitzgerald had a free and Kerry needed a goal. Jack Fitzgerald saved in the Kildare goal but a green flag was raised to signal a goal. Kerry led by a point and their fans had seen enough. They ploughed onto the pitch, swarming around players in a scene of bedlam. The referee, Pat McGrath, couldn't regain control of the situation and blew for full time.

Things hadn't settled before Kildare objected. The Central Council of the GAA ordered a replay and netted a record profit of £123 in the process. Again, it ended in a draw.

By now, fascination in the game had snowballed.

Kerry regrouped for a third game. So did Kildare. The Leinster champions trained together, while the Killarney and Tralee contingents of Kerry trained separately. In a large, sparsely populated county of peninsulas and mountains, the need for proper collective training was being forecast.

In 1963, Denny Breen from Castleisland, who played on the team of 1903, spoke to *The Irish Press* about preparations.

'Approaching a big game our employers would allow us to leave work early on Tuesday and Friday evenings. The team then travelled to Killarney where the Probables played the Possibles. That was as much collective training as we ever did.'

Kerry's preparations didn't hinder them. A disagreement over where the third final would be played added more spice and gate receipts of £270 for the final – played in the Cork Athletic Grounds – bombed the previous record out of the water. As Thady O'Gorman was hoisted off the field in Cork on 15 October 1905, the game was catching on. The bonfire was just about to blaze.

And, just like J.P. O'Sullivan, Thady left behind a son, Jimmy 'Gawksie' O'Gorman. He went on to win three All-Ireland medals with the county, strengthening the chain even more.

TJF

Rody Kirwan

More than anything, Rody was a sportsman. He travelled to every Olympics from 1924 to 1956 and took in the 1908 Games for good measure.

He was an Olympic judge in 1932, and was trackside as Bob Tisdall hurdled into history and Dr Pat O'Callaghan threw himself there by winning his second gold in the hammer.

Four years later, when Ireland boycotted the Games, Rody was spectating when Hitler left Berlin's Olympic Stadium rather than shake Jesse Owens' hand. Rody stayed around to see Jesse, shook his hand and got the signature of the most famous Olympian of them all.

Rody's marathon ended in Melbourne – an adventure that was nearly the death of him. On the return journey, the luxury liner *Arcadia* was tossed about like a cork by giant waves in the Bay of Biscay. Passengers were terrified, furniture flew and was reduced to matchwood. Some were badly injured – Rody just dodged his way out of trouble.

'I was used to tough situations on the football field,' he said of his ordeal. The gap of danger in the Bay of Biscay was nothing new – it's why football followers christened him Kerry Stonewall.

Kirwan got the nickname soon after coming to Kerry. The man from Kilmacthomas in Waterford worked for the National Bank and moved to Castleisland in 1903. He had already played inter-county football for Waterford and Wexford, so it was no surprise when Kerry called on his services.

Kirwan's reputation landed in Castleisland before he did. Big and strong, but an athlete as well. A 100-yards and 220-yards man, a hurdler, a high jumper, a hockey player and a rower. He didn't steal it – younger brother Percy won gold medals in the 100-yards, 220-yards and long jump at the 1906 Papal Games and won three British AAA championships in a row.

Percy Kirwan was also a footballer, captaining Waterford against Kerry in the Munster championship clash of 1903. Rody was selected on the Kerry team the same day but refused to play, saying he'd never line out against his own.

But it didn't stop the Kerry selectors picking Kirwan at full-back for the 1903 All-Ireland final and the Kerry Stonewall was born in the trilogy against Kildare.

He wasn't just a strong man, he had skill as well. In a famous incident against Kildare, Kirwan dribbled out of defence, kicked the ball past the

Facing page:
The Kerry team that won the 1903 All-Ireland title after three epic games with Kildare in 1905. Rody Kirwan is fifth from left in the second row.
(Seamus O'Reilly)

11

crouched Joyce Conlon and then jumped over him.

Kerry supporters roared the Waterford man on as one of their own. Soon after that game he produced a National Bank ledger in the dressing room. It was a famous day; Kerry's first All-Ireland was captured and Kirwan wanted to record the moment for posterity. He passed the ledger around and every man scribbled his name.

By the end of the decade, Kirwan had left Castleisland, but the names remained in his book.

He carried it everywhere with him. By 1948, the names of Jesse Owens, Dick Fitzgerald, Fanny Blankers-Koen, Dr Pat O'Callaghan, Pavo Nurmi and other superstars were also scratched between the covers of his book.

In September that year, Kirwan rapped his knuckles on the dressing-room door of the Waterford senior hurlers, after the county won their first All-Ireland senior hurling title, having won the minor title earlier the same day.

Kirwan was in his seventies by now but his face was known across Waterford as an All-Ireland medal winner and sports enthusiast. The door swung open and Kirwan flashed his most prized possession – the ledger.

'He embraced John Keane and Vin Baston and Rody asked the players to record their thoughts in the wake of what was an historic Waterford day,' explains his nephew, Jim Kirwan.

'He would have always said those notes and signatures were more important to him than Owens' or Nurmi's. But he brought his Irish roots with him whenever he travelled to Olympic Games. He said he cried whenever he heard the national anthem. And when "God Save the King", or "Queen" rang out, Rody stayed rooted to his seat.'

This is what his great friend from Waterford, Peter O'Connor, had done when he won gold in the hop-step-and-jump in the 1906 Intercalated Olympics in Athens. Rody Kirwan was true to his friend, in the same way he was true to Kerry. His time in Kerry may just have been an interlude in his travels but it stayed with him.

He carried memories of the county wherever he went. On Olympic or All-Ireland days Kirwan wore a gold chain watch presented to him on leaving Castleisland, as well as a chain carrying his Munster and All-Ireland medals.

Whenever Kirwan wanted a new suit of clothes he travelled to a drapery on Grafton Street owned by Kerryman, Dan Lyne. Kerry had seeped into Kirwan's blood, part of what he was.

Kilmacthomas was just as important. Nearly 40 years after winning his first All-Ireland he trained Erin's Hope, a breakaway club in his home parish, to win the 1942 Waterford junior hurling championship.

It was like an All-Ireland to Kilmacthomas and the parish's first All-Ireland man inspired them. 'He was full of enthusiasm for that team – running up and down the line like a teenager,' says Jim Kirwan. 'He was so fit that, when he was well into his seventies, he could straighten his legs and touch the ground with his fists.'

Fitness had him out on the field with players half a century younger than him. He was still the Stonewall.

He was eagerly looking forward to the Rome Olympics of 1960. He'd seen his brother Percy win his Papal Games gold medals there, but a return to Rome wasn't to be.

He died in January 1959 and the heavyweights came from Kerry to pay respects. Kerry GAA president John Joe Sheehy led the convoy, chairman Frank Sheehy was at his shoulder.

Kerry and Castleisland teammates Denny Breen and Denny Curran represented the 1903 team. When the coffin was going into the ground Curran and Breen produced an old Kerry jersey and draped it on the coffin. The jersey was being buried with Kirwan until his nephew Padraig Kirwan grabbed it for posterity. That jersey and those medals were Rody's badges of honour and they're still in the Kirwan family to this day.

JÓM

Batt O'Connor

How to Play Gaelic Football was written in 1914 by Dick Fitzgerald. GAA books were born with Fitzgerald's tome, an instructional manual for aspiring champions everywhere, and it was published just as Kerry won their fifth All-Ireland in eleven years.

'Such is the genius of the game itself,' wrote Fitzgerald, 'that while combination play will always be prominent, the brilliant individual gets his opportunities, with the result that, after the match is over, you will generally have a hero or two carried enthusiastically off the field on the shoulders of their admirers.'

He was writing from personal experience. His time on the field taught him values and foremost among these was the importance of fielding the football. It was the foundation of Kerry's dominance.

'We feel bound to maintain stoutly that the fielding of the ball should ever be recognised as an essential and most attractive feature of our game, and the rules which secure this attribute of Gaelic football should be allowed to stand in the Gaelic code.'

This simple philosophy made Fitzgerald a huge fan of Batt O'Connor. O'Connor wasn't Fitzgerald's exact midfield prototype in that speed wasn't his forte, but he was still one of the best because of his ability to field the football. According to Fitzgerald, 'our very best midfielders, like Buckley, B. O'Connor, C. Murphy and O'Shea' were 'sure fielders of high balls, full of vigour, able to tackle well, quick on the ball and great stayers'.

O'Connor had these qualities and bucked the trend by making the Kerry team despite coming from the footballing outpost of Dingle. Because of its location, Dingle had little impact on Kerry's early story but it did have tradition. The peninsula was a stronghold of the game in the decades before Michael Cusack and Maurice Davin drafted the first set of football rules in 1885.

West Kerry's game was called caid – they were crude, rough-and-tumble affairs that took up Sunday afternoons. Possession was everything; holding on to the pigskin and crossing the opposing parish boundary meant victory.

Fielding was caid's most spectacular feature and O'Connor used this background to put Dingle on the Kerry football map – he was the first Dingle man to wear the Kerry jersey. He did that in a brief but spectacular career where he was said to be without peer as a fielder of the football.

*Facing page:
In O'Flaherty's Bar in Dingle, Gerry O'Connor admires the Croke Cup won by his father Batt in 1907 as Fergus O'Flaherty looks on.*
(John Kelly)

'Dick Fitzgerald's book says it all,' says Batt's son, Paddy O'Connor. 'Fielding has always been a west Kerry thing, but what has been forgotten is that Batt learned a lot of his football in Cork when he played with the famous Nils Desperandum team like Dick Fitzgerald before him. When he came back to Kerry he started making county teams.'

The Nils were Munster champions in 1901 but, at sixteen, Batt was too young to make the team. In the following years he was drafted onto the team during his four-year stay in the city where he served his time as an apprentice bootmaker.

'When he came back to Dingle he really started making a name for himself as a footballer,' says another son, Gerry. 'People told me that through his performances for Dingle there was no keeping him off the Kerry team.'

The first great Dingle team – The Gascons – was built around O'Connor. In time, they became known as 'the princes who never wore the crown' because, despite valiant effort and heroic performances with O'Connor in the gap, they couldn't break John Mitchels' stranglehold on the county championship.

However, such was O'Connor's impact on club football that the Mitchels, who had control of the selection of the Kerry team back then, turned around and gave him his inter-county spurs in 1907.

Kerry were in transition, having lost the 1905 All-Ireland to Kildare and the Munster final to Cork the following year. In 1907, Kerry didn't even reach a Munster final. The county board went into meltdown that year after county secretary, T.F. O'Sullivan, left Kerry for Dublin and it wasn't until September 1907 that the board was up and running again. So was Batt O'Connor.

By then, he had set up his own bootmaking business in Dingle. Business and football flourished. On the field he won Munsters, a Croke Cup and an All-Ireland. Following these successes, he won a lucrative contract to boot the British Army garrison billeted in Tralee.

'The British Army were good to Batt,' says Paddy O'Connor. 'At one stage he had ten or twelve tradesmen in his workshop making boots and Sam Browne belts for the British. Then he got the Dingle team going. He was captain and organiser of the team.'

It was west Kerry's first coming – a Lispole team trained by Thomas Ashe reached the county final in 1907, but were beaten by Mitchels. That same year, Lispole's Paddy Casey won his second All-Ireland with Dublin Kickhams – he was west Kerry's first All-Ireland winner.

Batt O'Connor was the second in 1909 after his performances with the Dingle Gascons, on their march to the 1908 county final, won him rave reviews. Mitchels beat them that year, but they then turned around and made O'Connor vice-captain of the Kerry team they picked.

The biggest review of all came in death, as the Iveragh correspondent of *The*

Kerryman penned this tribute in 1931:

'As a footballer on the Kerry team his exploits were second to none. In fact, our victory over Macroom at Cork Park in 1909, which was won by Kerry in the last three minutes, was entirely due to Batt's long and brilliant kicking from the centre of the field to our forwards.

'We were beaten and badly beaten by the Macroom men for 55 minutes, when somebody in the stand shouted 'lash, Daddy lash', as the fair-haired Gascon raced for the ball. He lashed and what a lash.

'It reached Dickeen [Fitzgerald] and as Carberry [renowned GAA correspondent P.D. Mehigan] said, "The old dog settled himself. It was his or his county's last chance. Right across the goalmouth he swung it with beautiful accuracy. In raced Sullivan and Skinner and the goalie stood no chance".

'What splendid fielding and kicking there was for the remaining two minutes with Batt's fair hair waving amongst our men, who now pinned the Corkmen to the posts.'

It was O'Connor's finest hour. Kerry beat Louth in the final and he had Dingle's first All-Ireland. Ten other Dingle players have done the same on the field of play in 100 years – Batt O'Connor at midfield through to Tommy Griffin at midfield. Among the ten is Batt's grandson Vincent O'Connor – another midfielder who came in at full-back in 1979. Then there was John 'Connie' O'Connor – Batt's son and Vincent's father – who won his All-Ireland with Galway in 1938 against Kerry.

'It could be unique that the three of us have All-Irelands,' says Vincent. 'Batt started it all by getting the Gascons going way back then. That's where we got our football. He showed the way for a lot of people around here.'

Showed the way in America too, as Batt's son, Micheál O'Connor, found out in the '50s. He was holidaying in San Francisco, where Batt died and was buried. 'My father lived here for a few years,' Micheál told a bartender in the city's Sunset district, 'O'Connor was his name and he was big into football.'

The bartender remembered the man as Batt. It turned out he had a bootmaking shop across the road and trained the local football team.

'Everyone knew him as the man who won an All-Ireland with Kerry,' he told Micheál.

He was Sunset's prince.

JÓM

Austin Stack

Austin Stack turned 21 in 1900. He had been brought up with the GAA and the dawn of the new century brought new hope for old dreams. Like everyone associated with Kerry football, he wanted to win All-Irelands, but realised that a new approach was needed.

After a glorious start, Gaelic games in Kerry had fallen on lean times. That start came when Stack's father, Moore Stack, founded the county's first ever GAA club in Tralee. It started with a bang when Moore Stack organised the first athletic meeting under the auspices of the GAA on 17 June 1885.

There were running, jumping and throwing events, games of hurling and football. The GAA sports day caused uproar among Tralee's upwardly mobile sporting elite because it clashed with the annual jamboree organised by the County Kerry Athletic and Cricket Club under the auspices of the Irish Amateur Athletic Association.

The GAA even won the day, drawing a crowd of 12,000 while only 1,000 turned up at that IAAA event. It was expected that Gaelic Games would sweep through the county like a bush fire, particularly with the high watermarks provided by the Ballyduff hurlers and Laune Rangers footballers.

But, towards the end of the decade, the fires had almost burned themselves out as clubs from other Munster counties doled out provincial football titles between them.

Erin's Hope of Waterford, Nils, Dohenys and Fermoy of Cork, the Commercials of Limerick and Arravale Rovers of Tipperary all won titles in the mid-to-late 1890s. Kerry was being left behind while Tralee, where it all started in 1885, was dying.

'He was appalled by the Cinderella status of the national pastimes, in particular Gaelic football and hurling, vis-à-vis rugby and cricket in his native town and resolved to do something about it,' wrote Stack's biographer, Anthony Gaughan.

Against a backdrop of mounting apathy towards the GAA and possible extinction in Tralee, Austin Stack decided to act. He called a meeting in the old National League Rooms on Tralee's Mall in 1900.

The meeting came about after a chance encounter between Stack and Maurice McCarthy. They talked for hours about the decline in football standards in Tralee and the surrounding district. To bring structure to their debate they convened a special meeting.

Facing page:
*Austin Stack
– footballer,
administrator and
a fighting man who
became a minister in
the First Dáil.*
(Seamus O'Reilly)

Austin Stack took the chair, while Maurice McCarthy came in from Castleisland. Others around the table included James and Thady O'Gorman, Denny Curran and Con Healy. All of them went on to win All-Irelands.

The meeting ended with a resolution to reform the Tralee John Mitchels club that had lapsed for a number of years. It was here that Thady O'Gorman was appointed captain, while Austin Stack and Maurice McCarthy were made honorary secretaries.

A new era dawned. Within two years, Stack cemented his place on a Kerry team led by the Mitchels, while he organised the team off the field and his private purse paid for expenses incurred during the training of the Kerry team. It was a similar story on his regular excursions to Munster Council and Central Council meetings.

Stack's most important journey of all was to the 1903 Leinster final between Kilkenny and Kildare that went to three games. Stack was the Kerry spy in the crowd to note the handpassing and combination play of the Kildare men. It made for a well-prepared Kerry in the All-Ireland final against Kildare.

'The series of matches between Kerry and Kildare did a great deal to further the development of the GAA,' noted Anthony Gaughan, 'as the fixtures attracted the biggest attendances up to that time and the association was given much favourable publicity in the press.'

Kerry retained the title the following year with Austin Stack as captain. At the same time, he was honorary secretary of the Kerry County Board, later serving as chairman and president and representing the county on the Munster and Central Councils.

'At the 1908 Congress,' says Gaughan, 'as a result of a motion passed by Stack, it was decided that all GAA accounts should be audited by chartered accountants. Largely owing to his initiative, the Kerry team was given a period of training in preparation for the replay of the Croke Cup final against Louth in 1913.'

Collective training was born and, for two weeks before the game, they came together in Tralee under the supervision of noted athlete Jerry Collins, who acted as coach, and Billy 'Boxer' O'Connor who trained the team.

'The training became a ritual,' wrote Pat 'Aeroplane' O'Shea in his unpublished memoirs. 'Sprints, skipping, physical jerks, practice with the ball and trial games twice a week.'

It was Kerry's training template for the next 50 years, modified and perfected by Dr Eamonn O'Sullivan.

There was also another side to Austin Stack. Like his Fenian father, he embraced the freedom movement. The GAA volunteer became the Irish Volunteer and commandant of the Kerry Brigade in 1916.

For planning to spring Roger Casement from Tralee Barracks in 1916, Stack was given twenty years in jail, only to be released under the general amnesty in 1917. He was arrested again in 1918 for Sinn Féin activities and went on hunger strike in Crumlin Road Jail. By 1919, he was made Minister for Home Affairs in the First Dáil, but also spent time in Strangeways Prison before escaping.

Stack was one of the key figures in the prosecution of the War of Independence, but football never left him. The respect in which he was held was such that Kerry refused to play the 1923 All-Ireland until he was released from Mountjoy Prison and, in 1925, the Rock Street club was renamed Austin Stacks in his honour.

Kerry footballers of all political colours also turned out in force at Stack's funeral in April 1929 when his hunger striking ways of old took the ultimate toll. He was only 49 years old when he was buried in the patriots' circle next to the republican plot in Glasnevin Cemetery.

Ireland lost a republican diehard; Kerry GAA lost its president. To republican and GAA man Brian O'Higgins was left the last word at the graveyard.

'One of our greatest of our beloved dead lies in the grave – great in his patriotism, great in his fearlessness, great in his unselfishness, great in his humility and greatest of all in that glorious charity which governed every action of his life and won for him that love that cannot die.'

He was talking about Austin Stack's football as much as his politics.

JÓM

Paddy Healy

Paddy Healy was a turf-cutter, otter-snarer and two-time All-Ireland medal winner who lived in the heart of east Kerry on the banks of the Abhainn Uí Croí River, at the foot of a mountain with a wild and beautiful name, the Token Fire.

It was here, on his farmland, that he and his brother, Con, founded the Headford GAA Club in 1925 which, in turn, gave life to the present day Glenflesk Club.

Headford thrived in post-Civil War Kerry. The rough political climate had eased and, in the shadows of the Token Fire, there was a hunger for games.

Headford filled a huge void. Camogie, football and hurling were all played. Hordes travelled to Healy's field on the edge of the river for tournaments and training, and things were progressing better than anyone could have imagined until the club ran into some competition.

A dance hall opened at nearby Balnadeega and a large chunk of the Headford players scattered from the field for the vices of music and porter, which were available at the new establishment.

Immediately, the Headford club was in a bind. Some Sundays they couldn't even muster a full team and something had to be done to bring the locals back to the football field.

A meeting was called and a light popped in the head of one hardcore Headford man. 'Give them the music while they're playing the football,' the genius suggested. His advice was heeded and the Headford men began building a wooden platform at one corner of the field.

When it was complete, it was large enough to hold eight set dancers and a fiddler, who was paid each weekend to play music, while the footballers of the club competed or trained. Slowly, the players came back to this scene of madness and beauty. Music wafting through the air while out on the field, they divided their attention between the dancers on the stage and the flight of the pigskin.

'They kept it going for a while but something like that couldn't last long term,' said Paddy's son, Timmy, who also played for Kerry. 'Growing up, I remember the platform lying idle for years.'

Long before the Headford team sprang up, Paddy Healy made a name for himself with the Dr Crokes Club as a high-fielding centre-back.

He was on the cusp of his prime as a footballer when a series of dramatic

Facing page:
Paddy Healy's daughter Bridie O'Shea, mother of Kerry manager Pat O'Shea, pictured with the Croke Memorial Cup in Killarney. (Shelagh Honan)

events halted his progress with Kerry. In 1910, the county failed to defend their All-Ireland title. For years they had complained to the Great Southern Railway – seen to be hostile to the national games – about travelling conditions. Players were herded into cramped carriages for long journeys and the situation finally came to a head that year.

A week before the All-Ireland final with Louth, Kerry pulled out of the game until the company improved travel conditions. The Railway chiefs didn't budge. Louth were declared All-Ireland champions and the move shocked the people of the county. A public challenge was later made by Kerry for Louth to put the championship on the line in a one-off game, but the Leinster county didn't reply. It left a bitter taste in Kerry.

Then, the following year, more calamity arrived. Just as the county final between big rivals Tralee Mitchels and Dr Crokes was coming to an end, the Killarney players walked off the field in another protest, automatically suspending themselves for six months. Kerry lined out without their Dr Crokes contingent and lost to Waterford in the Munster semi-final.

By 1912, all squabbles had been put to bed and a united effort was being made to find glory once more.

When Kerry faced Antrim in the All-Ireland semi-final, they knew nothing of the Ulster team and expected to brush them aside with ease, like Cork had done the previous year.

The team stayed at Caffrey's Hotel in Dunboyne the night before the game and one of the travelling party got married that evening. A chunk of the Kerry squad went along to celebrate.

'Paddy didn't drink at all but he said the players came in at all hours that night,' revealed Timmy. 'The next day, one of the lads was still half-drunk. He [Paddy] had to fish him out of the Kerry net at one stage and get him back on his feet.'

Writing in his memoirs, Kerry midfielder Pat 'Aeroplane' O'Shea also gave a nod to the laxed attitude. 'One of our backs, who had to work until six o'clock [the day before the game], travelled all night and arrived at the hotel as the sun rose over Dublin Bay. A very poor team could have beaten Kerry that day.'

It wasn't surprising, then, that Antrim made it to the final and Healy was still waiting for his first shot on the big stage.

Things improved after this. For three years, the GAA had spoken about financing a fitting memorial for the first patron of the association, Dr Thomas William Croke. The idea festered until a national tournament was announced in 1913, to be run using a similar format as the championship.

When Kerry and Louth made the final, it was time to settle old scores. The game was vigorously advertised and both teams promised victory. The Croke Memorial

Cup final caught the imagination of the Irish public like no other game before.

What's more, it was the first game when teams lined out with fifteen players, as opposed to the traditional seventeen. More space, therefore better football and more entertainment the GAA said. The people bought in and the largest crowd to ever attend any sporting event in Ireland showed up that day. Healy was at midfield for Kerry but the game ended in a draw. Seven weeks passed before the replay went ahead on 29 June.

In the meantime, the fires were stoked some more. Louth had employed two soccer coaches from Belfast to help with preparations. Kerry went on the record saying they wouldn't leave a final after them this time. The atmosphere sizzled. If they had the media and technology that's available today, this would be pay-per-view stuff. Premium rate.

Close to 50,000 paid in – twice that of the drawn game – and thousands more looked on from the banks of the canal and rooftops of Jones' Road. Gate receipts alone allowed the GAA to purchase the field at Jones' Road and turn it into the biggest tribute possible to Dr Croke.

Aeroplane O'Shea recorded the hours before throw in:

'At twelve, we had a light meal – tea and buttered toast. About one o'clock we were driven to Wynns Hotel, taken upstairs, ordered to tog out, but without boots and then went to bed. As zero hour approached we put on our football boots, donned our overcoats and were driven on sidecars to Jones' Road.'

They walked out onto a field that had been transformed into a Gaelic coliseum. The game had atmosphere and hype. Kerry won and the frustrations of the two previous years were washed away.

Healy had secured a medal he always considered more precious than any All-Ireland.

TJF

Maurice McCarthy

Dick Fitzgerald and Maurice McCarthy won five All-Irelands each and dominated Kerry football in the first two decades of the twentieth century. Fitzgerald was the superstar of his day whose fame spread way beyond Kerry. McCarthy's part in the story was just as significant but was left on the shelf of Kerry football history.

In other ways, they also inhabited different worlds.

Fitzgerald was the star forward imbued with style and dash – a 'scientific footballer' the language of the day called him. Then, off the field, he enjoyed as big a media profile as any player of his era.

Maurice McCarthy was a back, square-jawed in attitude, and one who favoured steel over style any day. As for media profile, it was virtually non-existent as McCarthy didn't court publicity like Fitzgerald did.

Yet, media attention eventually came his way over 40 years after he had retired from inter-county football for the last time. It happened in the mid-1950s when McCarthy was into his seventies and out to prove that he was a throwback to a time when men were made of steel.

Despite his advancing years, McCarthy had the physical fitness of many people half his age. It came from his obsession with cycling, he eschewed the mod con of the motor car and didn't have too much time for trains either over the railway company's treatment of the Kerry team in 1910.

The years rested very lightly on his saddle, as one famous excursion that finally had him thrust into the spotlight proved. It came about after McCarthy's son, Dan Joe, who was a principal teacher in Liscannor, County Clare, took ill and was taken to Merlin Park Hospital in Galway.

Ireland had a proper railway network back then and a train to Limerick with a connection to Galway would have had Maurice in Merlin Park in four hours. However, Maurice wouldn't hear of the train, or the car either.

'When he got something into his mind, that was it,' says his granddaughter Catherine O'Connor, 'and straight away he said he was cycling to Galway. He was out the back making sure his bike was ok.

'My father Bill Myers got him a good bike for the journey, one that belonged to the insurance agent John Fitzgerald who looked on it as a great honour to give his bike to my grandfather.'

Facing page:
Maurice McCarthy, second from right on back row, with family in the 1950s, at the time they tried to dissuade him from cycling from Tralee to Galway.
(Maire Vaughan)

McCarthy left Tralee at 4am with a handful of sandwiches on his back carrier. 130 miles were ahead of him but he faced into the journey as if it were a short sprint up the road. It helped that he knew the track ahead – not that he stopped to admire the familiar territory en route.

In 1907, Maurice had captained Kerry to Croke Cup success over Mayo in the Ennis Showgrounds. Still, there was no time for a stopover down memory lane when he landed in Ennis.

'My father couldn't believe it when he arrived at the hospital,' says Dan Joe's son, John McCarthy. 'Straight away he tried to convince him to get the train back instead of cycling. In the end, he nearly had to force people in the hospital to put him on the train and not let him cycle home.'

It was a rare defeat for McCarthy but, by the time he arrived back in Tralee, word had spread around the town of his marathon journey. He was a topic of conversation at street corners. They talked about him from the altar as well.

'I went to evening devotions in Boherbee Church with him the Monday after he came back from Galway,' says Catherine O'Connor, 'and they were talking about him there too. He became famous for what he did, a bit of a hero but he just passed it off.'

Maurice McCarthy also made light of his football ability, despite a career that spanned fifteen years. He was there when it all started, one of the pioneers who opened a window to a new world with the all-conquering Tralee John Mitchels club.

The new Mitchels entered the county championship in 1901 but were beaten by Killarney Crokes at the semi-final stage. So began the first great club rivalry in the county, with the Mitchels having the whip hand for the rest of the decade, winning five championships.

It meant the Mitchels picked the Kerry teams, captained Kerry teams and got to choose the colour of the jerseys. They wore red and green in the All-Ireland wins of 1903 and '05, but by the time the third title was won in '09 had settled on green and gold. Four years later, the colours were officially ratified by the county board at the request of Dick Fitzgerald.

Tom Costelloe captained Kerry to victory over Louth in '09, but the big news came the following year when his brother-in-law, Maurice McCarthy, walked away from the game at 28 years of age.

Kerry football was thrown into shock – it was like D.J. walking away from Kilkenny in 1998. McCarthy had been looking ahead to a fifth All-Ireland appearance in 1910, but was deprived of the honour by the Railway Row.

The Central Council voted by a 7-6 majority to award the title to Louth. McCarthy walked away from football in disgust.

However, the decision by Louth to take the title also sowed the seed for McCarthy's dramatic return to county football. It didn't come in 1911 when Kerry failed to get out of Munster or in 1912 when Antrim ambushed them in the All-Ireland semi-final, but the Croke Memorial final did it for McCarthy. Once Kerry were pitted against Louth in the final he came back, ending a three-year exile with a couple of weeks' training before making his way to Jones' Road.

Louth may have enlisted the services of George Blessington and James Booth of Belfast Celtic F.C. to train them but having Maurice McCarthy back in their ranks was good enough for Kerry.

'With Maurice McCarthy's dramatic comeback after an absence of three years, our backline was again complete,' wrote Aeroplane O'Shea.

McCarthy won his fourth All-Ireland later that year, but by 1914 he had retired for the second time. When Kerry drew with Wexford on 1 November, McCarthy had reduced himself to the role of bystander but, for the replay four weeks later, he made another dramatic return to the full-back line to claim his fifth medal.

McCarthy had done it all and in his own way. In his own quiet manner he walked away for the last time in 1915, leaving the limelight and hero worship to Dick Fitzgerald and others.

Maurice McCarthy never was one for hero worship but he got more of it for cycling to Galway in the mid-1950s than he ever did in a Mitchels or Kerry jersey.

JÓM

Pat 'Aeroplane' O'Shea

Pat O'Shea was a great man for pounding the pavement that hugged the tracks of the Cnoc Glas to Castlegregory branch line of the Dingle Railway. He knew this road like farmers know their land. He loved rambling the road. Loved rambling over the humps and hollows of his long life.

Footballing and fighting weaved in and out of his days at the top. Occasionally, the lines between the two were blurred. There was no hurling in Castlegregory but O'Shea and his contemporaries used hurleys when drilling with local Volunteers.

By 1921, he was a prisoner on Spike Island, a senior IRA officer in charge of a company of sixteen Volunteers in his hut. It was one of the few internment camps where hurling was allowed and one of O'Shea's responsibilities was to keep the men under his command active. This was done through hurling and football.

The afternoon of 1 June that year was given over to 'the game of sticks', as the prison guards labelled it. O'Shea looked on as his close friend and fellow Volunteer, Patrick White, from Meelick in Clare, hurled for all his worth.

'The sliotar had been pucked under the strands of barbed wire and White went to retrieve it with his hurley,' wrote O'Shea in his memoirs. 'No warning was given, the minute the hurley touched the coils of wire, the sentry fired at a man who he would have never met on equal terms. The shooting was deliberate murder. The breakout of three IRA musketeers was made level by the blood of Pat White.'

As White lay dying, he called for O'Shea and after that, the Kerry footballer always thought of Patrick White when he thought of Ireland. The struggle. The fight. They were as important as football.

It's why O'Shea answered Austin Stack's call to arms in 1916. The Kerry GAA chairman told a startled O'Shea about Easter Week and the part he had to play. A German vessel, the *Aud*, was arriving off Inis Tuaisceart in the Blasket Sound on Easter Monday. On it were Roger Casement and a shipment of arms. O'Shea's job was to find a pilot in the Maharees to guide the vessel to Fenit.

O'Shea found his pilots in Maurice Flynn and Mortimer O'Leary, and they were to flash two green lights to guide the *Aud* ashore. On Easter Saturday, O'Shea travelled to Tralee by train to collect the lamps. He was walking down

Facing page:
Football's only Aeroplane who said, 'I had springs in my heels that helped me to rise from a standing position or when running.'
(Padraig Kennelly)

Nelson Street when he saw a group of RIC men on the march. They were escorting a moustachioed stranger to the 10.30am Dublin train.

O'Shea didn't know it, but it was Roger Casement; the *Aud* had been captured at the mouth of the Shannon. His two lamps were blown out. His 1916 battle over before it started.

By then, O'Shea's name was known all over Ireland. Thing was, people rarely called him by name. Aeroplane was enough then and still is to this day.

Gob a Riasg was the name given to a field close to O'Shea's home. It was a fairgreen hard by the sea that became a meeting place for footballers on holy days. The sandy soil of the place meant the ball hopped high in the air and it's there that football's first aeroplane was constructed.

'When I was a boy of sixteen the drop-kick was first seen in Castlegregory and at once became all the rage,' O'Shea wrote. 'One of the most expert practitioners was Ed Courtney and we used to play a little game. He drop-kicked the ball to me and I fielded it, standing very close at first, then gradually increasing the distance between us.

'After a while I found myself rising to meet the ball without conscious effort on my part. I had never seen any footballer do it, but I persisted. I soon found that I had springs in my heels that helped me to rise from a standing position or when running. I tried out the new technique when playing with grown men and I found it gave me a great advantage over taller players.

'One-handed fielding was the natural development. This enabled me to catch balls at greater heights while one hand and arm protected the side exposed to tackle. I did my fielding at full speed where possible and, thus, added impetus to my kick on landing. In my day, there was no such thing as breaking the ball. A clumsy phrase to describe a clumsy tactic.'

A footballer made, not born. It wasn't long before Kerry came calling. It helped that O'Shea cycled in the road or hopped on the Tralee train to play with the Mitchels. They had the O'Gormans, Austin Stack, Maurice McCarthy and Tom Costelloe. All-Ireland men the lot of them and Pat O'Shea was about to join the club.

'I first wore the Kerry jersey in a match against Cork in the spring of 1910,' he wrote, 'and I travelled to that match on a pushbike, complete with overcoat and football outfit.'

O'Shea had been at the 1909 All-Ireland final a few months before, standing behind the wire at the City and Suburban Sports Ground on Jones' Road with Jim Morgan, his classmate and footballmate from St Patrick's Training College.

Morgan was a Dundalk man and though Kerry played Louth in the final that day, their friendship survived the strain and tension.

When next they met in Croke Park, things had changed. This time, O'Shea and Morgan were on the other side of the wire. They were still friends but, because of the controversy of 1910, Kerry and Louth were far from brotherly.

There was no time for banter about St Pat's when O'Shea and Morgan went shoulder to shoulder in the Croke Memorial final and replay in 1913. These were Pat O'Shea's greatest days.

'During the course of a long life I cannot recall any event in this country which excited such general interest as the Croke Memorial matches. For my own part I hold that they were the greatest ever played.

'Winning the Croke Memorial final was set above the winning of many All-Irelands. This massed will to win undoubtedly had its effect on the Kerry players and no team at that time could have resisted them.'

Pat 'Aeroplane' O'Shea was irresistible in full flight, but grounded himself in 1915 after winning All-Irelands in 1913 and '14 and that precious Croke Memorial medal. He was only 27 but his country called as the Easter Rising was around the corner.

Still, in football retirement, he pounded the pavement out Castlegregory way. Where once it was for football fitness, it was then for personal fitness. The Castlegregory branch line closed down in 1938 and he couldn't hug the tracks any more.

He died in 1980, aged 92, but the name still inspires Kerry footballers. The game's only Aeroplane.

JÓM

Phil O'Sullivan

In the summer of 1931, the *St Louis* steamed into Queenstown, or Cobh as three blueblooded Kerrymen on board called it. Jerry 'Pluggy' Moriarty from Tralee, Phil O'Sullivan from Lauragh and Dingle man Mickey Moriarty were home on an extended holiday.

Pluggy and Phil were All-Ireland winners; Mickey, who made his money selling under-the-counter hooch in a Manhattan speakeasy, was a fixture at All-Ireland finals in his latter years.

They left the Great Depression behind them when they arrived that summer and it was a long one for Kerry as they reached their third All-Ireland final in a row.

It was another Kerry/Kildare final – Pluggy's and Phil's first since emigrating to New York a few years before. The two former Kerry captains were home in style thanks to Mickey Moriarty.

Running a speakeasy in prohibition years had been good to the Dingle man and, on a final soireé before getting married, he brought his black Buick four-door sedan home on holiday.

'By all accounts, none of them were experienced drivers,' says Moriarty's nephew, Micheál Ó Muircheartaigh.

They had a smooth enough Atlantic crossing but their passage west to Kerry was a rocky one. A few hundred yards from the pier they crashed into a water pump.

O'Sullivan still made it to Lauragh though and the place had never seen anything like his arrival. Cars were few on these roads; big American automobiles were never seen.

Apart from a battered bumper, it was an entrance fit for a king and that's how Phil O'Sullivan was regarded in this fingertip of south Kerry. Phileen or Phil 'The Master', as locals called him, was an all-rounder. Footballer, hurler and swimmer.

Famously, part of his training was to swim to Oileán na Tighe in the middle of Glanmore Lake. He was fit and supple and also moonlighted as a professional athlete who plundered purses on offer at sports days at home in Lauragh and further afield.

Facing page:
Phil 'The Master' O'Sullivan, pictured with the ball in the front row, captained a Kerry team that did so much to heal Civil War divisions in the county by winning the 1924 All-Ireland.
(Weeshie Fogarty)

One athletics meeting O'Sullivan made his own is embedded in Beara peninsula folklore and across Bantry Bay into Kerry. To get to the Adrigole Sports, he trekked 6 miles through the Healy Pass in the Caha Mountains.

There's a road through the pass now – it was only a rough track in O'Sullivan's time, rising 334 feet above sea level and passing between the two highest peaks in the Caha range before descending into Adrigole.

O'Sullivan competed in sprint races and jumping and throwing events that day. The feature event was the 100-yards dash in which O'Sullivan was pitted against the local favourite. It was a Kerry versus Cork thing that caused controversy. Crossing the line, a fraction separated the two and a row erupted, with O'Sullivan demanding that he had won.

The hometown crowd said otherwise.

'Ok then,' said O'Sullivan, 'we'll call it a draw.'

'No, we'll race again,' said the Beara boys, looking for a Kerry scalp.

The challenge was down and O'Sullivan didn't shy away. According to the story, he downed whiskey to put fire in the belly, won the replay and headed for home, back over the Tim Healy Pass with his day's pocket money.

There was no money to be made out of playing football with Kerry, only medals and the All-Ireland Phil O'Sullivan won was significant in Kerry's history. It came as football helped heal the deep wounds of divisions opened during the Civil War.

Phil O'Sullivan was Kerry's leader in 1924, chiefly because he was the most senior member of the side. He had first worn the Kerry colours as a nineteen-year-old in 1915, playing centre-half-back on the team that beat Westmeath in the All-Ireland junior final.

He was also a veteran of Ballymacelligot's county championship winning side in 1918, having played with them while teaching in the local national school. Din Joe Baily of the county board was another Ballymac man and played his part in making O'Sullivan captain for the 1924 campaign.

Captaincy meant more than leading the team out. O'Sullivan also organised Kerry off the field. His friendship with fellow UCD graduate Dr Eamonn O'Sullivan was to have far-reaching consequences for Kerry football.

'Qualifying in my final medical examination in March 1925, I had arranged to take out a three-month postgraduate course in the world famous Coombe Gynacological Hospital,' Dr O'Sullivan recalled years later.

'It was immediately prior to this that my old friend, Phileen O'Sullivan, announced to the Kerry team that I would train them for the 1924 All-Ireland. Needless to say, I thought that Phil was joking but he soon set me right when I took my residence with the senior and junior teams in O'Grady's Hotel, Ashe Street, Tralee.'

In O'Grady's, Dr O'Sullivan put a blackboard up on the wall for the first time. On it plans were thought out and drawn and the first All-Ireland in ten years was won.

Old-timers in Lauragh always called that their greatest day because of the role played by Phil O'Sullivan. The little village that had a population of a few hundred decamped en masse to Croke Park to see their man lead out Kerry.

'We went up to the match on the train,' recalled one match-goer Joe Lyne. 'We left Lauragh in the early hours on the first leg of our journey to Kenmare, we then boarded the train at 7am, arriving in Dublin around one o'clock. The round trip cost ten shillings and six pence. This may not seem very much in our days of rapid inflation, but ten shillings at that time was considered a good weekly wage.'

It was worth the journey. Kerry beat Dublin and it was O'Sullivan's first, and only, All-Ireland win on the field. Another could have come his way in 1925 only for Kerry hopes of back-to-back titles to flounder amid objection and counter-objection.

O'Sullivan had moved to Dublin by late 1925, playing football for UCD and hurling with Faughs. That year, Cavan contended he lined out illegally for Faughs and claimed victory in the All-Ireland semi-final that Kerry had won by 1-7 to 2-3.

Kerry counter-objected on the back of O'Sullivan's contention that, 'If I'm illegal, Cavan's Jim Smith and P.J. Murphy are illegal too'.

Both Kerry and Cavan were thrown out of the All-Ireland race and Galway were declared champions, having beaten Mayo in the Connacht final. Worse was to follow for O'Sullivan. In 1926, injury came between him and playing in the replay against Kildare. He played centre-back in the 1927 final but Kerry went down to Kildare and, by the time the next Kildare game came around in 1929, O'Sullivan was in America with Pluggy Moriarty and Mickey Moriarty. It was the rivalry that dominated the decade and they made sure to be home for the 1931 instalment. When they finally returned to America after Kerry's third All-Ireland victory over Kildare in five years, the Buick four-door sedan was slightly the worse for wear.

Apparently, the three passengers were the same.

JÓM

Revolution Years

Jackie Ryan

As the 1920s were approaching, football had yet to get a real stranglehold on the county. Along the lanes and streets of Tralee and in the fields of north Kerry, some fine hurlers were emerging.

Jackie Ryan was still a teenager in 1919 when the county board called a special meeting to discuss the state of Gaelic games in Kerry. Din Joe Baily – a man under whose gentle and politically-neutral watch the games in the county prospered – was influential on the board at the time and after this meeting had concluded, Kerry saw a clear road ahead.

'This was an extremely important meeting in the development of football in Kerry,' says J.J. Barrett, author of the fascinating *In the Name of the Game* and son of Kerry great Joe Barrett. 'At this stage, Kerry could have embraced hurling in much the same way as they embraced football. Politically, it was difficult for games to go ahead around 1919, but there was huge enthusiasm. The likes of Jackie Ryan, Pluggy Moriarty and my own father, for example, would have hurled to a high standard for Kerry and all of these were men who won All-Ireland football medals. During that board meeting in 1919, it wasn't exactly discussed "will we go the football or the hurling way", but there certainly was a change in mood after it. Din Joe Baily was a strong football man and, as a result of that meeting, there was a definite leaning to football.'

Other events began to determine Kerry's sporting course. Post-1916, militant nationalism began to assume greater importance than football. Kerry didn't field in the 1917 Munster championship because many footballers were caught up with political activities. The silencing of *The Kerryman* newspaper by British forces for its nationalistic outlook meant games could not be organised and football temporarily ground to a halt.

But the real test came after the War of Independence when Civil War gripped the county for eleven months over 1922 and 1923. As it did, more and more young Kerrymen were interned as political prisoners.

Republicanism was strong in pockets across the county and numerous young men – among them emerging footballing greats – were captured and interned by the ruling Free State forces they were fighting.

Locked up with nothing but time and youth for company, these Kerrymen took the lead in the spacious Curragh camps – where they were largely interned

Previous pages:
Miko Doyle was a child of Kerry's football revolution in the 1920s, winning five All-Ireland medals over a ten-year career. He's pictured leading the Kerry team before the 1937 All-Ireland final against Cavan.
(Seamus O'Reilly)

Facing page:
Jackie Ryan (pictured fourth from right in the back row) was an ever-present on Kerry's great four-in-row side from 1929 to 1932.
(Weeshie Fogarty)

– and began organising and playing games. It was a throwback to the Frongoch days.

'Jackie Ryan and my father were staunch republicans and they spent time together in The Curragh,' says Barrett. 'He [Joe Barrett] told me they kicked football all day. They'd nothing else to do.'

Football was an easier game to organise than hurling. All that was required was a ball and some energy. For hurling, the prisoners needed dozens of hurleys and the difficulties involved in passing these into the camps was enormous, given their potential to be used as weapons.

And, so it was that football prospered in the prison camps of the Civil War. Football-wise, Kerry benefitted most as its republican prisoners came to the fore. Tactics were chewed over, skills were sharpened. The game gave the internees a common language, provided them with a cohesive bond. It linked young men from all parts of the county.

When the bulk of the political prisoners were released in late 1923, sport in Kerry was once again given breathing space. Football prospered in the emerging environment.

Late on in the year, the Kerrymen who had been interned got together and decided to put what they had learned in The Curragh into practice and in the process they felt they could secure some places on Kerry teams of the future.

They publicly challenged the established Kerry team to a game and the offer was accepted.

The game – played in February 1924 – stands out as a landmark in the history of the game in the county. Among those who lined out for the Ex-Internees that day were Jackie Ryan, Joe Barrett, Pluggy Moriarty and Johnny Riordan – each one an enthusiastic hurler who would help copperfasten football's grip on Kerry in the coming years.

The meeting of the Ex-Internees and the Kerry team was talked about with fever around the county and, with pride at stake, there was a hard bite to the contest.

'The game was robust, at times rather too much,' reads *The Kerryman* report, 'and from start to finish was keenly contested. The match was somewhat marred by a large number of fouls.'

The Kerry team – led by Con Brosnan – prevailed by five points to one, but it had rained torrentially in the lead up to the match and on the day the Tralee Sportsfield was a quagmire.

Shortly after, another challenge was thrown down and a second game was pencilled in. It went ahead on 23 March. This time, the young team of ex-internees gave the experienced heads of Kerry – who were missing some players – a hiding by 4-4 to 0-4. Both games were refereed by Tom Costelloe, Kerry's All-Ireland winning captain in 1909.

'The importance of those games can't be overlooked, because they laid the foundations for Kerry to move away from everything that went on during the Civil War,' says Barrett. 'A great Kerry team formed from those challenge games and the success that they brought meant football had a hold on the county. Things started to snowball after the ex-internee games.'

The following month, Kerry would travel to Croke Park for the first time in nine years to take on Cavan in an All-Ireland semi-final. The county team was made up of a selection of players from both the Ex-Internees and the established Kerry team.

A vibrant feeling was now coursing through Kerry. The semi-final line-up was a starting point for future tranquillity. The crippling effects of the Civil War were beginning to be straightened out, but there were no illusions about how difficult the process would be.

Importantly, the backbone of the team that would dominate the coming decade – with Ryan as a vital cog – was also forming.

The final with Dublin was scheduled for June, but didn't go ahead until October. Three men with huge links to football in the county were still being held as political prisoners – Austin Stack, president of the county board, Humphry Murphy and Moss Galvin, both members of the county team. Kerry refused to fulfil the final fixture until they were released and when the game was played, Dublin prevailed. Still, it was the beginning of a new era and one that would reap Jackie Ryan six All-Ireland medals.

On the field, Ryan was regarded as a crafty, scientific forward. 'When Mikey Sheehy was growing up, people in Austin Stacks used to say he's going to be another Jackie Ryan,' says Barrett. 'That was the cut of a player he was. Total style.'

Micheál Cotter lived 50 yards away from Ryan at the top of Rock Street. 'He had this extraordinary talent for chipping the ball when it was rolling away from him,' he says. 'That was his trademark. And we're talking about a time when players wore cumbersome, orthopaedic boots with big steel toe caps. I can still picture the Sunday morning when we were kids and Jackie was late going for mass. He picked out a ball from a bunch of nettles at the corner of the pitch for us in Hill's Field – which was behind his own house. He screwed the ball with his Sunday shoes – he was always immaculate – and it went right over a piece of rope we used as a crossbar. We cheered down the field after him and he turned and gave us a wave. All his life he was considered a star.'

One of those who shone brightly alright, and one who paved the way.

TJF

Johnny Riordan

'All I need to make a comedy is a park, a policeman and a pretty girl.' Charlie Chaplin

In the mind's eye, Johnny Riordan is a sepia-toned image from another time. He's strolling down Castle Street in Tralee, bedecked in the black garb of the 1920s, a throwback to another, simpler age.

It's lazy and easy to presume this was a quiet, workaday time populated by humourless folk. If so, Riordan didn't belong. He lit up his town and his football community with bright colours. He had character. He was a wit and a mimic, and he set standards for entertainment.

Charlie Chaplin was the big stand-up comic of the day and he made a huge impression on Riordan. The Tralee goalkeeper would bring out his Chaplin routine without much coaxing. Pádraig Brosnan, brother of Kerry great Seán, recalls seeing Riordan in action. 'One year Kerry were playing New York who were over for the Tailteann Games. It was on in Tralee and Johnny was in goal doing all sorts of contortions – hanging off the crossbar and standing on his head. That day he performed a most extraordinary feat. A long ball was coming in and Johnny let it go over his head, judged that it would hit the crossbar, turned, and caught it when it came back out.' On other quiet occasions, the crossbar doubled as a chin-up rail, the crowd bellowing out his progress.

Riordan had form. Writing in his memoirs, Pat 'Aeroplane' O'Shea recalled his first encounter with Riordan before the Croke Memorial Finals of 1913.

'The most regular to the training camp was a red-headed, merry-eyed schoolboy named John,' he wrote. 'He was never referred to by his surname. John had a nice singing voice and often sang for us when we were resting. He tolerated me although he knew I was a schoolmaster and, as such, the natural foe of all right minded boys. Years passed and one September day I watched the Kerry/Kildare teams march past the Hogan Stand. There was my merry-eyed friend of long ago, John Riordan who, that day, defended the Kerry citadel.'

There were times when his own playing colleagues required the light mood that radiated from Riordan. In May 1927, Kerry, then All-Ireland champions, crossed the Atlantic to take on the cream of America's Gaelic talent. It was an historic trip, the first of the county's voyages to far off lands.

Ambitious plans had been made to travel all the way to Australia, but a New York sports promoter, Ted O'Sullivan, stepped in and arranged the fine details of a whistle stop tour of the east coast of America. Australia was cancelled.

Facing page:
Johnny Riordan was a star of Kerry's American tours of the '20s – he's pictured here, second from right in the second row, as Kerry made their way to New York on the 1929 tour. (Micheál Cotter)

An army of support turned out at Tralee train station on 14 May, a day before they set sail from Cobh, to see the team away. The large crowd suited Riordan. He revelled in the backslapping and hand shaking and as the train was pulling away, he was still on the platform, entertaining and cajoling. Eventually, a group of teammates had to drag him aboard the train through a carriage window.

The attention was just the beginning.

The *SS Baltic* – one of the few ships to make contact with the *Titanic* on the night it sank – carried the team to New York. It was a long, eight-day journey. Tedium reigned. Kerry, under the control of Dick Fitzgerald, had a 90-yard promenade deck at their disposal. They trained out there in the bald Atlantic sun every day, beneath the gaze of a crowd of curious onlookers. Another blast of faces for Riordan to amuse.

PF, *The Kerryman*'s well-known GAA scribe, made the trip as well. 'He was the life and soul of the party [on the *SS Baltic*],' he wrote, 'and Irish-Americans returning to the States found him a source of never-ending laughter and fun.'

On Sunday morning, 23 May, the *Baltic* docked in New York. For most, it was their first glimpse of craning skyscrapers and city life. Not just that. Almost to a man, nobody had ever seen traffic lights before.

There was an other-worldly edge to the place, but still, some familiar faces were perched on the pier to help ease the team into their new surrounds. Among a horde of Kerry exiles awaiting the arrival of the ship were Jerry 'Pluggy' Moriarty and Bill Landers, All-Ireland winners now emigrated.

A large motorcade was ready to bring the team to their first official meeting. They nosed through the southern tip of Manhattan, landing at City Hall in the heart of the civic centre. Arrangements had been made to meet the New York mayor, Jimmy Walker, but a late change was made to Walker's schedule and they were welcomed, instead, by his deputy. A gaggle of cameramen had tailed the group to City Hall and now, after the reception, here they are, standing outside the Woolworth Building – tallest skyscraper in the world! – flash bulbs popping in their smiling faces. The pictures were syndicated in the next day's newspapers right across the continent. With this superstar treatment, Riordan must have felt at home.

Unknown to most of the travelling party, the trip had generated an avalanche of publicity Stateside. This was, after all, America's most glorious sporting era. Jack Dempsey and Gene Tunney were in the middle of their renowned two-fight meeting and Babe Ruth was on his way to firing 60 home runs for the Yankees, a record that stood for 34 years. Americans revered their sports stars and, in a town teeming with first- and second-generation Irish, the arrival of the All-Ireland champions was a big deal.

Prohibition or not, saloon doors were thrown open and the following day, they were toasted once again. The banquet area of the Commodore Hotel – largest dining room in the world – was packed with over 1,000 guests as the players and Dick Fitzgerald paraded to their table. More backslapping and handshaking. Even Broadway can't be this good!

Perhaps the attention and the hooch took its toll on the Kerry psyche. Their first outing against the New York exiles provided a shock result. New York scalped them by double scores, 3-11 to 1-7. Or perhaps it just went to show the pocket of talent that had left the country.

Kerry marched on through those places where the Irish had settled. They visited Boston, Chicago, Springfield, Hartford and New Haven, and were met by mobs of emigrants at each city. Under this magnified spotlight, Riordan basked in the opportunity to entertain. They returned to New York for a second game against the locals on Independence Day, 4 July. Kerry went down again but the crisis was only beginning. When they rose the following morning, they heard that O'Sullivan, the promoter, had fled New York with the tour funds. Kerry couldn't pay their hotel bill and they didn't have the fare for passage home.

Led by Kruger Kavanagh and the Kerryman's Association in New York, they eventually rounded up enough dollars to pay the bills.

When Riordan passed away in 1965, PF remembered his energy and enthusiasm during the trip four decades previous.

'Those who saw him perform for the first time were amazed,' he wrote. 'Had he gone on the stage instead of the football field, I have no doubt he would have made a name for himself.'

Riordan's departure from the inter-county scene was filled, appropriately enough, with plenty of drama and a touch of slapstick. On the eve of the 1931 All-Ireland final against Kildare, he was in line to collect his fourth Celtic Cross. The morning of the game though, the chance had vanished. Unexpectedly, Dan O'Keeffe was named between the posts and news swept through Croke Park that the Boherbee goalkeeper was dropped. The story went that Riordan, along with several others, supped a few pints of stout the night before and woke on All-Ireland day under the weather. Riordan wasn't in any state to play.

It filled conversations for the entire day and long after Kerry had secured the title. His club lodged a complaint with the county board and demanded a full inquiry into the selection committee's decision for axing their man. After a strong fight from the club, the board eventually dismissed Boherbee's call.

He wasn't even playing, but still he had the masses talking.

TJF

Paul Russell

The *Sunday Review* was ahead of its time in many ways, even though its reign on the news-stands lasted only seven years from 1957 to 1963.

The redtop briefly challenged the supremacy of the heavyweight titles on Burgh Quay and Middle Abbey Street for a slice of the competitive Sunday newspaper trade and they looked to an old Kerry footballer to corner its GAA share of the market.

Selecting Paul Russell to write a flagship GAA column in this new tabloid was a clever ploy. The man from Mangerton View in Killarney was a much-travelled ex-Garda with fingerprints everywhere. As a writer, he wasn't afraid to air controversial topics and take on the conservative elements within the GAA.

He also wrote from the perspective of one of the most decorated players in Kerry history as well as being a key figure for other counties. Russell had turned his hand to hurling in retirement when training Waterford to the 1938 All-Ireland final and also lined out for the football team.

A decade later his job as a Garda sergeant took him to Oldcastle in Meath and his arrival there was the catalyst for the county's emergence as a football force. Meath threatened to win an All-Ireland in 1939 but Russell was later seen as the missionary to lead them to the promised land.

'We'd no All-Ireland,' says Paddy O'Brien, Meath's famous full-back, 'so Russell being around the team had a huge effect on us. He knew about winning All-Irelands and getting him to train the team was very important. He brought something new to the county.'

Meath won their first All-Ireland in 1949, with Russell as the guiding force, and his name is spoken of in the county ever since. He also played county football with Dublin and was selected to represent both Munster and Leinster in the same year. Russell had the cult of celebrity about him and cultivated it through the pages of the *Sunday Review* every week.

He told yarns about his time at the top, from his days as a child prodigy through to pocketing six All-Ireland medals by the time he was 26.

There were other stories about his famous duels with Kildare's Paul Doyle, and the year he was forced to turn his back on Kerry and declare for Dublin by Garda Commissioner Eoin O'Duffy who was trying to build an All-Ireland team of Gardaí.

Facing page:
The Kerry team in 1953 were trained by Dr Eamonn O'Sullivan with Paul Russell, pictured second from left on the front row, his assistant.
(Jerome O'Shea)

The *Sunday Review*, through Russell, became a platform for radical and anti-establishment thought within the GAA. He was a longtime activist against the Ban – Rule 27 of the GAA that banned the playing of 'foreign' games – and used his column to campaign for its abolition.

'He was going against the grain in taking this stance,' says fellow activist Tom Woulfe, who eventually succeeded in having the Ban rescinded at the 1971 GAA Congress in Belfast.

'He was never afraid to tackle powerful forces within the GAA like his former mentor, Dr Eamonn O'Sullivan, and all the hierarchy who were strong proponents of keeping Rule 27 in place. Writing regularly in the paper about how draconian the Ban was gave a huge boost to the campaign.'

Russell blazed a trail that other newspapers followed and he also blazed a trail out on the field.

His emergence was extraordinary by any standards. At seventeen, he was cannon-balled onto the Kerry team for the 1923 All-Ireland final. He'd never played for the county before or even had a trial for the team.

Selection came on the back of a challenge game for Dr Crokes against Castleisland on 21 September 1924. The game acted as a curtain raiser to a trial between Kerry hopefuls seven days before the final against Dublin. Russell was an interested observer during the trial and afterwards, as he lazed about near the River Maine, he was approached by a stranger who just asked him his name.

Russell later found out the stranger was Dick Fitzgerald. Two days later Fitzgerald had convinced the county board selection committee to pick Russell at right-half-back on the Kerry team. Local blacksmith Frank O'Shea broke the news to Russell as he went to school on Wednesday. By the time he reached St Brendan's College, the celebrations had already started. College president, Canon John Breen, proclaimed a holiday to mark the occasion.

Three days later, Dick Fitzgerald personally escorted Russell to Killarney train station and introduced him to his teammates. They'd never heard of the new kid; the newspapers hadn't either and referred to him as John Russell.

'I was very nervous, going up on the train,' he recalled, 'and my nerves got worse as the match approached. We were staying in Barry's Hotel and I couldn't sleep. I found the whole thing a huge ordeal. In the dressing room beforehand, Jack Prendergast – "Pendy the jerseyman" he was called – threw me the number five. He then had to lace my boots because I wasn't up to it with the nerves.

'After that I raced out of the passageway to cool down and famous Dublin trainer, Joxer Kavanagh, came up to me, wished me luck and sprinkled me with holy water.

Then I went out and played my first All-Ireland.'

When Russell got possession for the first time, he eschewed Kerry's traditional long kicking game and, instead, went on a solo-run up the field. Captain Jerry 'Pluggy' Moriarty admonished him on the field; county board official Din Joe Baily did the same at half-time, roaring, 'Who the hell said you could go out and play football?'

Russell had learned his lesson and, in the second half, stuck to his position, marking dual All-Ireland medalist Frank Burke from the O'Tooles club. His days as an attacking and scoring wing-back came later.

'I loved going up the field and going for scores. The drop-kick was my favourite,' he wrote in the *Sunday Review*. 'The game I pick out is the Railway Cup final for Leinster against Ulster in 1928. Ulster had controversially beaten an all-Kerry team in the semi-final so I had something to prove and scored three points in the final out of vengeance.'

Vengeance of a different kind greeted Russell after his All-Ireland debut against Dublin. He went from Croke Park straight back to St Brendan's and was back in the classroom on Monday morning.

A lot had changed in a week. There was no public holiday for students in honour of Russell's achievement, instead he was asked by one of his teachers to produce his homework. He hadn't got his Greek exercise done and the leather was taken out.

Maybe, mused Russell years later in his column, he was punished for losing the All-Ireland and it had nothing to do with the Greek exercise after all.

JÓM

Jack Walsh

Andrew Volstead's Prohibition Act, passed into law by US Congress in 1919, didn't apply to Kerry teams that toured America in the '20s and early '30s. Drink was their American dream as much as playing football in Yankee Stadium or Soldiers Field.

By the mid-1920s there were 100,000 speakeasies in New York alone. Dan Breen, who fired the first shots of the War of Independence in 1919, had one in Manhattan. Not surprisingly, the Kerry boys on tour aired many republican songs there. Like Breen, Kerry footballers weren't afraid of the law.

They also showed their spirit in Boston where the bootlegging drinks trade flourished. During the 1931 tour, one night was spent in a Dorchester speakeasy but when that closed its doors, some Kerry players had no homes to go to.

Jack Walsh, his full-back line colleague and drinking mate Dee O'Connor, Eamonn Fitzgerald and Paul Russell were in top form. They found more drink at a party hosted by a few Killarney lads in an apartment block in downtown Boston.

The party was going strong and a call came for Jack Walsh's party piece. The week before, Jack sang 'My Old Fenian Gun' in Dan Breen's. This was his encore:

> It hung above the kitchen fire. Its barrel long and brown
> And one day with a boy's desire, I climbed and took it down
> My father's eyes in anger flashed. He cried what have you done?
> I wish you'd left it where it was, That's my old Fenian gun.

Walsh's son Eddie regaled this story at Walsh's Bar in 2004. It had travelled all the way from downtown Boston to downtown Craughdarrig – a crossroads in rural north Kerry.

There was much more to the story. Walsh was giving the singing performance of his life at that Boston Beer Party as he built to a crescendo but he was stopped in the middle of a line.

A door opened and three hefty cops, armed for action, stormed in with truncheons raised and gun holsters swinging from their hips. The party was in full swing and the prohibition breakers looked to be heading for a night behind bars. Then, Paul Russell intervened.

'How did you get here?' he said to the sergeant in charge. 'It's a long way from Killarney.'

A smile came over the sergeant's face – he was a New Street man and an old classmate of Russell's in St Brendan's College.

Jack Walsh broke back into 'My Old Fenian Gun' and the sergeant and his two lieutenants joined the party.

The republican air was suited to Jack Walsh – he was a strong republican who never hid his politics and this is what gave him his breakthrough with the Kerry team.

'He always said John Joe Sheehy was the man responsible for getting him on the Kerry team,' says Eddie Walsh. 'He came to Craughdarrig Cross regularly during the War of Independence and Civil War. These visits continued when he went on the run. Our house was a safe house and there was always a place here for John Joe.'

Sheehy came running in April 1925. During his few days in Craughdarrig, one of the many conversations he had with Tom Walsh, Jack's father, paved the way for Jack's introduction to Kerry football.

'My grandfather, who was a schoolteacher, asked John Joe out straight to try to get Jack a chance with the Kerry team,' says Eddie Walsh. 'John Joe's reply was, "Where is he and how big is he?" When Tom Walsh told him to look out the window and see him drawing turf, Sheehy commented, "He's a fine cut of a man for a footballer, tell him to come to Tralee next Sunday where there's a trial game."'

Jack Walsh had never played a proper senior football match in his life. Up to then, football amounted to kick-arounds in Mac's Field. The field was a great breeding ground and one that helped Walsh become the first man from the area since Jack Moriarty to make the Kerry team. Moriarty was one of the stars of the Croke Memorial Cup victory in 1913, while Walsh was a star in the making after a 60-minute trial in Tralee.

The following Sunday, he was thrown the number six jersey for the All-Ireland final against Dublin. Bob Stack from a few doors down the road in Doon was another debutante. Neither had been to Dublin before.

It forged a lasting relationship. They soldiered together on Kerry teams for the next eight years, winning everything along the way. They travelled to games together, they got mass together on match days.

One Munster final morning, Walsh cycled 7 miles out to Doon for a rendezvous with Stack. Andrew Beasley from Ballybunion was giving the two of them a drive to the match in Killarney and the local curate came along for the mass and the free ride.

'The curate was Fr Stack and he said mass that morning in seven minutes flat,' says Eddie Walsh. 'It was the quickest mass ever in Doon Church, which was right beside Bob Stack's house.'

Both Stack and Walsh won six All-Irelands each, with five of Walsh's medals coming in a full-back line made up of himself, Joe Barrett and Dee O'Connor. Walsh was moved back to corner-back in 1926 for the replay against Kildare.

He had a hard act in following the performance of Jack Murphy, who was man-of-the-match in the drawn encounter. Murphy, from Caherciveen, was dying of pneumonia by the time the replay came around.

Walsh starred in the corner and played there for the rest of his career. He also held on to the number four jersey in retirement. When the great Kildare player Paddy O'Loughlin died, Walsh made the journey for the funeral and had his number four thrown over his shoulder. He didn't have to announce himself – he was 'Craughdarrig Jack at left-full-back'.

That was the line ballad writer Pat Connor penned in Jack Walsh's honour after the 1929 victory over Kildare.

JÓM

Three legends with eighteen All-Irelands between them, from left, Con Brosnan, Jack Walsh and Bob Stack.
(The Kerryman)

John Joe 'Purty' Landers

The shrill whistle sounds. Knifing the air, it carries on the wind and against. Time to clear the lines as the narrow gauge gently steams out of the station and heads for the west country of Dingle.

The tracks dissect Rock Street and therein lies football's finest fable. One big Rock when it comes to town leagues. Solid. Two smaller rocks when it comes to intra-street sporting rivalries. Just as solid.

The steam age and an exciting age. A train steams by every few hours and the Rock Street kids chase it down the tracks. Upper versus Lower. Sleeper to sleeper. Good young fun in a young place. Rock Street is bubbling with adolescent enthusiasm.

The houses are young, the people are young, new Ireland is young. Reidy's Terrace, Dawson's Terrace, Casement Avenue and Urban Terrace that's surely the Daddy of them all. The first block was laid in 1912, a foundation stone for football's most treasured terrace. Twenty houses of bricks and mortar but also much more. The people make the bricks and mortar breathe, make the Urban Terrace a living place.

Gal Slattery lives in number three; Miko Doyle in five; the Landers brothers in seven; the O'Gormans in ten; the Drummonds in twenty.

The street is their playground. Footballers and hurlers are crafted on Urban Terrace. It's only a long puck or punt away from the tracks that divide them from the Lower Rock.

This is where hurlers and footballers gather. Upper meets Lower at a signal box beside the tracks. Miko Doyle with his pigeon-toed walk leads the Urban Terrace boys out to the signal box – the Landers, Drummonds, Slatterys and O'Gormans are in tow. The O'Regans too. They pick up Jackie Ryan and Pedlar Sweeney on the way.

They talk about games and play games – hurling and football. When they haven't a football or sliotar, coddling is the game they play – the 'football' of the streets.

The Landers love this game – Bill, Mick, Garret, John Joe and Tim. John Joe loves coddling so much that he spends his time gathering newspapers – not to read but to ply and play. John Joe's a master craftsman – he rolls the paper in a ball, soaks it in water and ties twine around it until it looks like a big sliotar

Facing page:
John Joe Landers got his nickname from 'Pluggy' Moriarty who said, one day: 'Who's the pretty boy?' It was shortened to Purty.
(Padraig Kennelly)

without its casing.

John Joe produces this ball at the signal cabin and the game of coddling is on.

Upper versus Lower. The Barretts, Jerry 'Pluggy' Moriarty and others from the Lower Rock are older and stronger. John Joe is a boy, but plays football like a man – buffeted but still brave.

Pluggy hammers into John Joe one day, because Pluggy hammers into everyone. 'Who's the pretty boy?' he roars. The Rock Street wags hang on to Pluggy's panegyric – 'Pretty boy,' they echo. John Joe has a new name.

As Pretty Boy grows, it's shortened to Purty.

'I played in my first final in 1927,' he told Micheál Cotter from Rock Street in a recorded interview. 'Kildare captain Jim Buckley marked me and in the first couple of minutes sent me spinning. I was frightened of the crowd and very nervous. My old lad said afterwards, "John Joe, that's your first match with the seniors and your last match."'

Purty was twenty. The All-Ireland was lost and his big chance was gone. Leaving Croke Park, he swore that if he ever got back, he'd be a better player. More training, more coddling, more football.

That was life on Urbran Terrace – there was no work so Purty played.

One day in Hill's Field behind Jackie Ryan's house – two stumps of trees for goalposts, a rope for a crossbar. Another day, the game would move to Denis 'Rory' O'Connell's field. Another day to the greyhound track – then on to Urban Terrace and then to Garret Cotter's field. Garret also had a gym open to everyone on the terrace and, inspired by this, the Landers built their own private gymnasium.

Their garden on Urban Terrace measured only eight paces, but it was enough to build a small shed. Inside, they lifted heavy weights and had a bullworker tied to the wall.

Purty, Roundy and Bill were ahead of their time off the field. The 1932 All-Ireland final showed how advanced the Landers were on it.

JNS, *The Irish Press*: 'This pair found each other by neat sliced kicks, by clever short punts, and worked in such perfect harmony, that some of the Mayo men must have become dizzy trying to stop them.

'Tim dribbled as though the ball was tied to his toe. Furthermore, this lithe young man was forever holding the ball that exact second to draw his rivals upon him. Then he released the ball, more often than not to his unmarked brother, who dived through the ruck like a rat up a sewer pipe.'

Purty's last game for Kerry was the 1938 drawn All-Ireland with Galway. The sides were level when Kerry were awarded a 50 in the final seconds.

'Sean Brosnan kicked and it broke to me,' recalled wing-forward Tony McAuliffe years later. 'I gave it to Purty and he kicked over what everyone thought was the winning point.'

Purty's joy was over before it started. Referee John Culhane from Glin had blown his final whistle as the point was in flight. A sixth All-Ireland medal was whistle-blown away.

A turbulent finish in turbulent times and Purty was dropped for the replay. By the time the 1939, '40 and '41 titles were won, he was getting used to life in prison.

Purty the IRA man was arrested and interned under the Emergency Powers Act in 1939 – he was in Arbour Hill in '39 and The Curragh from '40 to '44. But he was still a star.

'Purty worked in the kitchens,' revealed fellow internee Pierce Fennell, from Carrigaholt in Clare. 'He was one of the best and tried to dig a tunnel out of the place. There were 30 men to each hut and space to play football. He was in charge of a hut and got lads playing. He was great.'

It was a Rock Street thing. Jackie Ryan, Joe Barrett, Pluggy Moriarty and Bill Landers were 'Tin Town's' best in the '20s. Now it was Purty's turn.

A Street of Champions thing – because Rock Street had more All-Ireland medals than any other place in the country. A conversation between Purty, Bracker O'Regan and well-known Tralee character 'Blood' Moran, explains the street for what it was.

Purty and the 'Blood' were talking one day when Bracker breezed by.

'Which club has more medals, Strand Road or Boherbee?' said the Blood. 'I can't help you with Strand Road or Boherbee,' said Bracker, 'but, I can tell you about the Rock. The other day I was coming down the Rock and there was a crowd of young fellas playing pitch and toss.'

'For money?' wondered the 'Blood'.

'No, they were playing for All-Ireland medals because Rock Street has so many of them.'

From the twenty houses on Urban Terrace came 22 All-Ireland medals between 1924 and '41. Purty Landers and Miko Doyle led the way with five each. No wonder Kerry winning captain Miko gave a loan of Sam Maguire to Purty after the 1937 final.

Sam was perched inside the window of number seven Urban Terrace for weeks, before going back to the captain's home two doors down in number five.

Back then, Urban Terrace shaped the landscape of Kerry football.

JÓM

Miko Doyle

They still tell stories about Miko Doyle's hair. He had a dark, wavy, luxurious mop on his head. He looked after it tirelessly. Before games, he would wax and comb it. After games, he set it back into place, ensuring the angles and creases were all correct.

That's what those who knew him remember first. Not the four All-Irelands he won by the time he was 21. Not the small, but significant, role he played in quenching the last of the Civil War flames when he cycled a return trip of 48 miles in 1936 to Johnny Walsh in Ballylongford and asked him to return to the county team – a Rock Street man, living in the heart of republican Kerry, reaching out to a Free State man.

It's always the hair they recall. And the good looks.

'There was no one more flamboyant than Miko,' says Padraig Kennelly of the *Kerry's Eye*. 'He spent a long time in the States and when he came home, he dressed like a Texan. Stetson hat. Big cigar. We had a routine where we'd meet in the Royal Dublin when Miko was back for a game. He'd always be in the thick of things – a crowd around him. His face was enough to earn money. Miko was one of the glamour men for a long period and he even remained good looking into his latter years.'

He made his way onto the Kerry team, aged just seventeen, at the beginning of the first four-in-a-row in 1929. Doyle climbed his way up the Rock Street academy, making use of the advanced facilities that were available at his club. For years, Hill's Field was used as one of the main training grounds for the Rock Street players. They took things seriously there.

A fellow clubman, Garret Cotter was working on opening a gym to be used by the players. By the time it was finished, he had free weights, parallel bars, Olympic rings and he found a bicycle to add another tangent to Rock Street training sessions.

In time, Cotter's Field, owned by Garret, would take over from Hill's Field as the mainstay for the Rock Street club and when they trained in Tralee, all of Garret Cotter's facilities were open to the Kerry players.

Those early days with the club remained important to Miko Doyle. In 1937, Kerry played Cavan in the All-Ireland final. The game ended in a draw but the stand out event for Kerry was the poor treatment one of their forwards

Facing page:
A dapper Miko Doyle, on the left, pictured with Jack McCarthy, secretary of the Munster Council, after captaining Kerry to the All-Ireland in 1937.
(Weeshie Fogarty)

was receiving from a Cavan defender. If they were to overcome Cavan in the replay, Kerry figured they would have to show a heavy hand early in the game. The week of the game, the Rock Street contingent gathered and formed a plan. Joe Barrett was a selector. Miko Doyle was full-forward and captain, and Purty and Roundy Landers were on the half-forward line.

They fixed their attention on the burly Cavan full-back, Jim Smith, and reckoned if they could quell him, a clear message would be sent out. The first high ball that came in, Doyle – Kerry's enforcer – was to take him out of the game.

'My own Da and Miko were supposed to have discussed the plan for the last time in the dressing room before the throw in,' says J.J. Barrett. 'The idea was that Kerry would go out and let Cavan know they wouldn't stand for being pushed around.'

Joe Barrett positioned himself on the sideline behind the Cavan goals for the start of the game. As the first ball came in towards Smith and Doyle, Doyle threw a fist and Roundy Landers charged in. Just as a fight was kicking off, Barrett, dressed in a heavy overcoat and a hat, ran onto the pitch, ready to get involved.

J.J. Barrett still has a photograph of the incident, and on the outskirts of the skirmish, you can see Purty Landers running, ready to defend his club men. A Rock Street move, planned and executed. Kerry went on to win and years later, Doyle, on a return trip from New York, met Smith after an All-Ireland final.

'I saw Miko and Jim Smith meet for the first time after that final in 1953 in the Shakespeare Bar in Dublin,' says Johnny Foley, goalkeeper for Kerry in '53 .

'People were aware of what went on and they were looking to see what would happen. The two just shook hands and chatted for a while.'

When his playing days were over and, once he arrived in New York, he began job hunting and made for John 'Kerry' O'Donnell. Shortly after, he was working in the Waldorf Astoria on Park Avenue, one of the plushest hotels on the planet.

His neighbour from Rock Street, Micheál Cotter, landed in New York after the 1953 All-Ireland final. His uncle was Jimmy Snee, the famous dual player who won 22 New York senior championship medals in hurling and football. To help familiarise him with his new home, Snee brought his nephew downtown to meet Doyle.

'You couldn't believe how fancy the Astoria was,' recalls Micheál Cotter. 'I just thought that Miko would be in his element in a place like that. He kept himself in shape. A six-foot build, with big wide shoulders and powerful thighs. In the Astoria, they probably had some sort of a gymnasium and I'm sure he would have made good use of that. But it was his tremendous wavy hair that really stood out. I remember speaking to Dan Ryan, the former Kerry player and All-Ireland referee, and Dan shared digs with Miko for a while. Miko never stopped combing his hair, he said. It used drive the lads in the digs mad.'

He dipped back home as often as he could, planning his trips whenever it looked like his county would find some glory in September.

'Myself and Miko were going to the All-Ireland final of '79,' says Padraig Kennelly. 'When we got to the barrier, I had to show my press pass to a cop to get in. Miko had a ticket in his pocket but didn't bother showing it at the gate. That would be his style – looking for a bit of banter. Next thing, all the Dubs behind us saw what was going on, that this man hadn't shown any ticket to get in. They were shouting, "Oi, Oi, what's he doing copper – you're letting him in for free." And the cop turns around and says, "Hey, this guy helped build this place." Miko loved that. He was known everywhere. If you saw his face only once, you didn't forget it.'

TJF

John Joe Sheehy

John Joe Sheehy retired from his post as chief inspector for the Irish National Insurance company in the early '60s. He led an active retirement. It came from his time on the run and his career on the road selling insurance. Wanderlust was in him.

He wandered many roads with Pádraig Kennelly, then a freelance cameraman who worked for Teilifís Éireann. Tagging along with Kennelly was Sheehy's way of time travelling.

The television camera attracted attention, but never as much as John Joe. In nooks and crannies of Kerry, they flocked around the old footballer like he was the prodigal son or prophet. 'Everyone courted him,' says Kennelly.

In Ballinskelligs, Barraduff, Dingle, Duagh or any place in between and beyond, the old man was worshipped. It was for deeds in the green and gold and on the fighting fields. He gave both equal importance.

Causes consumed the man from Boherbee. Winning All-Irelands and an all Ireland state.

RTÉ's GAA *World of Sport* programme in 1964, presented by fellow All-Ireland winner Jerome O'Shea, told this story; Sheehy proudly showed off trophies in the family treasure chest, but one jewel had a special place.

It wasn't the massive McGovern trophies presented to Sheehy after Kerry's unbeaten tour of America in 1931 or the minature Sam Maguire given to his son, Seán Óg, as a permanent memento of his All-Ireland winning captaincy in 1962.

The Casement Cup was the one. It was presented to first son Paudie in 1953. 'That's a little bit of our lost province [the six counties] and was won at the opening of Casement Park in '53,' Sheehy boldly told Jerome O'Shea.

That national question inspired a remarkable chapter in John Joe Sheehy's sporting and political life. Back in the 1920s, when football and fighting ran in tandem for many Kerry footballers, Sheehy was a wanted man. As an IRA man, he was an enemy of the fledgling Free State but still played football with Gardaí and members of the National Army whose job it was to quench the IRA. This unlikely alliance was forged over a ten-year period between 1924 and 1934, when those who played football for Kerry put their politics aside when they donned the jersey.

People like John Joe Sheehy and Con Brosnan placed football on this pedestal.

Facing page:
John Joe Sheehy with the family silver.
(Brian Sheehy)

67

Con Brosnan was a Free State army captain in the mid-'20s; Sheehy was an active IRA man who didn't recognise the legitimacy of a 26-county state, much less its army. But, Brosnan looked at the bigger picture of county football.

The Munster final between Kerry and Clare in the Market's Field, Limerick, on 12 October 1924 stands as an example. Unlike most footballers in Tralee who took the republican side in the Civil War, Sheehy escaped internment after the Civil War by taking to the Kerry countryside on the run.

For this reason, he wasn't named in the Munster final line-up, but unknown to everyone except an inner-circle of Kerry football men, Con Brosnan hatched a plan. Through a third party, Sheehy was given a guarantee of safe passage to and from Limerick on the day of the game.

Sheehy was believed to be hiding out in north Kerry at the time. He made his own way to Limerick, appeared out of the crowd in football boots, was handed a jersey and played his game.

As soon as the final was won he disappeared into the throng and was back on the run. It was a watershed moment.

The same happened in Croke Park on All-Ireland final day that year. John Joe paid his way in as a supporter, but underneath his street clothes, he wore his football gear. He may have been trying to overthrow the institutions of the State at the time but that had nothing to do with football and allowances were made for his subversive activities.

These activities even extended to gun-running all the way from America during Kerry's many visits there. Sheehy asked players of various political backgrounds to smuggle Thompson machine guns back to Ireland in their football gear.

And, according to GAA scribe, Carberry, he was as plucky on the field.

'Imagine a well-proportioned man of 5 foot 11 inches, weighing 13.5 stone, always in the pink of condition, of active and abstemious life, speed of a 100-yards man, and all the football of the best Tralee tradition. Imagine him in all the exuberance of hefty virile manhood, tearing in at the head of a pack of resolute Kerry forwards. That was John Joe Sheehy, captain of winning Kerry teams in their best years.'

These budding qualities first caught the attention of the Kerry selectors in 1915. Kerry were All-Ireland champions with veterans like Dick Fitzgerald, Maurice McCarthy and Tom Costelloe still backboning the team. Eighteen-year-old John Joe was on the cusp of greatness, but he put football to one side.

By the following year he had Ireland and not All-Irelands on his mind. Along with Aeroplane O'Shea, he was a member of Austin Stack's Tralee battalion that was to oversee the attempt by Roger Casement to land arms on Banna Strand.

It ended in disaster but it didn't finish the young Boherbee man's freedom fighting. It was Sheehy, as Assistant Commandant of the Tralee battalion, who planned and executed the assassination of the British Army's Major McKinnon at Tralee Golf Club in 1921.

When he wasn't plotting against the Tans and Auxilliary forces, Sheehy kept his eye in by playing street league football in Tralee. His Clounbeg home was only a kick away from the patch of ground called the Gardens and his team was known as the Garden Boys.

It was Sheehy's launching pad and by 1931, he had four All-Ireland medals. Kerry were embarking on their quest for a first ever three-in-a-row, but they had to do it without Sheehy who shocked the football world by announcing his retirement on the eve of the championship opener against Tipperary.

'I retired because in a match on the American tour, someone passed me out,' he said. 'That never happened me in a Kerry jersey before. I knew it was time to go after that. I was going slow.'

The county was in shock. Players and officials pleaded with him to change his mind. The Bishop of Kerry, Dr Michael O'Brien, even called to his door.

John Joe was polite and he brought his Lordship in for tea in Clounbeg but the bishop's efforts were all in vain. There was no comeback.

Instead, the ex-footballer turned his attention to GAA administration and again, his hardline principles shone through. Like Dr Eamonn O'Sullivan, he was vehemently opposed to ending the Ban on foreign games, a stance that put him at odds with former teammate Paul Russell.

When he died in 1980, his influence had seeped into every corner of Kerry football and he passed away as President of Kerry GAA. It was soon afterwards that Kerry County Council named a new road, going from Casement Train Station down to Boherbee, the John Joe Sheehy Road.

Sheehy would have purred approval, for the road leads all the way to the gates of Austin Stack Park.

Two unrepentant republicans. Two unrepentent footballers.

JÓM

Con Brosnan

Christy Ring was no fan of football, despite playing for many years with St Nicholas in Cork City. He once famously said that the best way to promote hurling was to 'stick a pen-knife in every football west of Youghal'.

Ring was a fan of Con Brosnan though. He never saw him kick ball in his prime but Brosnan's reputation alone reeled in the hurler. Whenever Ring's work as a driver for Shell Ireland took him to north Kerry, he always made it to Moyvane.

'There were twenty years between them, but they were one and the same,' says Con's son, Jerry. 'Total fanatics. Ring always had his hurley with him. My father was the same with football. He was always in the field. It was his life. He was always bringing people to the football field and if they hadn't boots, he would get them boots. Football kept him going in later years, kept him alive.'

When Ring and Brosnan hooked up, they retreated to the field that's now Con Brosnan Park.

There they talked. Tactics. Team formations. Collective training. Individual training. Two different games, but common themes.

'Con would tell him always about the few different drills he performed with the aid of enthusiastic helpers in Jack O'Connor's Field,' says Jerry. 'Thomas Mahony, who was a few years younger than Con, used to drive the ball high out to him at centre-field and he always said that's what perfected his fielding. Later on, Eddie Walsh and Jack Flavin would have joined the two of them.'

Brosnan was a noted all-rounder and returning the ball over the bar from the ground perfected his place kicking.

'Con Brosnan was a stylist,' says Liam Hanrahan, a friend of Brosnan's. 'A great fielder, with perfect delivery with both feet and very accurate. His partner, Bob Stack, was a rough, tough, hard man. They complemented each other.'

'Con Brosnan of north Kerry was reckoned by many critics as the best centre-field man that ever played,' wrote Carberry. 'Brosnan was beautifully moulded. Con was a polished footballer, grand fielder, clever anticipation, kicks perfectly placed. He could lace home a point from 50 yards on demand, drop kick, break, pass cleverly, race through in long solo runs, grand feeder of forwards, fast ground shots for goals or points.'

No point was more important than the one Brosnan scored to win the 1924

Facing page:
Con Brosnan, second from left, pictured with other Kerry greats in 1946. Others in the picture are, from left Denny Curran, who was on Kerry's first All-Ireland winning team in 1903; 'small' Ger O'Leary from Killarney, who was chairman of the Kerry Selection Committee in the '30s; Paul Russell; and Jerry 'Pluggy' Moriarty. (The Kerryman)

All-Ireland final. Kerry and Dublin were tied at 0-3 apiece – Dublin going for a four-in-a-row; Kerry, for their first title in ten years.

Referee Tom Shevlin awarded a free to Kerry 50 yards from goal. John Joe Sheehy took frees, so did Jackie Ryan; Con Brosnan always took the important ones. It wasn't the call of captain Phil O'Sullivan, it was Brosnan's own decision and he drove the ball over the bar to win the All-Ireland.

It was enough to have a poem penned in Kerry's honour. Brosnan was its headline act:

Hats off to Brosnan that midfield wonder,
He's par excellence with feet and hands,
Where is the Gael can bring down the number,
Of Kerry's idol from Newtownsandes.

Newtownsandes was the old name for Moyvane. It was also called Newtownclarke for a while. Brosnan lived through all the name changes that occurred during the Troubles and he came out the other side of these to play for Kerry. He was one of the lucky ones.

Brosnan was the leader of a raiding party from Newtownsandes that attended the Big Fair Day in Listowel on 19 January 1921. They weren't there to trade cattle but to take out a new RIC District Inspector.

Brosnan and others got their man in the town centre – 50 yards from the RIC Barracks, 300 yards from a garrison of British Army Auxiliaries and Black and Tans. It's a famous story in Moyvane.

'He was one of four men from Moyvane who volunteered to shoot this RIC inspector who was held responsible for killing an IRA man in Kilmallock the previous year,' says Jerry Brosnan. 'They drove into Listowel on their bicycles, shot him and went away on the run.'

When Con eventually made it back home, the Black and Tans had been there before him, sacking the village and setting the Brosnan family home ablaze.

Brosnan played little football in these years. He was too busy attacking the British, from the day in 1919 when he left his books and football boots behind in St Michael's College in Listowel and enlisted in the North Kerry Brigade of the IRA and the local Thomas Clarke Sinn Féin Club. It was a move that was mirrored across the county at the time.

'People's politics never bothered Con,' says Jerry. 'What people did in their time away from football held no interest for him.'

Crucially, it was that attitude, held by such an influential player, which helped

Kerry dominate during these revolutionary years.

Brosnan became a captain in the Irish Free State Army after the Civil War and some of his Kerry teammates were members of the Irish Republican Army that refused to acknowledge the very legitimacy of the Irish Free State. It was the John Joe Sheehy situation, only in reverse, but just like Sheehy, Brosnan had more interest in football.

'People say Con and John Joe hated each other,' says Jerry Brosnan, 'that they couldn't bear each other's company. That's not true. Even after they stopped playing, they were selectors on Kerry teams for decades afterwards. They'd be in here in the bar. They wouldn't mention politics but they'd be locked together talking football. They couldn't do that if they hated each other.

'Sheehy stood for the IRA, Con was a Blueshirt. Clashes between these organisations in Tralee eventually brought Kerry GAA to a halt in 1935, but even that didn't affect their football relationship.'

They were opposites. Sheehy was teetotal all his life – Brosnan liked his pint. 'He'd have to get a drink of porter before he'd go out,' says Jerry Brosnan. 'He couldn't lace his shoes unless he got a pint. He had no nerves going out on the field then.'

A cool head helped Brosnan kick the point to win the All-Ireland in 1924 and win five more medals afterwards. Helped him become the first All-Ireland winning captain to train an All-Ireland winning team when he led Kerry off the field in 1939. He showed the way for Kevin Heffernan, Tony Hanahoe, Billy Morgan and Páidí Ó Sé.

He shone a light for others, too. Those days in Jack O'Connor's Field had a lasting influence.

Jack Flavin is the only man in the history of the GAA to win back-to-back All-Irelands with different counties; Tom Mahony fisted the winning goal in the 1926 final against Kildare; and Eddie Walsh was one of Kerry's greatest wing-backs.

Con Brosnan helped make them.

JÓM

Joe Barrett

In his day, Joe Barrett was reputed to be the fittest footballer in Ireland.

'The remarkable thing,' says Barrett's son, J.J., 'is that, in all his time with Kerry, he never once trained with the team. He was too busy with his work as a cattle dealer, so he trained on his own.

'His most popular training routine was to walk from Tralee to Ballyheigue where he'd down an egg in sherry and then turn for home again. That was a round trip of nearly 22 miles. The egg in the sherry at half-way was the extent of his drinking.'

According to the last Street of Champions survivor, Bracker O'Regan, Barrett was given a free hand to undertake his own personal training regime. 'He could do what he wanted,' said Bracker, 'because he was the boss. I called him that all my life. He was the greatest leader Kerry ever had.'

These leadership qualities first emerged in The Curragh internment camp in the early '20s. He was there from April to December 1923 and those with him included Jackie Ryan, Jerry 'Pluggy' Moriarty, Gal Slattery and Denis 'Rory' O'Connell.

Barrett shared a hut with Tim Hurley from Cork. Hurley went on to win four hurling All-Irelands but Barrett went two better by winning six football medals.

'I consider Joe Barrett of Tralee the soundest and best full-back I've seen in Gaelic football – strength, courage, resource, judgment and football skill,' wrote Carberry in his 1947 *Gaelic Games Annual*.

'From his earliest appearance at inter-county, he seemed to fit in instinctively to the vital full-back position for which his physique and mental equipment admirably suited him. He had the strength and pluck of a lion. He was both cool and resolute. He tore his way out of difficulties, he could soar for a high ball, never missed a catch, his kicks were long and winging,' he added.

He was the Rock from Rock Street.

Joe Barrett's introduction to county football came via the first Kerry versus Ex-Internees match. He met Con Brosnan for the first time in Tralee Sportsfield that day and, for nearly 30 years afterwards, Barrett and Brosnan were inextricably linked together in Kerry's football story. They were on opposite sides on their

*Facing page:
Joe Barrett, pictured left, before the 1929 All-Ireland final against Kildare when he captained Kerry to their first Sam Maguire Cup success. (Seamus O'Reilly)*

first day because of their political beliefs, but soon afterwards, they put politics aside for the good of Kerry football.

1931 proved a monument to this commitment to football over politics. Barrett captained Kerry to the 1929 All-Ireland and, after Rock Street's county championship win of 1930, he was given the captaincy again for 1931.

Barrett accepted the honour, but immediately handed it over to Con Brosnan. They were sworn enemies off the field – Barrett had been a member of the IRA that fought the National Army Brosnan was part of.

Barrett was militant. He once went on hunger strike for sixteen days to highlight the republican cause he was willing to die for. However, Barrett the footballer still turned around and embraced Brosnan the footballer in giving him the Kerry captaincy.

'No Free Stater will captain Kerry,' was the cry in Tralee, a hotbed of republicanism at the time. Barrett's move was seen as high treason to many but he stood his ground and Kerry won another All-Ireland under Brosnan's leadership.

'He threw republicanism away for football,' says J.J. Barrett. 'In football there was no politics or factions with him. He looked on everyone as the same and this meant getting on with old foes. But there were people very much opposed to this conciliatory stance, as he found out in later life.'

J.J. Barrett first learned of his father's exploits when he was nine years of age. Joe Barrett was only 49 but was confined to his bedroom at 67 Rock Street after suffering a stroke.

On his deathbed, he summoned his youngest son, J.J., and, without saying much, pointed to the wardrobe at the foot of the bed. 'At the bottom of it, get it,' he said.

There, J.J. found a neatly-folded velvet cloth. It told J.J. more about his father than words ever did. He'd heard snippets from the streets of his father's part in the Rock Street story, but first sight of the medals made him realise how huge a figure he was.

Barrett's exploits continued after his retirement in the wake of Kerry's shock defeat to Dublin in the 1934 All-Ireland semi-final. He was a Kerry selector for over fifteen years and, in that time, five more All-Irelands were won.

At 49, he was looking to the future, until illness struck. His stroke left him partially paralysed – he was carrying an arm and a leg and only had half-speech. It meant he was never going to be able to take up his role as a selector in 1952.

'This is when the vultures gathered around,' says J.J. Barrett. These were members of the republican rump within the Kerry County Board who never forgave Barrett for giving the captaincy to Con Brosnan twenty years previous.'

At the Kerry GAA convention held at Killarney's Glebe Pavilion in January 1952, the move was made to rid Kerry football of Joe Barrett. The coup initially succeeded and Barrett was voted off the selection committee. But, in an amazing turnaround,

Con Brosnan brought his old friend back and made him chairman of the Kerry selection committee for 1952.

'Con Brosnan was appalled by what some people were trying to do to Barrett,' says Con's son, Jerry Brosnan, 'and, as a senior selector, he ensured that Barrett was co-opted back on to the committee.'

'The whole thing showed that politics was always underneath the surface of Kerry football,' says J.J. Barrett. 'Giving the captaincy to Con Brosnan in 1931 eventually brought the bitterness out in people. Some never forgave my father for what he did. They couldn't understand that Joe saw Con Brosnan as a great man because of his contribution to Kerry football.

'They wouldn't come up to him and say, "You're making a mistake with the captaincy." If they were going to do anything, it would be behind his back. It took twenty years. They waited until he was nearly dead. That hurt.'

Barrett's hurt was lessened in his last days. Con Brosnan was one of the regular visitors to 67 Rock Street. Little was said between them but what mattered was that Brosnan was there for Barrett. Their football friendship lasted a lifetime.

It's a scene that symbolised the true spirit of Kerry during a turbulent period in its history.

Barrett and Brosnan encapsulated what Kerry football had gone through – the black hole, and the emergence out the other end.

JÓM

Martin 'Bracker' O'Regan

Martin 'Bracker' O'Regan was peering out the window of his home – 249 St Brendan's Park in Tralee. Small in his prime, much smaller now in his ninety-fifth year.

Bracker strained his neck to see – impatient, waiting to talk some more about Kerry football. Bracker was ready. His interviewer was late.

'I'm waiting,' he says smiling out the window. Inside, he hands over four foolscap pages.

'That's me and Kerry football. I wrote it all down. I must be the greatest Kerry footballer ever because I'm the oldest one alive with an All-Ireland,' he says, still smiling.

Bracker's essay goes from the 1920s to the '30s. His playing days and before. Hill's Field, Slattery's Field, Denis 'Rory' O'Connell's Field, Cotter's Gym, Dr Eamonn, Kerry, Croke Park.

It was Bracker's written history but he had plenty of oral history too. Long before St Brendan's Park estate was built, there was field upon field. 'Out there,' says Bracker, pointing to St Brendan's greenbelt, 'was Slattery's Field and one day in 1921, when we were playing football there, Michael Collins came walking across it. He was looking for Mary Brigid Slattery, she was married to Fionán Lynch who was one of Collins' right hand men. Collins stopped off and had a kick with us.'

Bracker was eleven. Kicking ball with the Big Fella was a big day but Bracker got used to them.

His first was in Croke Park five years later when Kerry and Kildare clashed for the All-Ireland.

Bracker was peering that day too. He was too small for Hill 16 because there was no terrace there, only a mound built up with rubble from the Easter Rising. The Hill wasn't high enough, until someone produced a bucket.

'I travelled to that match on the train with my father – it cost five shillings. That bucket made my day, I could see everything. I could see Pluggy Moriarty standing down on Larry Stanley. He did everything on him. Phil O'Sullivan also hit him a wollop and nearly killed him.

'Jack Murphy was left-full-back and was a star. He played Kildare on his own and I remember him winning ball after ball and clearing down the field but

Facing page:
Martin 'Bracker' O'Regan placed a bet every day because it kept him young – he lived to 95.
(John Kelly)

it wasn't enough. Kerry were being beaten in most places all over the park.

'We had left the field before the end. Kerry were three points down and looked beaten. Then we heard a roar and we thought it was a roar for a Kildare win. Little did we know that Bill Gorman had got a goal to snatch a draw for Kerry.'

Bracker was back in Croke Park for the replay – this time he brought his own bucket and waited until the final whistle. Kerry were champions and the youngster from Rock Street went home dreaming his own All-Ireland dreams.

Being from Rock Street, he was already on his way.

'We played on the greyhound track – that was where all the stars played football. One time there were seventeen All-Ireland men out on the field at one time. I'd say it was the biggest number of winners ever having a kick around.

'We used to go up to Garret Cotter's field as well – that was a great place for the IRA. There was a gym there. John Hickey and Joe Síochrú built it.'

John Hickey from Rathmore was the man who stopped Bracker on the street and broke the greatest news he ever heard. It was a Sunday morning in July 1931. Bracker had come out of mass, where he whispered a few prayers that a Kerry call-up mightn't be too far away. It was closer than he thought.

'I met John Hickey below at Hilser's clock. He was a cabinet-maker down in O'Keeffe's. He stopped me as I was going down to the Green [Tralee CBS] for religious instruction. "You're on today – John Joe Sheehy has retired." I couldn't believe I was replacing one of my heroes on the Kerry team. It was a shock that John Joe retired, a bigger shock that I was playing. Tom Costelloe, who captained Kerry to the 1909 All-Ireland, got me on the Kerry team.

'I got four goals that day and Paddy Foley gave me a right good write-up in *The Kerryman*. "Auspicious debut" Paddy said. John Hickey came up to me after the game and said I should have got more. "Who do you think I am, Cúchullainn?" was my answer to that.'

Bracker was part of the Kerry set-up until 1938.

'I played the first All-Ireland with two odd boots. I couldn't afford a new pair. I had one boot of my own and Denis "Rory" O'Connell, who was a great player with the Rock, gave me the other. I was a young fella playing with my heroes. I did what I was told.

'Not long after my debut, I was playing centre-forward and that time, if you left your position there'd be trouble. I did and Joe Barrett came down the field and gave me a kick on the arse. Joe Barrett was captain and manager on the field.'

Bracker was full of stories.

'Another time we went up to play Dublin in a challenge game in Croke Park to raise money for the Killarney Sportsfield. We were staying in Barry's Hotel which was a great IRA house. They came into the hotel on the Saturday night.

'They said: "For the honour of God, don't let Dublin win." Dublin were very unpopular because they had guards and soldiers playing for them.

'We were winning by five points – the ball was kicked in and Dublin got a goal. Then, with the last kick, Dublin got another goal. The IRA crowd came in again that night – "Ye threw away that match," they roared. They grabbed the silver medals we had got and threw them down on the ground. If they had guns they might have shot us – they were disgusted.'

It was an eventful experience, just like the time he played before 90,000 in Yankee Stadium.

'It took us fourteen days to get to New York in 1938. We were like baseball players – superstars. We played football but enjoyed ourselves. One day in New York, Johnny Walsh said he'd do a parachute jump. Before going up in the plane Gega [Tom O'Connor] piped up: "Johnny, if it doesn't open, I suppose you'll get your money back." Sean Brosnan was in hysterics at that one.

'Coming home from America, we saw the picture, *A Night to Remember*. I was in the same room as Paddy Kennedy. And Paddy was in the top bunk, I was in the one beneath. In another bunk was Charlie O'Sullivan and underneath him was Billy Myers.

'What did Paddy Kennedy do only cut every second strap on Charlie's bunk bed. Charlie came in singing a Barber Allen song. He hopped into the bunk and fell straight down on top of Billy Myers. "Oh God almighty," said Billy, "we've hit an iceberg like the *Titanic*."'

Laugh-a-minute stuff.

Bracker was still laughing as his latest interview drew to a close.

Then he got serious. 'Drop me down to the bookies on Rock Street,' he said. 'I have to have a bet. I bet every day of the year.

'Keeps me young.'

JÓM

Eamonn Fitzgerald

It had all the ingredients for a Hollywood epic. The plot had triumph and tragedy cloaked around four men who made up Ireland's track and field team for the 1932 Olympics in Los Angeles.

They were Dr Pat O'Callaghan, Bob Tisdall, Eamonn Fitzgerald and Michael 'Sonny' Murphy, and they were the most successful Irish track and field team ever.

The picture makers wouldn't have had far to travel. Down Olympic Boulevard to the Los Angeles Memorial Coliseum before a six-figure audience.

In the lead in to the Games it appeared there would be no hope of attracting such crowds. They came in the middle of the Great Depression that bored craters in the American dream and six months before the opening ceremony on 30 July, no country had responded to invitations to participate.

'In the spring of 1932, it was the freely expressed opinion of disinterested observers that the Games either would not be held at all or, if held, would be a farce,' noted technical director of the Games, Bill Henry.

Everything changed when positive responses slowly trickled back. President of the Olympic Council of Ireland, General Eoin O'Duffy, entered an Irish team. There were 36 other entries that helped make the Games the most successful in the 36-year history of the modern Olympics.

Over 100,000 people attended the opening ceremony; there were eighteen world records; for the first time the Games finished in the black; medal winners stood on a rostrum for the first time and had their national flags raised; the photo-finish camera made its debut, as did the Olympic Village, while Ireland's quartet made their mark over sixteen remarkable days.

For 29-year-old Eamonn Fitzgerald, it was a long journey to the Coliseum from Castlecove on the Ring of Kerry. A stone plaque on the side of the road in Castlecove notes his journey, as does a stained-glass window in the church across the road. Down the road in Bunaneer National School is where it started. Fitzgerald's athletic ability flourished there before he got a scholarship to St Enda's in Rathfarnham.

He was a student of Pádraig Pearse, Thomas McDonagh and Joe Plunkett in the months leading up to Easter Week 1916, but was more interested in football than fighting.

Years later, Fitzgerald joined the staff at St Enda's. He had All-Irelands by then,

Facing page:
Eamonn Fitzgerald remembered – pictured from left are Sean Walsh, Kerry County Board chairman, Michael Farrell, president Athletics Ireland, Pat Hickey, president Olympic Council of Ireland, Ronnie Delany, Dan Keating and Eugene O'Sullivan, president of the Kerry Association in Dublin. (Kerry Association)

prompting PF to select him on his greatest Kerry team of all time. 'A wonderful high jumper who could literally sweep the ball out of the clouds,' he said. He also won Irish high-jump, long-jump and triple-jump titles and represented Ireland in the Tailteann Games in both football and athletics.

In 1932, Fitzgerald left football aside in an effort to make the Olympic team. He'd tried unsuccessfully to make the grade for the 1928 Games in Amsterdam but earned selection for 1932 by winning the hop-step-and-jump title in Croke Park with a leap of 48 foot 2 inches.

From there, Fitzgerald went straight into special training in Ballybunion with O'Callaghan, Tisdall and Murphy. Jim Clarke was a local publican and coursing trainer who was handed the job of training the Irish team before they left from Cobh on their Olympic adventure.

Clarke took them to the Ballybunion sandhills and the local greyhound track that was renamed the Great Olympic Greyhound Track in honour of Ballybunion's famous guests. It was there that fate conspired against Fitzgerald's ambitions. On the greyhound track he hurt his ankle for the first time and his Olympic participation was in doubt.

Rest and the salt water eased the injury and Fitzgerald was feted with the rest of the Irish team after landing in New York at the end of the first leg of their journey. In New York, public imagination in the Games ignited and it gathered momentum as teams crossed America over five days.

They took the famous Water Level Route from Grand Central Station that snaked along the Ontario, Erie and Michigan lakes before landing in Chicago. Then they travelled the Grand Canyon Route with stops along the way in Kansas City, Dodge City and Las Vegas. It wasn't just a sightseeing adventure though, they trained on stopovers. On one stop in Colorado, Fitzgerald twisted his ankle again, all but leaving his Olympic ambitions behind him in the Rocky Mountains.

But he still didn't give up hope. When the team reached the Olympic Village he got the best medical attention. The village on Baldwin Hills was built on 321 acres and had over 500 portable bungalows for the athletes – it also had a hospital and Fitzgerald spent much of his time there.

He marched into the Coliseum at Pat O'Callaghan's shoulder and then gave the performance of his life in the sandpit. Peter O'Connor acted as Fitzgerald's unofficial coach – the hop-step-and-jump champion from the 1906 Intercalated Olympics in Athens was also an Olympic judge and was beside the pit when Fitzgerald came tantalisingly close to a medal.

Despite his ankle injury he finished fourth, 1¼ inches behind Kenkichi Oshima of

Japan, who won bronze. His jump of 48 foot 2¾ inches would have been good enough to win six out of the previous nine Olympic titles.

Fitzgerald struck up a great friendship with Michael 'Sonny' Murphy on his Olympic adventure. Murphy from Killnaboy in north Clare played some football too but it was the tragedy that befell both Olympians afterwards that really welded them together.

Murphy competed in the 3,000-metre steeplechase. Temperatures during the race rose to over 100 degrees and they took their toll on Murphy. What made it worse was that officials got their measurements wrong and athletes were forced to run 3,460m instead of 3,000m and Murphy collapsed with exhaustion. His health never recovered. He died four years later and was buried in Deansgrange Cemetery in Blackrock. Eamonn Fitzgerald was one of the few people to attend the funeral.

Fitzgerald met a similar end. He went back to teaching in St Enda's after the Olympics but in the '40s contracted TB and died in 1958, aged only 55. With teachers Sean O'Neill and Fionán Breathnach, Dan Keating helped remove Fitzgerald's remains from his house in Beaumount Avenue in Churchtown and then shouldered his coffin into Deansgrange Cemetery. There were only eight other people at the funeral and Fitzgerald was forgotten for over 50 years with no proper headstone over his grave.

It only changed in 2004. Radio Kerry broadcaster, Weeshie Fogarty, saw the stained-glass window when passing through Castlecove and wondered who this man had been. Gradually, the Eamonn Fitzgerald story began to re-emerge.

The chairman of the Kerry Association in Dublin, Eugene O'Sullivan, used his Garda contacts to research the story and eventually discovered Fitzgerald's grave in Deansgrange.

A fitting headstone was erected in Fitzgerald's memory on 15 May that year. 102-year-old Dan Keating was back in Deansgrange for the ceremony – this time there were over 200 people with him.

Ronnie Delany gave the graveside oration, just as he had done in Deansgrange five years before when Michael 'Sonny' Murphy had a proper headstone erected in his memory.

The long forgotten Olympic teammates were remembered again and were in paupers graves no more.

Olympic heroes every bit as much as 1956 Olympic champion Ronnie Delany, or Dr Pat O'Callaghan and Bob Tisdall, both of whom won gold in 1932.

Delany said so himself.

JÓM

Tim O'Donnell

1935 was a strange year for Tim O'Donnell. He was a six-year veteran of Kerry teams and had stayed loyal to the green and gold despite pressure to declare for Dublin.

For young Gardaí, transferring county allegiance brought quicker promotion through the ranks of the force. Paul Russell bowed to pressure from Garda Commissioner Eoin O'Duffy and in 1927, played for Dublin. It didn't work out and he returned to the Kerry fold in 1928.

It seemed Tim O'Donnell would never make the same mistake. He was steadfast to Kerry, whatever the cost to his career. All that changed in 1935 but O'Donnell's decision to play for Dublin was made for him by those at home.

The 1934 county final between Austin Stacks and O'Rahillys was never played as Tralee was embroiled in political controversy for the first time since the Civil War.

Tralee republicans took the law into their own hands in October 1933 by facing down Eoin O'Duffy's Blueshirt movement when he came to address a rally in the town square. For these and subsequent manoeuvres, many republicans were arrested.

'We members of the Kerry County Board protest against the imprisonment of men of the IRA who are jailed in Belfast, The Curragh, Arbour Hill and Mountjoy. We view with alarm the news of torture in the infamous Glass House, The Curragh, of Tadhg and Pat Drummond, P. Curran, J. Devane, R. Eager, M. Quirke and M. Evans, Tralee,' said a resolution passed by the county board on 7 January 1935.

On 1 February, the Stacks took the next step at their AGM and endorsed the following motion: 'In view of what we consider the wrongful detention of some of our club members in the Military Detention Barracks, The Curragh, Kildare, more notoriously known as The Glass House, we members of Austin Stacks FC are unanimous in our decision not to take part in the games of the GAA for the coming year until we are assured that the lot of those mentioned in the said Glass House are removed to a different prison, or else released. We also call on Convention to take like steps.'

Next up were the O'Rahillys and John Mitchels. Competitive football in the capital town ground to a halt and the rest of the county took its lead from these

Facing page:
Tim O'Donnell, celebrates being 90 years young, in conversation with RTÉ's Des Cahill.
(Kerry O'Donnell)

Tralee clubs who ruled Kerry football at the time. The county didn't field a team in the All-Ireland that year.

O'Donnell was glad to be away from it. Had he been stationed in Tralee, he would have been one of the arresting officers, forced to arrest footballers and possibly teammates. Being away from it meant he could still play competitive football in 1935.

O'Donnell played for Dublin that year, but like Russell, he returned to Kerry and won another All-Ireland in 1937. 'The politics was taken out of Kerry football again when Kerry came back to play in the 1936 championship,' he revealed.

'I came onto the Kerry team after winning an All-Ireland junior medal in 1929. Myself and Miko Doyle came onto the team the same year. We knew not to talk about politics in the dressing room because we were warned beforehand. That was the unwritten rule in Kerry football always.'

According to O'Donnell, his journey to the Kerry team started with fireside stories from his father, Micheál, in Gleann na nGealt near Camp. It was there that he educated the five O'Donnell brothers about Dick Fitzgerald, the O'Gormans from Tralee, the Rices from O'Dorney and Aeroplane O'Shea from back the road in Castlegregory.

'I saw the Aeroplane in action,' Tim said. 'He was a small man but he could jump. I watched him take off for a ball and was captivated. It was a great name he had.'

O'Donnell could also take flight. He was self-taught but schooled very well too. 'We called school Aughcasla University. Master Rohan was a noted teacher – odd in the right direction. If you were late, he'd put a barrier across the school door. On a fine day he'd haul the *clárdubh* (blackboard) over into the yard and dare us to jump over it. Anyone who succeeded got a bit of silver. I won a few shillings myself.

'I used to train on my own – a 3-mile run along the road to Camp and back. I'd run hard between two telegraph poles and walk the next. When I'd train at home, I'd go out into the field in the middle of the day. I'd kick the ball up in the air as high as I could and run and catch it coming down. I'd do it again and again. If you were a good fielder you had a great chance of getting on the Kerry team.'

All O'Donnell needed to perfect his technique was a proper football. To make the price he went to Tralee town market every Saturday with his mother to sell butter and eggs. He deserted his post when he thought he had enough money.

'The ball cost ten shillings, but I had only seven or eight bob collected with a few friends. The shop owner, Arthur Caball, was the man I was looking for and eventually, I found him. He was a decent man and said, "Here, you can have the ball for that amount, sure, you might make a footballer and play for Kerry some day."'

Arthur Caball was right. O'Donnell first saw Kerry play in the 1924 All-Ireland final. He got the Ghost Train to Dublin that left Tralee at midnight on Saturday. The seven-hour journey in an unheated and jam-packed train was an endurance test.

The next time O'Donnell went to Croke Park he was on the Saturday Special for the 1929 All-Ireland – the 2pm train that always left at ten minutes to two – and he stayed in Barry's Pioneer Hotel.

'There was mass in Aughrim Street on Sunday morning and then a trek up the road to Parnell Park to watch a club match to try and kill time and take our mind off the game. When the club game was over, it would be time for Croke Park.

'That 1929 final is the one I remember most. John Joe Sheehy was my idol and the idol of Kerry. I remember we were getting it very tough that year. Kildare were leading in the last ten minutes but John Joe inspired the whole team. He left his corner-forward position and came out to all the players and appealed to them for a final effort.

'It so happened that while he was up in the backline, the ball broke in front of him. He was a master dribbler and dribbled the ball way down the field, dodging here and there, and passed it to Purty Landers and the ball went over the bar. Even now, I can still hear the stands shaking – it wasn't come on Kerry or the Kingdom, it was come on John Joe and we went on to win the game. That win was the beginning of the four-in-a-row.'

JÓM

Johnny Walsh

There were similarities between the two but how many noticed on that hot afternoon in a dusty New York ballpark?

If the fighter's grandfather hadn't left Kildare for Logan County, West Virginia, if the footballer had chosen to pursue his boxing career, perhaps the two would have crossed paths before that day in 1933.

Jack Dempsey, the boxer, always punched above his weight. Back in 1919, he gave seven inches to heavyweight champ, Jess Willard. After three minutes in the ring, Willard was on the Ohio canvas, a case for the coroner, the big time fight writers said, and the Irish Americans had themselves a real hero.

Over a dozen years later, Walsh pounced on the sporting world just like Dempsey. It was 1932 and the 5-foot-10-inch Ballylongford boy was cast among the giants in midfield for his first Kerry championship game. It was a significant moment. Not only was it an All-Ireland final, his appearance ended the renowned centre-field partnership of Con Brosnan and Bob Stack.

'I don't remember much about that final against Mayo but I was under pressure,' he said, years later. 'I had broken up the famous partnership of Brosnan and Stack. At the time, they had a great reputation so I had a lot to live up to.'

The final whistle that day brought Walsh an All-Ireland medal – his first of five – and bookended Kerry's four-in-a row run.

With victory came an eight-day voyage to the US and a whistle stop tour of America's east coast.

It was on the final leg of the journey, in Manhattan, that Dempsey and Walsh shared a sporting arena for the first and only time.

The Manassa Mauler, still the pride of the Irish, was called on to throw in the ball for the New York game, an exhibition between Kerry and the ex-pat community.

Dempsey obliged and minutes before the game, he walked up to Bracker Regan and wondered had he any advice on how to throw the ball in.

'Jack was talking to Bracker,' Johnny Walsh recalled, 'and he asked Bracker, "What am I supposed to do?" Bracker told him, "Throw in the ball then run as fast as you can because you might get hurt."'

Dempsey, who drew boxing's first million-dollar gate followed Bracker's instructions.

Facing page:
Johnny Walsh presents Bernie O'Callaghan with a plaque. Others in the photograph are Con Brosnan (extreme right) and Eddie Dowling (on right behind Johnny Walsh).
(Jackie Walsh)

As the game wore on, Dempsey could see that Bracker wasn't joking. This was a man's game.

Walsh and his firm political beliefs were being singled out and not for the first time. 'A New York player came on to mark me,' Walsh said after. 'He said to me, "You are an effing Blueshirt. I will send you back in a coffin."'

It was a threat Walsh could live with. He'd prospered as a boxer at college in Dublin and a few months earlier, with the help of a hurley, he kept a group of IRA men at bay as they tried to vandalise his parents' bar in Ballylongford.

Across the ocean in New York, the response to his marker was swift.

'I told him he had an hour to send me back in a coffin and let the best man jump the fence. The first ball that came in, he drew a clout at me but I sidestepped him and caught him. I staggered him and he began to get very quiet. I beat him for another ball and I pretended that I didn't see him coming and as he approached, I picked the ball and met him and he was carried off. That sorted him out.'

With Walsh still some years short of his prime, it appeared that Kerry had unearthed an uncompromising midfielder to lead the county through the decade.

But with the political climate reaching crisis point, Walsh's beliefs led to more confrontation. 'I was dropped from Kerry because of my politics and became exiled from the county team,' he said.

Meanwhile, other codes devoured his time.

He began playing rugby for Garryowen and vowed never to play Gaelic football again. Every Saturday for two years, he boarded a bus to Limerick for training. He played in two Munster Senior Cup finals and was capped by Munster in 1935. Rugby was in his blood and had been since his school days in Rockwell College. He'd transferred from St Brendan's, where his appetite for football had been fed. Dr Eamonn O'Sullivan had begun school leagues during Walsh's time in Killarney and he prospered. 'I was three years on the senior side in St Brendan's. There were boys three years older than me on the team.'

During the Garryowen days, he struck up a lifelong friendship with another GAA legend, Mick Mackey.

'We would meet after rugby games and have a drink,' Walsh said. 'Then we'd meet regularly at Railway Cup matches when hurlers and footballers would travel together.'

Mackey was known all over Limerick for his passion for rugby but his talents and name were too dear to be lost to the Ban. Through the forward thinking of one official, the GAA deployed him as a member of a Vigilante Committee to feed his love of the foreign code. His brief was to attend rugby games and watch out for GAA men who played or paid into the games. It was an in-joke that, during his time as an association spy, he never found a single GAA man at a rugby game.

Walsh wasn't so lucky. After he left the Kerry scene, it seemed there was no way back. Playing rugby and openly criticising the GAA powers in his own county was seen as a bridge too far. But the peace handshake came from an unlikely source.

The reconciliatory nature of the game was always evident in Kerry and Walsh's case adds to the picture with another scene. His political beliefs were in total opposition to Austin Stacks club. The Rock Street club, led by Purty Landers, was full of IRA sympathisers, but as the sun was coming up on 1936, Kerry were hungry for success after the stand down the previous year.

If they were to contest another All-Ireland, they needed all the picture cards in the deck. Walsh had to be talked back.

Amazingly, it was the Rock Street club who would instigate his return when they sent their clubman and captain, Miko Doyle, to meet him.

Though regarded as being headstrong, Walsh accepted the olive branch.

All that was left was to pay his time for playing rugby. He was handed a six-month ban by the county board and lined out for his second spell with Kerry for the 1937 championship.

'I was lonely leaving the rugby,' Walsh said. 'A man should be put in a field and let him play what he likes so long as he keeps out of trouble.'

A plain sentiment in complicated times.

TJF

Peace & War

Bill Dillon

Bristling with energy, Fr Jackie McKenna emerges from his back room in Baile na mBuaile holding an old and faded photograph of a Dingle team with whom he shared the good times. He points to the legends snapped in the frame, locating Bill Casey, Sean Brosnan, Gega O'Connor and Paddy Bawn. Men who helped Dingle win their first county championship in 1938, men who laid the foundations of a football legacy back west.

'And look,' he says finally. 'There's Bill Dillon – Billimite.'

He settles back into his chair and pulls the cork from his bottle of memories. Himself and Dillon go way back. He remembers him first as a man of Dingle, of the place from where he came. 'A real home bird,' he says.

Back when the town's beauty and solitude was a secret kept by those within earshot of the ocean, Dillon's was a face recognised by all. To McKenna's young eyes, the footballer, a few years his elder, had giant-like qualities. 'I can still see him, a big, strapping fella, standing at the top of Main Street after first mass on a Sunday. He'd stand there calling his dogs with a bugle to bring them beagling up Conor Hill for the day. I was only a small lad then and never thought I'd end up winning county medals with him.'

Conor Hill. Fr McKenna brings the place to life, says the men of Dingle wandered its unfenced surface with their beagles and got lost in the quiet of the place. They hunted foxes, hares, rabbits, whatever scent the dogs could pick up. But it wasn't about the hunting. It was about the feel of the place, the sound of the earth crunching beneath their feet.

'Bill had many dogs and he was at home on those hills. Much more at home than when he climbed the steps of the Hogan Stand to collect the Sam, as he did in 1941.'

A little yarn has grown up around Bill and that year. By now, it's woven into the folk history of the town. Plenty will swear it's true, but Fr McKenna isn't so sure.

The story goes that on the morning of the semi-final replay with Dublin, which took place in Tralee, Bill was nowhere to be found. Gerald Fox was the hackney driver charged with bringing the Dingle players to the game and at the appointed hour, they arrived for collection on Bridge Street. All except Dillon.

A few minutes passed and then a few more until the occupants became

Previous pages:
Kerry contested five All-Irelands in a row from 1937 to 1941. This is the team that played in the famed 1938 All-Ireland final replay against Galway, the only final they lost in this period.
(Seamus O'Reilly)

Facing page:
A Munster versus Leinster Railway Cup game in 1936 while the Cusack Stand was under construction. Bill Dillon is pictured second from left, challenging for possession.
(Vincent O'Connor)

twitchy. No captain in sight and what sort of reception would the selectors give them if they arrived in Tralee without Dillon? They got the idea that he had to be on top of Conor Hill so they sent a delegation up the mountain to retrieve him.

'There's no doubt that the mentors would have had a hard time keeping him off the mountain before games, but I'd doubt if that tale is true. It's probably grown legs. For a semi-final, the mentors would have held him in Dingle. He couldn't have got away with something like that.'

Whenever he came down from the mountains, Dillon spent time on the boats that departed Dingle pier. These were war days, fishing was a means of survival and jobs at sea were plentiful. When work eventually tapered off, Bill, like his brother Jack, found a job with Córas Iompair Éireann, conducting on the Dingle to Tralee bus route. For years, his face was the first glimpse of home for those returning to the town. 'He never strayed too far from Dingle,' continues Fr McKenna.

He recalls the trips the Dingle crew would make to play county championship games in Tralee during the storied decade between 1938 and 1948.

Dillon had enough clout to dictate who travelled in the hackney along with himself. 'Petrol was scarce then, you see, but we had a permit for four hackneys to take us into Tralee for games. Dillon insisted that fellas like me would go in the same car as himself. He knew I didn't drink and he didn't want to be with fellas who would stay in Tralee for a few pints in Quinlan's on Rock Street after the game. Some lads would be mad to go on the town in Tralee afterwards but Bill's idea was to play the game and get back as quick as possible. He just wanted to get back to Dingle.'

The old Ashbourne Hotel, beside the courthouse in Tralee, acted as the Dingle base before and after championship games. Dillon's routine remained constant. Tog off, drink some tea, play football and return to the Ashbourne where he washed up on an outside tap. The bright lights of the county town never held his fascination. 'He never married, you know,' adds Fr McKenna. 'And 'twasn't for a shortage of admirers.'

When Dingle's finest day arrived, the day they finally annexed a county title, Fr McKenna was too young to play and too far away to see the game. It was billed as the big one. North Kerry against Dingle. Con Brosnan's final opportunity to win an elusive county medal and Dingle's chance to make history.

Fr McKenna was finding his way in Maynooth, ensconced in religious studies but his mind was at home that evening in 1938.

'There was huge interest in the game in Maynooth,' he recalls. 'There were five lads from north Kerry in the college with me and we were very anxious to get the result. Of course, we weren't allowed a radio so the following morning after breakfast we all rushed to another building to meet the janitor. He'd jot the results down from

Sean Ó Ceallacháin on the ten o'clock news and pass them on to all the students. He was sweeping the corridors this morning and we came galloping down to him. Dingle won. A great day.'

The void was filled and Dingle's era was beginning.

Dillon backboned the team and three years later, he was All-Ireland captain. This time, Fr McKenna, now a young priest, had some heavenly intervention. Foot-and-mouth disease swept the country and, in an effort to curb its spread, the All-Ireland football final was brought forward to the first Sunday in September. 'Only for the switch I wouldn't have been able to see that game. It wasn't one of Bill's best performances but he played fine and I was back to Maynooth the following day.'

The Sam Maguire found a winter home on Dillon's windowsill along Green Street. Passers-by would drop in to admire the trophy but at times they'd see it was filled with meat. Curious, they thought. Then they'd glance at Dillon's dogs that had the run of his house and it would seem strange no longer.

'It keeps the dogs from getting at the meat,' Bill would explain.

The priest smiles at the story and takes one more glance at the Dingle photograph before he gets to his feet and returns the snapshot back to his room.

'A photo full of memories,' he says. 'A different world.'

TJF

Sean Brosnan

The declaration of the Second World War on 3 September 1939 didn't have much impact on Dingle. In time, the distant drums of war on the Atlantic could be heard and German airmen crash-landed on Brandon, but even then the impact was negligible.

It was football, not war, that had tongues wagging in 1939. The upcoming All-Ireland final against Meath; Dingle's All-Ireland in many ways. The spine of the team was Dingle. Bill Dillon, Billy Casey, Tom 'Gega' O'Connor and Sean Brosnan. Paddy 'Bawn' Brosnan was first sub.

There was more. Kerry and Meath both wore green and gold. This clash of colours helped make it Dingle's day. Kerry officials favoured wearing Munster blue but Dingle dug in.

'As county champions, Kerry will wear the red and white of Dingle,' insisted club secretary, Jimmy McKenna, in a letter to the county board. 'The Dingle lads won't play unless it's in the Dingle colours and we won't travel,' he added. Officials relented. The red and white of Dingle it was.

The first Dingle jersey out of the dressing room and behind the Artane band was to be that of Sean Brosnan, Dingle's captain. The midfield man and master fielder. He was very young when his fielding prowess became apparent. His game was all about catching the caid.

Sean and younger brother Pádraig taught each other with a ball made of paper wrapped in twine. Codball, the boys called it. Number six Strand Street was home, which doubled as a shop, with the hallway given over to codball. A tight field where you had to have good hands. This is where Sean Brosnan learned to catch and kick.

'We always played in the hallway,' says Pádraig Brosnan. 'And we always kicked the ball high even though the shelves around us were stacked with lamp globes that my mother sold in the shop.

'One day, sometime in 1923, the ball crashed into a shelf but Sean threw himself and caught a globe before it crashed to the ground. This was the first time he showed what a great pair of hands he had. He was only eight.'

After a while, Sean took his talents to the open air. He didn't have far to travel. At the back of Strand Street, there were two fields owned by Jonathon Moriarty.

The playground nearest Strand Street was the Bog Field and the ground

Facing page:
Midfielder Sean Brosnan is swept off the field by enthusiastic supporters after the 1937 All-Ireland win over Cavan. (Tony Honan)

between the Bog Field and the hospital was called the Green. The Bog was Sean's field – four stones would be thrown down on the grass for goalposts.

Occasionally the Strand Street boys would venture the 100 yards up to the Colony where the locals had their own field and team. This was the team led by Paddy Bawn who was another All-Ireland winner in the making. Sean Brosnan showed Paddy Bawn the way in the 1937 All-Ireland final when he was midfield with Johnny Walsh.

'Sean Brosnan brought down ball after ball with a reach that seemed magical, while his long punts goalwards gave the Cavan backs little peace or ease,' enthused Green Flag, a GAA correspondent in *The Irish Press*.

That day, his one-handed catches earned him the moniker of the one-armed man. Up he'd soar with one hand and then let the ball roll down his arm into his chest. A sight to behold, but he always seemed to need motivation.

'Brosnan never came out of his shell until he got a few hard knocks,' noted PF in his 1937 All-Ireland final report for *The Kerryman*.

They knew this in Dingle. In one county championship match in the early '40s, Dingle needed Sean to perform, so Tom 'Gega' O'Connor hatched a plan.

Brosnan went up for a ball, but Gega had no eyes for it. Thinking about his own man, he thundered in from behind and took Brosnan out of it, leaving him in a heap on Austin Stack Park.

A ball didn't pass Brosnan for the rest of the game – he took vengeance out on the opposition without ever knowing that Gega was the culprit.

It was Dingle's way of handling Sean Brosnan but it was something the Kerry selectors couldn't always do.

The All-Ireland semi-final against Galway in 1942 was one occasion and it almost brought Kerry football to its knees.

Brosnan had played a good Munster final but was curiously dropped for the semi-final. There was mayhem in Dingle and the semi-final was lost. Ironically, the scores that won it for Galway came all the way from the Dingle peninsula – Dan Kavanagh from Dun Chaoin got the equalising goal while Connie O'Connor from the Mall in Dingle stroked over the Connacht champions' winning point.

The chance of a four-in-a-row was gone and Kerry football was in crisis over the treatment of Sean Brosnan.

'The dropping of Sean Brosnan will be the biggest surprise for all county followers,' commented *The Kerry Champion* in their preview to the game. 'Kerry were beaten at centre-field in this game. I can't see where Sean Brosnan would have failed,' the *Champion* noted afterwards.

It prompted the Dingle club that had won three county championships in four years to throw down a challenge to Galway. A team made up of residents and non-residents from the Dingle area west of Camp wanted to play Galway to prove Sean Brosnan's worth. They even gave the Tribesmen their choice of venue but Galway shied away from the challenge and Brosnan was left disappointed again. It was a feeling he was familiar with during his inter-county career but 1939 was worst of all and this time it had nothing to do with the whims of Kerry selectors.

Brosnan was fated to miss out on playing in the All-Ireland final that year and instead, he was forced to re-live another part of his youth.

In the '20s Sean would gravitate to the radio in the Strand Street post office operated by Elizabeth Goggin, who was a sister of *The Kerryman*'s football correspondent PF. It was there that Sean heard about the fielding exploits of Larry Stanley and Con Brosnan.

'Carberry's commentaries were like a dream to young ears,' says Sean's brother, Pádraig Brosnan. But listening to Micheál O'Hehir's commentary in 1939 was a nightmare.

Sean caught the flu the day before the game. He was in his sickbed in the Grand Hotel in Dun Laoghaire Hotel as Gega O'Connor captained Kerry to the All-Ireland. Gega, when it should have been Sean.

'Sean Brosnan Robbed of Great Honour,' roared an *Irish Press* headline.

Gega brought the cup out to Sean's bedside and presented him with Sam Maguire. It wasn't the same as getting it in Croke Park but it still went down as Dingle's greatest day, though everyone in his town felt for Sean Brosnan.

JÓM

Tom 'Gega' O'Connor

Gegas is Greek for giant and Gega was the nickname given to Tom O'Connor from Goat Street in Dingle from an early age. The local wags may not have been talking about his football, but they could have been.

A giant Gega was but he never boasted about his football or his many other sporting pursuits when holding court behind his bar counter in New York, drinking pints of piping hot tea.

O'Connors in Rockaway, Queens was owned by Gega in partnership with Mickey O'Connor from Ballydavid, 7 miles west of Dingle. Gega had no Kerry memorabilia on the wall, no boxing snaps either. Nothing.

But Kerry people who called to the bar knew how famous Gega was. Some even knew of his boxing days and there was plenty of boxing history in O'Connors – Mickey O'Connor sparred with Joe Louis in his day while Gega fought for an Irish middleweight title.

'I was Gega's best friend growing up,' recalled Mick Falvey, 'but I didn't know about the middleweight title fight. He never told me even though I was in digs in Rathmines just down the road from the National Stadium. One night, my landlady came into my room and said, "There's a gentleman at the door for you."

'Who was it but Gega with a big swollen eye that was going black. "What happened you?" I said. "I was boxing, do you mind if I stay a few nights, I want to get rid of the black eye." He had a half-pound of steak up on his eye to bring the swelling down. I asked why he didn't tell me about the fight but he didn't want to be bragging. That was his way.'

Same way when Gega went to St Francis De Sales High School in Far Rockaway to kick some ball. It's where his son, Tommy, and daughters, Mary, Patty and Catherine, went to school. Tommy played gridiron and Gega took more than a passing interest.

He was regularly down on the field with the team, showing the kicker how to fire field goals, showing others how to gain yards by punting from the hands. He knew a trick or two about kicking ball in New York. He scored a goal in the Polo Grounds All-Ireland and had another disallowed.

'In Gega, St Francis had a new kicking coach,' says his brother, Fr Paddy O'Connor. 'He must have imagined he was in the Dingle Sportsfield again, learning his football from Brother Brennan. But a priest came up to him and

Facing page:
Captain Tom 'Gega' O'Connor chaired from the field after captaining Kerry to victory over Meath in the 1939 All-Ireland. (Jo O'Connor)

said, "What would you know about football?"

'Gega didn't explain, instead he just walked away. That was his way. His own kids didn't even know what he had achieved.'

Gega's first big day was in 1937, he was a year out of school and part of the revolution that was forming in Dingle. The town teemed with footballers. The Colony, Strand Street, John Street, The Mall. They all had teams.

'I lived opposite the Market Field that was a couple of miles up from the Holy Stone,' recalled Mick Falvey. 'I'd meet Gega every morning. Foxy John, Gega, Joe Adams and myself would go to school. There were 100 young lads on Goat Street that time. We played football everywhere.'

Then Gega did his own thing. Boxed in the Scout Hall on the Mall and later in Garret Cotter's gym in Tralee; weight-trained with anvils at the back of his house; kicked ball in the Upper Grove Field and Cnoc a' Charan behind the house when everyone else had gone home. All to be a Kerry footballer.

Bill Dillon used to go beyond the Conor Pass with his beagles; Billy Casey trained as he farmed near Strickeen; Sean Brosnan went to Jonathon Moriarty's Field.

These were Kerry footballers before Gega but O'Connor was determined to be one of them. It happened in 1937 by sheer persistence, even though he wasn't even at the drawn All-Ireland final against Cavan.

He was at home listening to Canon Michael Hamilton's commentary. Hamilton declared Cavan the winners after Pakie Boylan punched a point. What the Clare cleric didn't know was that Boylan had thrown the ball over the bar. The score was disallowed, the game ended level and Gega was in Croke Park for that replay.

First, he was in Austin Stack Park in Tralee when collective training for the replay started on 4 October. Gega travelled there with Sean Brosnan, Billy Casey and Bill Dillon. He was there to watch but was asked to join in and make up the numbers.

Dr Eamonn O'Sullivan was impressed. Kerry were already without the injured Paddy Kennedy and Billy Casey and, with this in mind, Gega was drafted on to the Kerry panel days before the replay.

It was too late to earn mention in *The Kerryman* and the official match programme had gone to print by the time Gega was given his first senior jersey.

It was a commentator's nightmare for the second match running – the bonfires had to be doused in Cavan after Canon Hamilton's blunder the first day. His second and last day out was marked by another blunder that happened when Tim O'Donnell suffered a career-ending knee injury after Jim Smallhorn crashed into him five minutes into the match.

'Jimmy "Gawksie" O'Gorman is on the Kerry team for Tim O'Donnell,' Canon

Hamilton roared. Gawksie from number ten Urban Terrace wasn't even among the five listed subs but Hamilton was convinced. 'The son of Thady O'Gorman who captained Kerry to their first All-Ireland title,' he explained.

They celebrated on the Terrace in Tralee but it was only in the following days that they found out it was Gega and not Gawksie who played. Gega slotted in at right-half-back and won the first of five All-Ireland medals. It was a quiet beginning. Kerry supporters, let alone the commentator, didn't know his name.

It was a lot different two years later. The unknown from 1937 was Kerry captain, bringing Sam up Main Street, Dingle, behind a procession of sod turfs on hay pikes that were soaked in paraffin oil and lit.

Canon Thomas Lyne led the convoy to the Temperance Hall and introduced the Dingle players one by one from a first-floor window to the crowd below.

Paddy Bawn, Bill Dillon, Billy Casey. Then Sean Brosnan and O'Connor came to the window together. Both captains held Sam aloft.

JÓM

Billy Casey

The sun was shining on Strickeen. A day to make hay, thought Billy Casey, as he rambled down to his field on the Dingle Road out of Lispole. *'Tús maith, leath na h-oibre'*, 'a good start is half the work'.

Casey was the best of these intentions as he forked hay. Nothing better than working the field. Solitary confinement but as soothing as the shine on Strickeen.

No interruptions until a car pulled up on the roadside. It had come a long way – the Northern registration gave that away. The accent of the occupant too. The driver abandoned his car and climbed the ditch. 'Do ya know who I am?' he roared.

Billy Casey recognised his man straight away. It was Harry O'Neill of Antrim. They shook hands in the middle of the field, then Casey drove the hay fork into the ground and hopped into O'Neill's Hillman Hunter and headed for Dingle. Casey took O'Neill on a tour. Into Tom Long's in the Holyground and down Strand Street to Paddy Bawn's.

Gega O'Connor was long gone to America but they still made off his family pub on Goat Street. They shook hands many times that day. They were making up for lost years.

Casey and O'Neill hadn't met in well over two decades and their previous encounter was fractious instead of friendly. The 1946 All-Ireland semi-final between Antrim and Kerry was a tempestuous affair. Of the 30 players on the field, the most hot-headed were Harry O'Neill and Billy Casey.

They didn't shake hands as they left the field, but they were shaking fists after being sent off for fighting. Pub-crawling around Dingle over two decades on was the making up after the breaking up.

The tour around Dingle brought back happy memories for Billy Casey. He was centre-back – in the thick of things when Kerry won their sixteenth All-Ireland in 1946, his greatest year in football – when he shone in the final replay against Roscommon.

When Kerry lost to Roscommon in the 1944 final, they did so without Casey, who was ruled out through injury. Martin McCarthy from Castleisland manned the gap but Roscommon punched holes down the middle all day.

Two years later Casey was back and Roscommon wished that he had stayed away. Footballer of the Year before such an award was ever dreamt up, Casey

Facing page:
Billy Casey at home, working the land in Lispole with two of his sons and a neighbour.
(Riobáird Casey)

put the shackles on Roscommon captain Jimmy Murray. It was a day to remember Billy Casey by.

Fifty years on, his son Riobáird Casey learned something of his father's greatest day. He was in the stand in Thurles at the 1996 All-Ireland Under 21 final between Cavan and Kerry. Joe McCarthy, a past pupil of his in Mary Immaculate College, Limerick, was in the same stand.

Sitting beside Joe McCarthy was his wife, Eileen Conneely, and her father, who had a story to tell.

'Myself and my brother shouldered your dad off the field in '46,' Conneely said to Riobáird Casey. 'I had a needle in the lapel of my coat and it went into Billy's thigh and the needle was the only thing that hurt Billy that day, he was brilliant.'

Casey won his fifth All-Ireland medal that October afternoon. Not bad for a bashful footballer. That was Billy Casey. He didn't live for football like many of his Dingle CBS teammates. Couldn't afford to. Farming took precedence over football and, as a boy, Casey stepped into a paternal role. His father passed away before he was born, while his older brother, Jack, died of pneumonia in his twentieth year. Jack was a good footballer, they said, but Billy would be better. It was just a matter of getting him to play the game.

When school was out, Casey always made a dash for his bicycle, only for Brother Micheál Brennan to block the way. It was a game within a game that they played most days. 'Just play today,' was Brother Brennan's begging line. 'Just today.'

Casey always played but it didn't stop him having one eye on the Lispole road out of Dingle. He regularly played with his jersey on over his shirt so that, when the game ended, he was already dressed for home.

Brother Brennan was such a perfectionist when it came to the attire of his footballers on the Dingle Sportsfield that he was infuriated by Casey's antics but he always shied away from taking action against the young Lispole footballer.

What mattered was he had Casey playing ball and that Dingle CBS had a star who came from great football stock: Casey's uncle, Paddy Casey, won two All-Irelands with Dublin before going to fight in the Great World War. He was gassed on his first night on the front but it didn't sap his strength.

Many years later, he was in Yankee Stadium. Kerry had just beaten New York before 60,000 spectators on the 1933 tour and Paddy made his way down from the bleachers. He picked up Roundy Landers as if he were a child and shouldered him around the field.

His nephew was just as strong. He had to be to man the centre-half-back spot almost uninterrupted for thirteen years from 1936 to 1949. One of those few interruptions came in 1942 when Dingle player-power came between Kerry and a four-in-a-row.

Some of the Dingle players went on strike, instigated by Sean Brosnan, who was dropped from the starting fifteen. Brosnan asked his Dingle colleagues not to travel to the All-Ireland semi-final against Dublin. Billy Casey and Paddy 'Bawn' Brosnan stayed at home in solidarity, while Bill Dillon and Gega O'Connor went ahead and played.

'It was the only regret of Billy's football life,' says his son, Riobáird. 'After Billy had a bypass operation,' says Fr Jackie McKenna, 'I used to go to visit him in Lispole and he said Brosnan should have been on the team but shouldn't have asked others not to play. He was still very disappointed he had stayed away that day.'

He had a long career that made up for this blip and went through it all that day with Harry O'Neill on their crawl around the pubs of old Dingle.

JÓM

Tim Landers

Roundy. He revelled in the bestowing of the name upon him. It gave him character and in time, he filled the word out and made it his.

Roundy. In Tim Landers' world, a kid with a nickname had his head a few inches above the crowd. It was the brand of individuality, catapulting him alongside his brothers – Lang and Purty.

In the years that passed, a cottage industry of theories surrounded his second christening. Roundy told only one.

He was whiling away his summer days with the rest of the Rock Street crew, kicking ball on a field called Barrett O'Leary's, later to become the Tralee Greyhound Track.

Tim was fifteen years of age, sixteen at the most and had reached a stocky 5 foot 6 inches in height. He would grow no more but he didn't know that at the time.

Denis 'Rory' O'Connell was a character and wit, living within kicking distance of the field. He was tired of the sight of this youngster, eternally out on the grass, ball at his feet.

One evening, he saw the youngster approach the field once more, boots slung over his shoulder. 'Here comes the roundy arse again,' O'Connell bellowed. The crew heard the shout. The name stuck and Roundy was born.

His stature wasn't a deterrent but he was aware of the difficulties it could bring on the field. He was smaller than his two brothers who had already worn the Kerry jersey. Bill 'Lang' Landers was a tall, square-shouldered man, with an ample reach. John Joe 'Purty' had 6 inches over his younger brother and Roundy knew if he was to follow this duo onto the county scene, he needed an extra edge.

'A small man had no chance at that time, if he didn't produce something out of the ordinary,' Roundy said years after he found his alter ego.

He set about uncovering some alternative talents and took dedication to new heights. For months at a stretch, he camped on the beach at Banna Strand, sleeping in a concrete hut beneath a tin roof, honing his skills in the morning and evening and cycling to work to break the day.

Sometimes, he had part of the Rock Street crew in tow. On other occasions, the crashing waves were his only company. One year, he stayed out on the beach, training like a fanatic, until the cold nights of November made a

Facing page:
Tim 'Roundy'
Landers.
(Tim Landers Jnr)

113

return to Urban Terrace the prudent decision. Five months had passed since he had spent a night in Tralee.

The special, extraordinary gift he sought was tailored on the sands of Banna – the ability to dribble the ball soccer-style, like a loping wizard from Brazil.

Out at Banna at the time, lobster pots and fishing nets were marked with bright glass spheres. For Roundy, they doubled as a football. Over a 3-mile patch of sand, he would dribble and dribble with this bright ball at his feet. His control was perfected and honed to a fine art and the toil was always worth it. In 1937, he scored one of the most individual and talked-about goals Croke Park had seen.

Two weeks before that final against Cavan, while the rest of the team trained collectively under Dr Eamonn O'Sullivan, Roundy was given permission to stay at Banna, where he pounded the sand alone, a ball stuck to his toe. The subsequent Cavan game saw him put practice into play.

It wasn't unusual for Roundy to claim a high ball from the air, drop it to his foot, then weave in and out between defenders. It was the most vicious weapon in his arsenal and this is what he did in the final, collecting the ball at midfield, then nosing all the way to goal. On the 14-yard line, he struck and buried to the net. Nobody had seen such a goal.

Word spread of his soccer prowess and an approach from England was made. The exact details of the offer and interested club are lost in the mist – not surprising, given the stifling climate of the Ban, coupled with local republican affiliations.

'Somebody from England came and made an offer to him,' recalls his wife, Noreen. 'But Roundy wouldn't even think about it. He refused straight off. You'd be shot back then if you played soccer.'

His soccer was on Banna. Those sessions with the weighty fishing buoys provided other important qualities and enhanced leg strength. On both sides of the field, Roundy became Kerry's free-taker-in-chief and even with the heavier leather of his time, distance wasn't an obstacle. He had range from 45 yards out and to further impress his audience, he always took just one step in the run up.

But the alternative training sessions weren't welcomed by all and there were times when some Kerry players didn't entirely approve of his custom-made drills.

When Roundy joined the rest of the group for collective training, he often forfeited drills involving ball control. Instead, he would don a pair of running spikes, break from the group and work on improving his speed, sprinting in bursts while the others went through handling and kicking exercises.

Some of the players began to complain that Roundy was opting out through laziness and at one point, while training in Tralee, matters came to a head. Roundy's independent state was invaded.

Out in his own patch, running by himself, a ball was bombed into his territory. A few comments passed. He ignored them. It happened again and on the third occasion, Roundy trapped the ball with his spikes, slamming his foot down and burst the leather in the process.

'That was the end of that,' Roundy explained to *The Irish Press*. 'Someone was sent in to Arthur Caball's to buy a new ball.' He wasn't bothered again. Roundy did his own things in his own way.

'In their young days, they'd kick on the street in front of the house on Urban Terrace,' continues Noreen. 'The bacon factory in Tralee was right beside number one on the Terrace and Roundy was in number seven, so he was just around the corner from it. Himself and the rest of the young lads would go down and ask for a pig's bladder. They'd usually get one too. I remember Roundy telling me about those games around the Terrace. They'd blow up the bladder and he said it was lovely and light to kick, but very tough. That's how he spent the early years of his life. He'd only venture into town the odd time, maybe to see the pictures. It was the pig's bladder that took up his time. Nothing else.'

He ran the gamut of footballs. Leather, pig, lobster marker. He mastered them all.

TJF

Dan O'Keeffe

A couple of facts to quickly paint a picture: Dan O'Keeffe minded the Kerry net from 1931 until 1948; he won seven All-Irelands; played 66 championship games and pocketed a dozen Munster medals; displayed longevity at a time when players in his position had no protection, when forwards hurled themselves at the goalkeeper every time he had possession; played senior football with Kerry until he was 42 and was the obvious choice for the number one spot on the Team of the Millennium.

Twenty years after he retired, *The Kerryman* ran a series of full-page articles on his life and career. It lasted four months; a mini-novel in itself.

Those who knew O'Keeffe recall firstly a modest man. When the Kerry team stayed in Scott's Hotel, Killarney, as part of collective training, O'Keeffe's noble ways stood him out from the crowd. He didn't drink. He wasn't loud. He was always the quiet gentleman. It impressed Mrs Scott, the lady of the premises, and she gave him a present of a horseshoe for his good behaviour. He brought it into the goals with him for luck and in 1946, his last successful All-Ireland for Kerry, Dan's son, Dónal, the mascot, famously carried the horseshoe in the parade.

Seven years later, the horseshoe was passed onto another Strand Road goalkeeper, Johnny Foley, and it rested again in the Kerry goals.

O'Keeffe rarely gave interviews to the press – it was standard for retired players to give their opinion on the current game of the '50s and '60s and their take on the rules of the day. They would normally reveal something about their own playing days as well. O'Keeffe shied away from this. On one rare occasion, he broke his embargo and gave a few soundbites – in 1952, he told a reporter from *The Sunday Press* that his competence as a goalkeeper was down to the backs in front of him.

'I always had great protection from my full-backs,' he said. 'It was their only method of giving me a fair chance to clear the ball. When the ball passed them, they concentrated on keeping out the forwards.'

But his relationship with Kerry full-back lines that included Joe Keohane and Joe Barrett is far from the full story.

O'Keeffe was born in Fermoy, north Cork, and landed in Tralee as an eight-year-old obsessed with hurling. It was 1915 and Kerry had just secured two All-Irelands as well as the Croke Memorial Cup. Football was becoming the

Facing page:
All-Ireland gold –
Dan O'Keeffe and
son Dónal with the
family gold.
(Maura O'Keeffe)

117

currency of all conversation in the county town. He kicked some ball for Tralee CBS but his teenage years came and went and O'Keeffe still hadn't joined any of the three Tralee clubs.

His schoolfriend, Charlie Crimmins, recalled that O'Keeffe had no ambition to make a name for himself with any recognised team. 'He was content to knock a ball about with his own cronies and practice with them in the evenings.'

The Kerryman series tells of one Sunday in February 1926 when the band of footballers gathered in Tralee. They rented a lorry and travelled to Killarney for a challenge game against the students of St Brendan's. It was the first time O'Keeffe would line out in anything resembling an official team. It was nearly his last.

The Tralee outfit was well beaten and as the lorry returned for Tralee, Crimmins produced an accordion to keep spirits up.

Halfway home, at the Farranfore level crossing, the lorry overturned and catapulted all passengers onto the road. Some landed in a nearby field and two were trapped beneath the vehicle. One escaped unhurt, the other, Joe O'Gorman, a nephew of Kerry's first All-Ireland winning captain Thady, suffered a severe leg break and spent weeks in hospital. His football days were ended for good.

Months later, that team, made up mainly of players from Ballymullen in Tralee, applied to the Urban Board for official recognition. It was accepted and the town had a new junior club – The Rangers. They began training at Barrett O'Leary's field in Rock Street and during his shift in goal, O'Keeffe's untapped abilities became recognised.

He was asked to take on goalkeeping responsibilities for an upcoming town league game and agreed on condition that he could wear long trousers and a peaked cap. The trousers remained only for a few games but the cap became part of his regular playing garb.

Scouts from Tralee's three big clubs noticed his league performances in bringing The Rangers up to senior grade and by 1929, he was lining out for Strand Street. He won a junior All-Ireland in 1930 and that campaign secured his place aboard the *St Louis* that carried the senior panel to the US in May 1931.

The trip lasted most of the summer with O'Keeffe deputising for regular goalkeeper Johnny Riordan in Boston, Philadelphia and Chicago. When he landed back in Tralee, the Atlantic air still in his lungs, O'Keeffe could smell his senior championship debut. But his stateside performances were tempered with news that the extended trip had lost him his job.

Still, his debut wasn't far away. Kerry/Kildare rivalry was at its height in the autumn of 1931 and 75 trains made use of Ireland's sprawling rail network to head to Croke Park for the All-Ireland final between the two counties. Kerry travelled more in hope than confidence. Pedlar Sweeney had been injured in a serious car accident in Brooklyn and the weekend of the final, the influential Tim O'Donnell had withdrawn from the team with knee problems. John Joe Sheehy had retired following the US trip and the local press didn't hold out much hope. 'A Kerry team without John Joe Sheehy is like an All-Ireland final without Kerry,' said *The Kerryman*.

The morning of the game, another bombshell was dropped. Riordan was off the team and O'Keeffe was in. He kept a clean sheet the same day and his story was just beginning.

Others tried to tempt him away from becoming the first footballer to win seven All-Ireland medals.

Celtic trainers came to Croke Park one day in the '30s to see him play. They were impressed and approached him after the game.

'He was married at the time and it was a chance to get a house, money and a car,' recalls Dan's daughter, Maura. 'A lot of his family were living in Glasgow at the time. His aunt and uncle were there so it would have been home from home.'

He stayed put. In 1946 he picked up that seventh medal. When the Kerry train pulled into Tralee after the game, a huge gathering lay in wait to welcome O'Keeffe back.

'My mother told me he jumped off the train and ran all the way home,' adds Maura. 'A crowd of supporters followed him back and the place outside the house was packed with people. He went upstairs to the window and waved down at them. There were bonfires lit for him but that was Dad. He always wanted to escape the crowd.'

TJF

Murt Kelly

Lismacfinnan lies on the Killarney side of Killorglin. The townland is an idyllic, gleaming speck on the map. It rests within grasp of Macgillycuddy's Reeks and in summer days when the sun spills out, the big mountain throws a soft shadow over the place. Nobody with their senses would wish to leave here. Plenty were forced to though.

Back at the start of the twentieth century when Murt Kelly was still a little wisp of a lad, more people said goodbye to Lismacfinnan than stayed to bask in its rolling landscape. Young Murt saw plenty nose off for faraway places. Nine of his ten older siblings were cast out upon all latitudes of the globe while they were still teenagers. They worked their way out of Kerry, succumbing, like many others, to the ruin of emigration. There was nothing, absolutely nothing to keep them clothed and fed in Lismacfinnan.

It was a familiar chain. The eldest would earn a few shillings and send back the fare for the next to follow. So it worked and a string of Kellys had left before Murt began school.

His elder brother by nineteen years, Jimmy, who he had never laid eyes on, eked out a living on America's east coast. His sister, Sheila, became Superior General with the Sisters of Nazareth and the others spread like wheat seeds.

Murt, the youngest, was lucky and so was his brother Joseph. Joseph became a farmer and Murt turned his hand to teaching and both were spared the boat trip.

For years, the old sages of Lismacfinnan reckoned the place could have backboned a couple of Kerry teams only for the sting of emigration.

All around it seemed like kids were kicking ball one day, preparing to board the ship the next. Leaving became woven into the fabric of the community and those who stayed behind reckoned they would never again see those that left.

In 1938, when Murt was 26, he went on a trip of his own and travelled to New York as a member of the Kerry team. Word of the visit arrived stateside before the ship did and Jimmy Kelly was waiting on Yankee soil to welcome his little brother to his adopted homeland.

A long time later, Murt's son, Colm, asked his old man what it was like seeing his brother for the first time.

'What was it like?' Murt pondered. 'It was like seeing my own father. It was like seeing Dad turning up again.'

Facing page:
Heavyweights all – from left, Teddy O'Connor, Johnny Walsh, Tadhg Crowley, Dr Jim Brosnan and Murt Kelly, at a Kerry trial game in 1965.
(The Kerryman)

Swings and roundabouts and some soft negotiating ultimately landed Murt Kelly on that tour. When he left St Patrick's Training College in 1932, a job in the city came his way. He grabbed it and after college days were over, began to kick football with the Geraldines, a club with a large number of Kerry exiles. Life was good. A few coins in the pocket and a place on the Kerry panel.

But the Kerry connection didn't last long. Soon after finding his way into the system, he was hit with a bombshell. His services were no longer required. Dropped. Good luck. It came from the blue and shattered his hopes.

'He always felt there was an element of local politics involved in that decision,' says Colm. 'He told the story that Tralee dominated Kerry football at the time and if you weren't from there, you had to be twice as good to play for the county. He was very annoyed over the whole thing.'

Word seeped through to the Dublin County Board that Kelly of the Geraldines was a free agent. They approached him to play for his adopted county. Headstrong and still disillusioned with Kerry, he accepted. In 1934, the unthinkable came to pass. Dublin won Leinster. Kerry won Munster. A semi-final featuring both was set for Tralee. And, cherry on top, Kelly was named captain for the day.

As Dublin paraded through the town en route to Austin Stack Park, Kelly could feel the glare of eyes fixed upon him. He heard the whispers – that there was the Kerryman who had defected to Dublin.

No matter. Two hours later and to the dismay and surprise of the local constituency, Dublin were heading back home with thoughts of an All-Ireland final to warm the journey.

They routed Kerry 3-8 to 0-6. It was an emotional day as most realised it was the end of the road for the four-in-a-row team.

'I remember saying to him, "God, ye must have got an awful bad reception in Tralee after ye beat Kerry." And he said, "Well, we changed out of our Dublin jerseys in Limerick on the way back." The Kerry crowd wasn't happy and the Dublin lads didn't hang about after the game. They made a quick exit.'

Dublin, patched together with footballers from all corners of the country, felt the final against Galway was a foregone conclusion. Galway surprised them, though. Beat them by two points and came away with the prize. It was Murt Kelly's first All-Ireland final but many more would follow.

Towards the end of the decade, a peace deal was finally brokered with the Kerry selectors and once more Kelly declared for his county. He excelled on his return and felt it was imperative to prove his detractors wrong. From a variety of forward positions, Kelly helped fire the county to a three-in-a-row run from 1939 to 1941. He dominated proceedings in '41 and finished the championship as Kerry's top scorer.

In the semi-final they faced Dublin. Trailing by a point, Kerry had a last minute free to level the game. Kelly nailed it.

On the toss of a coin, Tralee was chosen as the venue for the replay. By now, a petrol shortage had swept the county and transport was scarce. Still, 15,000 spectators pedalled and walked to the game. Kelly was a home hero this time. No whispers or glares. At half-time, Kerry led 1-3 to 0-3, all points coming from Kelly and the goal a creation of his. They tacked more nails into the Dublin coffin during the second half and beat Galway in the final. Kelly's wheel had come full-circle.

Two lean years followed before Kerry reached another final and when they were beaten by Roscommon, Kelly decided he had enough. His inter-county career was tapering away and those long journeys home were jangling the bones. He stayed put in Dublin and again gave his services to the capital men.

After a few years, the call of mid-Kerry began to find him again. He moved to Beaufort before the end of the '40s, married and bought himself a Volkswagen Beetle. He trekked the few miles west each day to Fybach National School in Keel, where he worked as headmaster. Beyond the rusty schoolyard in Fybach lay a few small acres of paradise. A patch of hard, dry bog was transformed by the school kids into two football pitches; Croke Park and Casement Park they called them. When an age of maturity was reached, the young footballers graduated from Casement Park to the larger, firmer ground of Croke Park. Those lunch times when the headmaster would wander onto the bog, stoop low and impart a shot of football wisdom were treasured and the advice was stored away and put into use on the dreamy pitches of Fybach.

Kelly spread his gospel further still, took up as a selector with Kerry in the mid-'50s and spent his last day on the sideline of the real Croke Park beside Mick O'Dwyer in 1977.

Dublin beat Kerry that day in an All-Ireland semi-final. Just like they had in Tralee in 1934 and the irony of the thing wasn't lost on the headmaster.

TJF

Charlie O'Sullivan

The place is pedestrianised now, but there was a time when two-way traffic flowed on Grafton Street. Pedestrians were pushed onto paths by passing cars. Austin A 40s, Anglias, Ford Prefects, Mini Minors and Morris Minors ruled this road. But even the cars had to defer to the higher authority that was Charlie O'Sullivan, the traffic cop. Charlie stood sentry on Grafton Street for decades.

He was known as Bonny Prince Charlie because of his permanent smile. A man as much a part of Grafton Street history as Brown Thomas, Bagatelle or Bewley's.

One of the singing Dubs called Luke Kelly used to slag Charlie about Kerry. Paddy Kavanagh would stop to talk up Inniskeen and Monaghan football. Taoiseach Jack Lynch played the Cork card. O'Sullivan was an institution.

'Going to Dublin meant meeting Charlie at his perch on the top of Grafton Street,' said Joe Keohane after Charlie's death. 'Twisting the words of the "Mountains of Mourne" a little, "There we'd stand talking of days that were gone, while the whole population of Dublin looked on."'

Those days started for Charlie in Camp National School. His father was the principal and a football man. Older brothers Tom and Gerry were on the greatest Camp team of them all – the 1928 side that won the West Kerry League final.

They talk about that final in Camp to this very day. Tim O'Donnell, Tom and Gerry O'Sullivan, Jackie Murphy. John 'Kerry' O'Donnell had come from America to tog out.

Fourteen-year-old Charlie looked on that day. Within a couple of years, he was out there with his brothers – they looked after him while fatherly protection was never far away.

It was needed. Camp football historian Eugene Deane remembers one day. 'Camp were playing a local derby against Baile Dubh and a bit of a fight rose between Charlie and a Baile Dubh fella. Charlie's father was in on the field and he pulled an umbrella across your man's throat and dragged him away. That finished the fight.'

In Tralee CBS, O'Sullivan was a hero to young players like Joe Keohane, Paddy Kennedy and Tadhg Healy. He led the Green to Munster glory and the Kerry minors to the All-Ireland. The senior selectors soon wanted Charlie to lead their attack. He travelled to America with Kerry in 1933 as the child of the new

Facing page:
Kerry's 1939 All-Ireland winning team in Dingle jerseys, with a smiling Charlie O'Sullivan pictured second from right in the front row.
(Seamus O'Reilly)

generation of Kerry footballers.

In time the child became the man and the 1940 All-Ireland would become known as the Charlie O'Sullivan All-Ireland, just like 1959 was the Sean Murphy All-Ireland. A Camp thing.

Kerry and Galway were deadlocked in time added on. One last Galway attack saw Brendan Nestor pick out John Burke. The army man from Clare glanced over his shoulder at the posts and screw-kicked for the All-Ireland. It looked like the winning point until the ball drifted at the last second, hitting the top of the post and bouncing back into play.

The ball hopped and another army man, Joe Keohane, fly-kicked it down the field towards the Canal goal. Charlie's All-Ireland was rubber-stamped with one lash of the sweetest left peg in football.

'Dan Spring got injured and Paddy Bawn came on as a sub at centre-forward,' said Charlie after the game. 'I went full-forward on Mick Connaire. The ball came from Joe Keohane's long kick to Paddy Kennedy who sent it to me. As Connaire closed to tackle me, he slipped on the wet turf. I palmed the ball over him as he slid past. I was clear, collected the ball and kicked it over the bar.'

The whistle sounded and O'Sullivan's hero status was certified.

Things were slightly different two years before that, the year Kerry lost an All-Ireland to Galway in a replay. O'Sullivan missed an opportunity to win the game the first day out but some said it wasn't his fault.

It was Micheál O'Hehir's maiden All-Ireland commentary and he was painting pictures for the first time. O'Sullivan stepped up to take a free that was well within his range and one that could snare another All-Ireland.

'I built up the excitement in my box as Charlie prepared to take the free,' recalled O'Hehir later. 'The run up, the kick. Charlie sent the ball wide. The result was an abusive letter from an irate Kerry listener. "Why did you not keep quiet when Charlie was trying for that point? All your noise put him off. How could anyone expect Charlie to score from that free with you nattering away?"'

Charlie and Micheál laughed about that All-Ireland incident on their Grafton Street meetings. Time was a tool with O'Sullivan, never a crutch.

That was the memory of O'Sullivan that Moss Walsh took with him from their friendship. The two went back a long way and joined the Garda Síochána on the same day.

'Charlie lived on Baggot Street and after getting sick later on in life he was brought to the Meath Hospital. When he landed there they sent him back to Baggot Street Hospital after discovering he was treated there previously. The ambulance passed his house en route and Charlie roared, "Goodbye number 52, I might never see you again."'

He fought on and returned home to Baggot Street before eventually retiring to Sneem. It was short-lived. He was only 64 when he died suddenly.

'It's hard to believe he's dead,' wrote Joe Keohane in a newspaper column. 'Charlie represented everything that was finest, not only in Kerry football but in Kerry manhood of any generation. Whenever and wherever Kerry football is discussed, his name and his contribution to Kerry's record will loom large.'

Joe Keohane, Donie O'Sullivan, Seamus Murphy and Tim O'Donnell carried Charlie's coffin out of Sneem parish church. The coffin bearers represented four generations of Kerry football and Charlie was surely smiling.

JÓM

Billy Myers

Nobody, not even one in the crowd of almost 20,000 that showed up in Fitzgerald Stadium that July day, could have foreseen the fallout. They came to watch Dick Fitzgeralds play Killarney Legion in a county championship quarter-final and what they witnessed helped decorate the summer.

The game itself had a weighty backdrop. Over twenty players on show had worn the county jersey. Dr Eamonn O'Sullivan had charge of the Dick Fitzgeralds for three weeks' intensive training and the season was seen as a springboard, particularly for the Dr Crokes, the main branch of the Dick Fitzgeralds.

When the '40s broke, Dr Crokes were going through a dark lull. At times, they struggled to piece together a team and in 1944, on the suggestion of the club, an amalgamation was formed.

The arms of the Dick Fitzgeralds spread wide. Like the Legion, players were legally recruited from beyond the traditional boundary of east Kerry. Lines were blurred.

One story goes that Mixie Palmer, from outside Sneem, was coaxed into playing for the Dick Fitzgeralds. He arrived from college in Cork and was met at the train station in Killarney by a Legion man. He was asked if he was the student from Sneem in town to play football. Palmer said he was. 'Come on with me, then,' he was told. Palmer was loaded into a car, brought to a game and was handed a Legion jersey. He lined out at centre-forward in the green and white that day in July 1946.

Central to that game and what came after it was Bill Myers – the only constant Dr Crokes player on the Kerry team that took four All-Irelands between 1937 and 1941. Off the field as well as on it, Myers helped keep the club ticking through the tough times. Unusually for an All-Ireland winner, he was involved in all the large and small committees that gave Dr Crokes life and hope.

And by the time the amalgamated side reached the closing stages of the championship, Dr Crokes were getting strong again. Dan Kavanagh was on the team and Teddy O'Connor was breaking through.

If the Dick Fitzgeralds could win the county championship, it would tip the balance for the town club.

The Legion were beaten in the previous year's final, so they had business to

Facing page:
Paul Russell passes on some of his knowledge to Billy Myers, left, and Paddy Kennedy.
(Seamus O'Reilly)

129

take care of as well. Both outfits spread their tentacles across the county and beyond looking for talent.

'The Dr Crokes still have a record of John F. O'Sullivan's trip to Killarney for the game,' says Fr Tom Looney. 'He was a nephew of Phil O'Sullivan and his travel expenses were paid for a trip from his home in Lauragh, south Kerry, all the way to Killarney. He came by the mail car from Kenmare, stayed overnight and went back the same way after playing for the Crokes.'

The game itself was won by the Dick Fitzgeralds (1-5 to 0-4) with the form of Bill Myers highlighted as their path to victory. But things didn't end there. The Legion pulled out the Dick Fitzgeralds team sheet and ran their fingers over the names. They stopped on Jimmy Joy. Joy was from Killorglin but had won an All-Ireland with Dublin in 1942 and was seen as a quality addition to the Dick Fitzgeralds. After the game, Legion heard that Joy had broken Rule 27 by playing rugby in the capital.

The Legion appealed to the county board but their fire was returned. Dick Fitzgeralds lodged a counter-objection. They had been overlooking the presence of Fr Mikey Lyne on Legion teams for the past few years, they said, but they weren't willing to keep their eyes closed any longer.

Fr Lyne was chaplain of Glasgow Celtic Football Club and was deemed a member of a foreign code. If Jimmy Joy had broken Rule 27, then so too had Fr Mikey Lyne, the Dick Fitzgeralds argued.

The fallout was seeping through the cliques and crevices of Killarney town and under a stifling arm of the GAA, the county championship stalled. The board ordered a replay of the game but their request was met with refusals.

In the meantime, Kerry had advanced in the championship and the Killarney dispute dragged for three months until Kerry had won the All-Ireland.

Even in autumn, when the debate resumed, the Dick Fitzgeralds had grown more militant, refusing to a replay on principle.

They continued with their argument. For three years they said, they had been beaten by Legion teams they considered illegal but they were always willing to let the scoreboard dictate who had won each game.

Billy Myers led their campaign and had the last word at the county board meeting that discussed the affair. The chairman, Din Joe Baily, called for the game to be refixed for 24 November. 'You need not be wasting time fixing it,' Myers said defiantly. The game was forfeited. Legion walked on and won the championship but Myers' club had made their statement.

Myers himself was used to ethical debates. In 1942, like Dan Spring, he secured a county council seat for the Labour Party and the following year, he narrowly missed out on a place in the Dáil.

His name was known across the county and had been for years. Jack Myers, Billy's father, was one of those who sailed the *Mayflower* in the 1903 campaign and helped navigate the promised land for Kerry. (Billy later married Joan McCarthy, daughter of Maurice who also played on the 1903 team.)

Jack's All-Ireland medals were things to behold. Little nuggets of gold from the beginning of the county's story.

Shortly after Jack Myers won his second All-Ireland medal, his two brothers took the boat for New Zealand. Pockets of Killarney had emigrated to the islands on the other side of the world and Bill and Dan Myers were following their trail. To remind them of home and the good times, Jack pressed a medal into the hands of Bill. Said take it with him and fish it out whenever he felt the pull of life in Kerry.

When the brothers landed in their new world, Bill made a life for himself in Wellington, marrying a lady from just outside Tralee and working on the city's wharf. Dan foraged up the coast of the North Island and settled in Taranaki. The medal stayed with Bill.

A century later, Jack's great-grandson from Killarney, Dónal Kavanagh, also moved to Wellington. Shortly after he arrived, he looked up his cousins and knocked at the door of his grand-uncle, Tom Myers, a son of Bill.

They were not long chatting when Tom walked down the corridor and came back holding a box. He peeled away a layer of cloth and fished out Jack's gold medal, still shining and bright.

Still a link to home. Through generations and across the oceans.

TJF

Dan Spring

Dan Spring said goodbye to football with his hands clasped on the Sam Maguire. In 1940, he captained Kerry to their fourteenth All-Ireland title. It equalled Dublin's record but Spring picked up an injury that forced him to retire immediately after the one point victory over Galway in the final.

In the previous year's final, Spring was a one man wrecking ball and produced one of the greatest individual displays in the history of the county. When he packed in the game after the 1940 campaign – even though he had just passed 30 – his departure was a blow to Kerry. Spring had the physique and power of a bulldozer, important attributes for a full-forward in the bustle of his day. On top of that, he was mobile and could score freely and he used these qualities to destroy Meath in 1939.

That year, Meath made a significant breakthrough. They won the Leinster title for the first time since 1895 and they were being talked up as genuine contenders for the crown.

One man was painted as the hero, the rock on which their path to glory was being laid – Tom 'The Boiler' McGuinness. He had a reputation as a full-back of Goliath proportions that stretched all the way back to the mid-'20s. He was tough and strong with Popeye arms – a boulder in defence.

Meath fans saw 1939 as the year when The Boiler would finally get his reward for carrying the county down through the years.

If Kerry were to take down Meath, they would have to find a way past The Boiler. Dan Spring was given the task. At 6 foot 3 inches and 14 stone, he was in the Goliath category himself and that day he out-fought and out-fielded McGuinness, and slashed Meath on his own. Kerry came out winners at 2-5 to 2-3 and Spring racked up a personal tally of 2-3 on one of the country's best full-backs.

When it had all finished, when 1939 and 1940 faded into the record books, Spring wouldn't really labour over those days. Even when he had a mind for relaxation, when he went on one of his trips to his bog in Lyrecompane with his radio and newspaper, not even then would he use his familiar face and frame to talk football with the workers saving turf beside him.

*Facing page:
1940 winning captain Dan Spring is introduced to the crowd at the Centenary All-Ireland in 1984.*
(The Kerryman)

There was plenty else to occupy his mind.

Two years after he finished with football, he secured a seat for Labour on the county council. The following year, he was elected to the Dáil. He married in 1944 and in 1945, his first child, Arthur, was born.

If Spring reckoned craters of time would open up after he moved away from the game, he was mistaken and he didn't leave politics until 1977. His political days were as well known by then as his football, particularly back west.

'It's something I can never explain, but my dad and the people of west Kerry had a great relationship,' says Arthur. 'Before elections, he'd get the train to Dingle and spend five or six days cycling around the peninsula campaigning and staying with supporters along the way. To say that it just had to do with football would be too simple. He had an affinity with the people there. In the early '60s, Neil Blaney was Minister for Local Government and under his constituency review, the west part of Kerry was taken from the north Kerry constituency and annexed to south Kerry. It was felt that it would cost my dad a seat. But the people of Tralee really rallied around him because they saw it as an anti-Spring move. His people kept faith in him.'

Time moved on. His kids were growing up and branching into sport. Football was the tradition, the lifeblood, but paths were easier carved away from the game that their old man dominated.

Arthur spent time with his mother's family on their farm in Crotta – hurling country – where his uncles were hurlers of note. Dick Laide had ten county championship medals with Crotta O'Neills and his brother, Pat, had six before emigration took him to Romford in Essex, England.

On the Crotta farm, Arthur had hurleys and sliotars to occupy him and he hurled at minor grade for the county. Shortly after that, he got hooked on golf and about the same time, his other brothers, Dónal and Dick, were immersing themselves in rugby. Along the streets of Tralee, both pursuits were seen as white collar and upper-crust.

Not for the first time, some soothsayers were saying Spring would lose his Dáil seat, this time because of his sons' sporting habits.

'When I was studying in Cork a few of my classmates brought me out to play golf in places like Bandon or Skibbereen or Mallow,' says Arthur, now a noted golf course designer. 'I fell for it completely. Loved it. Actually, my first set of clubs I got while going to play hurling. Dan was driving me and up in front, about 300 yards ahead, somebody was driving with a golf bag on the roof-rack. The bag fell down onto the road, we stopped and he kept going. Couldn't catch up to him. I brought them into the garda station and ages passed but nobody claimed them and they were given to me.'

Word of his golfing days did the rounds through the neighbourhoods of his town. His mother, Anne, was going about her business when the topic came up one day.

'She was at the hairdressers and somebody said, "Anne, I heard Dan bought Arthur a set of golf clubs for £200. That's going to cost him votes." At this time, Tralee would have been the only course around and people wouldn't like to be seen going in there to play. They'd go up to the gates of the club and if they saw somebody along the road, they'd double back and wouldn't go in. Golf was seen as snobbish but Dan was his own man and he didn't care what we played once we were happy. He saw it as a game to be played and enjoyed, irrespective of the social stigma that surrounded it.'

Even from his early days, Dan Spring had progressive and inclusive ideals. That's what pushed him towards politics.

He began working at Latchford's Mill in Tralee when he was barely fifteen and the well-being of the worker became his concern. 'There were fourteen in his family and about half had to emigrate. He would have been thankful to get the job at the mill and stay in Tralee. His involvement in the union would have started then and that's what edged him into politics. He learned a lot there. In many ways, the mill would have given him his outlook on life and politics. Maybe prepared him for the future.'

Plied him with muscle and commitment too, which he used that day in 1939 to cool down The Boiler.

TJF

Dan Kavanagh

They called it An Muantán, a piece of barren commonage that sloped down towards the cliffs that looked across to the Great Blasket. No man's land but there always seemed to be plenty of people there.

Young and old gathered at An Muantán at a moment's notice and it was there that they'd kick caid.

Local legend Muiris 'Kruger' Kavanagh returned from America in the early '30s and watched games at An Muantán. Then he joined in as a way of introducing his young relative, Dan Kavanagh, to the game.

'We had two posts that were made of limbs of trees that were stuck into the ground with a *sugán* tied across at the top,' recalls Dan.

'All you'd be doing is kicking in and kicking out. If there was a goal down the other end the ball would be gone over the cliff.

'My recollection is standing behind the goal and the ball coming over the *sugán*. Fielding was the thing at that time. There'd be about three of us behind the goal fighting hard for every ball. It was a great start.'

This start had Dan Kavanagh playing competitive football in Croke Park at a younger age than most Kerrymen. At fifteen, he secured a scholarship to Cólaiste Caoimhín in Dublin and within weeks he was playing football in Croke Park with the Dublin Colleges team.

One of his teammates was Johnny Carey, who attended Westland Row CBS. Carey went on to become a Manchester United legend in the years before Matt Busby gave birth to his Babes. Kavanagh became a legend in his own right too.

Johnny Carey's journey led to him captaining Manchester United to FA Cup and League successes; his old comrade was on a circuitous journey that finally yielded an All-Ireland in 1946. It was a long time coming for Kavanagh.

He played football in a generation when Kerrymen spread their wings. An era when there were as many Kerrymen playing senior football with other counties as there were with Kerry.

The county's diaspora were football missionaries and it's an overlooked part of football history. Kerry gave to others and plenty of them. Gave them All-Irelands and plenty of them too.

Mick Falvey and Joe Fitzgerald learned their football in Dingle CBS with

Facing page:
Dan Kavanagh and his wife Nellie, whose father, Jack Myers, was on Kerry's first All-Ireland winning team in 1903. Her brother Billy won All-Irelands in the '30s and '40s.
(Shelagh Honan)

137

Paddy Bawn and others. They left Dingle and Kerry football when they left school, ending up at midfield together on the Dublin team that won the 1942 All-Ireland. Jimmy Joy from Killorglin was the third Kerryman on that team. Sean Moriarty from Castlegregory was a sub.

Jack Flavin from Moyvane won an All-Ireland with Kerry in 1937 and then helped Galway beat Kerry in 1938. Mick Ferriter from west of Dingle was another to win an All-Ireland with the 1934 Galway team. Jim Cronin from Miltown also changed colours, crossing over to Cork to win his All-Ireland in 1945.

Dan Kavanagh took flight as well but it didn't bring him an All-Ireland. He became a Galwayman like Flavin and Ferriter before him. He had Kerry company on the Galway panel in Jim Clifford from Cahirciveen and Connie O'Connor from Dingle.

'I was a proud Kerryman like every Kerryman is but I was a long way from home. I was studying engineering in UCG and playing Sigerson football. While I was there, I looked for a job with Galway County Council. When I gave in my name, I was told I'd have to wait. I went into a pub next door to the council called the Old Malt. It was a GAA house and in there I met Mageen Ashe from Kerry and told her my story.

'I was told to come back the following Friday night, and that the County Engineer, a Mr Lee would be here. "He'll be coming down on the evening train and will be here at five o'clock. Come in and meet him."

'I did what I was told, met him and he said to call up to his office the following Monday morning. That's what I did and I had a job with the council and started playing with Galway.'

It brought Kavanagh to two All-Ireland finals. It meant playing against his own, beating them too when they were trying to emulate the achievements of the 1929–32 team and win a four-in-a-row.

Kerry's three-in-a-row came in 1941 when Kavanagh's friend from Dingle, Gega O'Connor got the crucial goal. A year later, with some of the Dingle boys turning their backs on Kerry, it was the turn of the Dingle peninsula's diaspora to take centre stage.

Kavanagh goaled for Galway near the end of their All-Ireland semi-final against Kerry, then Connie O'Connor kicked the winning point. West Kerry again flourished in the final but this time it was the turn of those wearing the Dublin colours.

Kavanagh was marking fellow Gaeltacht man Joe Fitzgerald. Fitzgerald lifted the cup for Dublin while Kavanagh left Croke Park with nothing. It was the same in 1944 when he returned to Kerry and it wasn't until 1946 that he finally left Croke Park a winner.

'I don't want to be overly critical but there was a lot of poor management in Kerry at the time. We should have won in 1944 but the wrong team was selected and we were anything but footballers that day. In 1946 we levelled it by bulldozing home two goals near the end thanks to Paddy Burke and Gega O'Connor.

'Before the first game in 1946, we trained in Tralee and were put up in the Park Hotel on Denny Street. We'd go training in the morning but the discipline wasn't there. You'd have a couple of pints before lunch in Jess McCarthy's. It was very careless. Dr Eamonn O'Sullivan took over the training for the replay and it made a huge difference. We were in Killarney staying in Scott's Hotel and were going to bed at half ten or eleven o'clock at night. Everything was marshalled to the last – what we ate and what people drank if they were allowed to take a drink. It was Dr Eamonn's way. The drinker was allowed a few pints at night without over-indulging. It worked and when it came to the replay, we won well.'

Dan's journey was complete. He's still the most westerly man in Europe with an All-Ireland, the only man from An Muantán with one. Football wasn't about All-Irelands for Kavanagh though, or wearing the Kerry jersey.

'Others grew up dreaming of the jersey but I didn't. I was never too worried about winning an All-Ireland. Football was always just fun, but we knocked as much fun out of hurling.

'We'd be looking for things to do when we weren't playing football. We had a game, pucking a little ball. We'd make it out of a stocking and tie a bit of twine around it.

'We didn't know what hurleys were back then. When they'd set a ridge of potatoes, sometimes cabbage plants would be stuck into the sides of the ridge. The cabbage would grow with a very long stem. We hurled on the roads with those cabbage stumps. There was no such thing as a hurley with a boss. I remember hurling with cabbage stumps as much as winning an All-Ireland.'

JÓM

Gus Cremin

Gus Cremin has a Sam Maguire in his living room and it sparkles. The replica is a cut glass chalice and it's a daily reminder of the best of times and the worst of times.

Cremin was central to Kerry's story but still a bit player. He's always been politely angry about it, when he was playing and even now.

His Kerry career wasn't much in game time. He played three games in 1946, broke a leg in 1947, was a sub in 1948 and gone in 1949. Brief statistics on the yellowing pages of Kerry history.

Cremin gives meat to those stats by laying the blame on Dr Eamonn O'Sullivan. He's no fan of the master trainer and organiser who drifted in and out of Kerry's story for five decades from the 1920s to the 1960s and Cremin is one of the few who doesn't speak highly of Dr Eamonn.

'I was never in my life talking to Dr O'Sullivan,' he says. 'In my time with Kerry he never spoke to me. He never really saw me. He saw nobody only Paddy Kennedy, Dan O'Keeffe and Gega O'Connor. That's the way I feel about it. It was off a blackboard he did his training.'

By mid-August 1946 Gus Cremin had never trained with Kerry. He had a run against Tipperary in the National League and was a sub for the Munster final against Cork.

While Johnny Walsh trained the Kerry team in Tralee for the All-Ireland semi-final against Antrim, Cremin was at home in Lissleton, Ballydonoghue, playing another game.

He was up against nature, fighting the weather to bring home his crops. This battle was being lost all over the country as 1946 was the year of the bad harvest.

Then a piece of paper changed his life.

'Take it easy for the rest of the week, you may be playing on the Kerry team on Sunday,' said a telegram from Din Joe Baily of the county board. His roller-coaster ride was beginning.

'It all happened so quickly. I saw Kerry play in the 1938 All-Ireland final but never thought I'd get there as a player. Now, I was going to Dublin with the Kerry team in 1946, but I couldn't take it easy. I was picking corn up until 10pm the night before I went to Dublin. With the weather, the work had to be done so I had no time to think about playing.'

Facing page:
Mick Finucane (left) and Gus Cremin, two Ballydonoghue greats who came to the attention of the Kerry selectors after Shannon Rangers' epic 1945 county final win over Killarney Legion.
(John Kelly)

Cremin has had the intervening 60 years to think about it. He came on as a sub against Antrim and kept his place for the final.

He was selected at midfield with Dan Kavanagh, while the man to lose out was his clubmate and team captain Eddie Dowling. Crucially, Cremin was also handed the captaincy for his first championship start.

'Eddie didn't like being dropped. The vice-chairman and secretary of our club came down to me the Friday before the final and asked me to stand down because Eddie was dropped. It was an awful thing to be asked to do.

'I was foolish enough to tell Micheál Ó Ruairc and John Joe Sheehy about it before we went to Dublin. John Joe turned to Eddie and said, "Is it a fact what I'm after hearing that people in the Ballydonoghue club want to deny Cremin the honour of captaining Kerry next Sunday?" Eddie didn't say, "Go and captain the team." He didn't want me to be captain.

'What I recall about the game was that we were lucky to get a draw, but at the end the Kerry crowd were so delighted with the result that they rushed the field and shouldered me off. It was said that I had played a captain's part but I didn't know what was ahead of me. My football world was about to fall apart and it was Dr O'Sullivan's fault.

'Johnny Walsh trained the Kerry team for the drawn game but for the replay Dr O'Sullivan was brought in. He wasn't a selector but he picked the team. I was dropped. If I was from Tralee or Killarney, it would never have happened.

'Joe Barrett and Johnny Walsh, particularly Joe, made a show over what happened. During the replay there were several times when Joe was on the sideline pushing me on to the field. He wanted me on at all costs.'

Joe Barrett was used to getting his way and Gus was thrown in for the second-half. His time had finally arrived. He forgot about the bad harvest, his dislike for Dr O'Sullivan and helped win the All-Ireland for Kerry.

'It was very tense and we couldn't get ahead. There was a free outside in the middle of the field. I took it and it dropped between the fourteen and the 21. Bill Carlos went up for it, got it, tore through and ballooned it out the field, where I got it again.

'Boland made a drive on me and I saw him coming and just took a step back and let him pass. I could see the goalposts opening up and just steadied myself for a second and let fly. I could see Gega roaring at me to give him the ball but I was determined to have a go. I was 60 yards out from the Hill 16 goal. It was the point that turned the game.

'John Joe Sheehy said to me afterwards, "When I saw you steadying yourself, I couldn't believe it – you were so far out. I put my hands up to my head. I couldn't watch it and missed the ball sailing between the posts. That's the greatest score ever to win an All-Ireland."'

It was Paddy Kennedy who lifted Sam Maguire though. Gus Cremin felt the honour should have been his. He still does.

'Once the game was over, that was it for me. I went to the banquet but came away home on the train on the Monday morning. The Tralee crowd were disgusted to see me going away. When the celebrations were going on in Tralee, I was at home. I didn't want to be with them.

'To this present day, there are people who say to me that I should have taken the cup when I came on the field. I should have been captain once I played. The cup never came to Ballydonoghue. The county board rang me several times to bring out the cup but when I wasn't captain I wouldn't do it.'

The only Sam Maguire that came to Ballydonoghue was the miniature crystal replica given to Gus in the GAA Centenary Year in recognition of captaining the side in the drawn game.

Back in 1946, he turned his back on the real Sam Maguire and went to face his fields of corn.

JÓM

Ballydonoghue legends, from left, Mick Finucane, Gus Cremin and Eddie Dowling. (John Kelly)

Paddy Kennedy

There were twelve minutes left in the 1946 All-Ireland final when Jimmy Murray had to leave the field with a facial injury. The Roscommon captain had a bloody face after a clash with Paddy 'Bawn' Brosnan but he was still smiling. So was all of Roscommon.

One first aid man going to work on Jimmy remarked, 'I'd better wipe the blood from your face so you'll look presentable when you receive the cup.' Another attendant combed Jimmy's hair ahead of the presentation.

At the same time, Dan O'Rourke was going from his seat in the Cusack Stand to the old Hogan Stand. He went around by the Canal goal and his smile was as wide as the canal itself.

For good reason. O'Rourke was Roscommon's first ever president of the GAA. The highlight of his presidency would be to present Sam Maguire to Jimmy Murray who was minutes away from emulating Wexford's Sean Kennedy as a three-time All-Ireland winning captain.

It never happened. Roscommon led by 1-7 to 0-4 when Paddy Kennedy took over the management of the Kerry team on the field and changed the course of football history. By proxy, Kennedy was already a selector. Fr John Beasley, part of the backroom team, had nominated the player to take his place on the selection committee when he was transferred to Rome mid-season. But late on against Roscommon, Kennedy was taking total control.

'Come out from the corner Gega,' roared Kennedy. 'Play centre-forward. I'll go midfield and we'll get a goal to make it respectable.'

Gega did what he was told and it won Kerry their sixteenth All-Ireland.

Act 1: Paddy Kennedy fields a ball underneath the Cusack Stand and heads goalwards. Bill Carlos and Brendan Lynch close in for the hit but before impact, Kennedy offloads to Paddy Burke from Killorglin who crashes home a goal.

Act 2: Kennedy leaves the field with concussion and an injured ankle. He has barely reached the sideline when Gega lofts a 40-yard ball that evades all and somehow ends in the net for another goal. Jimmy Murray comes back on the field but Roscommon's chance is gone. The game is a draw.

Act 3: It's two weeks later. Kennedy's ankle has healed sufficiently for him to line out at midfield for the replay. He's now captain in the absence of both Eddie Dowling and Gus Cremin. Kerry never look like losing and Kennedy brushes through Roscommon and accepts Sam from Dan O'Rourke. He brings it back to Annascaul on Tuesday 29 October while Gus Cremin is busy with his corn.

The convoy started at the gateway to west Kerry at Blennerville Bridge, where the first bonfire blazed. There were more in Derrymore, Lower Camp, Upper Camp and Gleann na nGealt.

There was even a fire in the townland of Ráth Dubh, a mile and a half east of Annascaul, the place that gave Paddy Kennedy to Kerry football. But the biggest fire of all burned at the bottom of the village beside Tom Crean's South Pole Inn. It was in the right place. Kennedy and Crean were cut from the same countryside, the two greatest figures in Annascaul history.

Kennedy was even like Crean, leaving Annascaul to earn fame. Crean, the adventurer, went to the harsh environment of the South Pole; Kennedy, the footballer, went east to the friendlier landscape of the Green CBS in Tralee.

Kennedy was another child of Kerry football's new revolution. Things changed after Kerry stood down from action in 1935 in solidarity with the interned republican prisoners, and the following year, Kennedy was part of an emerging team that shook up the world.

Early that summer, the new Kerry travelled to Tipperary town to take on the home side in a challenge game. The Tipperary hurlers played Limerick as a curtain raiser but all eyes were on the football match. Tipperary were Munster champions while Kerry were rebuilding.

Sean Brosnan, Paddy Kennedy and Bill Dillon were young guns, people like Miko Doyle, Tim O'Donnell, the Landers brothers and Martin 'Bracker'

Facing page:
Paddy Kennedy, described by Mick O'Connell as the greatest of them all.
(Lila Kennedy)

O'Regan were the old hands with All-Ireland medals.

The Bracker was the last survivor and recalled a significant day in the story of Kerry football.

'A Tipperary priest was behind that tournament game. He was interested in greyhounds – like myself – and I got talking to him before the game. Anyway, he said, "I've a lovely set of watches for the winners and you've got no chance with your young team." I just said to him, "Have you a notebook? Take down these two names – Paddy Kennedy and Sean Brosnan. They're Kerry's new midfield men and every bit as good as Con Brosnan and Bob Stack." Somebody had arranged that the game would be started with the ball being dropped from an aeroplane up in the sky. When it was dropped for the throw-in, Paddy Kennedy caught it.'

Kerry won the game by fifteen points and the Tipperary hurlers put nine goals past Limerick. When the watches were handed out Bracker's clerical friend remarked, 'You're right about Kennedy, he's special.'

Paddy Kennedy's special qualities are still talked about. There are still people around who played with him and against him. Sean Connolly from Clifden played with Westerns in Dublin and marked Kennedy regularly; Moss Walsh played with him at Geraldines, Kennedy's Dublin club after he left Kerin's O'Rahillys.

'Paddy Kennedy taught me the greatest ever lesson on a football field, when to jump for a ball,' says Connolly. 'Midfield wasn't about size but timing your jump. He was the best at this. His jumping from a standing position was unbelievable.'

Connolly learned well. The Galwayman went on to play county football for Clare and took part in two Railway Cup finals for Munster.

'He could field a ball like Mick O'Connell but was as tough as Gega O'Connor in the boxing ring,' says Moss Walsh. 'He could mind himself. One day Geraldines were playing against O'Tooles in a Dublin senior league game in Croke Park. Paddy was lording it at centre-back but the word came from Murt Kelly that there was trouble coming down the field. Mick Wellington was coming down to put manners on Paddy. Wellington ended up landing in one of the sideline seats that ringed Croke Park.'

Hard to get the better of Paddy, harder still to beat his Geraldines team. Kennedy, Sean Brosnan, Joe Keohane, Murt Kelly and Charlie O'Sullivan were down the centre. Throw in Galway's Frank Cunniffe and Dublin's Joe Fitzgerald and you had a team good enough to win All-Irelands.

Little wonder that crowds flocked to Harold's Cross Greyhound Track and Rathmines Technical School just to see Geraldines train. One year, 45,000 – all on foot or by bicycle – travelled to Croke Park to see Geraldines take on UCD in a county semi-final.

Kennedy came to Geraldines in 1940, one of three west Kerrymen who joined the Garda Síochána on the same day. Charlie O'Sullivan and Joe Fitzgerald were the others and they travelled to the Garda depot on the Tralee train on 28 February 1940.

Moss Walsh from Knocknagoshel was with them. There was fun all the way to Dublin. Charlie smiling, Paddy thinking up ways of wiping it from his face. Cigarettes were scarce in these war years so Paddy nipped them from Charlie's pocket and passed them around as his own. Charlie went mad but not for long.

'The first day we were in Dublin we all played ball beside the Garda Depot in the Phoenix Park,' recalls Moss Walsh. 'All football. Years and years later myself and Paddy would go to Murphy's of Rathgar for a drink. Taoiseach Jack Lynch, Dublin's Pat "Beefy" Kennedy and Big Tom O'Reilly from Cavan would join us in the snug.'

Paddy died in May 1979 and the Paddy Kennedy Memorial Park in Annascaul is his monument. It was opened in 1984, thanks to Fr James Curtin from the village.

He was a contemporary of Kennedy's growing up in Annascaul but left home to minister parishes in England.

For fun at weekends he filled pools coupons. One day in 1969, Fr Curtin's luck came in. He won the pools and donated £2,000 of his winnings to the Annascaul club. With it, they cleared debt on land they owned and built Paddy Kennedy Park.

The field is in the area of the village called *Breach Luan* – The Speckled Meadow. Paddy's place.

JÓM

Joe Keohane

In the history of Kerry football Joe Keohane is a huge figure. PF labelled him 'a latter day Horatio who defended his square forcefully, fearlessly and flamboyantly'.

He was as controversial as he was flamboyant during an amazing life that saw him involved in 23 All-Ireland senior finals as a player or a selector over six decades.

In the '70s he lambasted Kerry's handpassing game, while that same decade saw him court-martialed on a charge of misappropriating rounds of Irish Army ammunition. Sean McBride defended him and General Tom Barry took the stand and boldly declared that the court martial wouldn't have happened in any other army in the world.

Keohane never bored and always made headlines.

The Boherbee man had a meteoric emergence. By seventeen he hadn't played senior football with John Mitchels but his breakthrough at club level was quickly followed by a call up to the Kerry senior squad in 1936.

He came up the hard way, learning his football at the Staff Barracks field in Tralee that only measured 50 by 20 yards. It was here that Keohane and contemporaries like Tadhg Healy, Eddie Dunne and Chipsie Donohue educated themselves in games between Upper and Lower Boherbee.

'We used to play for a penny a man, so the games were very competitive,' he said recalling his playing days in *The Sunday Press*. 'Everyone hit hard and got rid of the ball quickly, there was no time for messing around.'

Keohane's learning curve reached its apex on a summer's evening in 1936 when a surprise excursion to Listowel made a full-back out of him.

'I was sitting outside our house in Boherbee when a bus with a crowd of footballers in it pulled up. The Mitchels club secretary Gerry Flynn opened a window and hollered, "Young Keohane, get your boots and come to Listowel. We're short."

'That day I started my senior career. They only had fourteen players so they put me in at full-back. I was standing there and who came in to play full-forward only Con Brosnan. He was coming to the end of his career. That was my first game at full-back and I stayed there for the rest of my career. Within a

Facing page:
Joe Keohane with Mick O'Dwyer and Mick O'Connell.
(Padraig Kennelly)

year I had an All-Ireland medal.'

But by 1938 Keohane threatened to throw it all away. He moved to Dublin after leaving school and secured a job in the Civil Service. He joined the Geraldines club, but unlike many other members of the Kerry diaspora, declined overtures to play with Dublin, staying instead with Kerry.

This meant a lot of travelling to matches and to collective training before All-Irelands. Between the drawn All-Ireland final and the replay in 1938, Keohane approached the county board for expenses. When they refused, his mother tackled John Joe Sheehy on the matter but came off second best. With no money forthcoming, Keohane withdrew his services to the Kerry team. Murt Kelly, who was also based in Dublin and a sub the first day, did the same.

'I had made my decision but on the morning of the match I regretted it very much,' Keohane recalled decades later. 'Knowing that I wasn't going to play in the final broke my heart. All during the morning of the match I was saying, "You big fool Joe – why did you do it?" How could I have been so stupid to pull out of the Kerry team?'

Keohane made his own way to Croke Park that afternoon and paid four shillings six pence for a sideline seat on the Hogan Stand side of the field. It was the start of a remarkable day in Kerry football history. Keohane became the first player since John Joe Sheehy in the 1924 final to go into the All-Ireland as a spectator but end up a player.

With Keohane in the stand Kerry were outclassed by Galway – only Sean Brosnan's brilliance kept them in the game but they still trailed by 2-4 to 0-6 with three minutes remaining.

'The referee blew his whistle,' reported The *Irish Independent,* 'but the whistle sounded for just the slightest bit longer than usual. With one bound some people on the sidelines rose from their seats, and, cheering loudly and waving flags, dashed onto the playing pitch. In a matter of moments the pitch was a mass of surging humanity.

'The Galway players were hoisted shoulder high around the field and borne towards the dressing rooms. Then came the voice over the loudspeakers declaring that the game had not finished.'

Keohane was on the field but when it was eventually cleared, most of the Kerry team were missing. 'All our boys had got into togs back at the hotel and had no reason to stay in the pavilion to dress,' revealed selector Jerry O'Leary.

With Bill Myers, Billy Casey, Bill Dillon, Paddy 'Bawn' Brosnan and others gone, Keohane, the spectator, ended his self-imposed exile from the Kerry team. Brendan Murphy, Eddie Walsh, Gerald Teahan, Mick Raymond, Con Gainey and Jack Sheehy also made up the numbers. Keohane had no boots but found a pair in the dressing room.

'My appearance made no difference though, as we couldn't catch Galway. I felt like crying after that All-Ireland and have never forgiven myself for letting down my county,' he later admitted.

Keohane had learned an expensive lesson. He left Croke Park vowing to make amends and did so for ten years. In that time, he became the full-back rock to rival Joe Barrett on the edge of the square.

But he was always the rogue. Against himself, Keohane always told a story from the 1947 Munster final in the old Cork Athletic Grounds. The going was heavy by the Lee that afternoon but Keohane famously did his bit to make it that bit heavier when Cork were awarded a penalty near the end after Jackie Lyne jumped on the ball to save a certain goal.

'Straight after Simon Deignan [the referee] stretched his arms I confronted him. We were army colleagues in the 12th Battalion in Limerick.

'The ball was placed for the penalty and I argued the call, but when I was doing it I stood down on the ball, driving it into the mud. It went unnoticed to everyone and when Jim Aherne eventually took the kick he only succeeded in splattering mud in Dan O'Keeffe's direction. The ball trickled into Danno's open arms. It was the easiest save he ever had to make. I did it because I could see the Statue of Liberty.'

Keohane won the tenth of eleven Munster medals that day but in New York, a sixth All-Ireland wasn't to be. He was a marked man in the Polo Grounds and sensed this beforehand.

'Before the game GAA secretary, Padraig Ó Caoimh came into the dressing room and stressed the need to make this a showpiece. He emphasised that it must be played by the book as the eyes of the New World were on us. I was distinctly uncomfortable for, while he was addressing the team, he kept looking at me. It put me off my game, maybe with what happened in the Munster final it was a bit of poetic justice.'

JÓM

Batt Garvey

The day of 14 September 1947 had dust and heat, a bone-hard field and an ocean-coloured sky. Some Kerry players wore white jockey style caps to protect themselves from the sun and in this strange, mishmash world, Batt Garvey could already peer ahead and feel the pieces clicking together.

Quarter of an hour gone and Kerry were up by eight. They were eating through Cavan like termites through plywood and Garvey was whaling it up. He was scorching. After four minutes, he went on a typical Garvey solo run for 50 yards, slalomed between the Cavan defenders and buried to the net.

Right after, he pulled down a raker, looked up and found Gega O'Connor with a pinpoint 35-yard pass. Gega fielded, then dropped the ball to his foot. It was the perfect move. They had never seen the like of this on Yankee soil but after Gega's shot hit the net, the goal was disallowed.

Right after that, Garvey went on another run and rattled the net again, but his goal, too, did not stand.

Years and years later, when he spent his summers in Ventry taking time away from Dublin where he was headmaster at Terenure Boys School, Garvey would tell his friend and former Dingle teammate, Fr Jackie McKenna, that the goal should definitely have been given.

Martin O'Neill, the Wexford referee, was making sure the American public and their Irish brothers who paid into the Polo Grounds that autumn day got value for money. No point in a Kerry rout, was there? Almost to a man, Garvey's Kerry colleagues would agree.

Two weeks after they returned to Ireland, Cavan and Kerry met in Croke Park with nothing but a set of suit lengths and some pride at stake. Kerry won easily, adding to the conspiracy theory.

Still, back in 1947 with fifteen, sixteen, seventeen minutes gone in New York, Kerry were rolling. Coasting along. The thing was, nobody realised that was going to be it. The apex. Everest.

Within the hour, Micheál O'Hehir would bawl down the microphone to the radio powers in Dublin, pleading with them, begging them even, for more air time. The radio men had a schedule to keep but the New York game still wasn't up and the result hung in the balance. 'Five minutes more,' Ó Hehir roared.

Cavan had done a Lazarus on it. With life running out of the game they led

Facing page:
Batt Garvey, Kerry's speedy wing-forward who was the master of the solo run, seen here in action (with the ball) against Mayo in the 1951 All-Ireland semi-final.
(Seamus O'Reilly)

153

by two. A few moments later they would add another two and win the most hyped football game since the Croke Memorial Cup of 1913. Then, they'd sail back to Ireland with some of the Kerry boys, dock in Dun Laoghaire with the Sam Maguire beside them, make for town and celebrate like crazy.

In three years, Garvey would play his last game for Kerry. His speed was dying, they said, and he had put on some extra weight and the move from wing-forward to the corner wasn't working. Anyway, all around him, the air was going out of Kerry.

1948: hammered by Mayo in the semi-final, 0-13 to 0-3. 1949: humiliated by Clare in the Munster championship. 1950: surprised by Louth in another semi-final. Five years Garvey spent playing at the top and he left a legacy as a high-fielding, quick-thinking speed merchant. He reached his peak during that baking game at the Polo Grounds.

It didn't take Cavan long to realise the havoc the Ventry man was wreaking. Because of him, they rearranged their half-back line. John Wilson, normally a corner-back, was on the wing beside Garvey and he was being eaten alive. P.J. Duke, the regular number five, was switched from midfield back to shepherd Garvey. It gave Cavan a strong buffer against Kerry's onslaught. Neighbouring Duke on the half-back line now was captain John Joe O'Reilly and Simon Deignan – the latter, incidentally, had refereed the Kerry/Cork Munster final that year.

Crucially, even at eight points down, Cavan didn't panic. 'I knew we had a battle on our hands but I had noticed the Kerry backs were very jittery,' said Mick Higgins, who played centre-forward for Cavan that day.

Things were getting worse for Kerry. Eddie Dowling, tormentor-in-chief with Garvey, banged his head on the pitcher's mound and had to go off injured. Three more Kerry players – Eddie Walsh, Paddy Kennedy and William 'Bruddy' O'Donnell – followed him. In the smaller confines of the baseball park, the 30 men were running into one another with more frequency and, given the talk surrounding the game, with more ferocity too. Souped-up Irish dodgems on Manhattan's West Side.

Writing on page 22 of the following day's *New York Times*, renowned American sports columnist Arthur Daley commented on the physicality of the game: 'Considering the fact that Gaelic football is what would technically be described as a "non-contact sport", there was more violence than you'd find in [an American football] game between Army and Notre Dame. The busiest man on the field was Dr Thomas G. Dougherty. He was the official physician.'

As the game wore on, Kerry began to wilt. Buckets of water and bags of oranges were flung onto the pitch to rehydrate the players. The majority of the Cavan team had travelled to the game by air, in a trip that took 29 hours. Things were worse for Kerry – half of the team came by long-haul boat and the travel exertions were beginning to tell.

Before half-time, Cavan bagged two goals to drag themselves back into the game. They trailed by one point at the break, and then outscored Kerry 0-8 to 0-3 in the second half beneath the backdrop of the Manhattan skyline.

By right, the game should never have been played there. For years, Irish emigrants in the States had petitioned to get the centrepiece of the GAA calendar stateside. Every time their motion reached the GAA Congress, it was strongly rebuked. Things changed for 1947. Just before the vote on the matter was due at Barry's Hotel that Easter Sunday, an adjournment was announced. Delegates gathered to burn off the minutes when Clare delegates Bob Fitzpatrick from Miltown Malbay and Canon Michael Hamilton from Clonlara – who were canvassing to bring the All-Ireland out of Croke Park – passed a letter around. They said an Irish exile penned the letter and it told of the positive effect an All-Ireland in New York would have on ex-patriots. They just wanted a little slice of home between the city's skyscrapers, the exile wrote. He added it was exactly a century since the famine, the defining event that forced the Irish to flock to the States in the first place, and what better gesture to mark their arrival than staging the All-Ireland final in New York?

When Congress resumed, to drive the point home totally, Fitzpatrick, a noted orator, read the letter aloud. He produced a handkerchief at the most emotional lines. When he was finished, the atmosphere among delegates had shifted. They were sombre, more reflective.

They thought of their American cousins across the ocean and, when the result of the vote came in, the motion carried. (Amazingly, on the same day, Kerry were playing Cavan in a tournament game in London.)

Right after the decision, word broke that the letter – the mood swinger, the deal-getter – had been a set-up. A hoax. The exile didn't exist. It was a crafty, heart-tugging ploy by Fitzpatrick and Hamilton, but the decision still stood.

The Irish in New York and those at home became twinned in hysteria over the game. They expected 50,000 to flood into the ballpark that September. Less than 35,000 came. The turnout was a disappointment but the game had class. A massive lead, controversial refereeing decisions, a major comeback, the underdogs upsetting the odds. And Garvey's early brilliance.

TJF

Eddie Dowling

Friday morning is pension day in Ballydonoghue. It's the best time to catch Eddie Dowling. He's always on the road early, cycling four miles up to Ballylongford Post Office to collect his money.

Passing cars beep hello and one of Eddie's huge hands always returns the compliment. He's cycled these roads for over 70 years now. Cycled everywhere. To mass, to see his cattle, to football matches.

In 1946, Eddie was 23. Fit from football, farming and his bike. Kerry were playing a National League game against Clare in Tralee that spring and Eddie was called up to the Kerry team for the first time.

On the eve of the match, some of the north Kerry contingent gathered in Ballybunion and bussed their way to Tralee. Eddie wasn't with them as he was up in the bog to draw home some turf. Tralee had to wait.

He cycled the twenty miles in the road to Tralee on the morning of the match and started his Kerry career. Eddie won on the double that day.

'Paddy Bawn and myself had a couple of pints after the game. I took out a slag bag. "Holy Christ," says the Bawn, "not only do you drink the same as me, but you smoke the same Woodbine cigarettes as I do." We were great friends from then on. Small things like that are very important.'

Their friendship lasted a lifetime and when the Bawn passed away in July 1995, Eddie was in Dingle to shoulder his coffin. He drank to the Bawn with old friends and toasted football.

The game gave Eddie everything but treated him very badly. It brought him to Dublin, London and New York but brought no All-Ireland medal. He's not bitter but very disappointed. Still smiles though.

The journey; the games; the drink; the Polo Grounds.

This was Eddie's All-Ireland.

'I was part of the group who flew over and we were to leave Shannon for New York on a Sunday night, but the flight was put back to the following day. We were driven to Shannon for ten the following morning, but that flight was then put back to seven that evening. There was nothing to do only drink.

'I had 30 glasses of beer before getting on the plane. When we got to the Azores to refuel, Eddie Walsh and myself went into a café and called for two beers. I put a five dollar bill on the counter and was told I was short. I turned to

Facing page:
Eddie Dowling who touched the Manhattan skyline in 1947 before coming crashing to earth on one of the Polo Grounds' baseball mounds.
(John Kelly)

157

Eddie and said, "We won't be getting drunk here I tell you."'

The drink was well out of Eddie's system by match day on 14 September. Eddie's All-Ireland: 'We were flying it. We were all over them and had two goals disallowed in the first half. I caught a ball at midfield in front of John Joe O'Reilly and made off with it. Next thing, I was right in on top of the goalie and shot for a goal. It was my last kick.

'The next ball that came out was going to be mine, I was going that well. I crossed the field to go for it. It wasn't straight ahead of me, but to the side and I was over stretched. "You came from nowhere and your shoes hit my forehead," Cavan player P.J. Duke said to me afterwards. I came down and hit the baseball mound. I was out cold for a while.

'I was brought off the field and only for my Aunt Dolly, I'd never have seen home again. I was in the bus after the game and all the talk was about where they were going to go drinking. They took no notice of me – I didn't know where I was. At times I'd be alright, then I'd black out.

'Dolly took me off the bus and brought me to this fella in Harlem. He put me on a couch, put an ice bag on my head and gave me a few drops of whiskey. Dolly then took me to St Mary's Hospital in Brooklyn where she worked as a nurse. I got an injection and didn't wake up until Monday evening.'

Only then did Eddie find out that the All-Ireland had been lost. He woke to another nightmare, to park alongside his experience from the year before. And he had six days in hospital to think about both years.

After his debut in 1946, Eddie cycled back home to Ballydonoghue as Kerry's new captain. Shannon Rangers were county champions in 1945 and nominated Eddie as Kerry captain for the upcoming championship. He started the year as captain and midfield partner to Paddy Kennedy – he ended it with nothing.

'I brought the Munster Cup home to Ballydonoghue and captained Kerry in the torrid semi-final against Antrim. Then I was dropped for the final but came on as a sub in the drawn game against Roscommon. I went very well in the final trial game the Sunday before the replay. I would have been on the team and would have been captain again.

'On the Tuesday night we were playing backs and forwards, just tipping around. I was picking up the ball and Teddy O'Connor came in and hit me on the shin. "That hurt, Teddy, you son of a bitch," I roared. The next ball came in and I put my weight on the leg and the bone came out through the skin. That finished it.

'I went to the All-Ireland on crutches. Rory O'Connell was a selector and after the game he said, "I've an announcement to make. Eddie Dowling will get the first subs medal – only for the misfortune of breaking his leg last Tuesday night, it's the cup he'd be carrying home to Ballydonoghue." It was unanimously accepted and there was a big cheer. The medal never came – it's a bit late now, but after 60 years I'm still waiting.'

Rough justice but they're used to it in Ballydonoghue. Another great from the area, Mick Finucane, who also distinguished himself in the Polo Grounds, was a Kerry sub in 1946 with number seventeen on his back. After the final, he received a letter from board secretary Micheál Ó Ruairc saying he wouldn't receive an All-Ireland medal. Lots were drawn to see who got a subs medal and Tom Long from Dingle was picked ahead of Mick.

'It was wrong,' says Eddie, 'very wrong that they took away my medal. But they can't take away the football. They were great days man.

'I just loved when Bill Delaney from Stradbally in Laois used to come down to Johnny Walsh in Ballylongford every year. It made our year when we'd head to Dingle for a night or two.

'Into the Bawn's pub we'd go to meet the man himself. Billy Casey would come in, Tom Ashe and Tom Long would be there too. If Gega O'Connor was home from America, he'd be there. We'd do a round of the pubs – Bawn's, Long's, O'Connor's and Ashe's. We enjoyed ourselves. Mighty.'

That's what football has been about for Eddie Dowling, not missing out on an All-Ireland medal.

Time is moving on now and Eddie glances at the clock in his kitchen. 'Jesus, you've kept me late this morning. I enjoyed our little journey but I've to go and collect my pension. I'm late, fierce late. We'll have a drink when the book comes out.'

With that, Eddie is on his bike. Out the gate and gone.

JÓM

Eddie Dowling heading to Ballylongford on pension day. (John Kelly)

Eddie Walsh

A little over a year before Eddie Walsh passed away a photographer visited him at his home in Knocknagoshel. By then, Eddie was spending some of his day in bed, reading the paper, keeping an eye on Kerry's progression in the National League, prophesising that Colm Cooper would go down as one of the greats of the game.

Anyway, the photographer arrived this Friday evening and knocked on Eddie's bedroom door. Eddie called him in. They talked for a few minutes about what the photographer would need in order to get some nice shots and Eddie listened to what he had to say.

After their discussion, he rose out of the bed, combed his hair carefully and made his way to the bar, a little stroll down the hall from his bedroom. It was close to six o'clock and a handful of locals sat at the counter. When Eddie walked in, he was greeted with a giant welcome. Smiles. Handshakes. Quiet whispers of football. From the reception he received, it seemed like Eddie hadn't been in the bar for a little while.

When he had finished shaking hands he sat facing the door, his back to a wall that doubles as a library and museum of Kerry football. Photographs and clippings. Team lists from years back. Stories of victory and defeat captured in picture frames.

Behind the bar is the main attraction – the football used in the 1947 All-Ireland final in the Polo Grounds. It was given to Eddie by John Kerry O'Donnell fifteen years after the game, during the year Eddie gave working the bar at Gaelic Park, New York.

Shortly after Eddie sat down, somebody poured him a glass of Guinness and he didn't wait long for the drink to settle before he brought it to his lips. From time to time, Eddie's young grandson would come and chat to him and every so often a local who hadn't seen him in a while would sit down and catch him up on happenings. From an odd snippet of conversation, you knew the talk always wound its way to football and the championship Kerry were facing into.

Every few seconds, a camera flash lit the air but nobody took any notice. Eddie told his friend he hadn't been to a game for a while but it was surprising the knowledge and opinion he had of players and games – even those not involving his own county. His advice and words were taken in very earnestly by

Facing page:
Eddie Walsh surrounded by football memories at home in his pub in Knocknagoshel.
(John Kelly)

161

the small audience.

Eddie is a legend in these parts, known as the best wing-back to come out of Kerry and there's no need arguing the point in Knocknagoshel.

He came from good stock. Eddie's own father is still remembered in the village as a big, strong man. Ned Walsh moved from Knockaclare near Lyrecompane to Abbeydorney, where Eddie spent his early years.

'If I stayed there I'd probably have been a hurler,' Eddie said quietly and with a smile. As it was, when Eddie was six his father moved the family to Knocknagoshel. Traded in a few acres and bought the pub. In his free time, Ned Walsh was taken up with throwing free weights. 'A huge man,' says Eddie's son Eamonn, a former Kerry selector. 'A champion plougher and a champion weight thrower.'

Competitively, he once threw a free weight of 56 pounds over a 7-foot bar. It's a feat that has seeped into oral history in Knocknagoshel.

Eddie wasn't blessed with his father's bulk or brawn but he was swift and fast and had a silk touch on the football field. After he came to Knocknagoshel he, too, found something to do with his spare time. In his mind's eye, the sloping streets of his village doubled as a green sward where football names were made. It's on those streets Eddie first kicked ball.

The game in Knocknagoshel was a raggle taggle affair until a young curate, Fr Bob Walsh from Lisselton, arrived.

He began organising games and established a local team that he affiliated with the Tralee District Board. He ferried footballers all over north Kerry and across the border into Limerick in search of matches. It wasn't long before Eddie started making a name for himself for real.

The first to uncover his emerging talent was Con Brosnan who moved to sign him up for duty with his own club in Moyvane, a fair trek from Knocknagoshel.

For years, boundaries were blurred in this part of the world. In 1942 when North Kerry and Castleisland clashed in the county championship, Eddie and two other Knocknagoshel players were on the North Kerry team. Three more Knocknagoshel men lined out for Castleisland. All six travelled to the game in the same car. Football yarns are scattered all across the rolling countryside of the place.

Down the road from Walsh's bar, Luke Keane farms some land and milks a few cows but his real passion is local folklore. He'll tell you Eddie was the king of them all but with a broad sweep of his hand he says a few princes were reared on this land as well.

'You'd pick a team from Knocknagoshel that would win you an All-Ireland,' he maintains. 'We had lads from here that went on to play for other counties and they'd say we had no one at all. Jack Murphy for Dublin. Jack actually played for the

Dubs in 1942 but didn't make the team for the final and he never got a medal. He wouldn't stand in on the photograph either and he told me once he always regretted not standing in. Bertie, his brother, played for Dublin and Leinster as well. And Denis Roche was a great Knocknagoshel man who played for Tipperary along with his brother, big Ned.'

There's another gem and Keane revels in its telling. It shows the status that Walsh commanded during his playing days.

'Way back in 1948, this would be when Eddie's playing career was coming to an end, I went with a group into Killarney to see Eddie play in the Munster final. A trip to Killarney was a big thing then. We left Knocknagoshel at seven in the morning on a donkey and cart and went the 6 miles to Abbeyfeale. Then we got on the train, it was known as the Iron Horse, and travelled to Listowel. From there, onto a train to Killarney. It was just to see Eddie playing but when we hit Killarney we were told Eddie was a sub. We nearly didn't bother going to the game when we heard that.'

Keane is just getting started.

Up the road at the bar, the photographer is leaving now and Eddie is on the move, passing by those photos of him and his teammates in their prime. He gives the photos a quick scan, says goodbye to his constituents and walks back down the hall.

TJF

Eddie Walsh's grandson with the ball used in the Polo Grounds in 1947. (John Kelly)

The Comeback

Donie Murphy

Mayo were All-Ireland champions when Kerry faced them in the semi-final of 1951 but Kerry had them on the rack all through the game. With three minutes left, they led by five. Mayo clawed a point back and for the only time in the game, left-corner-back Donie Murphy didn't take the kick out.

Paddy Bawn collected the ball, spotted a man out the field and tried to pick him out quickly. He didn't hit his target. Eamonn Mongey won possession, saw Tom Langan at full-forward free from the shackles of Paddy Bawn and lofted a long ball in for Langan.

Liam Fitzgerald, in the Kerry goal, raced out but Langan got there first and palmed the ball to the net. The stadium rattled and shook. Mayo were back in it. A minute later, Paddy Irwin pointed and the referee blew time. It finished a draw, 1-5 apiece.

The month before the game, Donie Murphy was in Ballina, working as a potato seed inspector as part of his college training.

There was a big, sprawling field on the edge of town and every evening with the sun still high and a few miles road-running under his belt, Murphy would gravitate towards the field. A few balls would be hopping about and all Donie wanted was to get his hands on the leather and stay sharp. He mainly played among the kids and young teenagers of Ballina but after a few days, he noticed a group of men at the other side of the field going through some serious training drills. He made enquiries and was told it was the All-Ireland champs preparing for the upcoming semi-final with Kerry. He never did wander down to them but recognised the faces when they met in Croke Park on 12 August.

After the draw, he went to Ballyheigue for two weeks' collective training. Ballyheigue was an unusual choice but this year, the county board had a strong north Kerry presence and they wanted to bring the stars of the team to their locale. They paid the players their full wages for the duration and put them up in Lawlor's Hotel where essentially, the team split into two groups. Roundy Landers was manager – a mild-tempered man who didn't have the cut-throat attitude to keep a tight rein on some of the older, wiser players.

Some took advantage and spilled out into the drinking houses of the area. Others took things more seriously. Out the back of Lawlor's Hotel was a field where a core of six or seven would train religiously. 'A rough meadow' is how

Previous pages:
Kerry versus Dublin in 1955 was the All-Ireland final that defined the decade – Kerry's traditional catch-and-kick methods up against Dublin's new approach to football. The older prevailed. (Jerome O' Shea)

Facing page:
Donie Murphy, who had an eventful career in a Kerry jersey, pictured with his wife, Pauline, just after his induction into the Legion Hall of Fame. (Tommy Regan)

Seán Murphy remembers it. 'I think a few of us over-trained during those weeks,' says Donie Murphy. 'Things weren't very strict.'

Meanwhile, back in Ballina, the Mayo team were staying in Gaughan's Guesthouse mulling over what Eamonn Mongey described as 'the toughest game we ever played'.

This was a Mayo team made up of intelligent, deep thinkers. They decided that, to overcome Kerry, they would need a totally new approach. They sat in front of a blackboard for three weeks talking tactics and eventually settled on a plan of attack. They would use the wide open prairies of Croke Park to open up Kerry. Play fast, early ball into space. It was the first time any team concentrated on this approach.

'We had a fairly straightforward regime,' recalls Paddy Prendergast, Mayo's most respected full-back. 'Jackie Carney and Gerard Courell were over the team. They had us up for eight o'clock mass every morning, then it was back for a bit of breakfast and maybe a twenty-mile round walk after that. Sometimes we nearly walked as far as Foxford. Then we'd rest and train for two or three hours with more discussion on Kerry. There was no going out at night. We'd stay in and play a few cards and talk about the match. We might have gone to the films once or twice at most.'

The contrast with the Kerry approach was sharp. Come the replay, Kerry couldn't keep pace with Mayo, who executed their new plan to perfection.

After five minutes, Tom Langan collected the ball on the wing and played it first time into space. Mick Flanagan came onto it at speed and drilled it to the net. The same two repeated the same move before the half was up and Kerry hit the rocks.

Having left Ballina in the summer of 1951, Donie Murphy returned to Mayo in 1968 with his wife, Pauline, and has been there since. From his home in Castlebar, he puts together the pieces of the events that happened after that game.

He was studying in Dublin the following December, living in digs on the Norfolk Road, opposite Dalymount Park. Cycling to lectures in the morning, there was a hill that he found difficult to climb.

'For no reason I used be out of breath. It would kill me to cycle up that hill. You were of the age when you'd hardly ask yourself, "What's wrong?" I was sharing a basement with Hugh Scanlan from Cavan and one evening I was walking back down to the room. I almost collapsed. I thought I'd never get down the stairs.'

He was disgnosed as having pleurisy – 'I maintain I got that from wearing damp clothes' – and he spent that Christmas, and seven weeks in total, in Jervis Street Hospital.

When he was fit to play for Kerry again, Jerome O'Shea had taken his place. Donie couldn't budge him from corner-back. That was until the fortnight before the semi-final of 1953 when O'Shea was stricken with the same ailment. Murphy was back in and collected his first All-Ireland medal.

At 25, it looked like he would be a staple of the Kerry team. The Munster final of 1955 saw Murphy in his prime. He was man-of-the-match and life tasted sweet. He couldn't have seen that TB was waiting for him around the corner.

Two weeks after the Munster final, he was in a sanitorium in Dublin where he spent the following seventeen months.

'The pleurisy had left a shadow on my right lung. After the game against Cork, I was living in Rathkeale and didn't feel well one evening. My doctor was Jim McCarthy – an All-Ireland hurler with Limerick – and he lived next door to me. He knew what the problem was and sent me up to St Michael's in Dun Laoghaire. After a few days they transferred me to Our Lady of Lourdes.'

The players daytripped out to him with the Sam Maguire that September. He never dwelled on what might have been. Just kept on the road to recovery and reached his destination.

Four years later, he lined out for his club again before marching off to eventually settle up west.

In the football pockets of Castlebar, they know Donie Murphy as the Kerryman who worked hard at underage level for the local club, the Castlebar Mitchels. Scattering seeds in his new home and planting for the future. Just like he would have done in Kerry.

TJF

Paddy 'Bawn' Brosnan

By the time Paddy 'Bawn' Brosnan travelled up the coast from Dingle to Ballyheigue in August 1951, his football career was in its final phase. There were just a few more acts left to play out and, as ever with Brosnan, they were in uncut technicolour. The Bawn never did black and white.

When Kerry were drawn together in Ballyheigue for collective training before the All-Ireland semi-final replay against Mayo, the Bawn didn't go the direct route over water in his trawler. He was without a vessel for much of that summer after it was wrecked one night on rocks off Brandon Creek, west of Dingle.

It was a hard luck story but one that suited the big man's image – a chieftain of the high seas surviving a shipwreck to take his place on the Kerry team. He loved it and milked it.

The Bawn travelled to Ballyheigue with fellow Dingle man Tom Ashe. They were there for the grand plan of winning an All-Ireland but also out to have a good time. On their journey, they took a detour via Ballydonoghue, found Eddie Dowling forking hay and dragged him away for a fortnight's training with the team. The detour set the tone for the two weeks in Ballyheigue.

Some players were more interested in the social side of things than football and had started on the night of the drawn game against Mayo. Goalkeeper Liam Fitzgerald from Ardfert had a dog running in Shelbourne Park on the eve of the game.

'Fitzgerald was having a big bet and he said if his dog won and we made the final, he'd buy us all a bottle of whiskey,' said Timmy Healy, who played in the full-back line with Brosnan in 1951. 'The dog won and we only drew but we still went to The Moy across the road from Barry's Hotel and started drinking whiskey. We got fairly drunk that night.

'Then we went back to Barry's where you couldn't get a drink. It was a dry house. But the Bawn brought some back with him. The following morning, he had the most of a bottle of whisky left and anyone that was sleeping, he'd lift his head up like he was dosing a calf and he'd give them a shot. If he didn't wake, he'd give him a second one. That was the Bawn, a right character.'

The party continued in Ballyheigue where the Bawn's hard luck story with his boat began to strike a chord. Subscriptions of a pound here and a pound there rolled in to help buy him a new boat and his Kerry teammates soon

Facing page:
The best known fisherman/footballer in Ireland, Paddy 'Bawn' Brosnan (fourth from the left) with fellow fishermen in Dingle.
(Padraig Kennelly)

resolved to play their part.

Under Roundy Landers, some players ran amok through the bars of Ballyheigue and beyond. Brosnan had ordered a boat from a Glasgow shipyard and was in the process of getting the payment together.

'Some of us went drinking,' said Timmy Healy, 'because we decided we'd help the Bawn buy the new boat. We went to bars and halls all over north Kerry to drum up money.

'We all had party pieces that we sang. I used to sing the 'Headford Ambush' and people went mad for it because there were a lot of republicans in north Kerry. Then the cap would be passed around and the money came in. By the end of the two weeks, we had a deposit for the Bawn's boat. They all wanted to give the Bawn some money.'

As Brosnan was fighting a losing battle against Tom Langan in Croke Park, his brothers, Timineen Deas and Tommy Blocks, and two uncles were at sea, guiding the Bawn's latest fishing smack, the *Ross Dubh,* from Glasgow back to Dingle.

They berthed on the Dublin docks on the day of the game and a few days later, made the last leg of the journey to Dingle. The All-Ireland semi-final was lost but the Bawn had his new boat. He had his livelihood back, thanks to football.

Football gave Paddy 'Bawn' Brosnan more than a new fishing trawler. He wasn't the greatest player to wear the Kerry jersey but was the most colourful as myth merged with man during his fifteen years on the county team.

John B. Keane: 'I remember when I was a gorsoon to be in great demand after my arrival home from a football match. In my street there were many football fanciers starved for news on the game. No matter what question I was asked I obliged, even if the answer was more indebted to the imagination than to fact. It went like this: "And Paddy Bawn, now when he came out with the ball after saving the goal was he hit hard?"

"Hit hard is it? If he was a stone wall he'd be in rubble."

"It had no effect on him, so?"

"No effect at all, sure it only straightened him."'

The Bawn cultivated this image and bucked convention. Fishermen never had much time for football but Paddy 'Bawn' Brosnan changed that. He came from the Colony, a row of artisan dwellings off Strand Street in Dingle.

Nine were reared in the three-room Brosnan cottage, but this was luxury by the Colony's standards. In one house, there were eighteen Flannerys. The Flahertys and Moores were other fishing footballers and they all came under the influence of Brother Micheál Brennan in Dingle CBS.

'The Bawn was ten years ahead of me but I know that Brother Brennan was responsible for getting him to stay with football,' says Tom Ashe.

Others helped too. Paddy O'Donoghue from Dykegate Lane in Dingle provided a pair of boots, as Brosnan was famously reputed to have never owned a pair in his life.

'The only training I need for football is a few days on dry land to stretch my legs, borrow some boots and play away,' he once said.

'A lot of it was a myth,' says Mick Falvey, who was a year ahead of Paddy Bawn in Dingle CBS. 'He trained hard when he had to and even though he wasn't as good a footballer as Gega O'Connor or Billy Casey he made a huge impression on Kerry football.'

And, like all good stories it had its ups and downs. The Bawn was a forward in his early days but found himself relocated to full-back for the All-Ireland final replay in 1938 to plug the gap left by Joe Keohane who was missing for the day.

It was a disastrous debut as he dropped the ball for Galway's first goal and was bustled in over the goal-line for another. Brosnan was blamed for losing the All-Ireland and his inter-county career seemed over. It was only starting though, as he returned to the forward line to win All-Irelands in 1940 and 1941.

'He was moved again to the full-back line and that made him,' says Mick Falvey, 'especially when he took over from Keohane for a second time in 1948. He became this warrior fisherman who held the Kerry ship afloat at the back.'

He revelled in it.

JÓM

Tom Ashe

Father Mikey Lyne was a VIP long before directors' boxes and corporate suites were built. As chaplain of Celtic Football Club, this status allowed him have a unique view of matches in Parkhead.

Lyne enjoyed celebrity status within Scottish soccer for a few years and it wasn't because he defied the general law of the land by making the move from Gaelic football to soccer.

'It was his armchair,' says Tom Ashe. 'An armchair went everywhere with him and was brought down to the sideline for games. He stood out because of that and everybody knew him.'

Ashe lived in Glasgow for two years in the late '40s, serving his time as a beer bottling apprentice. He served a different kind of apprenticeship with Celtic, thanks to Fr Mikey Lyne and his uncle Canon Thomas Lyne.

Canon Lyne was Kerry GAA president and stalwart of the Dingle GAA club. He alerted his nephew to Ashe's burgeoning talents as a footballer and within weeks of landing in Glasgow, Ashe was wearing the famous green and white hoops.

'I played in a cup final with them,' says Ashe. 'It wasn't a Scottish Cup final but a final with the reserves. They were my team and I played with them in midfield first.

'I had one big problem though in that I had never played soccer before and when the first couple of balls came my way, I just went up with the hands and fielded them. That's what you did with a football in the air.'

Ashe's midfield career was over within minutes as his mentor, Fr Lyne, relocated him to goal where he played in that 1947 Reserve Cup Final against Dumbarton.

'They had a big brute of a fella playing centre-forward. He was an ex-German POW. I wasn't going to stand back from him. That would be giving in. He wasn't going to stand back either.

'One ball came in and I just took him out of it. It was a way to let him know I was around. He was lying on the ground and the referee came running in. The referees that time wore a blue suit, with a white shirt and a collar. "You might be able to do that over in Ireland but not here," he said.

'Fr Mikey rushed onto the field. "What, in the name of God, are you doing?"

Facing page:
Tom Ashe in Páirc an Ághasaigh, Dingle, where he learned his football.
(John Kelly)

175

he roared. "Don't do that again." The ref heard Fr Mikey and didn't send me off. But he wasn't finished and whispered to me after the ref had gone, "By Christ, if he comes in again, make sure to kill him."'

Tom Ashe was well able to take care of himself. Two years previous, he debuted for the Kerry seniors and squared up to Mick Mackey. He was only sixteen and played minor and senior on the same day in the Gaelic Grounds in Limerick.

After playing midfield with Tom Moriarty in the minor victory over Clare, Ashe was drafted into the senior dressing room because only fifteen of the panel had showed for the Munster semi-final against Limerick.

Joe Keohane, Jackie Lyne, Tom 'Gega' O'Connor, Martin McCarthy and James 'Gawksie' O'Gorman were missing. Before he knew it, Ashe was playing with Paddy Kennedy, Eddie Walsh and Paddy Bawn and against Mick Mackey, Jackie Power and Dick Stokes.

'Eddie Dunne got injured and I ended up going in on Mackey,' he recalls. 'He was wearing a new pair of boots. When Limerick were awarded a penalty, Mackey stepped up. The crowd came on to the field and Mick came in and hit a bullet of a shot with the top of his big toe. Dan O'Keeffe blocked it but Mackey followed up and scored.'

Limerick celebrated; Mackey scored 2-4 but Kerry won. 'I won on the treble that day,' says Tom, 'the minor and senior and a friend for life in Mackey. We were great pals after it.

'We'd meet at matches and I remember the 1952 Munster final because of him. I played the match in the Athletic Grounds with a sore leg. I hurt it against Legion the week before and leading up to the final, I put all kinds of liniment on it. I burned the leg off myself but still played. During the game, I got kicked on the exact same spot and had to come off.

'Who was on the sideline only Mick Mackey. Kerry were being hammered and at half-time he turned to me and said, "We may as well be drinking, rather than being here." He had a dozen of stout inside in a suitcase and we went down to the banks of the Lee and drank the lot.'

Ashe then washed himself down in the river and gave a new meaning to the term an early shower. It wasn't the first time he had one.

'One day, Neilly Duggan of Cork was marking Tadhgie Lyne and giving him a hard time of it. I was a kind of a hit man, so I was switched out from corner-forward onto Neilly. After a while, Neilly wasn't getting his way anymore. We went for this ball and he hit me right across the mouth. If he did, I went after him and gave him two or three good ones.

'The same referee warned me during a game in Tralee when McAndrew of Mayo threw the ball in my face and I went after him. I didn't get a second chance after hitting Neilly but as I was going up through the crowd, the Bishop of Kerry, Dr Denis Moynihan, shouted over, "You were right Tom, dead right." It was like getting absolution there and then.'

Dr Eamonn O'Sullivan wasn't so complimentary – foul play wasn't part of his *Art and Science of Gaelic Football* manual. It wasn't Ashe's only transgression as he found out during the 1953 All-Ireland semi-final against Louth.

'I came off at half-time and was delighted with myself – I'd kicked a point but Dr O'Sullivan gave out to me. I'd left my area to score the point. You didn't leave your area under Dr O'Sullivan.'

It wasn't all bad as Ashe held his place on the team for the All-Ireland final. It was his first All-Ireland appearance, eight years after he first lined out with the county and a winning performance that meant he could hold his head high in Dingle.

'You were nothing in Dingle if you didn't have an All-Ireland at that time. I played club football with all the Dingle greats and now had an All-Ireland like them. It was important. I had to win one and one was enough for me.'

And, like all Dingle folk, Ashe repaired to the Shakespeare Bar on Parnell Street to celebrate his All-Ireland success.

'It was the place to go,' he says, 'and myself, Gega and Paddy Bawn had a great time there when we played on the Railway Cup team in 1949. The final against Leinster on St Patrick's Day, a Thursday, finished level. Rather than go home, we stayed in Dublin for the replay on the Sunday. We had a good drink of porter. We were in the Shakespeare from Thursday to Sunday, came out of it and won the Railway Cup by fourteen points. A great few days in Dublin they were. I'll always remember Dublin and football by those four days. Great days. Jesus, they were great.'

JÓM

Paudie Sheehy

Even in later years, the five selectors never told the players exactly what happened when they met to pick the team in the Park Place Hotel just over a week before the All-Ireland final of 1953. As far as anyone can remember, nobody ever really asked them either.

It took a while for news to break that Paudie Sheehy wasn't on the team for the final against Armagh. His father, John Joe, was part of the five man selection committee, along with Fr Denis Curtin, Paddy 'Bawn' Brosnan, Murt Kelly and Johnny Walsh.

As the players heard that Paudie hadn't made the cut, word also reached them that when it was time to select the six forwards – Paudie played wing-forward and captained Kerry up to that point – John Joe Sheehy excused himself from the task. Most players recall hearing that he left the room and gave directions to the remaining four selectors, saying they knew what to do with Paudie.

His son was now an established player but, by all accounts, hadn't played well in the semi-final against Louth.

'He marked Denis White in the semi-final, and White was a fabulous player who put in a great display against us,' says goalkeeper in '53, Johnny Foley. 'Paudie would have accepted it wasn't his day. It was suggested at some point that John Joe told the rest of the committee what to do.'

If so, it wasn't the first time John Joe Sheehy showed caution in selecting his son. For the replayed semi-final of 1951 against Mayo, John Joe asked for Paudie to be overlooked for the team, saying he was too young to start. He was eventually overruled but his advice was acted on two years later.

'We heard John Joe asked to leave the meeting,' recalls corner-back, Jas Murphy. 'He probably knew what was coming because Paudie didn't have a good semi-final. He was a great footballer but nothing went right for him that day. He ended up paying the price.'

'Competition for places was huge that year,' says Dermot Hanifin, who played midfield in the final. 'We had a special game about a fortnight before the final, just so the selectors could make a decision on who would play midfield.'

For a few days, the starting fifteen was kept under wraps. The players were winding down their two weeks of collective training in Killarney when Jas Murphy was approached on the street.

Facing page:
Clan Gathering – 1962 All-Ireland winning captain Sean Óg Sheehy, holding Sam Maguire aloft, is flanked by his brothers, Niall and Paudie, during the homecoming in Tralee.
(The Kerryman)

179

'I was walking through the town and somebody came up to me and said I was captain for the following Sunday. It was news to me. It was also the first I heard that Paudie wasn't playing.'

Even though his semi-final performance wasn't impressive, a few players sensed Paudie would still make the cut.

'You knew that if John Joe wanted to keep Paudie on the team he could have,' says other corner-back, Mixie Palmer. 'John Joe had that kind of power and respect and he could pull strings – a father and son could have captained Kerry to All-Irelands. But you also knew that John Joe would only have the best for Kerry at heart. We all felt for Paudie. At the same time, you had to respect John Joe as well.'

'John Joe walked out of the meeting in 1953 when it came to selecting Paudie's position,' says Paudie's brother, Brian. 'Not being picked was a huge disappointment to Paudie. After that, all he could do was stay with it, keep plugging away with the county.'

The evening the team was made official, the squad left their digs at the Park Place under the watch of trainers Dr Eamonn O'Sullivan and Paul Russell. They went for their usual walk after tea, this time scaling the boundary of Killarney to trek along the roads of Aghadoe, with the town twinkling away below them, oblivious to it all.

'I can remember that evening well,' says Johnny Foley, 'and I spoke to Paudie about what had happened while we were out on our walk. He told me he'd love to be playing next Sunday. He'd played every game that year and, needless to say, it would be difficult for any fellow to lose out for the final. But he took it on the chin. You have to remember that Paudie was Kerry to the fingertips. That would have been passed onto him from his father.'

For Jas Murphy, his role of captain for the final was tinged with thoughts of Sheehy.

'Myself and Paudie were both from Tralee and we went back a long way. Friends for life,' he says. 'I used to travel from Cork with him, down to Kerry for games and I felt bad for him missing out. He was devestated but he was very even tempered and though he was down, he accepted it. When I captained the team to win, he was delighted for me even though he was the one who had lost out.'

'At the function after the game, Paudie was crying with disappointment,' says another brother, Seán Óg.

He didn't play any role that day against Armagh. Gerald O'Sullivan came on for Dermot Hanifin and Paudie stayed on the bench. The whole episode was a personal setback but it didn't define him. He went on to win All-Irelands in 1955, 1959 and 1962, starring in all three campaigns.

'Paudie was an exceptional man,' adds Seán Óg. 'His attitude was that he took the beating and came back. Others would have walked away and played no more.

Not Paudie, though.'

Commitment and application coursed through his blood, as it did through his father's. The easy option for John Joe Sheehy was to select his son at wing-forward for one more game, a final Kerry were generally expected to win anyway.

But the word 'easy' wasn't part of John Joe's lexicon, or his son's either. Paudie had a slight frame at a time when brawn and physical presence were required features. Instead of bustle, he used speed and craft, and excelled on the field. He forged his own way. Eventually, he got a chance to lead Kerry out in an All-Ireland final seven years later, when Down beat Kerry.

The father and son combination didn't come that day – it arrived two years later in 1962 when Sean Óg captained Kerry to win the All-Ireland.

'Paudie was running out onto the field beside me before the final and I actually thought about asking him to be captain. [But] I felt it would upset the whole thing if I did, considering how things had gone wrong in 1953. Paudie had a great game that day, too.'

If he excelled on the field, then he also stood out away from it. In between All-Irelands, he finished with the country's best marks in accountancy and secured a postgraduate seat at Harvard University in Massachusetts. That they had a Harvard scholar for a brother didn't surprise Brian or Séan Óg.

'He had a record that he never missed a day at school,' says Séan Óg. 'One time when he was a kid, he broke his leg playing a game of football but he still used to cycle his bike to school. Never missed a day – broken leg or no broken leg.'

Always persevering. Always pushing on. That attitude stayed with him.

'In the spring time, a few of us used to run up Carrauntoohil for training and to keep ourselves fit,' recalls Brian. 'We'd start off together but, after a while, Paudie would edge away from us. It got to the stage that, when we'd be halfway up the mountain, he'd be halfway down. He'd pass us coming back and we'd shout over to him, "Ah Paudie, sure you weren't up at all." It was always the same though when you'd reach the top. There would be a new set of stones on the ground marking out the letter P.'

Always staying with it.

TJF

Jas Murphy

Jas Murphy has lived in Cork for over 60 years. Over the decades he has become part of the place.

He played most of his club football there between the St Nicholas and Garda clubs, pulled on the Cork jersey and has been president of Nemo Rangers. A Corkman even taught him how to kick ball back in Tralee.

Jas Murphy is still Kerry though and every now and then, affirmation of Kerryness comes his way. Reminders that he never really left Kerry and Tralee behind.

The train from Cork to Tralee takes just over two hours. Jas takes it every few months to meet up with Johnny Foley and Mixie Palmer for a few hours to chew the fat.

'I was walking down the street one day with Johnny Foley,' says Jas, 'and this woman came up to me with her arm out-stretched. "Are you Jas Murphy?" she said, "I haven't seen you in 50 years!" It was Gerald O'Sullivan's sister and the last time I met her was after the 1953 All-Ireland final with Gerald.

'I can go back to Kerry and it's as if I never left all those 60 years ago. Kerry never forgets its footballers. If you wore that jersey, you can go down any time and you'll be one of their own – always. They'll remember you for that jersey.'

It means a lot to Jas. He lives alone in Turner's Cross. Ned Roche, who was beside him in the full-back line in 1953, was a neighbour but is gone now. So are the other Cork links to Kerry's win over Armagh – Tom Moriarty and John Cronin.

Jas' only real reminder is his replica Sam Maguire. It's in a cabinet in the front room of his house on Mount Pleasant and he catches a glimpse of it most days. It's also a reminder of the controversy that rocked Kerry football in September 1953.

'I didn't really want to be captain. I didn't think much of getting the captaincy because it was so controversial.

'Tralee people, who are great ball hoppers, made light of me getting it. They said I was made captain because Johnny Foley, our other Tralee man, was too small to be the first behind the Artane Boys Band. I know Jackie Lyne was very disappointed. He was the longest on the team and felt he should have got it. He would have been welcome to it. It was a big ordeal for an ordinary fella like me

Facing page:
Kerry captain, James Murphy, kissing the Archbishop's ring in 1953.
(G.A. Duncan)

183

to go up and collect Sam. But still, I was the first Strand Road man since Dan Spring in 1940 to captain an All-Ireland winning team and that was great.'

It was Jas' link to a golden period when Tralee captained All-Ireland winning teams most years: John Joe Sheehy in 1926 and 1930; Joe Barrett in 1929 and 1932; Miko Doyle in 1937.

Superstars walked through Tralee everyday. Jas remembers the Street Leagues that were played in Tralee Sportsfield every Friday night and the posters on shop windows, hawking the games. They were an easy sell. Rock Street versus Boherbee; Strand Road versus Rock Street. '*Bí ann gan teip,*' be there without fail the posters said.

They were. Crowds of up to 2,000 would show. Jas was always one of them and without a penny in his pocket, he'd loiter outside the entrance waiting for the stars.

'I'll take your boots in for you tonight, Miko.'

'Can I carry your bag, Purty?'

'My mother has a pub on the Strand Road side, Danno, can I carry something for you?'

Dan O'Keeffe never let Jas down. Jas stood behind the goal in the Tralee Sportsfield just to be close to the netminder. The scene was replayed in a field opposite the Brandon Hotel where Jas would sometimes kick ball with Danno.

'We played there on summer evenings in our ordinary clothes. I'd go in amongst the grown-ups to try and get the ball. I mightn't get a kick but I'd be learning about the game. Mixed matches we used to call them and you learned quickly. You had to. I was sad to leave it all behind when I joined the Gardaí.'

Jas went the opposite direction to Danno. Dan came from Cork – Jas went there. Brother Murray from Cork had taught Jas the basics of the game in Tralee CBS, so for a few years, he gave something back to Cork.

'I played against Kerry in the 1947 Munster final. I was marking Frank O'Keeffe, a school pal of mine. John and Jim Cronin from Miltown were also on the Cork team. I mustn't have done well because I heard after that Cork weren't too happy with the way I played. They lost faith and trust in me, they thought I wasn't giving my best. In 1949, Micheál Ó Ruairc asked me to declare for Kerry. John Cronin and Tom Moriarty and myself declared around the same time.

'We all had to wait for an All-Ireland though. In 1951, we were up in Ballyheigue training, but people were acting the fooleen. We should have won the All-Ireland in 1950 and 1951. In 1953, Paul Russell and Dr Eamonn took over as trainers. There was great drive, discipline and method. Players weren't doing what they wanted to do, they were told what to do.'

No one summed up this drive better than Jas, Kerry's player of the year up to the final.

Mick Dunne, *The Irish Press:* 'I thought I had seen everything from James Murphy in the Munster final but this was nothing to yesterday's performance. The 6 feet 1 inch garda was right-full-back on the programme but he was everywhere in defence when danger threatened. He outjumped and outreached Hugh O'Rourke, Peadar Smith and every other Louth forward who came to challenge him.'

That performance came in the All-Ireland semi-final and then came the captaincy he never wanted. 'It affected my game for the final. I didn't play well but I got through it. I would have rathered concentrate on my own game than be burdened with that.'

Jas carried the burden well when he got back to Tralee with the cup. His mother's pub, Babe Lucett's, stayed open through the night. Babe Lucett's was known locally as 'Lourdes' – the early house in Tralee where hard drinkers went for the cure.

It's just what Jas Murphy needed on the Tuesday morning after the All-Ireland. It had been one long session since Sunday but the party wasn't over yet.

'I had to do the round of the schools with the cup. Paudie Sheehy's brother, Brian, came up to my mother and told her to get me out of bed and down to the schools so they'd get a half-day. I was a sick man as I went around the town with the cup that morning.

'I brought the cup to the Listowel Races another day and to Con Brosnan's pub in Moyvane afterwards. We finished up in the ballroom in Listowel. It was a hectic few days. Eventually, my mother called me aside and said, "Give up the 'aul drink now, you're at it long enough."'

He took Babe's advice and the celebrations eventually died away. Not the memories though.

Meeting Gerald O'Sullivan's sister in Tralee brought them all home.

JÓM

Johnny Foley

He paid into the Munster final of 1953 and watched the game from the bank on the town side as Kerry took down Cork. Johnny Foley had no idea at the time but the best year of his life was about to kick off.

By right, Foley shouldn't have even been at the Munster final. A few months before that, he and his future wife, Mabel, had planned on moving to America but Johnny failed the medical test in Dublin. A spot on the lung kept him out of the States for the time being.

'Nothing to worry about, the doc said. Just come back in twelve months and you'll be ready for the trip. So that was the plan,' recalls Johnny.

He settled back to life on Strand Road, keeping goal for a side that was looking more and more like winning a county championship, and Foley was one of the leaders of the team. He played three years for the Kerry minors and was disappointed not to have made the step up to the seniors.

For sure, he was going to miss Tralee when he emigrated and he was going to miss the game too but at least he wasn't walking away on a Kerry career. He thought that boat had sailed.

But it rankled a little because Foley was a football fanatic and kept track of life's events by way of his football memories.

During his last year of school, he skipped class whenever he could. Kerry were training in Tralee for an All-Ireland with Roscommon and Foley was anxious to get a close-up look at the stars. He has a vivid memory of standing beside Billy Casey on the sideline as Casey lay stretched out on a plank between two blocks getting his shoulders rubbed after training. 'Those fellas were the Robert Redfords of their time,' he says. That was 1946.

His first pay cheque? That was the week he walked into Hurley's Music Shop in Tralee and bought a photograph of Paddy Kennedy kissing the ring of Bishop of Perth, Mundy Prendeville. Hurley's always published photographs of Kerry's games and usually had them for sale on a Monday morning.

Foley's second pay cheque? That was the week he bought the photograph of Dan O'Keeffe.

Foley always wanted a shot at the Kerry seniors but that chance hadn't come yet and before August 1953 it wasn't looking likely any time soon. So, when the possibility of heading to the States arrived, he and Mabel were ready to make the

Facing page:
Johnny Foley back to where it all started – the Strand Road club of Kerin's O'Rahillys.
(John Kelly)

187

jump. But it just happened that O'Rahillys were fulfilling their potential and had made the semi-final of the county championship. Foley had been awesome along the way.

It was still a surprise when he was called in for collective training before the semi-final against Louth and he hadn't yet twigged he was in line for a starting place.

'We were staying in St Finian's because the Park Place was booked out. It was tourist season,' he says. 'So we're having dinner after training one night and I hear Paddy Bawn say, "We're going to start Foley in goal." My heart was pounding. You should have seen me. I could barely swallow my food.'

His form continued against Louth and so did Kerry's. They were back in the Park Place for two weeks before a showdown with Armagh.

Crammed between these two games, Foley's club had reached the county final. It took place the Sunday before the All-Ireland final and the Kerry players travelled together to the game.

'I arrived with the rest of the Kerry lads just fifteen minutes before the game. Dr Eamonn had me warned that if we won, I'd have to come straight back to Killarney. Sure afterwards, all the Rahillys' lads were going out on the town celebrating and I was mad to go with them. But Dr Eamonn nabbed me. I'd two pints in the Royal Hotel in Killarney later on. That was my celebration.'

The trainer may have had a tight rein on the team but a renegade group did manage to break free before the semi-final.

'The Monday of Puck Fair, five of us said we'd chance going back. We got a lift that night with a milk truck, all the way to Killorglin. Three of us on the milk tank and two in the cab. God almighty, we suffered in training the next day.'

The week of the final dragged on and pressure on Kerry increased. It was 1946 since Kerry won a title and prior to that, they had claimed eleven out of 23 championships. In 1953, seven years was like a famine.

Foley became acquainted with the nuances and tics of the team. He knew who to room with if he wanted a decent night's sleep – Seán Murphy – and who was best for talking into the night – Mixie Palmer.

Mixie and Foley. The two of them have remained tight ever since those days. A few years back, when Palmer rang his buddy up to tell him he was returning to Ireland and moving to Blennerville, just out the town from Foley's Strand Road home, he could almost see the smile stretched across his friend's face.

When the mood takes them, they'll meet up in O'Dwyer's Bar in Blennerville – with its bare walls and good stout, itself a throwback to the good old days – maybe to share a nugget of racing information or to drag one of their own stories from the vault.

Often, their introduction to golf will get an airing.

'Dr Eamonn organised a little golf tournament in Killarney the Friday before

the Armagh final to take our minds off the game. He went to a lot of trouble, arranged a miniature cup for the winner and got real serious about it. So, we were taking this thing real serious as well. Normally the craic would be to see who'd drive the ball the furthest into the lake, you know. Not this time. We were immersed in it and eventually Tadhgie Lyne won.'

The final is remembered for dead ball expert Bill McCorry's penalty six minutes from the end with Kerry slightly ahead. Foley famously saw his two corner-backs, Mixie and Jas Murphy, heckle and tug the shorts of the Armagh man and then watched as the ball sailed a yard wide. He remembers most the sparkle of the crowd as they rushed behind his goal. 'They were so close you could hear their conversations. You could even start up one yourself.'

The penalty was the end of Armagh but the beginning of a bond between players from the two counties.

Whenever one of the Armagh lads holidayed in Kerry, Johnny and Mabel would put them up for a few nights. He has swapped Christmas cards every year with the bulk of that team, drove up to Pat Campbell's funeral a few years back.

In 2002, Foley, together with Mixie, Jas, Dr Jim and a few more, pensioners the lot of them, trekked all the way to Armagh for the opening of the Collegeland GAA pitch.

'I saw a sight that night I'll never forget. Sean Kelly and Jack Bracken, who marked each other in 1953, shaking hands. It was the first time they'd laid eyes on each other since the final whistle of the final. What a thing to see.'

The year after his two games with Kerry, he drifted out of the panel. He remembers playing an Easter Sunday tournament against Armagh in London in 1954 and hearing news that would have repercussions for Kerry.

'We were coming home on the boat after the game and it was just after Congress. We'd picked up an *Irish Press* at Marble Arch and saw in the GAA pages that collective training had been abolished. I won't say what some of the lads said to that. Collective training was our thing.'

Only a year with the team but his mind is dappled with wonderful memories.

And America? Turns out it was just a little footnote. 'After the All-Ireland we changed our plans. We never went.'

Noosed by home and the warm glow of his year. America, they thought, could stay waiting. It still is.

TJF

Tom Moriarty

They were running all their youth. Never stayed still. Mount Brandon weaved in and out of their days and they knew its haggards and slopes and every hollow from Cappagh to its peak. Eleven months separated Michael Moriarty from his older brother, Tom. 'When we were young we never stopped going,' Michael says.

He tells the story of Brandon and the Moriarty brothers. Says the obsession with running and athletics began there. Primed their fitness and expanded their lungs.

Five aeroplanes crashed into the humpy mountain when they were kids – at least, he reckons it's five, could be more, could be less – and each one lit a fascination within the brothers.

'We were going to sleep one night and heard this loud sound outside. Bang. Then everything fell silent. We knew what it was. The next morning we were off up the mountain before school, with a lot of the locals. Running. Never stopping. That one was a Polish crew on a British bomber plane, during the war. They were all killed and I can still remember the ammunition thrown all over the hill. Another time, a plane from Lisbon couldn't land at Shannon and was circling out at sea. That went down in a very heavy fog. We went up the hill for all the crashes.'

Wrecks of planes greeted them. Singed debris and often bodies scattered around the mountain. There was an innocence to their curiosity, though. Young lads with adventure on their minds, oblivious to the bigger picture.

Once, a German bomber sailed over their heads when they were saving hay in the fields. The Luftwaffe's finest was pursued by a plane from the RAF and they heard a loud shrill sound in the foggy air. Whoosh. Then came the familiar bang before everything fell silent.

They dropped their pikes and took off on the climb.

The crew had survived and as the brothers were scaling the mountain, the Germans were piecing their machine gun together, ready for whatever enemy greeted them.

'There were a few Gardaí and a Special Branch at the barracks in Clahane at the time. They were tearing up the mountain as well and made us turn back. I don't know how it happened but the Germans were captured and were interned for the rest of the war.'

Facing page:
Tom Moriarty goes highest for the ball in the 1954 All-Ireland against Meath.
(Seamus O'Reilly)

Extraordinary stories to make the days pass by quicker.

''Twas a fair run up that hill alright,' he says. 'But we were like mountain goats. We never stopped.'

Their fitness peaked when they wore the colours of Tralee CBS in those big time athletics meetings against St Brendan's of Killarney. Austin Stack Park was packed for the events. Marching bands, wedged crowds, knife-edge atmosphere. The works.

Tom dominated the high jump and the 100 and 200 metre sprints. 'He cleaned up. The only thing I could beat him at was the long jump.'

The Moriartys had football skill to go with the fitness and their brother, Sean, was part of the Dublin panel that won the All-Ireland in 1942.

Michael and Tom shared their moment to shine when both played on the minor team in 1945 against Dublin in the All-Ireland semi-final, Tom at centre-forward, Michael at full-forward. Dublin won by two points but the day stayed with them.

When they arrived in the capital that Saturday afternoon, the minors were split into two groups – ten going for Buswells Hotel and ten going for the Imperial. Tom and Michael were together in the group searching for the phantom Imperial Hotel.

'There was no hotel in the city by that name. We must have asked every Garda in Dublin.'

They were led in their search by a Boherbee man, an undertaker called Jimmy Foley.

The group spent five hours tramping around Dublin, looking for a hotel that didn't exist and eventually, as evening was coming in, Jimmy Foley said he had enough.

'Jimmy was a great man. He took us off to stay at the Savoy on O'Connell Street, in we went and had a mixed grill. We'd never even heard of a mixed grill before and by Jesus, we nearly ate the plate. We were so tired that night we couldn't sleep and the next morning, we were up early to walk to Croke Park for the game. It's no wonder we lost. But it turned out the county board had got it wrong and the hotel we were looking for was the Exchange, on Parliament Street. I passed it a few years ago on a bus. The whole story came back to me when I saw it.'

Soon after that episode, Michael's knees began to fail him and his days at the top of the football heap drew in. Tom kept on making a name for himself.

He moved to Cork with his banking job, won a junior All-Ireland with the county in 1951 and a year later had a county championship medal playing for Clonakilty. Other sports intrigued him. One day he travelled to Tipperary to watch his banking colleagues take part in a rugby game, a meaningless inter-firm encounter. It turned out the bankers were a player short and the footballer on the sideline was approached.

'What's the use in wasted talent?' the bankers said. 'C'mon and line out.' He'd never played before but what the hell? What's the worst that could happen? So, he gave it a shot and lined out at full-back, the perfect position for a 6 feet 3 inch high ball fielder.

The association had their spies for occasions like this, though, and when the game was done and dusted, he was told a priest had identified him as a GAA man and had informed the association. Tom was banned from playing football for the rest of the year.

Moriarty wasn't alone. Shortly after, the Cork County Board pulled a similar stunt on Ned Roche. The man from Knocknagoshel was playing his football in the county but a board official uncovered a photograph of Ned playing rugby – twelve years before.

They claimed Roche brought the association into disrepute and gave him a similar suspension from the GAA.

When Moriarty's blockade had finished, he declared for Kerry. Good days and accolades followed. His last game came on a bad day for the county, the All-Ireland semi-final of 1958.

'Tom was playing fantastically that day,' recalls Jerome O'Shea. 'What a pity we lost him.'

Michael Moriarty recalls the details. '1958 finished him. It was a wet, rainy day. Tom had a fierce stride and he stretched out for this ball. It was right in front of where I was sitting. A Derry fella came in over him and made bits of his leg. He was nine months out of work after that. He thought for a while he was going to lose his leg but they put a plate into it and he was fine after that. He had strong legs.'

Strong legs. Chiselled on the crags of Brandon.

TJF

James 'Mixie' Palmer

He was studying medicine at UCC and soon, he was the richest kid on campus. Mixie Palmer reckons he played for fifteen clubs in Cork while he studied in the city during the 1940s.

'You'd get a couple of quid for lining out with each club. If your team won and you played well, you'd get a fiver. That was roughly half a week's wages then.'

He wasn't the only Kerry exile plying his trade illegally with the clubs of Cork. On one particular day, Palmer was in the Inchigellagh colours. Another west Cork team provided the opposition. When Palmer was making his way towards his marker, he found Michael Moynihan, soon to become a TD, standing in wait. Palmer was officially a Legion player at this stage, Moynihan was a Headford man. Both exchanged looks, shook hands and never uttered a word.

'Back then, there was a lot of money gambled on games in west Cork, even junior games. So, clubs were always willing to bring in outside players.'

For Palmer, life as a football mercenary lasted about a year, until he was rumbled and landed with a twelve-month suspension.

But he'd made enough of an impression in Cork to merit a place on the county's minor team and in 1945, the student from Glenlough, outside Sneem, lined out at midfield against Kerry. A stint on the Cork senior panel was to follow and, in fact, Palmer ended his inter-county vocation in the colours of Waterford, playing with the county in the Munster final of 1957. The Deise had famously defeated Kerry in the previous round.

Wedged in between his Cork and Waterford days was a Kerry career littered with fun and fortune.

Palmer was studying in Dublin and playing with the Geraldines when he got the call to the Kerry seniors. But the tang of defeat was tasted before success came his way.

One of Kerry's darkest moments came in the 1952 Munster final. Cork handed out an unmerciful defeat to their neighbours, triumphing on a scoreline of 0-11 to 0-2.

To say that Palmer wasn't properly prepared going into that game is an understatement.

'The Killarney Races were on the week before and some of the team, myself included, spent a few days racing. The night before the Munster final, about six

Facing page:
Mixie Palmer had good reason to have the game of his life in the 1955 All-Ireland – he wagered £80, at 6/4 on Kerry to beat Dublin.
(Shelagh Honan)

of us decided we'd go to Glenbeigh. We stayed in Evans' Hotel, had a few pints and the next morning when we woke, the owner of the hotel had to drive us to Cork for the game. I slept the whole way there and when I got on the field, I was knackered after twenty minutes. We were hammered and it would have been worse but for Paddy Bawn and Marcus O'Neill.'

On top of the seven year All-Ireland famine, the Cork mauling meant there was added pressure on Kerry's campaign of 1953. Kerry came good, though, thanks in part to that infamous penalty miss by Bill McCorry. Palmer takes up the story.

'It was a huge kick and could have swung the game for them. So, I said to myself, there's no way he's going to score it. What I did you wouldn't get away with nowadays. I nearly had my finger on the ball when he was kicking it. I was one side of the ball and Jas was on the other. We gave Bill plenty of chat as well. I suppose, by right, the penalty should have been taken again but he blasted it wide and we won the All-Ireland.'

Three weeks before the Armagh encounter, Palmer was involved in another final: the Dublin Soccer Hospitals Cup Final, played at Dalymount Park. With the Ban still very much en vogue within the Association, word of Palmer's soccer exploits could have had disastrous results for Kerry. And worse was to come the following day, when *The Irish Times* ran a team picture which included Palmer.

'If anyone saw that picture I would have been run out of Kerry. And if Armagh had seen it after the All-Ireland final, they could have objected. But that wasn't something I thought about. I played in goal, which I really enjoyed, and all I wanted was a game. That photograph nearly ruined things but I wasn't too worried, because back then, supporters of Gaelic football would never buy *The Irish Times*.'

Nobody ever did get wind of Palmer's appearance at Dalymount Park and the Kerry celebrations began and ended uninterrupted. After the Armagh game, the Kerry team made their way to The Moy, beside Barry's Hotel. Over twenty bodies were stuffed into a room on the top floor and pints were delivered on the hotel's food pulley. With midnight approaching, hunger set in and mixed grills replaced the stout.

'We went to The Castle Hotel for grub. It was owned by a man from Sneem and had the best food in Dublin. The mixed grill was a huge plate of food. It was a great sight seeing the grub coming out and a great feeling with the medal secured.'

Two years later, after the Kerry/Dublin final of 1955, Palmer was joint sports star of the week in the *Irish Independent*. The performance he gave at corner-back was one of the reasons Kerry overcame the Dublin challenge, but unknown to everybody, he had added incentive.

A fortnight before the final, Palmer was on cattle dealing business with his brother-in-law in Kilmallock. They retired to Mooney's, a local establishment, and came across two Dublin cattle buyers with money burning their pockets. Talk wafted onto the upcoming final. The Dublin men declared a city victory. Palmer, who they didn't recognise, disagreed. The Dubliners offered odds of six to four against a Kerry win. Palmer took the bet.

'I put £80 behind Mooney's bar and the Dublin lads put £60 each, winner takes all.'

His confidence of a Kerry victory was based on that year's Whit Tournament in Killarney. 'We stayed with Dublin in the Whit Tournament for about three quarters of the game. They pulled away at the end. We were far from fit but the Dublin fellows were on top of their game. For the All-Ireland, we trained for two weeks solid, three times a day. The night in Mooney's, I was on my way to Killarney for the fortnight training so I knew we'd match Dublin for fitness and we'd beat them. I played my heart out. I had to. And I was back in Kilmallock the Monday after the game to collect my £200.'

The richest cattle dealer in Munster.

TJF

Jerome O'Shea

'*Enjoyed first kick of football with new Blackthorn boots.*'

He wrote that in his diary on 22 January 1955. The boots cost £2-2. The following day, a pair of basketball shoes cost 30/-, after which came his 'best ever training game of basketball'.

It wasn't just football and basketball though. He was also a voracious reader. On 23 January, he read *9.15 to Freedom* by Martin Fiala; two days later, he was on to Sean Ó Faoláin's *South of Sicily*. By month's end, he had read *The Vanishing Trick* by Harry Komichael and John Cassells' *The Grey Ghost*.

He'd also seen Maureen O'Hara and Errol Flynn in *Against All Flags*. Other movies were *My Outlawed Brother*, *Lily of Killarney*, *Under The Red Robe* and *A Real Blarney Show*.

It's all documented in Jerome O'Shea's diary of 1955.

Page 1: Diary 1955
Name: Jerome O'Shea
Address: 2 New Market St., Caherciveen
Trains: To City 7.40 am From City 10.30 am
Collars: 16½
Gloves: 10½
Shoes: 10

Above:
Jerome O'Shea still has the diary he kept from 1955, his greatest year in a Kerry jersey.
(Shelagh Honan)

Insurance Premium: '86
Weight: 13 stone 8 pounds. On 1st January
Height: 6 feet 1½ inches

'I don't know why I kept it,' says Jerome now, clutching the hard-backed book that measures 4 inches by 3 inches. 'Maybe I thought 1955 was going to be a big year for me.'

Previous years hadn't been. In the autumn of 1953, a group of football people gathered in John 'Bawn' Curran's pub on Main Street, Caherciveen. Bawner, as everyone in Caherciveen called him, was at the centre of things.

He was also convinced there was a hex on Caherciveen footballers. No one disagreed with his thesis. It went back to 1926. Jack Murphy was the hero of Kerry's drawn All-Ireland against Kildare, but come the replay Jack was on his deathbed – struck down with pneumonia. He died two days after Kerry won the replay. He was 22.

The same happened P.J. 'Peachy' O'Sullivan. He was a sub on the Kerry team that won the All-Ireland in 1931, but in March 1932, contracted meningitis and died. He was nineteen.

Jerome was 22 in 1953 – he got his first Munster final start that year and distinguished himself in the final in Killarney. Paddy 'Bawn' Brosnan was so impressed that he took him to Scott's Hotel afterwards for pints. Jerome was being dubbed Paddy Bawn's successor.

Kerry went on to win the All-Ireland but Jerome was only a sub. The Monday before the All-Ireland semi-final against Louth, he contracted pleurisy and Donie Murphy took his place at corner-back, holding onto the jersey for the final against Armagh.

'When Bawner heard I had cried off, he thought it was the end of the road for Caherciveen. He thought a Caherciveen man would never win an All-Ireland medal again.'

It wasn't the first time fate conspired against Jerome. In 1951, he was called into Tralee for a trial game as Kerry prepared for the All-Ireland semi-final replay against Mayo. He impressed and was invited to Ballyheigue for collective training.

'I thought I was up in Ballyheigue making up the numbers but one day when I was leaving the dressing room after training a selector said, "You'll be playing on Sunday." I was in a quandary – my Kerry career could have been over before it started. When Kerry were playing Mayo the first day, I played a North Cork final for Mitchelstown against Glanworth, which meant I was illegal. I had to make my excuses for Kerry and say I wasn't available.'

There were no hard luck stories in 1955. Diary entries:

Saturday 1/01/1955: Most important of my New Year resolutions is to make a serious effort to give up cigarettes.

Sunday 09/01/1955: Chosen as Munster's right back for Railway Cup.

Friday 14/01/1955: Selected captain of the South Kerry team for this year's Co. Champ.

Friday 21/01/1955: Snap appeared in today's Kerryman. *Helped at fixing the hall for Hurling 31 Drive at which I played. Bawner says 'You'll never be held this year'.*

Bawner was right. Munster, All-Ireland, county championship and divisional championship medals came Jerome's way in 1955. He shared Sports Star of the Week with Mixie Palmer after the All-Ireland and was The *Irish Independent*'s Footballer of the Year.

Monday 14/02/1955: Got a good write-up in Press *and* Indo *today. Blotted Langan completely out of the game.*

Tom Langan, the best full-forward in Ireland. It got better.

Saturday 23/07/1955: Had a very enjoyable evening at the White Strand. We played beachball game – fourteen all in. Palmist tells me my fortune – won't lose.

It was the day before the Munster final against Cork. The fortune teller called it right. Jerome didn't lose, with his finest hour coming in the All-Ireland final against Dublin on 24 September.

Saturday 23/09/1955: Filming of Spirit of St Louis *today at Portmagee. Staying in Portmarnock tonight. Game of croquet.*

There were no entries in Jerome's diary for Monday, Tuesday and Wednesday after the All-Ireland. *The Irish Press* told the story though.

Padraig Puirséil, *The Irish Press*: 'No man on the winning side jumped as high, or caught as safely, as did their fair haired marvel from Caherciveen, Jerome O'Shea, who served up two flying saves in the second half, which must be treasured in the memory of everyone who saw the game.

'One of the finest saves I ever hope to see was effected by Jerome O'Shea. A hard drive that looked a goal all the way, had beaten the rest of the defence and was flying for the net, just beneath the bar Jerome came with a tremendous leap to snatch the leather at the last moment and bring off a clearance as spectacular as it was dramatic.'

Thursday 28/09/1955: My spectacular saves towards end are talk of the county. Headlines of the Fair Haired Marvel.

Friday 30/09/1955: Sports Star of the Week.

Saturday 01/10/1955: Kerryman loud in its praises of team. My display reminiscent of Jack Murphy in 1926 famous games with Kildare.

Bawner's curse was broken.

'A football fever in South Kerry,' noted Jerome in his diary on 7 July.

Fever was pitched at its highest on 30 October – the day of the county final replay against North Kerry in Tralee. The train to Tralee left at 8.30am, prompting supporters to ask curate Monsignor Lane to bring the 8am mass forward. He refused.

8.20am: The whistle to announce the imminent departure of the train.
8.21am: Dan O'Connell stood up in Daniel O'Connell Church. He was 75 and hadn't seen South Kerry win a county final since 1896.

'He had been kneeling in the front row,' says Jerome, 'but got up, genuflected and walked out of the tiled aisle of the church with his cap in his hand. I can still hear the sound of his hobnailed boots on the tiles, as he walked out of a silent church. He wasn't going to miss the match.

'The doors of the church creaked as he opened them. In his own way he was challenging the church and many people followed. They saw no reason why the church should stop them getting to the match on time.'

Sunday 30/10/1955: 'South Kerry's Greatest day having first win in Senior Co. Final since 1896. Captained them to a two-point win over North Kerry in a typical Kerry final of text book football. Victory celebrations greatest ever in Caherciveen where bonfires blazed. Thousands gathered and candles smiled from their pedestals on every window as the triumphant parade passed through town. Three-mile streams of cars.'

No one held Jerome O'Shea in 1955 – people learned of his exploits in the strangest of ways. In the '80s Jerome was in Rome working for the United Nations and produced his passport when checking into his hotel.

'Ah it's you, Jerome O'Shea,' his Italian host said. 'I was educated by the Christian Brothers and we learned English by reading *The Kerryman*. You played for a great Kerry team in 1955.'

1955 never went to Jerome's head though.

Last Diary entry: 'Keep your own sector of play. Don't hop the ball. Don't drop kick. Don't foul. Chest the ball. Fullback not outside 21-yard line. Though beaten follow your man. D~~~~ ~~~~t R.F. [right field] if half-back beaten. Follow through with foot.'

Back to the basics after a superstar year.

JÓM

Ned Roche

A Saturday in early summer and a purple, cloudless sky. Ned Roche is directing you to his house, set among the patchwork of suburbia on the edge of Cork. His wife is out shopping, he says, so he has the morning to himself and there's time to talk.

You take a right, one more left and 50 yards down the road, you spot big Ned – a strong, muscular figure in the distance, fitter and younger looking than his years – waiting patiently for your car.

Those with an eye for such things would immediately, and correctly, assume he was, for a large part of his life, an army man. Tall, angled shoulders. Language that is straight to the point.

'I still don't know why you want to talk to me,' he says, by way of a greeting. 'The fellows that won five or six medals, they're the ones you want to talk to. The older men are forgotten about now. A fellow like me in Kerry with only two All-Irelands, well, the way things have gone … it isn't worth much.'

If the 1955 final against Dublin was a pivotal game in shaping the future of football in Kerry, then the role Roche played in securing that year's title was also pivotal.

He was to mark Kevin Heffernan, a man in the process of changing the way forwards and backs looked at the game. For the first time ever, a full-forward was roaming from the square, eating up space out the field. Heffernan was a wild cowboy on the rampage over the great plains of Croke Park. In the Leinster final, he had gobbled up the great Paddy O'Brien of Meath and in the two subsequent games it took Dublin to overcome Mayo, Heffernan proved to be the vital cog.

Against this man, Ned Roche wasn't given a chance. Too clumsy, they said. Not enough football in him, was the whisper. With day-glo colours, the national media painted Heffernan and his Dublin forwards as invincible. They were a machine. Fast and mobile. Poor Ned was about to get mauled. He proved them all wrong.

Roche came to the attention of Kerry's selectors in a roundabout way. In 1949, while still a teenager, he joined the army and moved from Loughfoudher, outside Knocknagoshel, to The Curragh. Up in Kildare he played alongside some greats. Sean Gallagher of Antrim, Sean Quinn from Armagh and Cavan's John Joe Reilly.

Facing page:
Johnny Foley clears while Ned Roche keeps an Armagh forward at bay during the 1953 All-Ireland.
(Seamus O'Reilly)

Among these Railway Cup men, the teenager from Kerry learned a few tricks and held his own.

Two years later, he was transferred to Clonmel and broke into the Tipperary county team. His brother Denis, a garda in Tipperary, joined him. 'That Tipp team was full of strong devils,' Ned said, 'and Dinny was one of the strongest.'

Together, they made inroads. In the spring of 1953, Tipperary reached the league semi-final against Dublin in Croke Park, losing by five points. Back home in Kerry, pickings were lean. They were also beaten in the league semi-final by Cavan and an All-Ireland hadn't come to the county in seven years. A call for the exiles to return went out and Roche was a wanted man.

'Back then, anybody living outside Kerry had to declare for their county. I was approached to come back but I was slow enough to declare because it would be difficult to keep your place. It took a while to decide, but I did [return]. So did a few others. John Cronin. Tom Moriarty. Several more came from Dublin.'

When 1953 had finished, Roche had togged out in Croke Park six times and for three teams: Tipperary, Kerry and Munster. He also had his first All-Ireland, bringing a breath of relief to Kerry and extended celebrations. A banquet was arranged for The Great Southern in Killarney and every former All-Ireland medallist was invited. The good times were being ushered in again and supporters lapped up the victory – hungry cats before a bowl of milk.

It didn't last. Meath took Kerry apart the following year and some feared 1953 was a once off, a flash in the pan.

In 1955 though, the seeds of hope began to grow again. Kerry hurdled past a strong Cork side in the provincial decider and now, Cavan stood in the way of an All-Ireland final. The game ended level but the stops were pulled out for the replay. Dr Eamonn O'Sullivan was brought back as trainer; collective training resumed. Cavan was overcome.

A week after the replay, Ned Roche received a letter from the county board. 'Please present yourself at the Park Place Hotel, Killarney, two weeks before the final to continue collective training.'

Though officially he wasn't a selector in 1955, Dr O'Sullivan's influence seeped into the team. He was a presence. He had a reputation and aura. He put a structure to things.

For two weeks before the final, each day was a mirror image of its predecessor. Rise at the Park Place at 8am for a three-mile walk; complete relaxation between 9.30 and 10.30am; 11am, assemble at the stadium for a short lecture and some light training; lunch at 1.30pm; rest from 2 to 3.30pm; return to the ground at 4pm for another lecture and intense, tough training; evening meal at 6pm, followed by relaxation and another walk; light supper at 10.30pm and at midnight, lights out. Day after day after day.

The rigid timetable was familiar for Ned, the army man. It was strictly adhered to by the twenty-strong group and the only thing to break the routine was an odd game of golf.

On those long walks around Killarney, the trainer would tail to the back of the pack and share his wisdom with each player individually. He gave special time to Roche in light of the publicised challenge of Heffernan but it was a course in psychology rather than a tactical conversation.

'Dr Eamonn gave me no instructions on how to mark him [Heffernan]. They say he told me to do this or that but he didn't. I just marked him like I'd marked anybody else. I followed him out the field when he moved but I didn't go too far out. I didn't want to get lost.'

Dr O'Sullivan had another surprise in store. He insisted on breaking with tradition and organised accommodation outside the city centre the night before the game, well away from the usual haunt of Barry's Hotel.

Barry's had a reputation as an unruly spot. There were a dozen men to a room, and one particular room, at the end of the corridor, was labelled 'Eejits Ward' by the kit man, Gaffney Duggan.

Players wouldn't find sleep until all hours. With excitement levels already high, it was a haven of nervous energy. Sleep would just be about to hit when BAM! your bed is overturned in the darkness and there's a fit of laughter from the other occupants. Good fun but it wasn't unusual to have to put your bed back together four times a night, just hours before an All-Ireland final. That was Barry's and it didn't sit well with Dr O'Sullivan.

So, the details of their new hotel were kept secret. Not even the players knew. Eventually, on the evening before the final, they rolled into the old Guinness House in Portmarnock on the bus that collected them from the train at Heuston Station. They had a restful evening.

'On the way up to Portmarnock, we heard Ned give an interview on the radio that was pre-recorded,' says Jerome O'Shea. 'He was being asked continually about Heffernan but Ned gave short, funny answers. His attitude put us at ease.'

It was billed as the biggest All-Ireland yet but Ned Roche recalls no nerves on the Sunday morning. His task was simple. Stop Heffernan. Stop the Dublin Machine.

His man moved, Roche moved. He shackled him totally.

Heffernan scored 0-2. Kerry prevailed and Roche had poked a finger in the eye of his detractors.

TJF

John Dowling

Trace a line through the history of Kerin's O'Rahillys and at some point, it will lead to one name. He's left a legacy and is remembered for the blood and sweat he drenched the pitch with, helping develop and tend it.

Back when the field on Strand Road was just a few acres of urban waste, John Dowling would wander down pushing a wheelbarrow. He'd fill it with stones and quarry the ruins of debris that were scattered across it. He dug drains and sprinkled seeds. An All-Ireland captain getting dirt beneath his fingernails.

'I'd go down to do the odd story as the pitch development was moving along,' says Padraig Kennelly of *The Kerry's Eye*. 'And in those days it was a pick and a shovel. Nothing was above him when it came to Rahillys. John was different to a lot of them who played for Kerry at that time, in that quite a few of his contemporaries just vanished after they finished playing. Not John. He gave back double what he took out of the game.'

Transforming the field into a playable area was a mammoth task. But Dowling was blinkered when it came to breathing life into the club, even when others doubted a field could be shaped out at the site.

'Basically, the Rahillys' pitch is on the site of the old town dump; the council gave them the land,' explains Kennelly. 'It was up to the club to make it into a GAA pitch and you can imagine the task they had. They did an incredible job. This was in a part of Tralee where facilities were needed most and the pitch had a very beneficial effect. Strand Road has never been known as a crime area down through the years and a lot of that is down to John. It gave the local kids a real focal point in the community.'

He grew up with the club and, in turn, wrapped himself around all aspects of it. The Dowlings came from Cockle Shell Road on the outskirts of Tralee, in the middle of the countryside when John was a colt still finding his legs. They were farmers first but the mould was soon broken.

'Really, he was the only one in the family to play,' says his daughter, Karena. 'He said it was a big thing back then, going off to the football because he'd only been seen farming cows.'

The first leather football that ever came into the house paints the times in which he lived. He badgered his father, William, until his old man gave in. A family goat was sold and part of the profit went for the football. When that was

Facing page:
John Dowling at work on the Kerin's O'Rahillys field.
(Padraig Kennelly)

207

worn to shreds, he got pocket money for chasing hares up the slipper for the local coursing club which funded another ball.

It didn't take long for organised games to open themselves up to him. When the club were short space in the '50s, the Dowling farm was made available. The team that won the 1953 county championship was selected one night in September in an outhouse on the farm. In Killarney, Dowling's teammate and Kerry goalkeeper, Johnny Foley, was bedded down in the midst of collective training for the All-Ireland final, separate from his club mates. Dowling should have been in a similar situation, part of both teams. But he made it onto neither.

He missed the entire season of 1953 because of a fifteen-month suspension. Word had leaked that he lined out illegally for a club in Cork and he was rapped on the knuckles. It hurt deep, especially since both club and county were on a roll. Years later, he said it was a whole new world living without football for those months. 'It was very, very hard,' he said. He bought a gun and took up shooting, rambling over the countryside while the rest of the county was taken up with Kerry's bid for an All-Ireland.

He was back the following year and had captaincy. Again, a final loomed. Meath were the opponents. Kerry were expected to account for them with ease but failed and most put it down to the abolition of collective training that year. But the captain took responsibility.

After the final, Padraig Kennelly arrived back in Tralee on the first train with the day's photos to develop. He was hanging the shots on the front window of his shop when Dowling passed by, just off the second train. His friend tapped on the window pane and though he couldn't hear him through the glass, the expression on his face and movement of his lips told Kennelly all he needed to know. 'Will I be run out of town, Padraig?' he asked, then wandered off alone into the Tralee night.

Dowling persevered. The next year, he was captain again. By now, he'd left his job at Munster Warehouse to open his own shop in Tralee, the Boot Cycle Store. He was juggling business and the biggest game in the GAA's history but he excelled. Those who were at the final recall Dowling's performance as being absolute and assured. He completely exhausted himself on the field (the presentation of the Sam Maguire was held up for five minutes because he was too spent to climb the Hogan steps) but two days later he was back at home, Sam sitting inside the shop window, drawing crowds from all over. He was making up for the previous two years until 1960 came and it looked like another dose of bad luck was going to keep him out of the final with Down.

The week before the game, the papers were filled with jibes about Kerry's full-back and full-forward lines. They were too slow, the papers said and they'd cost

Kerry the game. At the time, the Sunday morning routine was to have the team photograph taken at the Grand Hotel in Malahide before they headed for Croke Park.

'When we were breaking off from the photo, somebody threw out a quip about the speed of the two lines in question,' says Jerome O'Shea. 'We were having a bit of craic and John, as the full-forward, said the backs were slower. And as a corner-back, I disagreed.'

They decided to settle the debate. O'Shea and Dowling – togged out and ready for action because of the photograph – went head to head in a sprint around the hotel grounds. 'There was a half-crown at stake and some rivalry between South Kerry and O'Rahillys as well, so there was a competitive touch to the race,' continues Jerome. 'We were to run to a wall and back again but when we hit the wall, we got tangled and John fell.'

He ripped his shorts, tore his leg and was an instant doubt for the game. In the hours before throw-in, he was lying down with two selectors picking stones from his leg and ribs. Still sore and visibly limping in the parade, he played in shorts borrowed from a Cork minor.

He retired shortly after losing to Down that day, retreating to Strand Road.

'He'd go through *The Kerryman* every week to see what babies were born in Tralee and he'd be down to the house the week after, trying to claim them for Rahillys,' says Karena.

'With the six of us [daughters] all playing basketball, he'd have us out training at 6.30am every morning. You might get a Sunday off. He built us a floodlit court at the back of the house when nobody even heard of floodlights.'

They'd heard of the Dowlings though. They'd heard their dad had broken the mould.

TJF

Tadhg Lyne

It's 1953 and there's two-way traffic on High Street in Killarney. Business as usual, save the sounds of beeping horns. The noise is going all day. It's not '50s road rage, but people's way of purring approval as they pass. They're purring for the Prince of Forwards.

Others go the extra few yards and venture into Lyne's den – Tadhgie's High Street chipper. There's great trade in fish and chips after the All-Ireland final of two days previous. People want to see Lyne more than they want his fish or chips. It's the cult of celebrity.

One group of boys went on an extended lunch break that afternoon and headed for High Street. They'd no money for chips but seeing Lyne sated their stomachs. In Lyne's den they stood in silence, mouths open at seeing their hero in civvies, in an apron chopping potatoes and breading fish. 'What can I do for ye lads?' Tadhgie said to them.

The star-struck kids just stared, words failed them and all they could do was run out the door, giggling in excitement. They'd just stolen a few words from their hero and it made their day.

'I was a student in the Monastery School at the time,' recalls Weeshie Fogarty. 'Tadhgie was our hero even before the All-Ireland. We used to watch him up in Fitzgerald Stadium because he was always up there practising on his own. When he talked to us from behind the deep-fat-fryer that day, we didn't know what to say. It didn't matter anyway because seeing him was enough after listening to the match on the radio and reading all about what Tadhgie did in the All-Ireland final against Armagh.'

The final was Lyne's first. He marked it with a man-of-the-match performance but early in the game it looked as if the occasion would get the better of him.

All week, he was a bundle of nerves. At the time, it was an open secret among the panel that any player who was finding it difficult to sleep ahead of a big game only had to ask Dr Eamonn O'Sullivan for a tablet to help them get through the night.

The evening before the All-Ireland, Lyne knocked on the trainer's bedroom door in the team hotel and asked him for a sleeping tablet. He found Dr O'Sullivan reading the newspaper, with a few aspirins scattered on his table.

Facing page:
Prince of Forwards Tadhgie Lyne on the attack for Castleisland Desmonds against Dingle in 1961.
(The Kerryman)

211

The tablets were cut in two, harmless mouthfuls of medicine that the trainer had been pedalling as sleeping aids. Dr O'Sullivan was playing mind games.

Lyne's nerves still plagued him that night and the following morning as well.

Before the game and just after the throw in, he experienced tension like never before and his first All-Ireland appearance threatened to turn into a nightmare. The game was five minutes old and he still hadn't got a touch. Ten minutes passed and still nothing. Fifteen … Sixteen … Seventeen ….

When he roved for the ball, it went to where Dr Eamonn O'Sullivan's blackboard said he should be. When he held his left-half-forward position the ball found the open country of Croke Park where Lyne thought he should be. The game was passing him by.

'My father decided to take some action,' says Domo Lyne. 'He moved over to the sideline and begged Dr O'Sullivan to take him off the field. He felt he was letting the team down and was convinced it wasn't going to be his day. But Dr O'Sullivan had great time for him and just waved him away. Then he roared at Seán Murphy, who was playing in midfield, to play the ball to Tadhgie.'

'Tadhgie was a master at collecting the ball on the run and kicking it over the bar,' says Seán Murphy.

This mastery began in the 1953 final. Murphy found Lyne within seconds of being issued with instructions from Dr O'Sullivan and Lyne turned and kicked his first point in an All-Ireland final.

The cloud lifted and his nerves disappeared. Now, where Lyne roved, the ball followed. Five white flags later, and football had a Prince of Forwards – the name given to Lyne by *Irish Independent* GAA correspondent, John D. Hickey.

Like generations of Killarney folk, Lyne cultivated his skills in Fitzgerald Stadium that was only half a mile from his home on High Street. He also trained at home – by day, Jerome Lyne had a garage on the top of High Street, by night, the garage belonged to his son, Tadhgie.

'He used to park cars tightly and suspend a football by its laces from the rafters,' reveals Domo Lyne. 'Then he'd practice away for hours, kicking with left and right and catching it when it was coming down. If the ball came down low he used to trap it with his foot.'

The garage is where he learned ball control – a skill that brought Glasgow Celtic scouts to Killarney offering Lyne a professional contract. They came after him in 1955, but like Tim 'Roundy' Landers and Dan O'Keeffe in previous years, he turned them away.

'I asked my father about going over but he knocked it straight away,' revealed Tadhgie in retirement. 'He told me that if I went playing soccer I'd be letting the GAA down and letting Kerry down. My decision was made for me, but I wasn't that interested anyway.'

Lyne was top marksman in Ireland in 1955. He scored 5-42 and was named footballer of the year. His most important score came in the All-Ireland semi-final against Cavan when he punched a goal in the closing moments to earn Kerry a draw.

Lyne scored 1-6 that day and followed it up with six points in the All-Ireland final against Dublin. 'The first point he scored was his specialty and it set the tone that day,' says Seán Murphy. 'It came in the first minute when Tadhgie got on the ball nearly from the throw in and from over 40 yards, arced a great point over the bar. He drew it around like a golf shot.'

'Tadhg Lyne is a tall clumsy looking young man,' wrote Benedict Kiely in *The Irish Press* the day after the game, 'lazy looking even but he has an uncanny knack of doing the right thing at the right time and for getting there before anyone else. No Dubliner could deny that there is in him a possibility that Kerry may have found another legendary footballer.'

All this after a quiet introduction to county football. For two years in succession, Lyne had turned up in Fitzgerald Stadium for minor trials but had failed to make the grade while contemporaries like Jerome O'Shea and Seán Murphy stood out.

It changed in 1951 when the Dick Fitzgeralds won the county final. Lyne lined out at right-half-forward against Dingle and kicked 1-5.

He was a fixture on the Kerry team for ten years afterwards.

JÓM

Jim Brosnan

Over lunch in Lord Bakers on Dingle's main drag, Dr Jim Brosnan goes through his football philosophy. Slowly, eloquently and with yarns and facts he brings his thinking to life.

Kitty, his wife, sits beside him. She knows these stories and has lived through them. When her husband first arrived here from Moyvane and drove the area checking on his medical constituents, Kitty would come along for the spin and to bask in the splendour of the place.

Up and over the twisting roads of Conor Hill with the heather brushing against the car or back past Miltown bridge and out towards the rugged coast to watch the Atlantic rage. All around here, they drove and more often than not, Kitty's ears were filled with a football yarn. Ah, she knows these stories well.

At times now, Kitty wonders if the day would be more pleasant if Jim didn't get on his hobbyhorse again and bring out these old chestnuts. But she also knows her husband well and knows this will never happen. Dr Jim's universe is occupied with football.

During lunch, Marc Ó Sé wanders over to the table, asking after him, wondering if he's busy down at the Medical Centre.

Jim wants to know how Kerry are fixed at the moment and he's heard Marc is motoring well in training, that he's keeping a tight reign on the Gooch. Dr Jim has had a huge influence on the development of football in the county. Ask any man who played during his reign as county board chairman or anyone who shared the field with him back in the '50s and they'll have only good words.

'Dr Jim was the first to look after us with grub,' says D.J. Crowley.

'A very powerful but very stylish corner-forward' is the picture Johnny Foley has in his mind.

But from his trove of memories, Jim can recall times when he wasn't so popular. Still isn't with some people around here, he reckons. And it's all to do with his hobbyhorse.

Dr Jim is intrinsically interested in the welfare of the ordinary club player. He says this group needs most attention and deserves most games. When he arrived in Dingle he saw some fixtures weren't being fulfilled and players were missing out on game time. He set about fixing the problem.

'Now, there were two clubs in Dingle when I came here. St John's and Na

Facing page:
Kerrymen in Dublin for the 1965 All-Ireland – from left, Dr Eamonn O'Sullivan, GAA President Hugh Byrne, Dr Jim Brosnan, Paddy Moriarty and John Joe Sheehy.
(The Kerryman)

Piarsaigh. For a while, there was a problem getting fifteen players for each team and so there was a problem with arranging games. One day, St John's came up to the field with only eight players. I thought this was ludicrous. So at the next [board] meeting, I might have been chairman of the West Kerry Board at the time, I decided to put the two clubs together. Make them into one. Make sure they had players to play games. To this day, there are fellows and they hardly talk to me over that, because I did away with the St John's club. But I wanted to ensure games were played. For a while, there was some bitterness but then I got a slight break. Shortly after, didn't the combined team win a West Kerry minor championship. I was saved then.'

Dr Jim is a football socialist. Gather the people, organise them and give them ownership of the games. Let them have fun. That's his philosophy.

During the summer when Dingle teems with holidaymakers, kids from all over the country visit the Medical Centre to get their colds sorted or their bruises looked at. Before he's finished, Dr Jim has them peppered with questions. What county are they from? Do they play GAA? Do they enjoy the games? What are their leagues like?

The league. It's key to Dr Jim. It gives players games and doesn't necessarily emphasise winning. This is what Dr Jim had in mind when he set about establishing the league structure that exists in the county today.

'Championship is a word that causes an awful lot of headaches. I have no problem with playing the championship with as much ballyhoo and razzmatazz as you like but don't forget that it's the other player, the ordinary fellow, who is the backbone and the lifeblood. These are the fellows that need to be looked after.'

It's slightly strange, this concern with the average man, because Jim's football DNA is pure thoroughbred. He grew up with stories of his father, Con, and his exploits on and off the field. The Sam Maguire was a regular visitor to the house. Down the road, he first kicked football in a small corner of Stack's Field, where Tommy Stack, jockey of Red Rum, grew up and jumped piebald ponies while developing big dreams of his own.

Dr Jim has added a plate or two to the great buffet of sporting yarns himself. Back in 1955, as the whole country came under the spell of the All-Ireland final, Jim was studying in New York, quarantined from the hoopla.

He hadn't played for the county all year but was recognised as a vital cog if Kerry were to overcome the odds. A flight home was arranged for the Tuesday before the game but there was a snag. In New York that evening, a storm was raging. High winds and buckets of rain. It was forecast to continue for the week and it looked like there was no way out of the city. Planes were grounded. Rocky Marciano was also down to box Archie Moore for the World Heavyweight title the same evening in Yankee Stadium, and it was to be Marciano's last ever fight, but the event was postponed due to the weather.

Against the odds, Dr Jim's plane took off and landed safely on Wednesday morning in Shannon.

A few hours after touching down, he was training in Killarney and it was just as well his plane had made the journey. At half-time in the final, Kerry led by two but Dublin were raging back at them. Brosnan whipped over two quick-fire points after the break and with the cushion, Kerry didn't look back.

One game and an All-Ireland champion. Four years later, it came full circle. He played a full campaign but picked up an injury in the semi-final and didn't play in the decider. Kerry won and he never received a medal.

It's just a footnote, though. Medals? They don't matter to Dr Jim. They're the obsession of the elite.

From gently quizzing all who pass through his surgery, he believes Kerry has a strong structure. 'The organisation of games here is great but more could be done. Teams need 25 games a year. A long time ago, I drew up a very simple table that would keep track of how many games each team played. Championship, league and friendly. I thought the county board should know where teams are falling down in terms of playing games. That was one of the last things I did when I was involved but it wasn't accepted by the board.'

He's away again, still concerned with the state of the game and still full of enthusiasm for the potential in Kerry.

TJF

Above:
Jim Brosnan at home in Dingle
(John Kelly)

Seán Murphy

Micheál Ó Muircheartaigh launched his autobiography, *From Dúnsíon to Croke Park*, in the Hogan Suite of Croke Park in September 2004. O'Dywer was there, so was O'Connell and Jack O'Shea too. Photographers gravitated towards these three legends.

They left Seán Murphy alone.

They didn't know him and even if they'd heard of him, they didn't recognise him. Murphy was centre of attention in other circles though. He was the talk of a few women in their seventies at the back of the room.

Maureen Dunleavey from the Great Blasket and Eileen O'Shea from Annascaul knew Murphy in the '50s through teaching, west Kerry and football.

Eileen was in the crowd that broke the gates of the Canal End down in 1955. Maureen was in Croke Park that day too when Murphy gave another great All-Ireland display.

'That's Seán Murphy,' said Eileen at the book launch.

'I haven't seen him in years,' said Maureen. 'Oh Seán was lovely, he was a great footballer.'

Then, they approached their old friend and talked about times when their world was young and the price of an All-Ireland final programme was six old pence. It was a time when Seán Murphy was as well known as Nicky Rackard or Duncan Edwards. He was a poster boy.

Aengus Fanning, the *Sunday Independent*: 'Murphy was one of the handful of true greats in the game's history, one of the hallmarks of his dashing style being long, raking kicks from half-back, lowish in trajectory carrying 50 yards or more.'

That was Seán on big days. He, more than anyone, seemed made for them. Micheál Ó Muircheartaigh, who shared digs with Murphy in Phibsboro in the mid-'50s, recounts a familiar tone to their many match day conversations.

'Where's the game today?' Murphy would say.

'Portlaoise.'

'And will there be a crowd?'

'O'Moore Park won't hold it.'

Ó Muircheartaigh knew his last words meant no one would hold Seán Murphy. The day remembered by people of a certain vintage is the 1959 All-Ireland

Facing page:
Seán Murphy in the field behind Camp National School where he first kicked ball as a child.
(Shelagh Honan)

win over Galway. It's referred to as 'The Seán Murphy All-Ireland' and it was his greatest tour de force.

Mick Dunne, *The Irish Press*: 'When everything else is forgotten about a final which gave Kerry back this supreme football prize, the remembrance of Seán Murphy's part in it will still be a treasured memory. For the brilliance of the 27- year-old native of Camp sparkled unforgettably in a bafflingly disappointing final like a rare jewel cast among stones. And his display of insuppressible football was so typical of the Kerry power that crushed Galway that he will forever be associated with this latest triumph.'

Pádraig Puirséil, *The Irish Press*: 'If I were a Kerryman, I think I'd start a subscription to erect a monument to right-half-back Seán Murphy from Camp. I'm sure many of the neutral spectators would subscribe, for, on a day when close marking, keen exchanges and bone-hard ground often reduced even long famed stars into very run-of-the-mill footballers indeed, the UCD medical student gave us the most astounding exhibition of high catching, long kicking, clever anticipation and intelligent passing that I have ever seen in an All-Ireland.'

There's a similar story from one of Murphy's first big days. In 1949, he played for Headford in an East Kerry final against Dr Crokes. The Crokes had Dan Kavanagh and Teddy O'Connor. Headford had Timmy Healy but needed a few more. They got them when Glenflesk curate, Fr Michael O'Driscoll, cycled out to Ballyvourney to see Headford play Coláiste Iosagáin in a challenge.

He came back with the names of Seán and Padraig Murphy and the Laois minor goalkeeper. Murphy's first big day and he was a banger as Headford shocked the Crokes to win the East Kerry title. It was a close run thing, though. Dr Crokes were two points down when Teddy O'Connor faced up to a penalty with the last kick of the game. The Laois keeper saved to give Murphy one of his first big day triumphs. He got used to the big days.

'I was playing for the Camp senior team at twelve because on Sunday afternoons they'd fill up the team with people like me when they were short,' he recalls. 'We were always hanging around waiting to be asked to join in. I remember as a young fella, scoring a goal and a couple of days later one of the Camp regulars, who became a Kerry junior, was walking along the road and he saw me and said, "You'll make Croke Park yet." It always stuck in my memory.'

Other things stuck too, like his personal training regimes in Camp and UCD before the call came for collective training. Murphy trained in solitary confinement. 'At home on holidays, I walked for miles along the road,' he says. 'Wearing a pair of hobnailed boots, I'd walk anything up to twelve miles a night. If I hadn't been walking the night before, I would climb the foothills – a little hill overlooking Camp called Carraig – with a gun and a dog. I would roam those hills until nightfall and would often try to sprint up, so that I was very fit when I went in for collective training.

'When I was training in Dublin, I'd get a bus out to Belfield on my own. There wasn't any consensus between the Dublin-based players about getting together. There was no supervision of training – it was up to players to condition themselves. I trained three or four days a week, getting a ball and running along the sideline on the right-half-back side. I'd solo down the line to get a mental picture of my sector.

'Dr Eamonn O'Sullivan impressed upon us that your sector was your responsibility and you had to have a mental picture of that. Just as if you were driving a car, you're in a tight squeeze, you can't look left and right, you have to drive instinctively and get an instinctive feel for your position.'

Seán's position was right-half-back – he played midfield in the 1953 final but after that, became the greatest right-half ever.

'I insisted on playing there, I wouldn't move around. They moved my brother Seamus around but I refused.'

His own man, but a great team player too and one who stayed to his sector, as Dr Eamonn demanded.

'Dr Eamonn's presence seemed to dominate the footballers,' says Murphy. 'He was bigger than the team itself. His demeanour, the way he stood, the confidence he exuded. He immersed the team in a psychological process.

'You felt, with Dr Eamonn, that he was going to win this match for us. His personality, his very strong personality, dominated any gathering of footballers or officials, it didn't matter who.'

After 'The Seán Murphy All-Ireland' he had done it all and later that year, he was named Caltex Footballer of the Year. Murphy was in great company. Christy Ring got the hurling award beside him. Ring knew he was in great company too.

At the official reception, he caught Murphy by the arm and brought him out beneath a stairwell when the presentations were finished with.

'I want my photograph taken with you,' said Ring. It was one of Seán Murphy's proudest moments and the snap hangs on his kitchen wall in Oakpark, Tralee.

JÓM

Tom Long

Town versus country was the ultimate GAA game to many. Make it a local derby in Croke Park and it's better again. What harm if it's high winter with sleet sweeping over the Railway goal? It still draws a crowd of 16,000.

16 December 1956 and St Vincents are going for an eighth Dublin senior football title in a row. Standing in their way is a country coalition made up of trainee teachers from St Patrick's Training College who called themselves Erin's Hope.

Erin's Hope were the first ever Dublin senior football champions in 1887 – they were no hopers in 1956 against St Vincents, who represented the antithesis of all things country.

St Vincents were bluebloods and after their first ever championship win in 1949, they effectively assumed control of the Dublin County team when they insisted that the panel should be made up of natives only.

The sky blue jersey with its three castles was culchie free. It was bold, imaginative and isolationist and it changed the face of GAA in the capital. For years, Vincents dominated club football and the make up of Dublin teams.

Back in 1942, the Dublin team that won the All-Ireland had been metropolitan in name only but by 1953 things had changed. The team that won the National League had fifteen natives and fourteen of them were Vincents'. Then thirteen Vincents men played in the 1955 All-Ireland final against Kerry.

Kerry won by three points that day and Tom Long felt he could have been on the team.

He was a minor in 1954 but considered by many to be good enough for the seniors a year later. Long smiles over half a century on. Then he explains. 'I was suspended that year,' he says. 'The week after Kerry lost the minor All-Ireland in 1954 to two late Dublin goals, I was asked to play for Geraldines in the Dublin championship semi-final under my brother's name. Seán and Padraig Murphy, Colm and Brendan Kennelly were playing as well.

'Then the following Sunday, I was playing for Dingle in Tralee and Colm Kennelly was refereeing. "Keep your mouth shut about last Sunday," he warned. Twelve of that minor team were brought in for trials with the senior team but the word was out that I was suspended. No one informed me officially but I knew, so I suspended myself.'

Facing page:
'The greatest day of my career' is how Tom Long described being part of the Erin's Hope team that beat St Vincent's in the 1956 Dublin county final.
(Shelagh Honan)

It gave the Dublin county final of 1956 an added significance. Kerry were underdogs in 1955, Erin's Hope were that and more but Vincents were sucked in like Dublin.

'The two county semi-finals were played on the same day in Croke Park. We played the Gardaí in the first one. It was an awful surprise that we beat them. They had a very strong team – Paddy Harrington, Frank Evers and a few more.

'Vincents were playing Clan na Gael in the second semi-final and we waited to see the game. Snitchy Ferguson said afterwards, "That's the eighth in the bag." We used that sentence a lot before the final. They were over-confident. We were confident and got over them by a couple of points.'

Tom Long had arrived. His football education started with the football leagues organised by Fr Jackie McKenna. At the start, he used to watch the *coláistánaigh* play. These were the students who came to the Gaeltacht to brush up on their Irish. Then, he got to play in Fr McKenna's Under 14 league.

'I remember a league final Fr McKenna refereed in Gallarus. It was a rabbit warren then – no such thing as a level field. Two stones were thrown down and there'd be oars for goal posts. Jackie would trust no one to help him officiate. He'd be referee, linesman and umpire.

'I took most of the Ventry team to the match on a pony and cart. There were two cars in Ventry and one belonged to the agricultural instructor; the creamery manager had the other. Over a couple of pints, they promised one of the lads they'd bring us down to the match but they forgot.

'I had a cart at home and stole a pony to travel the four and a half miles back the road to Gallarus. Of the 28 or 30 that were playing, only one person had football boots. They were a luxury. We played in our bare feet.'

That rabbit warren in Gallarus, on the edge of Smerwick Harbour, was a school of excellence. Coláiste Iosagáin in Ballyvourney, which Long attended, was another and, with thirteen sets of goalposts, footballers trained there everyday. They got football in class too. Professor Dónal Ó Ciobháin, another west Kerry man, had the best story of all, claiming credit for enticing student priest, Mundy Prenderville, out of All Hallows College to play in the 1924 All-Ireland final.

'*Chuathas suas ann ar mo rothar,*' he used to tell his students, '*agus ligeach isteach sa pharlús mé, tháinig an t-óganach mór isteach agus dúrathas leis,* "Would you play for Kerry?" *Stáin sé ar ais orm agus a dhá shúil ag bolgadh amach as a cheann agus d'fhreagair sé,* "Would a duck swim?"'

All Ballyvourney boys loved the story. It was history and romance rolled into a football match. Kerry won that day too. But sometimes the history and romance was for others and Kerry didn't win.

Straight away, Long thinks of Down, those upstarts who wore tracksuits and had tactics. Kerry were ten years behind the times, Joe Lennon famously said in the late '60s. Just too nice, according to Long.

'Down were very good, the most professional crowd that ever hit the field. They came with a strategy and that was to nail the forwards, pull the jerseys off them. That's what they did in 1960. I remember my jersey was torn by Dan McCartan and I turned to the referee John Dowling and protested, "Look at my jersey." He just said, "Play away."

'There's no doubt Down were a great team. They had the most constructive forwards I ever saw but the most destructive backs. About five minutes from the end, I gave Dan an upper-cut and I closed his eye. It was frustration. If I had done that in the first five minutes, I think Kerry could have won that All-Ireland.

'In '64 I retired and I was only 28 but had my two All-Irelands from '59 and '62. I was sick of it. Things weren't very well organised then. I was going out to the Sem field in Killarney training on my own for the All-Ireland in '64. That's how bad it was. I had enough, even though they tried to get me back in '65.

'Johnny Culloty and Donie O'Sullivan called to my house in Killarney one day and I went over to the field with them. Tadhg Crowley said to me, "You can play any place you want. How about centre-forward? There won't be much on you." Dr Jim was training and playing backs and forwards – who did he put centre-back but *mé féin*. I didn't want to be there but I said nothing, played a bit of backs and forwards. I told the lads afterwards not to call for me again.'

Tom walked. Three years later, he scored four goals for East Kerry in the county final. He passes it off though. The only final for Tom is the one against Vincents.

'It was as good as an All-Ireland, the greatest day of my career. There were some great players on that team – Mattie McDonagh, Martin Quealy, Donie Hurley.'

Long is too modest to reveal he was one of the players shouldered by supporters from Croke Park back to St Pat's after the game. The story is part St Pat's folklore now.

Mick Gleeson heard it during his time there in the '60s. Plenty of other footballers have heard it as well.

JÓM

Garry MacMahon

It's a 50 mile drive from Killarney to a place called Gorta Dubh beyond Ballyferriter. It was one long *bóithrín na smaointe* for Garry MacMahon on 23 July 1995 as he travelled the road back west from Fitzgerald Stadium.

Kerry had been beaten by Cork for the seventh championship season out of nine. That was bad enough for Kerry supporters but it mattered very little in the broader scheme of football.

The big news was that Paddy Bawn had passed away. At once people knew that life in Dingle, in the wider Corca Dhuibhne barony, would never be the same.

'Start writing this down,' said MacMahon to his son, Rossa, as he drove back to his holiday home. He was thinking about the Bawn and the words tumbled. By the time MacMahon reached Gorta Dubh, 'A Lament for Paddy Bawn' was finished.

Two days later MacMahon sang his lament as Brosnan was lowered into the ground at Miltown Cemetery outside Dingle.

From '36 to '52 he graced the Green and Gold,
And parents to their children his mighty deeds extolled,
His fishing boat at Dingle Pier stands silent in the dawn,
No more will it be skippered by our peerless Paddy Bawn.

It showed what the Bawn meant to Kerry football and what the Bawn meant to Garry MacMahon.

He was everything to MacMahon and it was his life on the high seas as much as his football that inspired him when he was a kid.

'He was a huge presence to us growing up in Listowel. He was a craggy fisherman with the tang of the sea and the wild Atlantic about him and he cultivated it,' says MacMahon.

It was enough to get Garry and his friends out kicking ball.

'You had surround sound in the countryside because, at every open door, Micheál O'Hehir's voice wafted across the country. The whole of Sunday afternoon was dominated by his voice. We took every word he said as gospel and at half-time and full-time you went out the back and kicked the stuffing out of a football.

Facing page:
Garry MacMahon was just the son of a famous father until he made his mark with the Kerry team.
(Shelagh Honan)

227

'We started off kicking a pig's bladder. It's hard to imagine we had no football but we weren't able to afford one. We went around the town from house to house collecting money. On a fairday in Listowel we'd ask people for pennies – we'd have to make up fifteen or sixteen shillings.

'There was always an awful lot of people kicking around on the Sportsfield. Very few were togged and there would be people from fourteen to 50 there. You earned your kick in that company. As a youngster you'd be on the fringes of it, behind the goal.'

It seemed for a while that Garry MacMahon would always be on the fringes. He was a minor in 1955 but Tipperary beat them in the Munster final. MacMahon later expressed an interest in lining out with Tipperary, the county of his birth. As his parents' first-born, tradition dictated that his mother return to her native county for the birth. It still didn't matter. Tipp turned him down and with Tipp not wanting him, what chance was there that Kerry would?

That changed with time. Kerry eventually did call and MacMahon helped land two more All-Irelands for the county. His graph began to rise from the moment he started playing with the Clan na Gael club in Raheny.

'I started off playing junior in Dublin and it was tough. I played intermediate in my second year. The Ingles, the boxers, used to play with us. Gradually, I worked my way up to the club's senior team after two years.

'At that time, Kerry football was going through a bad period. It was around the time of the famous article with a big headline: "What's Wrong With Kerry Football?" The county board organised a match between the residents and non-residents. I got on the non-residents team in a match that was played in late '57 or early '58.

'After that, I got picked for the Kerry team. My first day was against Kildare in Newbridge and I had played a match for the club earlier that morning. After that, I was selected for the first round of the championship against Tipperary in Clonmel.

'In the Munster final against Cork I had a great first half and scored 2-2. That was the day Micheál O'Hehir said, "This morning Garry MacMahon was the son of a famous father, this evening Bryan MacMahon is the father of a famous son."'

Playwright Bryan MacMahon was 'The Master' whose ballads told the stories of some of Kerry's greatest days. One of his most famous ballads was penned the morning after Kerry beat Dublin in the 1955 All-Ireland. The next time 'The Master' put pen to paper about Kerry winning an All-Ireland he was writing about his son and his goal-scoring exploits.

MacMahon always had that goal touch in the old stadium. He even remembers his first visit to Dublin because of a goal in Croke Park, a thing of beauty from Christy Ring on St Patrick's Day.

'My father's play, *The Bugle in the Blood*, was on in the Abbey so we were in

Dublin. We went to Croke Park to the Railway Cup final and I remember seeing Ring score a goal I've never seen the likes of in my life.

'The ball broke to Ring after being thrown in. He was about 30 yards out on the right. Someone tripped him from behind and as he was falling, he took a scelp at the sliotar with one hand. It went into the net and I can still see it today.'

Then there was MacMahon's own famous All-Ireland goal of 1962 to go with the one he scored in the 1959 final. The '62 final was the first ever All-Ireland that was televised live and it couldn't have had a better script.

'I was watching your marker in the semi-final,' Johnny Walsh, the selector, told MacMahon before the game. He said that John Oliver Moran, the Roscommon corner-back, would go for a ball that wasn't his. 'The first ball that comes in,' Walsh told MacMahon, 'just stay back and stand your ground.'

In the first minute of the game, Kerry were awarded a free that was taken by Mick O'Connell. It was beautifully flighted and heading towards the goal. MacMahon was already there and thinking.

'I was about to move out but then I remembered what Johnny Walsh had said to me, so I stood my ground. Next thing Moran took off and jumped up on Tom Long and the full-back, knocking the whole lot of them.

'I let the ball hop and as I saw Roscommon goalkeeper, Aidan Brady, coming out towards me I just hit it handball style into the net. That was after 34 seconds. It was the fastest goal ever scored in an All-Ireland.'

Garry MacMahon had made his mark on Kerry football history. Paddy Bawn was a selector that day and proud of his pupil.

JÓM

Swings & Roundabouts

Mick O'Dwyer

The morning of Mick O'Dwyer's championship debut is remembered for a row in the south Kerry camp but some of the details have been clouded with the passing of time.

For one, nobody is quite sure how they got to Waterford for the opening round of the Munster Championship. Jerome O'Shea reckons O'Dwyer drove because, simply, O'Dwyer always drove.

'Even though he would have been young at the time and new to the scene, I'm sure it was Micko that drove to that game in a Buick. He was always into cars.'

Ned Fitzgerald thinks O'Dwyer drove as well but was behind the wheel of a Baby Ford. 'Micko was a man for the Babys,' says Ned.

The other passenger, Mick O'Connell, isn't sure one way or the other and O'Dwyer himself says Tom Cournane, the hackney driver who ferried the south Kerry players to games, was driver for the day.

Whoever was driving, the four players pulled in for one final pick-up before they began their journey. Goalkeeper Marcus O'Neill was the last man to board but before he did, he poked his head through the window and wondered who was captain for the coming year.

Jerome O'Shea, the senior player of the group, broke the news to him that a decision had been made to appoint Ned Fitzgerald as captain. Both Fitzgerald and O'Neill were in the running as South Kerry were county champions. O'Shea had captained Kerry the year before, ruling him out; O'Connell and O'Dwyer were too young for the responsibility.

When the goalkeeper heard Fitzgerald had the armband, he didn't take the news well. He turned away, walked back home and never travelled.

It was 2 June 1957 and a strange day for Mick O'Dwyer was just beginning – it would end at The Showboat dance hall in Youghal, late that night. Some of the crew got down to drowning their sorrows but O'Dwyer – a teetotaller all his life – remained on the fringes, wondering when things would come good for Kerry. Waterford had beaten them earlier that Bank Holiday Sunday, as big a shock then as it would be now.

'I'd say a lot of Kerry people mightn't have even known the game was going on, it was that much of a foregone conclusion,' says O'Dwyer.

A fortnight before the game, Kerry lost to Galway in the league final in Croke Park, so they had some form and a lack of fitness usually apparent in the early rounds of

Munster wasn't a real issue. But they also had a completely relaxed attitude.

O'Neill aside, they were missing a number of regulars. Seán Murphy was taking medical exams; Tom Moriarty and Mick Murphy were unable to travel; and Mixie Palmer, then living in Waterford, had left the Kerry fold.

The night before the game, the majority of the Kerry players stayed in Waterford. 'I met up with a share of them on the Saturday,' recalls Palmer. 'I'd made off a few haunts in the city and a few of us stayed out 'til one or two that morning. A right good night.'

When the players gathered at the Waterford Sportsfield, a head count showed Kerry didn't even have enough pleyers to field a team. They were one short.

Tralee's Tim Barrett, just out of the minors and at the game as a spectator, was given the goalkeeper's jersey. His brother John, sent to cover the tie for *The Kerryman*, was drafted in as a substitute. Half an hour before the throw in, one of the Kerry players realised he had left his boots back at the team hotel. The day was slowly turning into a black comedy. A sense of the pandemonium in the Kerry set-up was seeping through to some of the Waterford players.

'The secretary of the Kerry County Board was sent back to get a pair of boots down the town,' says Seamus Power, who played for Waterford that day. 'I heard the commotion and started to think, "These lads are really taking this game for granted."' There wasn't much fuss made of the game in Waterford either. Hurling dominated the sports landscape and only diehard football fans bothered to show up.

Mick O'Dwyer faces the throng in Tralee after the All-Ireland win in 1984. (The Kerryman)

'It was a beautiful summer's day,' continues Power. 'The train was still running from Waterford to Tramore at that time and it was packed because of the Bank Holiday. There were far more people heading out to the beach to get sunburned than what there was at the game. I even said we'd nearly be better off going out to Tramore rather than meeting Kerry. Even with their attitude, I still thought they'd make a show of us.'

Not long after things got underway, though, Waterford began taking the slingshot to Kerry. Goliath was having a hard time of it. Jerome O'Shea has a clear memory of playing the first ten minutes of the game with the realisation that Kerry were struggling.

Mick O'Dwyer was an unknown entity. He had played just once for the seniors in that year's league against Carlow. There were plans to stake a claim on the Kerry team from the Waterford game onwards, so it was vital his day went well.

His opposite number that day was Billy Kirwan. 'I was at wing-forward and Micko was a brawny fellow beside me. Good on the ball and a good pair of hands. He made a few superb catches but the game was being lost all around him.'

At half-time, Waterford were in contention and word began to sweep through the city that an upset was on the cards. Locals from the nearby estates began to teem into the ground during the break.

'I'll always remember the point that won it for them,' says O'Dwyer. 'Tom Cunningham came bursting through from about 60 yards out and scored a belter of a point from about 45 yards with the left boot.'

Nobody believed what had happened and the four south Kerry players didn't waste time getting away from the scene. They togged back in and hit the road. Meanwhile, the day was still being discussed in Waterford.

'We were given the night off, so a few of us finally got to go out to Tramore,' says Seamus Power. 'We met a few people that evening in the bars out there and they wouldn't believe that we'd beaten Kerry. That was the reaction. Most people didn't accept that we'd won until they read it in the national papers the next morning.'

Conversation in the south Kerry car was scarce, according to O'Dwyer, and the passengers were wondering how to break the news to those waiting for word at home.

Shortly after leaving Waterford, they decided to break the journey and gather their thoughts in Youghal.

'We stopped off anyway and the lads went and had a few drinks,' says O'Dwyer. 'I wasn't sure how to react after losing to Waterford. That night, I certainly didn't know where Kerry football was going to lead me.'

TJF

Jer D. O'Connor

It takes some time to make contact with Jer D. O'Connor but the battle is only beginning. Persuading him to sit and talk is the real task.

There are plans to meet in Ballydonoghue, Abbeydorney and Ballylongford. Each one is passed off with a necklace of excuses. 'Ah,' he says down the phone one day, 'sure nobody knows me.'

'Gus Cremin and Mick Finucane,' he says a few weeks later, 'they're the footballers you want to talk to from around here.'

Weeks pass by and eventually, O'Connor relents on condition that his story, isn't dwelt upon. The Listowel Arms is agreed as the meeting place.

It's a winter's night and there's a wind blowing all the way from the estuary and pools of water are spilling over the Square. The minutes drift past eight o'clock and, for a few moments, it looks like he's evaded the noose again.

But here he is now, in his long green coat, offering his big farmer's hands, apologising about the delay but the weather's awful and he had some work to finish, he says, and sure he's only a little late anyway.

Above:
Jer D. O'Connor, another great Ballydonoghue midfielder vying for the title of Kerry's greatest player who never won an All-Ireland.
(Shelagh Honan)

So he sits down and orders some tea. 'To warm the bones,' he says.

O'Connor's is a face not normally recognised in the large story of football. For certain, they know him in these parts. Some even saw him back in the day when his budding talent was the talk of north Kerry but in other constituencies, Jer D. O'Connor is an asterisk in the county's legacy.

Those who saw him play in three All-Ireland finals and those who tracked his career over the bumpy fields of north Kerry can quickly put his talent in context.

'How good was he?' ponders Mick Finucane. 'I'll put it this way. I still have a photograph of him playing. He was as good a footballer as ever laced a boot and gave the greatest display Austin Stack Park saw in the 1964 county final, against Mick O'Connell. Jer D. had the best jump for a ball you ever saw and he brought down some rakers that day. Whenever he played centre-back for Ballydonoghue, we didn't need anyone beside him because he caught every ball coming in.'

That day in Tralee, when he pulled scud missiles from the air, saw the creation of an intimate legend around O'Connor. Shannon Rangers had won their first championship in nineteen years thanks to the shy man from Ballydonoghue, and word of his exploits drifted up the western seaboard.

Kerry faced Galway in the following year's All-Ireland final; their second final meeting in as many years and O'Connor had captaincy.

'I was midfield for Galway that day,' recalls Pat Donnellan. 'Now, we'd beaten Kerry in 1964 and they didn't play well that day. But one of our lads was in Kerry on holiday and went along to the county final and saw the display O'Connor gave. So we were watching out for him in a big way in 1965, but before that, we hadn't heard a whole lot about him.'

There was a reason. O'Connor clawed his way onto the Kerry team that reached the final in 1960 but the headlines were suffocated by a Down side that won their first title.

He remembers the lead up to the 1960 final, the three weeks given over to collective training in Killarney. He was twenty years old and a touch of unease settled over him.

'You'd be shy enough going in. I used to hang off of Connell for a while. I hadn't a clue really and Mick was a very quiet individual himself but very sharp. After a while, you'd get comfortable with the lads though and in the end, I had great craic. Some fellows would toe the line for those weeks, others wouldn't. It was up to you.'

At the end of that year, Kerry travelled to Kildare for a league fixture. A nothing game in the big picture but it brought a significant shift in O'Connor's emerging career.

He recalls little about the incident, only that he went high for a ball, like he always did, but this time he landed on his knee. The pain is still burned in his mind and so too is the crack that rose from his right leg. Pat Daly, a trainee doctor and Kerry panellist, rushed over and winced at what he saw. O'Connor's cartilage had popped out. It resulted in the first in a series of operations that took place in the spring of 1961.

'I played shortly after the operations and I suppose I came back too soon. But nobody knew much about the injury then. I'd never heard the word cartilage until I had it taken out. Dr Jim Brosnan gave me weights to build up the leg but it was never right again. That year, the leg nearly fell off me after a game. It was going this way and that way. I'd no muscles in it.'

There was nothing he could do in 1962 but farm his land and watch from the sidelines as Kerry won another All-Ireland. He was young enough to carry the hope that the rest of the decade would deliver a medal to him, but it didn't come to pass. Galway blocked the path to the title twice more.

In 1963, he played only once for the senior team – in the successful league final – but he was slowly and painfully building up the strength in his leg.

Things only got worse though. After the All-Ireland final of 1965, the problems resurfaced and his left leg was also buckling. The cartilage was eroding and crumbling in both knees now, and the surgeon's knife beckoned once more.

'I had one last operation to try and put everything right but when the doctor took a look at the knees, he said I'd them torn asunder. I'd an old man's knees, he said and I'd worn them away to nothing. So, the last time I pulled on the green and gold was in 1966. That was the end of it. I was only 26.'

The game never really consumed him. He looks back now and reckons if the chips had fallen right, he could have more to show for his Kerry days – an All-Ireland or two – but it doesn't eat away at him.

When his own kids came of age and pulled on the local colours, he went along to help out and support but, in the back of his head, he wondered how so many parents could get so worked up. It's supposed to be about having a good time, he thought to himself.

These days, he plays the odd round of golf but there's no competitive itch baying him to lower his handicap. His world is temperate and content.

'I'm lazy with it [the golf],' he says. 'I've a few cattle and to tell you the truth, I'd rather be out the fields with them.'

Then he gets up, apologising about arriving late and departing early and behind him, a half pot of tea is slowly going cold.

TJF

Johnny Culloty

His face breaks into a smile when he thinks of the fuss made over the coexistence of basketball and football. When he stood on the Croke Park sideline for the 2006 All-Ireland final – 52 years after he first graced its surface – he watched the lithe figures of Kieran Donaghy and Ronan McGarrity and thought of the headlines both men filled in the weeks before the game.

The media had gone to town. A new era was being ushered in where the hardwood floor of the basketball court was the place to scout for new footballers.

Culloty had seen it all before. In the lead up to that final, he didn't comment one way or the other though, wasn't asked to really. For how many knew of his deep familiarity with basketball?

Things were different in Culloty's day. Calmer. Less intense. Nobody took to the hoop game to improve their handling or speed up their turn. When the autumn was coming to an end, basketball simply filled a vacuum but the rivalry was quick to spread.

For sure, the games around Killarney were tough and intense but they were filled with lively characters who drew swarming numbers to the old Town Hall. The walls would sweat with condensation and the fog from the crowd's breath would take a while to die off but these were good, unfussy times.

Things happened. It was a period when the whole town was dazzled with Manchester United and their young team. Two basketball powers emerged. The United and The Busby Babes, the team Culloty played for. Other striking names flitted in and out of competition back then. The Rockets. The Crusaders. The Battleships.

Funding for jerseys was always a problem but one of the Busby Babes came up with a genius idea. Write to the man after whom the team was named and see what he could do.

Two weeks later, a package arrived. Inside was a bright red strip for the Killarney Babes and a letter from Matt Busby himself.

In return, the club sent him an Irish *shilelagh* and a correspondence grew, but after the Munich air disaster in 1958, the club lost contact with Busby.

They ploughed on and made it to a Munster final in Cork against a favoured Blue Deamons side. Trailing by a point with time up, Culloty popped two free throws to capture the title.

Facing page:
Captain Johnny Culloty leads Kerry out in the 1969 All-Ireland final.
(D.J. Crowley)

It was a team littered with stars, like Paudie O'Connor, the only Irish basketballer to play for the European All Stars.

'It's funny how things change,' says Culloty. 'I played a whole number of sports back then but they'd nearly stop you from playing them now. Concentrate on the football they'd probably tell me. But you'd play against great footballers on the basketball court. Lads like John Dowling, Tadhgie Lyne, John C. Cooper and Jerome O'Shea.'

Culloty never stalled. He'd row the fifteen miles from Ross Castle to the Gap of Dunloe and back again, himself and another lad breaking through the water for a dozen tourists. Lung-bursting stuff and it only paid change but he liked it. These days, when it's a quiet hour he seeks, he still heads to the lakes for a peaceful wander.

Of all the hours on the field, it's a hurling moment he likes to turn to for satisfaction. It was 1958 and Kerry were playing Waterford in the first round of the Munster hurling championship in Kenmare and Culloty was corner-forward. This was a Waterford team of giants. The previous year, they were beaten by a point in the All-Ireland final against Kilkenny and in 1959, they were champions. But in '58 they only carried their legs out of Kenmare.

'They only beat us by about five points and we gave them a right good game. They had fourteen of the team who went on to win that All-Ireland in 1959 and we were short some great players. Brendan Hennessy and his brother, Frankie, had emigrated to New York. Great hurlers. Billy McCarthy was missing. He went on to play for Munster afterwards. We had John Mitchell at corner-back for us that day, he was working as a garda in Killarney and went on to win an All-Ireland with Wexford shortly after.'

He remembers the day hurling was given life in Killarney. A Galway man called Ben Campion moved to the town and opened a pub on High Street. Hurling was his tradition and he didn't want to let it go. 'One day he went up to the practice pitch in the park and around twenty or 30 young fellows followed him up. He threw out a rake of hurleys and sliotars and we all grabbed them. That's how it started.'

When Culloty was fourteen, he began to play in goal for the county minor hurlers and if it wasn't for that, maybe he'd never have had the goalkeeping career with the footballers.

In the '55 All-Ireland final against Dublin he was a light forward, the youngest player on the field but the following year he picked up an injury.

'I was told I damaged my cartilage. Today, it's nothing, but you could be out for a long time with it back then. It was a fairly serious operation and I gave the best part of a week in hospital. You're talking about the '50s when there weren't physiotherapists knocking each other over like they're doing now. Maybe there was one or two in the county hospital but that was about it. So it would take you a long time to recover if you picked up an injury like that.'

He was on the way back when the footballers were due to play Galway in a *Gaelic Weekly* tournament. The Kerry goalkeeper, Marcus O'Neill, wasn't available and there was an opening in goal. As Culloty had experience between the sticks in hurling, he was nominated for the position.

'I remember it well,' he says. 'I was down to play corner-forward and the fellow I was to mark cleaned up. Gave a great display. I was delighted I wasn't out the field. I wasn't picked in goal for the league but after that, I gradually came to play there. I suppose Marcus must have retired.'

He took charge of the team just before the Mick O'Dwyer dynasty changed the landscape forever and though he has no concern for reputations ('I'm too old for that, gone past it,') he says the team of the early '70s shouldn't be ignored.

'I trained them for three championships. We didn't win an All-Ireland but we won three leagues. There was a need to concentrate on the league then to earn money. The team had come back from Australia and the board lost a lot of money so the league raised finance. You'd hear people say there was no football in Kerry in those years but that's not the case. They say football was redundant then. It wasn't. Just look at our league record.'

Days crammed with sport. Although he moved away from the Kerry scene in 2006, he still makes it to more club and college games than most. It's not exactly an obsession, more a pure fascination.

TJF

Jackie Lyne

The background to Jackie Lyne's appointment as Kerry manager on 14 May 1968 is significant.

It was six years since the county won an All-Ireland, the stock of football had nose-dived considerably in the previous two years and the Kerry team was generally seen to be in disarray.

Leadership and structure had all but vanished as the following insight highlights.

For the only time in the county's history, the goalkeeping situation was up in the air. Five keepers were tried at various points between 1966 and 1967. In '66, Teddy Bowler started the season as goalkeeper; by the following year he was playing full-back, replaced in goal by Eamon O'Donoghue, himself a respected forward.

In the Munster final of 1967, played on a waterlogged Athletic Grounds in Cork, Kerry trailed Cork by a point with minutes remaining.

A kickable free, 25 yards out, was given to Kerry. Immediately, the strangest of substitutions was called – one that shows the bedlam that existed both on and off the field.

O'Donoghue was moved from goal to corner-forward to take the free; John O'Shea was called ashore, replaced by Josie O'Brien who then went into goal. The balance and shape of the team was completely distorted for one – albeit crucial – free kick.

Having run the length of the field, O'Donoghue was handed a sopping, heavy ball, not having kicked one free all afternoon. Unsurprisingly, his subsequent effort drifted wide.

The manner of the defeat led to a flood of criticism and in early February 1968, the board decided to put three training panels together at three different venues. Ned Roche would take training in Cork for those living there, Micheál Ó Muircheartaigh would do the same in Dublin and county board chairman, Dr Jim Brosnan, would look after things in Kerry.

Shortly after this, on 18 February, one of the most quirky but significant games to be played in Kerry went ahead at Austin Stack Park. It was seen as Kerry's Past against Kerry's Present but officially the game was advertised as an exhibition match in aid of the Lixnaw and Waterville Sportsfield Committees.

Facing page:
Jackie Lyne practices his putting in front of his Kerry colleagues, at Killarney Golf Club, the week of the 1953 All-Ireland final. (Domo Lyne)

Jackie Lyne arrives victorious into Killarney train station in 1953.
(Weeshie Fogarty)

Unofficially, it had a dual purpose. It gave some players who had retired the opportunity to cement their reputations and more importantly, it provided the possibility for Kerry to rebuild their national credibility.

By now, Mick O'Connell, Mick O'Dwyer, Johnny Culloty, and Seamus Murphy had all left the county scene so the team was essentially missing its spine. But all four were asked back for the one-off exhibition match and all played, except for Murphy who was unavailable on the day.

With pride at stake, the game was a rough and bustling encounter. The Past wanted to prove they still had talent and fitness. The Present, with the likes of Liam Higgins (playing in goal), Tom Prendergast and Pat Griffin (lining out) were anxious to save face given the Munster championship campaigns of the previous years.

Even *The Kerryman*, despite the sterilised nature of GAA reporting at the time, described the encounter as having 'a bit of needle, which gave the exchanges some bite'.

In the end, the Past won by 2-13 to 3-8, Mick O'Dwyer scoring 1-8 for the veterans, and the result reverberated across the county.

The public wanted the old heads back and the retirees in turn began to wonder if they hadn't something more to give.

Mick O'Dwyer and Mick O'Connell signed up for the championship but momentum was slow in coming. In early April, only two players turned up for training in Tralee – O'Connell and O'Dwyer (Murphy and Culloty hadn't yet given their commitment to the county). It left the two south Kerrymen wondering about their decision to return.

'I don't see the point of us coming in here anymore,' O'Dwyer was quoted as saying at the time. 'I just can't understand the lack of interest by the players.'

Enter Jackie Lyne. Over the course of the two previous years, Lyne had been openly critical of Kerry's performances.

After the Munster final debacle of 1967, *The Kerryman* newspaper carried an article in which Lyne wondered what had gone wrong with football in the county. 'Jackie laid it all out,' recalls Weeshie Fogarty, who was breaking onto the panel at the time. 'He outlined some problems and gave solutions and people sat up and took notice.'

In May 1968, realising that things were progressing poorly, the county board undid their earlier plans and Dr Brosnan – who was juggling two high profile positions – approached Lyne to take over the team.

Support for Lyne had grown in Kerry after *The Kerryman* article and this put him on the radar of the county board.

It was a bold, but telling, move.

Lyne was largely untested as a trainer. His only experience came in 1967 with his club, the Legion, who he led to O'Donoghue Cup success but the lack of experience didn't stop him and he accepted the offer. His methods were old-school and after his appointment, he instilled a strong ethos of discipline in the team, something that was seen to be lacking. Importantly, from his own time with Kerry, he was known and liked by the players.

They also understood the circumstances surrounding his departure from the county panel and respected his decision to maintain his close links with the green and gold.

In 1954, Lyne was controversially dropped from the team just before the All-Ireland final with Meath and it ended a nine-year inter-county career.

'He should have played that game,' says Mixie Palmer. 'In the dressing room just before we went out we were told he wasn't starting and a group of us were thinking about not togging out. We wanted to have some sort of protest but we were talked back into playing. I don't think anybody's heart was in the game after that.'

Almost immediately after Lyne's appointment as trainer, things began to progress again. Players didn't miss training and crucially, on top of the return of O'Connell and O'Dwyer, Lyne persuaded Murphy and Culloty to come on board for the season.

He had a tough task with Culloty. Kerry won Munster but the week of the semi-final with Longford, Lyne was still short an established goalkeeper. He called to Culloty's house in Killarney and managed to talk the goalkeeper into returning.

With the four older players back, the team was balanced with experience and emerging talent. Though Down beat Kerry in the final, credibility was slowly being restored and Kerry won the next two All-Irelands under Lyne.

'We were on a bus travelling to a game in 1969 and I remember somebody asking Jackie how long he would stay on,' says Fogarty. 'He said he'd stay on until the team lost another championship game. "This should be remembered as one of the great Kerry teams," he said. But even today, I don't think that team or Jackie himself ever got the recognition for what they did in those years. They lifted football in the county at a time when it was way down.'

Lyne's influence was huge. He made additions and changes in the team that would open up the world to them in the years to come.

TJF

D.J. Crowley

The weekend of his Kerry breakthrough, D.J. Crowley had played in Croke Park for the first time. That Friday, Munster won the Garda Interprovincial football title and Crowley produced an epic performance. He kicked 1-3 from centre-field and they said only a stone wall across Croke Park would stall him.

His name blazed across three columns in the *Irish Independent*. 'Crowley Was Football Star' it read. They wondered why his county had overlooked the smiling midfielder.

Garda medal secured, he hopped into his Morris Minor and set off to watch Kerry play Offaly in that weekend's Whit Weekend Tournament. On the Sunday, he was standing on the terrace of Fitzgerald Stadium when he heard his name on the loudspeaker.

'If D.J. Crowley is in the ground, please come to the Kerry dressing room.' He ambles over and is met by the team trainer. 'D.J., I'm Jackie Lyne. Do you have your boots?'

Lyne was a D.J. fan. He'd just taken over as Kerry trainer and had watched the Cork-based Garda line out for Rathmore. He also read the *Irish Independent*.

Did he have his boots? Course he did. They were still caked in Croke Park mud but he fished them out from the back of his car and put on the green and gold.

Two years earlier, in 1966, he'd played in another Whit Weekend Tournament. Didn't set the world on fire. Wasn't heard of for a couple of years. Thought that was that. But Crowley was wrong. And this time things would be different.

Look back through the list of those who pulled on a Kerry jersey and few will have logged more miles in one year for the cause.

In 1968, D.J. Crowley was stationed in Kinsale; a 180-mile round-trip to Killarney training. Jackie Lyne wanted charge of Ireland's fittest team and he began by calling his men for training seven nights back-to-back. The demanding regime lasted a number of weeks. For Crowley, that was over 1,200 miles every week. He recognised bumps on the county bounds like they were his own flesh and blood.

'I'd get off work at five o'clock, leave Kinsale at five past and wouldn't arrive back until after eleven o'clock that night. There were others travelling from Cork as well: Pat Griffin, Tom Prendergast, Mick Morris. After training, we'd only get a few sandwiches and you'd have worked up a good hunger by then. A few of us put it to Dr Jim, who was chairman of the county board at the time. We said we weren't getting enough to eat. And fair play, he came back the next night and said, "Ye're getting steak and chips from now on and as much as ye want." He said the only

Facing page:
'If D.J. Crowley is in the ground, please come to the Kerry dressing room' went the announcement at the Whit Weekend Tournament in Killarney in 1968. Minutes later, D.J. was togging out and never looked back. (Shelagh Honan)

247

problem was we'd have to win the league to pay for it, because the county board would get a take of all league games. And over the next five years, we went on to win four National League titles.'

They called it the elusive twenty-first and it didn't come until 1969. For seven years, Kerry had tried to wrestle Sam back to the Kingdom. Nothing worked and seven years was a lifetime in those days. Three All-Ireland losses had been chalked up in the search for number 21. Defeat was scratched into the Kerry conscience and the cloud had to be lifted.

'The pressure was unreal going into the final against Offaly. Kerry supporters need success like another person needs air. I remember after we lost the 1968 final, we arrived back into Killarney train station and there were about sixteen people waiting for us. And these sixteen were the remainder of the East Kerry team that had been in for training that night. There might have been a handful of locals as well, but that was all.'

Crowley changed all that the following year. He lit up Croke Park like a bright fireball. The wind blew on All-Ireland final day and the game was no classic, but Crowley, with that eternal smile, defined proceedings. He was on one of those meandering solo runs of his when the referee blew full-time, heralding an unusually enthusiastic response from the sceptical Kerry crowd.

He had excelled at midfield, outshone his opponents, surpassed all but a handful of final day performances. He even eclipsed the great Mick O'Connell.

Some men quote Shakespeare and others collect travel yarns. D.J. Crowley has a head filled with Mick O'Connell stories.

There's the time the two were changing after training in Killarney. O'Connell was putting his socks on when he noticed a new face in the corner of the dressing room. 'Where are you from, boy?'

Turns out he's from Tyrone, plays in goal with his club, is on holiday in Kerry and wants to see the great Mick O'Connell in action.

O'Connell shouts over to Crowley, 'Din Joe, we're going to give this fellow a try-out, see how good he is in goal.'

So, the two midfielders tog off again. Crowley stands behind the goal, the tourist is between the posts and O'Connell is on the 21 taking pot shots. He moves onto the fourteen, blasts a few balls towards the net and they stay like this for twenty minutes. No interruptions, just a ball whizzing past a Tyrone tourist in the Killarney goals on a summer evening.

'Sure, it made his holiday,' says Crowley, 'it was a lovely thing by Connell.'

Then, there's the opening game of the summer in 1970. Another Whit Weekend Tournament. Johnny Culloty is captain and leads the team from the dressing room to warm up at the near goals in Killarney.

O'Connell is four or five players behind Culloty going onto the field and keeps running towards the other end of the pitch. He gets a ball and beckons D.J. to follow. Now it's just the two of them out by midfield.

D.J. is still fresh from his man-of-the-match All-Ireland final. He's dethroned The King. But only for the time being.

They begin their warm up. O'Connell is whistling size five bullets into Crowley's chest. Fail to catch and the ball rebounds 30 yards. The crowd soon spot the duo and all eyes are locked onto them. Crowley and O'Connell, prince and king.

Suddenly, O'Connell takes a four step run and blasts the ball towards the sky. It takes an age to come down and when it does, he catches it at the apex of his jump. Poetry in motion. The crowd holler and whoop. O'Connell the King. He fires another bullet at Crowley. All eyes are on him, daring him to follow.

'I couldn't even try it', says D.J.. 'He had the crowd set-up brilliantly and if I dropped the ball, I'd look like an awful eejit. It was a rougish touch, a lovely touch. Pure Connell.'

Later that year, D.J. would make it to Croke Park again. He'd score the best goal that old stadium had ever seen in an All-Ireland final. Four minutes to go, solo with the left, bury it with the right. Bye-bye Meath. At that very moment, legend says Jackie Lyne had a slip of paper waiting to herald D.J.'s exit from the action. Lyne kept on waiting.

Crowley finished the game on the field and left, once more, prince of them all.

TJF

Mick Morris

Mick Morris was an international basketballer who ended up an international golfer. He also passed on an opportunity to play football internationally. The story of why it never happened is rooted in the politics of Kerry football.

Morris had no time for it. For the dressing room favourites. For Kerry teams that reflected geographic spread instead of talent. For the unequal treatment of players.

It all came together after Kerry came of age when they won their twenty-first All-Ireland in 1969. On the back of it, they toured the world in triumph. Morris toured too but he never togged out. On principle, he refused to play for Kerry ever again. He had his fill of politics.

'The board secretary, Tadhg Crowley, went to everyone who was going on the tour and said, "We'll be away four or five weeks, we're losing money, how much a week do you earn?"

'I'll tell you the exact words he said to me. "Mick, a certain player earns £150 a week and we'll be away five weeks, that's £750. Mick, you're a student, you earn nothing. Five times fuck all is fuck all." That's what I got going on the tour. Nothing.

'I wrote to the county board afterwards and said, "I really don't want the money but I want to be paid for the expenses I incurred while I was away." I had to have lecture notes photocopied and pay the rent when I got home. I wasn't in a position to do it. They were uncompromising and I said, "Lads, I'm being reasonable on this, if you don't want to be, that's fair enough."

'It saddened me, in the sense that my football ability might have been limited, but I gave 100 per cent playing with Kerry. I was always 100 per cent fit and I was never a sub, expect in my first match in Carlow in 1963.

'That was an indication of my dedication to the game. I was disappointed that the whole thing was blown away in one small bureaucratic decision. They had to make their decision and I had to make mine. That's why I had a premature retirement from Kerry football. I didn't line out with Kerry again.'

Morris was 26 when he walked away. He had four All-Ireland appearances behind him in six years. He was convinced he had four or five more good years in him but still found it easy to walk. All-Irelands weren't everything, he says.

'Winning an All-Ireland with Kerry didn't feel as good as it might sound

Facing page:
Mick Morris clears his lines in the 1969 All-Ireland final against Offaly.
(Seamus O'Reilly)

to somebody out there. Walking out onto Croke Park and winning an All-Ireland medal wasn't the pinnacle of my football career. Beating UCG in Croke Park to win a Sigerson was. I never trained as hard. I never vomited in training with Kerry but I vomited when I was training with UCC.

'We had a trainer, Denis Leahy – an army sergeant – he had us all over the floor. I'll never forget Billy Morgan [UCC goalkeeper] one evening. He was knackered and Leahy said, "Billy do you expect me to clean up your vomit because Moss Keane isn't going to do it?"

'Sigerson gave me a buzz – that's where it was. That's where the camaraderie was. When you're in college, when you've no money, when you're living on the breadline but all you know is win and you have to win, that's when a rapport and bond develops with a team.'

Kerry, meanwhile, stumbled through much of the '60s. The All-Ireland winning team of 1962 was considered poor by Kerry standards; the teams that lost in 1964, 1965 and 1968 thought to be poorer again. Morris played on all three and thought he'd never win an All-Ireland.

'In 1964, I was like a zombie on the field. I was marking John Keenan of Galway but I felt I offered nothing to the Kerry team because I wasn't experienced enough. I was shattered after 1965. Galway were a good side – they were able to put away our mistakes and we weren't able to put away theirs.

'We had a very good midfield and full-back line, our half-forward and full-forward lines were appalling. And we had no top class free-taker. If you look at the teams of the past, Galway had Cyril Dunne, Offaly had Tony McTague, Dublin had Keaveney, Kerry had Sheehy in the '80s. We had no one.

'I remember Jackie Lyne saying to me in 1968, "Don't leave the centre-half-back position." I just said, "Hold on a minute, Paddy Doherty is going to be down in the half-back line, the full-back line and in at corner-forward." "No, stay in your position," Jackie said.

'In the first half, Doherty ran rings around us – Paddy Bawn came to me at half-time and said, "Mick, you'll have to sail into that fella and stick with him."

'That was one of my better games. That day, we missed a critical free in front of the goal – a 14-yard free to bring us back to level. I won't say who missed it. Next thing, Down went and got a point. We weren't beaten in that match – we lost that match. Winning in 1969 was just a relief and I cried my eyes out when we won.'

Morris didn't know it but he had played his last championship game for Kerry. Instead of football, he turned to championship golf, setting himself a target of reducing his handicap from five to scratch in three years.

He did this comfortably and went on to win 31 Scratch Cups, the South of Ireland

and Irish Amateur Close titles. He overcame some more politics along the way.

'In the early years, I was having difficulty getting selected for Ireland because, obviously, being a footballer you wouldn't have the swing of Jack Nicklaus or Ernie Els. The selectors didn't like what they saw. My attitude was the game was about low numbers.

'In my speech after winning the Irish Close in Carlow in 1978, I was really going to go to town on the selectors for overlooking me up to that point.'

But one far thinking friend came to him, handed him a piece of paper and said, 'Mick that's your speech.'

'It was a very moderate speech but I did say, "Having won the Irish Close, it gives the selectors no embarrassment in having to select me for Ireland."'

Morris made his mark internationally, playing 39 times for Ireland – the pinnacle of which was a place on the Irish team that won the European Team Championship in Chantilly, Paris in 1983.

It might never have happened but for Kerry's world tour in early 1970. The county board played its part in turning an All-Ireland footballer into an international golfer. Professor E.C. Dillon of University College Cork did as well.

He gave Morris six weeks leave of absence from final year engineering classes in 1970 on condition that he'd bring him back an e-type boomerang. Morris brought home the biggest boomerang he could find in Australia and it hung over the door of Professor Dillon's UCC office until he retired.

The boomerang always comes back to Morris when he thinks of Kerry football.

JÓM

Tom Prendergast

Jim Foley was another mid-Kerry soul lost to the oceans of the world. Behind his eyelids, Tom Prendergast can still just about make him out and last he heard, Jim was over in San Diego, living a life of sun beside the blue Pacific.

What Tom remembers most about his old neighbour is the stylish manner of him. The sweet way he put a boot to a football.

Tom was of an impressionable age when Jim was getting strong.

He remembers that in 1953, Jim played in goal for the Kerry minors in the All-Ireland final. In the following year's minor final, he played midfield alongside Tom Long. It amazed Prendergast that a goalkeeper could transform into an outfield player – like Superman in a phone box.

A young Tom Prendergast – maybe eleven or twelve years old – would give hours watching Jim Foley kick ball around the fields of Keel. When he saw Mick O'Connell play for the first time, he thought it was Jim Foley back from America. Jim had that kind of class.

In 1956, just as Foley was about to burst onto the senior team, he was gobbled up by emigration. Same old story replayed over and over.

In the '50s, Tom knew parents from Keel who saw their twelve or thirteen kids pack up and leave their part of Kerry. Before he could really understand it all, he knew two things about the young men who lived around him. Football filled their days and long boat trips filled their future.

When he went to school in Fybach, Murt Kelly was the headmaster and Murt knew both topics by heart. 'Football and emigration,' says Tom. 'That was about the size of it back then.'

Tom moved away himself, though, he didn't have to cross any oceans. At nineteen, he went to college to study forestry and the move set in motion a series of strange but satisfying years on the fields of the country.

In 1963, he spent the year in Wicklow. Played National League football for the Wicklow seniors, finished college and in 1964, work took him to Donegal. He played in the Ulster championship for Donegal that summer and won a county championship with Ballybofey. The next year, 1965, he was in Cork and pulled on the red and white jersey for a couple of games in the National League.

By its own standards, football in Kerry was going through a slump. They hadn't won a title in three years and Galway had edged them out of things that

Facing page:
Kerry captain Tom Prendergast and his Offaly counterpart Tony McTague before the 1972 All-Ireland final.
(Seamus O'Reilly)

September. By now, Murt Kelly was a county selector and whenever Tom would visit home, Murt would tell him he had a hand in his transfer from Donegal to Cork, that it was part of his masterplan to get Tom playing for Kerry. Tom never found out for sure if Murt was having him on or not and before he got the chance to find out, Kelly invited him onto the Kerry team in 1966. Prendergast jumped at the opportunity.

He began to settle into the team and found a place at top of the right. The green and gold may have been on his back but not everything felt comfortable.

'Jackie [Lyne] came in as trainer in 1968 and his training was a big step up, a lot tougher, more focused and more organised but I wasn't a right-corner-forward. I was well able to get the ball but I couldn't score. I didn't have a strong left leg, which I needed for that corner and I always maintained if I was to play corner-forward, it should be on the other side. I told that to the selectors numerous times, told them I wasn't fulfilling my potential. But that position [left-corner-forward] was filled.'

Mick O'Dwyer had top of the left noosed by the neck. After Kerry lost to Down in the 1968 All-Ireland final, Prendergast began to slip off the team. Tom O'Hare, tall and sticky and one of the Down stars that season, marked Prendergast in the final and played well on him. Prendergast – along with a few others – lost their place when the championship clicked back the following year.

'We were after losing a bad All-Ireland to Down. It was probably felt we needed a new approach and I was one of three or four to lose out.'

Chance kicked open another door that July. The week of the Munster final, a space at wing-back became available after Micheál Ó Sé was ruled out with injury. The morning of the game, Jackie Lyne pulled Prendergast aside and told him he was starting wing-back. Lyne had heard that in 1966, the former corner-forward lined out for Kerry in a challenge against Down at right-wing-back and showed well. This was enough to give him the nod. Kerry came out of the province and faced Mayo in the semi-final. A.N. Other was listed at number five.

'This time, they told me the night before we played Mayo that I was starting. I was marking Joe Corcoran, a highly respected player with Mayo and Connacht and I held him scoreless. I kept my place for the final and was on Tony McTague – another prolific scorer. We won the All-Ireland. After that, I became the regular wing-back.'

He helped Kerry to the All-Ireland in 1969 and victory was enough to send the team globe-hopping for a few weeks in early 1970. They stopped in Amsterdam, Turkey, Singapore, Jakarta, Perth, Sydney, Melbourne, New Zealand, Fiji, Hawaii, San Francisco, Chicago and New York.

They lingered for longest in Australia where they played a few early hybrid games of international rules.

'That trip was something else,' says D.J. Crowley, Prendergast's teammate and travelling companion that year. 'We lived on barbecued steak for four weeks. We got a month's wages and a hundred quid on top of it. We lived like kings.'

In Australia, they blazed a trail across the continent. Travelled from Western Australia all the way to the east coast and began laying foundations for future series between the two countries.

Meath had ventured Down Under in 1967 and Kerry were the next to take the step.

Along the way, Prendergast made national headlines. The Aussies became enthralled with the punch he could pack into his frame – noticeably compact compared to the footballers from Australia. One newspaper featured Prendergast in an article and blazed a huge headline across the page. 'The Greatest Small Man To Ever Play In Australia,' it read. He still has the cutting stashed away in his attic.

When Kerry arrived back, things continued on their upward spiral. Kerry took the All-Ireland again. Prendergast was man-of-the-match in the final and later that autumn he was named Texaco Footballer of the Year.

The switch to wing-back sat well with him. Like the other young men from Keel, he was familiar with upping and moving. Donegal to Cork. Australia to Croke Park. Corner-forward to wing-back.

The road well travelled, as always.

TJF

Brendan Lynch

1968. Tough times for big ball lovers in the Kingdom. Cork ruled the province in 1966 and '67, and All-Ireland victories were a distant memory in Kerry. Worst of all, the Ulster invasion was creeping south. Over the past decade, Down had twice beaten Kerry so when 1968 broke, it was time to put the record straight.

Through the forward thinking of newly-appointed trainer, Jackie Lyne, the big names – O'Connell, O'Dwyer, Culloty and Murphy – were coaxed out of retirement and the juggernaut was beginning to chug along in early summer. But only just.

Kerry got through Munster for the first time in three years after a classic provincial decider against Cork but the clued-in could see the wheels were beginning to creak beneath the pressure of expectation.

In the semi-final, the minnows of Longford put up an unexpectedly strong fight in another quality game. With eight minutes left, the Leinster champions had a four-point lead. A late save from Johnny Culloty prevented a colossal day for Longford and with life going out of the game, Culloty's cousin, a kid called Brendan Lynch, popped up with two beautiful scores. It gave Kerry a narrow win on a scoreline of 2-13 to 2-11.

His reputation as a free-scoring right-half-forward was being moulded. The previous autumn, shortly after he finished his Leaving Certificate, Lynch helped Mid-Kerry to their first county championship and his name was beginning to sweep through the county.

The Kerry break came against Mayo in a league quarter-final on 24 March 1968. The performance was good and the right people were impressed, but his potential wasn't unfurled on the nation just yet.

A couple of hours before the Mayo game, a story broke which gobbled up airtime and vast tracts of newspaper coverage for weeks.

The *Viscount*, an Aer Lingus aeroplane en route from Cork to London, plunged into the Irish Sea just off the Wexford coast. The Tuscar Rock tragedy – in which 61 people lost their lives – had just occurred and all talk of football was shelved. Nevertheless, Lynch continued to turn heads.

The four points he finished with against Longford – he was one of Kerry's best players on the day – set his star rising even more but against Down in the All-Ireland final, the team was fighting a losing battle.

Facing page:
Brendan Lynch in action against Cork in the 1969 Munster final in the old Cork Athletic Grounds.
(Seamus O'Reilly)

The Ulstermen started well and overwhelmed the Kerry defence. Seán O'Neill and John Murphy slugged two early goals past Culloty in as many minutes. Wham. Bam. The Kingdom was reeling.

Like the last two games, Lyne's men started poorly and the backs were sinking again. As the game went on, Down were simply tapping the final nail into the coffin around Kerry's corpse. The stadium quivered and shook with northern roars. Three wins over the aristocrats and not one single defeat. That day, Kerry folk were left to wonder if they'd ever again see O'Connell, O'Dwyer, Culloty and Murphy in the county jersey.

Lonely times for the eighteen-year-old from Beaufort but he figured time was on his side and there would be other cracks at the big time. He was right.

Spool the story on seven more years. At 26, Lynch is Kerry's eldest head on a coltish team about to set Ireland's sporting landscape ablaze. Enthusiasm crackles about him and in some ways, his experience allows him peer beyond the horizon.

''75 was different to anything I'd experienced,' he says. 'There was more glamour [surrounding the final]. More excitement. Just different to the other years. Even though I was the senior player, I was surrounded by guys who had confidence. They'd experienced success at underage level and I felt we were certainties for the All-Ireland. We played Dublin early in the summer in a challenge game, lost by a few points and this was a full-strength Dublin side. There were a few missing for us and I felt if we had another go at them, we could beat them.'

When Kerry came off the train in Dublin for the 1975 All-Ireland, a group of photographers was waiting to collect shots for the Sunday newspapers. One walked over to Páidí Ó Sé and, thinking he was one of the Kerry minors, asked him on which carriage were the senior team. Young and fresh, they came in under the radar that year but Lynch's last days as an inter-county player were beginning to dovetail with the emergence of Kerry as the game's true superpower.

The year before Kerry's bachelors conquered Dublin in that final of '75, Lynch broke his ankle playing a challenge for UCC at the Mardyke in Cork. And, even though he also went on to play in the 1976 final, the injury was the beginning of his slide out of the Kerry scene.

'I never got back to that early sharpness [after the ankle break]. It set me back a lot. The career brought me to England shortly after it as well, so that kind of finished me. In ways, I felt I could have gone on for a bit longer, but the ankle started the decline.'

That injury may have happened in the college colours, but his playing days for UCC were speckled with big games and he provided one stand-out moment to the Sigerson Cup story.

The year is 1972 and UCC are playing UCD in the semi-final of the Sigerson Cup. The Dublin college – on the cusp of Sigerson dominance – are hosts and favourites for the title. They trailed well at the break but put in a storming second-half. Into injury time, they led by two points. Then, 14-yards from goal, the referee called a free for UCC. Lynch, true to his character, felt the burden of expectation and accepted responsibility.

'I remember it vividly,' says Eugene McGee, UCD's most successful Sigerson manager. 'It was into the lower goal at O'Toole Park. We had seven or eight on the line and as it happened, I was right behind the goal. I thought Brendan had no chance. But he had that sweet, powerful left leg. John O'Keeffe was playing for UCD the same day and the ball flew past him and into the net. Some goal. One of the great Sigerson images.'

The Cork outfit, with ten Kerrymen on the first fifteen, went on to win the Cup outright. It took sixteen years before they won it again.

When college and football were finished with, Lynch settled neatly into the world of medicine and psychology, taking up the same role at St Finan's once occupied by Dr Eamonn O'Sullivan. All through his career, the psyche of the sportsman enthralled him, kept him hungry and intrigued. His own father, Tom, played for the Dick Fitzgeralds and was on the fringes of the Kerry team. He could smell a regular jersey but he never quite made the breakthrough.

Having heard of Tom's fleeting involvement with Kerry, Brendan wonders if some switch didn't click inside his own head, spurring him on, motivating him to excel as best he could. But that's probably the psychologist coming out in him, he says.

Dr Eamonn would have understood.

TJF

Donie O'Sullivan

They were exciting times and they started with a small seed, a slip of an idea that had no right to germinate.

At the time, Spa was hemmed in by the town and for years, Killarney's two clubs, Dr Crokes and the Legion, were the only football outposts in the area. Back in 1948, after one or two false starts, Spa finally decided to do something about that.

They went about setting up their own club. The idea was that there were enough young men in Tiernaboul and Lissivigeen to kick football without them having to go into town to pull on a jersey. Some Spamen were even playing on teams against one another, so the pool of talent was deep.

He was only eight when all of this happened but Donie O'Sullivan remembers it clearly, the pleasure and anticipation that rose from forming the club and the fuss rubbed off on him.

Stories of how they got the club off the ground are still embedded in his mind. Fundraising and coaxing youngsters to come down and kick ball in Jack Doherty's Pit.

One time, Donie remembers, the elders of the club got together and rehearsed a play. When it was ready, they performed it before their own people, then took it to Listry, to Rathmore and to Glenflesk. After the few weeks of treading the boards, Spa had enough money to buy a set of spanking new jerseys.

He was there when the seniors pulled them on for the first time. Spotless blue and brilliant gold and the players inside them seemed like big hulks of men. Gods. These were great days but they didn't last. A shift soon came. Unemployment visited and blighted the fields of Lissivigeen and the hills of Tiernaboul and many had to emigrate, scattering in search of work. The locals got older and football stayed a young man's game and by 1959, Spa had folded.

Things just changed back to how they were. Save an odd junior team or an under-age amalgamation, the men from Spa went again to Dr Crokes and the Legion.

O'Sullivan had to do so himself. He picked up three East Kerry O'Donoghue Cup medals with Dr Crokes and enjoyed every minute too but it just wasn't quite the same as doing it with your own neighbours, your own men.

He was doing well too, taking significant steps with Kerry and with Dr Crokes.

Facing page:
Donie O'Sullivan captained Kerry to the 1970 All-Ireland and is pictured here, receiving Sam Maguire from GAA president, Pat Fanning.
(Seamus O'Reilly)

In this part of the world, an O'Donoghue Cup medal is the elixir, the giver of bragging rights and as O'Sullivan was collecting his third with his surrogate club, a map was being sketched out to resurrect the Spa seniors.

Mick Gleeson was maturing into a fine footballer, Paudie O'Mahoney was young but getting strong and, along with O'Sullivan, the backbone of a team was once again taking shape.

By 1966, Spa were on the road again and they started with the only competition that mattered – the O'Donoghue Cup.

The first game was drawing near when they hit a snag. No jerseys and the club coffers were empty as a desert. Couldn't even afford a pair of socks.

But a light went off and somebody remembered that set from 1948. So, the jerseys were fished out of some dusty place and given a second life. Lazarus in blue and gold.

They were quite old and faded by now. The dye had run and they were shapeless things but they did the job. Spa motored on and that autumn found themselves in the O'Donoghue Cup final.

Amazingly, they won and they celebrated hard but something still clawed at the back of the mind. They hadn't yet broken down the real barrier. That happened three years later when they reached another final, this time against Dr Crokes.

For years, the town side had a two handed Godzilla grip on football in east Kerry. Before 1966, Dr Crokes had won nine out of ten titles and Spa's win in 1966 was seen as a blip on the chart. Going into the 1969 final, Spa weren't given a chance. Somebody even offered odds of six to one on the new club winning.

'There were years when we underestimated ourselves in our own minds as well,' says O'Sullivan. 'This went back to the fact that we were a country, rural team and you were always second and third to the Legion and Crokes. Town teams. Whenever Spa managed to get a minor side together in my time, we'd get so far until we came up against Crokes and Legion and they'd hammer us. We were like lambs to the slaughter. In the end, we began to think, "If we just put up a good show we'll be doing well."'

The football landscape of east Kerry changed once more after that final of 1969. Spa toppled Dr Crokes and ended their domination of the competition. In the following decade, Spa won five titles and three new clubs shared the others.

'In ways, we gained real confidence after winning our first title in 1966. It was a huge achievement for us because we came from nowhere. It was so enjoyable for me, simply to be beside our own lads, the local boys.'

O'Sullivan iced the cake that year. Captained Kerry and lifted Sam.

It all might never have happened because of the most notable weapon in his artillery box – his dead ball kicking. O'Sullivan's free kick off the ground was like a scud missile. People paid through turnstiles just to see him blast the ball 60 or 70 yards. The story goes that he once tried to score a last-minute goal for his club from close to the half-way line to level a game.

Maybe that yarn has grown legs but that's the kind of energy he pounded a football with.

After O'Sullivan left Maynooth College, he studied psychology at St John's in Queens, New York. The campus is right beside Shea Stadium and in 1967, when O'Sullivan attended class at the college, the New York Jets played their home games at Shea. They also trained at St John's.

O'Sullivan had found a place on the college football team as a kicker and his style of kicking was drawing observers.

'Roundhouse, the usual soccer-style, wasn't widely used in American football at the time. They had straight kickers, who basically kicked it with the big toe.' As a publicity stunt, the college newspaper wrangled the Jets into freeing their kicker for an afternoon to take some photographs beside O'Sullivan in order to compare their kicking styles.

A few Jets coaches turned up out of curiosity. After O'Sullivan had blasted his first scud, they sat back and gawped. They hadn't seen anything like it. Their boys had been pinging seven irons all along. O'Sullivan showed them how to use a Big Bertha. Soon after, they approached him with a contract and O'Sullivan was interested.

'This was in November and I was to start with the Jets in June. I agreed to join but when June was coming, I reckoned I was finished with America and I backed out.' It was a brief glimpse into another life. He got his photograph taken with Joe Nameth, the Jets American Football Hall of Fame quarterback, packed his clothes and slipped the snap into the suitcase.

There was still unfinished business at home.

TJF

Seamus Murphy

At first, he played with giants. Big, hulking bruisers of boys who populated Camp's daylong games. His father, Jackie – a founding member of Camp GAA club – had passed away when Seamus was still a young buck, so his football education was entrusted to his older brothers, Pádraig, Seán and Tomás. They were happy to oblige.

Beside their house, beneath Carraig Hill, Jackie had secured a patch of land, about 6 acres in size. When his sons' legs had enough strength to walk, they and plenty others helped give it life. It whizzed with games. Such a facility was a rarity at the time and soon, the grass was bald from football activity.

One week, the River Finglass was the dividing line. East versus west. Another, the road to Dingle provided the boundary. Uppers against Lowers.

There were plenty of local footsteps to be followed. Tim O'Donnell and Charlie O'Sullivan. Mythical figures. Names to make a kid's heart skip. He didn't know it at the time but by acquiring that piece of land, Jackie Murphy had created Camp's very own football nursery.

'It might be five-a-side one hour, seven-a-side the next,' recalls Seamus' brother, Pádraig. 'And these games would go on for days. Literally days. Seamus was seven years younger than me and he'd follow us out to the field to play in those games. That was his introduction to football. That was his start.'

All the while, between these epic games, interest was stoked like a fire about to blaze. On Sunday mornings, Seamus would serve as altar boy at Camp church. There were perks.

For big Kerry games – perhaps a Munster final in Killarney or a meeting with Dublin in Tralee – the local curate, Fr McMahon, would pack a lunch and he and Seamus would nose for the game. Great and exciting times. Travelling to any town was an event for a boy from Camp. The streets, the people and the green and gold in front of your very eyes. Faces, at last, for those magical names. Seamus was hooked.

When the time came, like his brothers before him, he took the road east to board at Coláiste Íosagáin in Ballyvourney. He mapped the route by the houses of those he knew had worn the county colours. John Cronin's, just by Miltown. Jackie Lyne in Clenagh. Paddy Healy's beyond the railway in Headford. Not too far to go now.

Facing page:
The Kerry team that played Cork in the 1969 Munster final in the Old Athletic Grounds – Seamus Murphy is first from left, on the front row.
(Seamus O'Reilly)

267

And in 1954, like his three brothers, he collected a Corn Uí Mhuirí medal with the school. He was on his way. Another great in the making.

It's August 1965 and Seamus Murphy has just married Joan O'Sullivan. The honeymoon is arranged for Jersey. Joan wouldn't mind venturing further, perhaps to France or even Italy, but in a few days, Kerry play Dublin in an All-Ireland semi-final and Seamus can't venture far from Croke Park. So, Jersey it is.

Before they set off, they fill a couple of suitcases, pack some books and, tucked under his arm, Seamus has a leather football. Can't afford not to train, he reckons. Not with the Dubs around the corner.

So most days, for an hour or two, Seamus takes off running across the sand dunes of Jersey. He's at home here. It's familiar terrain. If he were in Kerry right now, most likely he'd be pounding Inch Strand or scaling the tracks of Kinard Hill.

With the semi to navigate, the honeymoon is cut short and the newlyweds arrive back in Ireland, to the shadow of Croke Park, the night before the game.

As is the custom, a pair of tickets is waiting for Seamus but with a seat already obtained by Joan, it's decided the spare pair will go to two friends. Joan arranges to meet the couple an hour before throw in, outside the Hogan Stand but now they're 40, 45, 50 minutes late. Joan is pacing up and down the road, wondering will she ever catch sight of the two so she can take her seat and watch her husband play.

Time keeps ticking and still no sign. There's a roar from the stand behind her and she knows the teams are on the field. She thinks to herself, 'No way are touts getting their hands on these tickets,' and then she spots a couple of priests walking in her direction.

She asks are they going to the game? Yes.

Do they have tickets? No.

Would they like these spares? Course they would.

They offer money. Joan refuses, telling them to enjoy the game, she's off to see her husband, Seamus Murphy, play for Kerry.

She thinks no more of it.

At last she can take her seat and as she watches Seamus further his reputation for Kerry, she remembers the little stories he has told her. How on hackney trips to Dublin, Dr Eamonn would lead the car in saying the rosary *as gaeilge*. How he hopes one day to be mentioned in the same breath as those greats he obsessed over in his youth.

He must be mentioned with them, of course. When he finally leaves the Kerry scene, he will have eleven provincial medals to his name, all gained in a huge array of positions, never having lost a match in Munster. Near the end of this great spell, he made the tough decision – with three kids in tow – to come out of retirement and pin his name to the ship once more, to eventually pick up four All-Ireland medals in a career that spanned three decades.

But back in 1965, up in the Hogan Stand, all that matters to Joan is that Kerry have defeated Dublin and Seamus is on his way to an All-Ireland final.

Time passes. It's now late 2000 and Joan's phone in Tralee is ringing. Who's on the other line but one of the priests from all those years ago. He introduces himself as Fr Brendan Murray and says he's conducting a retreat in Ardfert.

He was sitting beside Canon Dennis Mahony from Castleisland and enquired if he knew of Seamus Murphy, the footballer, because he wanted to meet his kind wife who gave him two tickets 35 years ago.

'Course I know Seamus,' said the Canon. 'But sadly, he passed away in April.'

So, the Canon gave him a number for Joan and over the phone, she invited Fr Murray for a cup of tea.

He arrived in Tralee shortly after and explained how he was teaching English to Jesuit students from the continent in the summer of 1965, when one young French priest asked could he be taken to a football game. That Sunday afternoon in Croke Park, he said, was the highlight of his trip.

There was more.

'We were chatting away and Fr Murray told me he was the editor of the magazine, *The Messenger*,' says Joan. 'I couldn't believe it. I was getting the magazine for years so I went into the kitchen and got a copy. There he was, a picture of him inside the front cover. I was looking at Fr Murray's face all this time.'

A few weeks later, Fr Murray relayed the story in the pages of *The Messenger*. He gave it the headline 'Rose of Tralee'.

Later still, Radio One heard of the story and contacted Joan to see if she would like to tell the tale to the country. She thanked them for their interest but politely declined the invitation. Big audiences and the national spotlight didn't suit her, she said.

Unlike Seamus.

TJF

Liam Higgins

The old schoolhouse in Lispole is deserted now, a relic that's boarded up and blue. Decaying when it was once where football stories were made.

One story dates from 1979. Members of the Lispole club went into special session. They had a new pitch that was christened on a famous evening in late 1978 when Lispole shocked Dingle in the West Kerry championship final.

The night before that game it poured rain. 'Call it off, you couldn't play a game on that,' said Dingle supremo, Dr Jim Brosnan. 'That bloody pitch is playable,' countered Liam Higgins.

Weeshie Fogarty was referee and a friend of Higgins. He deemed the pitch playable and an hour later, Lispole were celebrating a famous first. The meeting in early 1979 had one item on the agenda. An official pitch opening.

Johnny Barrett, John L. O'Sullivan and Liam Higgins were among those around the table. John L. started to daydream.

'What if we could get the Dubs down here and have Kerry up against them?' said John L.

'You're dreaming, John,' said Johnny Barrett.

'Why not?' said Liam Higgins.

The Dubs, but how?

Liam Higgins got thinking. Paddy Moriarty, from a few fields away in Doonshean, worked with Kevin Heffernan in the ESB and knew Jimmy Grey, who was the chairman of the Dublin County Board.

'Any chance of getting Dublin for us, Paddy?' said Higgins. 'We'll do our best,' said Moriarty, who immediately set the wheels in motion and the Dubs landed on 30 July 1979.

'It was a tough game,' said Higgins, 'Brian Mullins was coming down to where we all considered he got his football and his uncle Billy Casey looking on. Dublin put out a full team and Kerry did the same. It was tough but it was great. We had 4,000 people in Lispole – lovely day, everything went right.

'Afterwards Dublin got straight on to the bus without togging out because the game was a small bit late in starting. They were racing for a train in Tralee, and missed it so they had to go to Mallow to catch it.

'And we never, ever, got a bill from the Dublin County Board. We were supposed to pay the expenses. The ESB even put up poles to bring the power to

Facing page:
Like most of the greats from west Kerry, Liam Higgins learned his football in Dingle CBS, where he later taught for many years.
(Shelagh Honan)

271

the pitch – that should have cost £1,500 but that was written off as well. We never got a bill for that either.'

Higgins was at the coalface of Kerry football for 40 years. Winning All-Irelands, selecting on the four-in-a-row team, commentating for Radio Kerry.

'The 1955 Munster final was my first memory – at nine years of age. I had to jump up and down on the terrace to see the game before my father would lift me up. I remember Mick Murphy from Ventry punching a point that day. It was a huge adventure – there were five buses that went from Dingle to the match. I remember the bus stopped in Crowley's of Inch, that was a stop for the men to have a pint.

'The first All-Ireland was in 1963 to see my classmate Tomás Ó Sé play in the minor All-Ireland. Pádraig Lynch from Dingle brought me up. We were staying in some guesthouse on the South Circular Road. Pádraig and a few others were going out on the town. I remember walking up and down outside the house, making sure that I wouldn't go more than 50 yards beyond it in case I wouldn't be able to find it again.'

The nervous teenager would get to know his way around Dublin as a Kerry senior but Higgins wasn't good enough to be a Kerry minor and Under 21 football also passed him by.

'I never thought I had a hope of being a Kerry senior – I was long, thin and scrawny.'

He got a run against Cork in Tralee in late 1967, thrown in at the deep end at centre-forward against Denis Coughlan. He was lost out there and by the time of the Past versus Present game in early 1968, he was in goal. He stayed on the panel until the end of the National League before bailing out to work on English building sites for the summer.

Higgins thought his Kerry career was over but he had friends in high places. Paddy Bawn was a Kerry selector and Dr Jim Brosnan was county board chairman. They got him back on the panel before the latter stages of the 1968/69 National League campaign.

'There were four or five minutes left in a play-off game against Cork and they got me on,' he recalled, 'and we were down a point at the time. Mick O'Dwyer got a ball over near the sideline. He crossed it over and Dominic O'Donnell who was playing corner-forward that time went for it with his man. It just broke to me – I was standing near the endline and I threw a left leg at it and it just hit the far post on its way to the net.'

Kerry played the National League semi-final two weeks later against Westmeath with Higgins named at full-forward for the first time. He stayed there for the next five years.

'Connell would stick the ball to your chest from 50 or 60 yards out and you'd offload to Dwyer. If you dared to have a go yourself and you missed, you'd get a bollocking from Dwyer.'

There was very little bollocking in 1969 or 1970. Higgins was still long, thin and scrawny but he was winning All-Irelands.

'I remember running out on the pitch for the 1969 All-Ireland. It seemed any time your boot hit the ground the noise of the crowd was going through your head. We were playing in the Munster jerseys and there was doubt in all the Sunday papers about whether Connell would be playing.

'We didn't know ourselves and were all out on the pitch kicking around. There was no Connell. Next thing, about five minutes after we went out, there was this huge roar. I'll never forget it. Connell had walked out on to the pitch and wasn't wearing the same jerseys as us.

'He was wearing his own personal jersey. It was blue alright, probably an old jersey he had worn with Munster. He insisted on wearing it. We didn't know until that minute whether he was going to play or not. Jackie Lyne, Dr Jim Brosnan or Paddy Bawn didn't know either. It was the cheer we heard first – we knew he was coming then.'

'Great, great,' he said of those days, over pints in O'Flahertys in Dingle in October 2005. Not as great as Lispole though. Liam made his debut as a fourteen-year-old in 1959 and played his last West Kerry championship game in 1990. In between, Lispole experienced everything.

'The club died for a while in the '60s but back we came and fielded teams when it was a real struggle. The day we won that West Kerry Championship in '78 on our own field with two famous Pat Begley goals was better than any All-Ireland. Much better.'

JÓM

Mick Gleeson

Mick Gleeson isn't anti-establishment. He's just his own man. Different. In politics and football. In football, when managing his club team Spa with his brother Jim, he was too much of a purist to pick a team. He left it to others. He was just interested in the game and how it was played.

The same with politics. He turned his back on the Labour Party after the 1991 Kerry County Council election. Gleeson's departure was sparked by what he describes as 'a very fine pincer movement' during the selection process for the election. He was selected at convention along with Michael Moynihan but Moynihan withdrew to contest the Killorglin ward and gave a spot on the Killarney ticket to his daughter, Breda.

Gleeson left the Labour Party after this experience and a few years later, joined the South Kerry Independent Alliance, contesting local and general elections on behalf of the party. An All-Ireland man to contest the Dáil like Austin Stack, Con Brosnan, Johnny Walsh, Seán Brosnan, Billy Myers, Dan Spring, Gega O'Connor, Mick O'Connell and Jimmy Deenihan.

Only Deenihan, Stack, Spring and Seán Brosnan were successful but Mick Gleeson still made his mark. It was his independent mind. As chairman of Killarney Town Council in 2001, he played host to a civic reception for members of the New York Fire Department, who worked at the World Trade Centre on 11 September. Less than two years later, Gleeson led a march in Killarney against the American invasion of Iraq.

'I saw no dicotomy between the two,' he says. 'Those firemen deserved to be honoured but Iraq was wrong.' Gleeson has held strong views all his life. In politics and in football.

He won his first All-Ireland in 1969. As Kerry celebrated in the Grand Hotel in Malahide after the match, the only survivor from the first All-Ireland winning team was there with them.

Denny Breen went back 64 years to Kerry's first triumph over Kildare. Denny did more celebrating with the team on the Monday night but Mick Gleeson wasn't with them. He was a teacher – he had to go to school.

It was a familiar routine for Kerry footballers in the teaching profession. Jerome O'Shea was teaching in Drimnagh Castle in 1959, he was at school on Monday after the final; Mick Murphy was in St James' Street CBS the day after winning in 1955.

It was Mick Gleeson's lot in 1969 – he had to be back in his classroom at St

Above:
The Department of Education's message to Mick Gleeson after winning an All-Ireland in 1970 was: 'We wish to inform you that you have been deducted two days' pay. On this occasion we won't break your service.'
(Shelagh Honan)

Fergal's NS in Finglas. Life went on. He was in his flat in Glasnevin on Monday night as his colleagues were rolling into Killarney on the train.

Mick was the only player missing when captain Johnny Culloty led Kerry's twenty-first All-Ireland winning team down the platform and up to the Great Southern Hotel.

He had the same routine planned out for himself in 1970. The Department of Education was his master, not Kerry football. For the second year in succession, he prepared to miss out on the celebrations back home.

'East Kerry were in the county final the following Sunday, so when I went down to Heuston to see the team off, I turned to Donie O'Sullivan who was also based in Dublin and said, "I'll see you on Wednesday night for a kickaround." Donie was Kerry captain and my clubmate at Spa and he said, "Well, if you're not going down to Kerry, I'm not going down." As Kerry captain, Donie had to go down so I hopped on the train with him and the rest of the team.

'At the end of the month, teachers had to sign a form for days missed at school. I put down 'Missing 27 and 28 September'. For the reason behind my absence I put "*Ag Imirt do Chiarrai i gCraobh na hÉireann*". I got back a note from the Department of Education saying, 'We wish to inform you that you have been deducted two days' pay. On this occasion we won't break your service.' Breaking my service would have affected my pension.

'It always riled me considerably – an authority like the Department of Education, that was supposed to be so focused on promoting Gaelic games, still docked me two days' pay for playing in an All-Ireland and, only that they were being nice, they didn't break my service. That's clear in my mind from 1970. I have a cynical view of a body that would do that.'

Cynicism never crept into Gleeson's football though. Firstly, he traces it back to his home in Minish, five miles east of Killarney. 'I remember the day a football came into the house,' he says, 'because it was my uncle, Dan, who brought it from Cork. He always brought something but this was the only present we got that was of real value from anyone. It was a wonder to behold. I was seven or eight.'

From there, Gleeson brought his ball on excursions to Killarney for the annual Whit Weekend Tournament – Tadhgie Lyne, Mixie Palmer and John Dowling are the names he remembers. 'They would have been my demi-gods, if not gods,' he says. 'Paddy Bawn was another – I went to school in Dingle one year from September to Easter to brush up on my Irish and remember sneaking on to his boat.

'Then, when I was at home for the summer I'd go to Horgans, a two-room cottage where Mrs Horgan manned a level-crossing and raised a family of nine.

Mrs Horgan had a radio and people gathered from everywhere to hear Micheál O'Hehir's voice. It's something that people nowadays can't understand. His voice was the magic of the day – whether he was exaggerating the reality of what was happening was not important.

'He was animating everything and giving life to names and games. I remember names like Thady Turbett, Iggy Jones of Tyrone and Dr McNight of Armagh. Then, I always think that, other than being allowed to listen to the radio, the greatest thing I owe my parents is that a paper came into the house everyday.

'I would have known the names of all the players through the papers. I knew the famous Wexford hurlers – the Rackards, Paudge Kehoe, the Morrisseys. One could say GAA was the total focus. It meant the one ambition I had in life was to wear the Kerry jersey. Having achieved that was enough for me and I feel enormously privileged to have worn that jersey.'

Mick first played for Kerry in a Grounds Tournament game against Down in 1965 and was marked by Leo Murphy. Then, he got a run in the league against Louth before his inter-county career ground to a halt.

He was back in 1968 but only on the fringes. 'Fifteenth sub,' he says of himself. 'I didn't even tog out.' By 1969 he had moved from the fringes to the frontline, playing in the full-forward line with Mick O'Dwyer and Liam Higgins. Training with UCD helped get him there as much as training with Kerry.

'I was in UCD and we trained early in the morning for Sigerson. We were the first team to do it. Benny Gaughran used to come to collect me at 7am. He had a scooter and he'd be flying through town to training at 7.30am in Belfield. That helped me make the Kerry team.'

The purist had landed.

'I remember meeting Gay O'Driscoll in Fagan's of Drumcondra in the early '70s,' he recalls. 'Gay had a young lad with him. I said, "Is he a relation of yours?"

"He's my brother," says Gay, "and I had him with me in Croke Park. Anything to keep him out of Tolka Park, you know yourself."'

JÓM

Micheál Ó Sé

Old socialist Peadar O'Donnell burned a phrase into the consciousness of emerging, independent Ireland when he said, 'The gates flew open and out they came'. Peadar was referring to the end of internment and the release of political prisoners after the Civil War.

His line had a totally different meaning in the Ireland of the late '60s. Whether by edict from Rome or Armagh, the gates of seminaries flew open. It was as significant for the church of the GAA in Ireland as Vatican II.

A stricture barring seminarians from playing football or hurling once their summer holidays were over had deprived many a man of an All-Ireland. Worse still, upon ordination, priests couldn't play any ball. Football or hurling weren't priestly pastimes – such enjoyment was out of bounds.

In 1962, Donie O'Sullivan was a young seminarian – he was also Kerry's right-corner-back. Donie played in the Munster final win over Cork and in the All-Ireland semi-final victory over Dublin. Come final day his football year was over – he was back in St Patrick's College, Maynooth, listening to the match on the radio when he should have been playing.

Mundy Prenderville was in All Hallows College in the early '20s but escaped to victory by scaling the college wall to help Kerry win the 1924 All-Ireland. As punishment Mundy was banished to Australia to finish his studies, only to return to Ireland as the Archbishop of Perth.

Micheál Ó Sé entered this underworld when he landed in Maynooth in 1964. The student priest with blackthorn boots.

He had come of age as a footballer when he was just a kid – had to, because he shared a field near Smerwick Harbour with men as old as 60. There was also plenty of ball on Béal Bán strand on the summer nights when All-Ireland men like Garry MacMahon, who frequently holidayed in west Kerry, joined in. The young Ó Sé wanted to win All-Irelands like MacMahon but Maynooth meant this might never be.

'In the years up to '69 there would be a retreat on All-Ireland weekends. You wouldn't even know who won the All-Ireland. You weren't allowed to talk for three days. You wouldn't know who won until Monday or Tuesday if the final clashed with a retreat.

'In the lead up to the '68 All-Ireland final, I was back in Maynooth. I had two weeks done back in college since early September and, on the Thursday, I was allowed

Facing page:
Fir na Gaeltachta – clubmates and countymates Seamus MacGearailt and Micheál Ó Sé (right) got to write Johnny Culloty's speech in Irish before the 1969 All-Ireland.
(The Kerryman)

out for a few days at home. It just so happened that the All-Ireland was on during my few days out. The team had been picked at that stage and I wasn't on it, even though I had a good semi-final.'

Twelve months later, everything changed. The gates flew open; internment on All-Ireland weekends was over; priests playing under assumed names was over. The great liberation.

Ó Sé could have been forgiven for screaming divine intervention as All-Ireland final day in 1969 dawned. No All-Ireland final weekend retreat. Instead, Croke Park was the place of worship. He had his bag packed the night before – was massed and breakfasted early as he set out for Croke Park. Going there in style too, courtesy of the Kerry County Board.

'I was at the gates of Maynooth at eleven o'clock, waiting for the taxi that the county board had promised me. Tadhg Crowley was the man to order the taxis – he'd never fail you but this was the one time he forgot. I was waiting and waiting and there was no sign of the taxi. Time was dragging on.

'I don't think I had enough money in my pocket for a bus and the buses weren't that regular anyway, especially on a Sunday morning. So I decided to go on the thumb. I was there for a good length of time before this man driving a Morris Minor stopped. "I'm going to Dublin," I said. "I'm going there myself, going to the All-Ireland," he said back.

'I said nothing to him about playing in the final. We were talking in English at first and then he revealed he was an Aran Islander. It was all Irish after that.'

Ó Sé was dropped at the Skylon Hotel where the rest of the Kerry team were waiting, passing the time and nibbling a few sandwiches before the journey down the road to Croke Park by bus. The crisis had passed for Ó Sé but this unusual All-Ireland build-up was far from over.

He was hungry after his journey and was eating a few sandwiches of his own when a worried-looking Johnny Culloty approached. Captain Johnny was the coolest of them all but was far from cool as he dragged Ó Sé and Seamus MacGearailt away to his room.

'We didn't know what was wrong but then he said quietly, "If we win, what will I say at all? – I don't have much Irish."'

Culloty was put right when the Gaeltacht boys scribbled down the *cúpla focail*. Then Culloty's great save from Seán Evans ten minutes into the second half had Kerry on their way.

What matter if Ó Sé's fun was nearly over with the final whistle. While his teammates celebrated for the week, Ó Sé was just given a few hours' grace before Maynooth's curfew called. He was allowed attend the post-match function but had to be back at Maynooth that evening for classes on Monday morning.

Ó Sé only left this life behind on leaving Maynooth in January 1970. He said goodbye to the priesthood for a broadcasting career in Radió na Gaeltachta that went to air for the first time in 1971.

A great career move, he says, but not a good football move. A radio day could involve a drive from the Radió na Gaeltachta studio in Casla, Connemara to the Donegal studio and then back to Killarney for training. It couldn't be done – Ó Sé could be a broadcaster or a footballer, not both. He played his last game for Kerry in the 1973 Munster final. He was only 27.

A way of life was over. Training seven days a week. Running in the dark on Inch Strand with Seamus Murphy; going back to Smerwick Harbour and the Béal Bán of his youth; up and down the Three Sister Peaks beyond Ballyferriter; training in Tralee or Killarney.

He loved training but it made for a poor patient in the run up to the 1970 All-Ireland. Five weeks before the final against Meath, Ó Sé's ankle gave way. Rest was the only prescription – Micheál had his leg up for four weeks, only returning to the training field on the week of the final.

'Dr Jim Brosnan said he'd give me an injection on the day of the match. He gave it to me in the dressing room just before the game but admitted to me afterwards that there was only water in the syringe. It worked though, I went out and played the game. It was all psychological. But afterwards, I had to have an x-ray. I had a bone broken and needed an operation.'

Playing in an All-Ireland with a broken bone was worth it. Of that, Micheál Ó Sé is still convinced.

JÓM

Micheál Ó Sé pictured in Baile na nGall
(Shelagh Honan)

Mick O'Connell

The ferry service from Reenard Point to Knightstown operates as a shuttle service. It takes five minutes to cross 900 yards so miss one and you're put out by ten minutes.

It's nothing, unless you're on a schedule. O'Connell's schedule. 'Meet me at eleven o'clock,' he says, so missing a ferry now means being late for O'Connell.

When his visitors finally arrive at Glanleam ten minutes late, O'Connell quips, '*Tá tú déanach*.' Then he returns to what he's doing. Whips back his throwing arm and arcs a chest high ball in the direction of his son, Diarmuid, 15 yards away.

The next ball is over head height, in the direction of the lighthouse at Cromwell Point. O'Connell is playing quarter-back with Diarmuid's American football.

'Have to hit it hard,' he says. 'No point lobbing a gentle ball into the arms. Hard like it's coming to you in a match. No easy ball. The old television pictures of me kicking the ball against the gable wall and catching it are bunkum. It was for the cameras. The ball comes back too dead. You want the ball coming flying at you.'

O'Connell is the same when an O'Neills is fished out of the boot of the car. He goes to work with it – punting hard ball with left and right. Wanting the ball pumped back harder.

Mick O'Connell. Seventy years of age in 2007. Still playing. Still training. Still talking ball. You can tell that he doesn't like today's football very much.

'Name five outstanding fielders in the 32 counties who can field the ball and kick off right and left. You can't. You're searching, you're searching. Darragh Ó Sé is one of the only ones. It isn't a feature now to go out there and catch the ball. It's bunching, *pádaling*, fouling, handpassing, soloing. The solo run is a man playing the ball to himself.

'Paddy Kennedy was the best fielder ever – people still talk about him. How many of the players today will be talked about? Kennedy was singled out all over Ireland.

'That was the time when you had to be able to field. Two men competing for the one ball. Man against man. It's nearly non-existent now. No pulling or dragging going for the ball back in our time. I win the ball, or Cathal O'Leary [Dublin midfielder of the 1950s] wins the ball. We didn't foul each other.

Facing page:
At home with Mick O'Connell, still leaping high for the ball in his seventieth year.
(John Kelly)

'In 1960, there were 28 fouls in the Down versus Kerry All-Ireland – someone said to me after it, "For a big game wasn't there a lot of fouls." That's small compared to now, you'd have up to 70 fouls in some games.

'Catching and kicking was the foundation of the game. What was the main thing one time was good fielding, good kicking off left and right, blocking down. I'm not extolling the values of the past but the basic foundations have been lost.'

O'Connell's time as a Kerry footballer was from 1956 to 1974. In that period, the cult of celebrity was a cottage industry that built up around him. Mick O'Connell. A footballer born, it was said. The perfect footballer.

Kerry captain Mick O'Connell shows off his fielding skills to team trainer Dr Eamonn O'Sullivan and some of his teammates in Fitzgerald Stadium during collective training before the 1959 All-Ireland. (The Kerryman)

'Bunkum,' he says on both counts. 'Even the greatest of soccer players will tell you that it wasn't natural talent but it was the practice they put in that developed their skill.

'You hear this thing, that if one fella is good at one game, he's good at another. A fella who's dedicated to every game, it will take him a very long time to perfect any game. Perfection is ideal for those who attain it. Who is the player with all the skills? In any game? I don't know that there has been such a person in any game.

'Glory to me is playing the game, not perfection. There is no other reason to be involved in football or any other sport unless you like it. That was my basic motive for playing the game. That was my only motive.

'If people are playing football for fame or for gain, they're in the wrong game. If that comes indirectly, well and good, but if your first purpose is to win a medal and get fame and gain, you're not going to get full satisfaction from the game.'

Mick O'Connell wasn't getting satisfaction from the game early in 1968. Thirty-one years of age and back on the carousel after a couple of years out. Soldiered with Mick O'Dwyer then, to matches, to training and O'Dwyer always at the wheel.

Kerry were training in Tralee that year, O'Connell and O'Dwyer having returned to the fray after the Past versus Present match in February. One night in early April, they were the only two to turn up for training – 52 miles for O'Dwyer, just ten less for O'Connell.

'I have plenty of other things to do at home besides coming in here and wasting my time. If this is the interest that's going to be taken, then we might as well forget about the whole thing,' O'Connell told *The Kerryman* afterwards. He says more now.

'I was finished playing in 1966, didn't play in 1967 and came back in 1968 and went to play a match in Portlaoise and there were only fourteen players. What does that tell you about Kerry football?

'League, championship match, challenge, I don't distinguish between any game. A match is a match, you go out there and play. League football isn't different to championship football. There isn't a different shaped ball.'

The shape of the ball wasn't different on All-Ireland days either. Still, O'Connell never liked them. As captain, he left the field injured in 1959; left Sam in the dressing room after the game and headed straight back to the island.

'I enjoyed local games much more than All-Irelands because the pomp and ceremony of All-Irelands was ridiculous. I felt you have the game first and the pomp should follow. I hated the pomp and ceremony.'

Still they flocked to the island.

'I was the only islander to play inter-county football while living on the island. That was unique. It attracted attention, just for the sake of people wanting to write something. There was some bit of a myth about it.

'Why didn't they talk about the person who lived on the side of a mountain? They thought the place a bit of a backwoods and with fellas riding donkeys. We lived a life here that was as advanced as anywhere else.'

So advanced that Valentia myth and legend has it that Olympic swimmer Mark Spitz came to the island en route to Munich in 1972. Trained on the island; went diving off Ballinskelligs; went on to win his seven gold medals.

'Came to see me? Mark Spitz the swimmer in Valentia? That's bunkum; maybe he did come to Valentia. I saw his name in the papers but I never saw him.'

Others definitely came though. They still do. 'There was a couple from Tyrone here yesterday,' says Mick's wife, Rosaleen. 'They just wanted to meet him but he wasn't around. They were happy to wait until he came back.'

Later today Fr Peter O'Loughlin from Kilmihil in Clare makes the journey. A pilgrimage of sorts.

There will be someone else tomorrow. And probably the day after too.

JÓM

The Golden Years

Mickey 'Ned' O'Sullivan

A lot happened in 1975. The Bay City Rollers were on their way to ruling the world, Dev died, and Georgie Best played soccer for Cork Celtic. They were all big deals in their own way.

So was Mickey 'Ned' O'Sullivan's captaincy of Kerry, but this role came to an abrupt ending when he lay sprawled between Alan Larkin and Sean Doherty in the All-Ireland final. The next thing Mickey Ned remembered was waking up in the Richmond Hospital with nurses around him.

'The final went to my head,' he laughs. 'It's still a blank you know. I remember John Egan's goal going in and after that, I instinctively knew we were home and dry. Next thing, I got a pass from Paudie Lynch and went on the run. Then I was down on the ground, I couldn't breathe and the lights went out.

'I was in and out of consciousness for a good bit. I remember at one stage the nurse in the Richmond coming up and smiling. "Stop smiling," I said, "we've an All-Ireland to win."'

The All-Ireland was captured hours previously, but O'Sullivan only played fifteen minutes. A cameo that's remembered and replayed whenever Kerry and Dublin are about to meet. His flowing locks that could have been modelled on the Bay City Rollers; Doherty and Larkin standing over him feigning innocence after the deed was done. It's a toss up between Mickey Ned and Mikey Sheehy's goal for the most aired Kerry versus Dublin moment of all time.

He tells it against himself now but it's not the real tale from 1975. That came long before he was cut down, just after Mickey Ned was confirmed as Kerry captain for the 1975 championship on the back of Kenmare winning the 1974 county final.

'Frank King [county board vice-chairman] rang me up and said, "You know you're captain and we've no trainer. With your physical education qualification, you'll go up to Gormanston and do a coaching course." I told him I'd no interest in coaching Kerry and just wanted to be captain.'

Despite Mickey Ned's protests, he knew after King's call that the captaincy meant much more than going up for the toss and being the first man behind the band. O'Sullivan was expected to be a leader off the field as well as on it.

His year started on a winning note with Kerry beating Dublin in a challenge in Croke Park on 5 January by 1-6 to 1-3, but the team had no selectors in place that day.

The Gneeveguilla club wanted Mick O'Connell appointed manager/trainer of the team; Frank King wanted Mickey Ned as captain/trainer; Mickey Ned wanted Mick O'Dwyer, especially after the Kerry Convention on 26 January.

Gneeveguilla's motion to the Kerry convention never made it to a vote but O'Dwyer, with 97 votes, topped the poll in the election of selectors. Pat O'Shea, Donie Sheehan, Murt Kelly and Denis McCarthy were also elected as selectors, while Johnny Walsh and Joe Keohane lost out.

Kerry still had no trainer until O'Sullivan made his move. The story of O'Sullivan and O'Dwyer is worn nearly smooth by now but it led to something of an epic.

O'Sullivan dragged O'Dwyer to a coaching course given by Joe Lennon in Gormanston. Beforehand, O'Dwyer had protested, 'There's no way I'm going up to the Gormanston professor.' He relented on the understanding that he wouldn't have to sit an exam at the end of the course.

On the return journey, Mickey Ned asked O'Dwyer to train the Kerry team. According to O'Sulllivan, the following day, the county board secretary, Gerald McKenna, travelled to Waterville and sealed the deal. McKenna has another take on the most significant appointment in football. He says he had O'Dwyer in mind for a while, asked him to take the job and without any fuss, O'Dwyer accepted.

Either way, Mick O'Dwyer was appointed Kerry trainer on 22 March 1975, the day before Kerry lost a National League quarter-final to Meath by 0-11 to 0-6. The following Tuesday, Kerry had their first training session under O'Dwyer. 'If we beat Cork, we will be well on the road towards regaining the Sam Maguire. Basically, the team is ok, it's more a question of getting fit than anything else,' O'Dwyer said after his first training session.

'I remember nights as a minor when we had no trainer,' recalls Tommy Doyle. 'In 1974, Gerald McKenna would take the odd night's session. It got so bad that myself and Sean Walsh took a session a few nights up in the park. As far as I can remember, it was only when Seamus MacGearailt got involved in 1975 that minor teams were looked after right. That year Dwyer also took charge of the Under 21s. Those were massive events for Kerry. Things really started to pick up after that,' he adds.

'I would have helped Micko make out the first training session,' says Mickey Ned. 'After that, he was on his own. We had the first session and he came over to me and said, "How was that?" It was hard but I said it wasn't half hard enough. He never consulted with anyone after that. We had seen Dublin train in Gormanston and came to the conclusion that the only way we'd beat them was to be fitter than them. We had to be the fittest team in Ireland.'

Not long in the job, O'Dwyer ran in 27 sessions in a row. Tadhg Crowley came to him halfway through and told him, 'Horse nor hound, nor man will stick that.' He was wrong.

The captain was fitter than anyone else, even though he missed a large chunk of O'Dwyer's brutal regime in between beating Sligo on 10 August and the final six weeks later. During those weeks Kerry trained 35 nights.

Mickey Ned was teaching in Coláiste Iosagáin in Ballyvourney that year, and teaching meant summer holidays. Even captaincy of Kerry didn't come between Mickey Ned and his holidays, and he toured around Europe for four weeks with his pal, Donncha Lucey.

'I told Dwyer and there was no problem. He let me go, knowing that I'd keep myself fit.'

Mickey Ned did that and more. Training as he travelled – morning and night. Taking in the sights but thinking of the game; of the Dubs he'd seen in Gormanston; of Dublin's right-half-back, Georgie Wilson. Mickey Ned had the legs on Wilson, he thought.

'I trained twice a day and became more fanatical. We were camping and wherever we were, I'd find a field to train. One day, it meant finding a field on top of the Alps.' He found others in Paris, Luxembourg, the Rhine Valley, Austria, Switzerland, Italy and the Dolomites in Yugoslavia to train.

'I was arrested one morning in the Rhine. I was up at six in the morning and strayed into a military compound. A soldier came up and brought me in for questioning. I told them I was training for an All-Ireland. They didn't know what I was talking about but they let me go. When I came home, I was even more obsessed as being away focused my mind totally. I was convinced we would win. I saw no pitfalls, no danger.'

Everyone felt the same. From Paudie O'Mahoney out.

'I remember telling the lads in the dressing room that we were born for this day,' says Mickey Ned. 'It's easy to say but I believed it was our destiny. I knew going out on the field that there wasn't a team that could live with us. It was the nearest I ever got to total cohesiveness with a team – every member was tuned into the moment.

'Contrast that to '76. Before the final, I remember going to the festival in Tralee and meeting the lads. I knew we were going to be beaten. We were on one big ego trip. The focus was gone for the All-Ireland and we were out socialising.

'Four guys in the '76 final had injuries. I was one. We told no one. I remember saying to myself, "You might never get another chance of playing in an All-Ireland." Mentally, we had gone soft. We were hard in 1975, very hard.'

JÓM

Paudie Lynch

Paudie Lynch and *piseoga*. It was his great friend, Páidí Ó Sé, who got the Beaufort man going with superstitions on their famous tour of pub duty down streets and up laneways of Killarney on 19 September 1975.

It was the Monday night after the All-Ireland win over Dublin when Paudie and Páidí jumped train in Killarney, crossed the tracks and did their own thing downtown instead of joining the masses in celebration outside the Great Southern Hotel.

They ducked into Eddie O'Sullivan's Tatler Jack on College Street; Teddy O'Connor's on High Street, with Teddy himself who won an All-Ireland in 1946 behind the bar; then up to Murphy's on College Street.

Jimmy O'Brien's on Fairhill is another football pub. It's where the two went before every big game. Not for drink but for green gloves in Jimmy's sports shop above the pub.

Jimmy could set his clock by them. Before Munster finals, All-Irelands semi-finals and finals, they always showed. 'I'd be waiting for them, with the green gloves,' recalls Jimmy.

After a kick-around in Fitzgerald Stadium and lunch in the Park Place, they'd land in Jimmy's. For the gloves and to lighten the mood with match day around the corner. They did this before the Roscommon All-Ireland final in 1980.

'Bomber had got his appendix out,' recalls Páidí Ó Sé, 'and there was A.N. Other as full-forward. There was all kinds of speculation about who would play there and Jimmy was quizzing us.

'Micko decided Tommy Doyle would go in there. Ogie would play on the 40 as usual but myself and Paudie told Jimmy that Ogie would be given the number fourteen. Roscommon had this big strong full-back Pat Lindsay, a big scopy fella. Now, when Jimmy heard Ogie was in full-forward, he'd have thought we were mad. Ogie wouldn't be near the size of Lindsay, but Jimmy goes, "Ogie'll do a great job, lads." We got a good kick out of it.'

There was something every year. *Piseoga*. They served Paudie Lynch well. Another was a special training regime he set himself every year. His own superstition, for fitness but a part *piseog* too.

'I had to be right for Micko's training,' he says. 'I made sure I was right by doing my own training before the season started and a lot of it too. You had to do it.'

293

Lynch's extra miles in training were as important as the green gloves. Dunloe Castle was his haunt for extra training. While Páidí was running over the Clasach from Ventry to Dún Chaoin in special sessions, Paudie was doing circuit training with Beaufort teammate Colm Kelly – son of Murt.

'Paudie was phenomenal in his dedication to training and getting himself fit for Kerry training,' says Colm. 'Dunloe Castle was owned by German people and they had a training circuit of about a mile there. It was cross-country, but every 400 yards or so there was a station where you stopped to do exercises – push-ups, chin-ups, squats. Even during the height of Kerry training under Micko, Paudie went there one night a week. He punished himself with a lot of hard work.'

This ethic paid off. The star minor from 1968 to 1970 was a senior in 1971 – looking for All-Irelands like other Beaufort men, his brother Brendan and Kevin Coffey.

Paudie Lynch was a nineteen-year-old midfielder in 1971, vying with 34-year-old Mick O'Connell for his place on the team. 'It was way more laid back then, compared to when Dwyer trained the team. I was delighted to be on the panel and take my chance,' he says of his induction.

Lynch took his chance, getting the number eight jersey ahead of O'Connell for the 1971 National League final against Mayo. He was the only player on the team without an All-Ireland. Overawed? No. He played a blinder.

'At midfield, Kerry's man of the hour was Paudie Lynch,' said *The Kerryman*. 'Brought in as a sub for Mick O'Connell, Lynch rose to the occasion in tremendous style, giving a display that even O'Connell would be proud to turn in. Lynch fielded like a man inspired. Altogether a display that must surely keep him his place for the Munster final.'

It wasn't to be. For the Munster final two weeks later, the old order prevailed. Jackie Lyne stuck with those who had won Kerry's twenty-second All-Ireland in 1970. The only change on the Kerry team from the league final was at midfield. Paudie Lynch was dropped. Mick O'Connell was brought back.

The consolation for Lynch was that he was number sixteen in the match programme. First sub – the only one brought on as Kerry surrendered their Munster and All-Ireland titles.

So began a remarkable inter-county career. Over the next dozen years, Lynch was never dropped from a Kerry championship team. In that period he became one of the most versatile players in the history of Kerry football. The Seamus Murphy of the '70s and '80s. A big-game player who could play anywhere and was picked everywhere. Scan Kerry's final days in those dozen years.

National League finals – 1971: midfield; 1972: right-half-forward; 1974: centre-back; 1977: full-back. All-Ireland finals – 1972 and 1975: midfield; 1978: left-half-back; 1980: left-corner-back.

'That he could play in so many different positions as that came against him in a way,' says Mick O'Dwyer. 'He performed well in every position he played and that's the real test of a great footballer.

'If he played in one position all his life he'd be regarded as one of the greatest players of all time. But he still is one of the great players in my book. He would be on any all-time great team of any period.'

Beaufort say the same, the small mid-Kerry club that punched way above its weight thanks to the Lynch brothers. Beaufort was their world, from the time their father, Tom, started telling them stories about football days past. Billy Casey's brilliance prevented him from making it at centre-back on the Kerry team. Nobody could stand in Paudie's way, but after his travels with college, county and province, he always retreated to Beaufort.

'There were days when Paudie played for UCC on Saturdays up the country but was back on Sundays to play with us,' says Colm Kelly.

'Paudie's first loyalty was the Beaufort team – winning Sigersons and county championships with UCC, Railway Cups with Munster and the Combined Universities and everything with Kerry came after Beaufort. He wouldn't miss a club game unless he broke a leg.'

Beaufort's first Mid-Kerry championship came in 1976, with Tadhg O'Sullivan as captain in deference to his long years of service with the club. Paudie took the reigns from 1977 to 1980, during which time Beaufort never lost a Mid-Kerry championship match.

They went from Division four to Division one in the county league, only losing to a crack Austin Stacks side in the Division one final at the end of their sprint through the ranks of club football. They won county junior and intermediate championship titles on the way.

'We went through a four or five year period that if we lost a match, there'd nearly be a public enquiry,' says Colm Kelly. 'Paudie Lynch was massive for the club.'

'Massive for the county,' says Mick O'Dwyer.

JÓM

John O'Keeffe

On the eve of the 1997 All-Ireland, there was a small gathering of golfers in City West Hotel. After a quick sandwich, they split into a couple of fourballs and played a game of skins.

John O'Keeffe was in the group, so was Páidí Ó Sé's older brother, Tom. Professional golfer Paul McGinley was there too, as were his fellow members of Grange Golf Club, Dónal Moriarty and John Nolan.

They golfed and talked football. Kerry versus Mayo. Maurice. Maughan. McGinley could hold his own in any football conversation because he had played the game. John Nolan couldn't and pretty soon, his hand was up to admit he knew nothing about the game.

'Did you ever play a bit yourself?' he asked O'Keeffe.

'Played a little bit,' came the reply

Typical Johnno. Quiet and modest. No braggadocio. Seven All-Irelands; twelve Munsters; six National Leagues; eight Railway Cups; four All Stars; two All-Ireland Clubs; four county championships; Texaco Footballer of the Year; Hogan Cup.

O'Keeffe never had need to say how much he played, what he won, what he lost. Saying so would be out of character with the man.

The real Johnno is out on the field. Inheritor of a tradition that has fed Kerry football intravenously for over 100 years now. The school system. The bedrock of Kerry GAA.

As a teacher, he is to Tralee CBS what Brothers Young and Turner were to the school in the '20s; what Brother Brennan was to Dingle CBS in the '30s; what Brother MacDonagh was to Caherciveen CBS in the '40s.

Brothers Young and Turner brought football into the classroom – John Joe Sheehy made regular guest appearances, using the *clár dubh* for football tuition. Brother Brennan carried a cutting from *The Kerryman* until the day he died, in which PF forecast a glittering future for his CBS players, Tom O'Connor, Billy Casey, Paddy Brosnan and Bill Dillon. Brother MacDonagh fought with his superiors to have football in Caherciveen – he had his way and Dunloe Cups came to the town.

O'Keeffe went to the biggest cradle of all, The Sem, where footballers were weaned on stories about a past pupil and the first superstar in Gaelic

Facing page:
John O'Keeffe
cultivating the youth
of Tralee CBS.
(Shelagh Honan)

297

football, Dick Fitzgerald, and what he could do with a ball. Dr Eamonn O'Sullivan remembered the school day Fitzgerald came among them.

'We met that wizard of Kerry football, Dickeen Fitzgerald,' he wrote. 'I recall distinctly that, equipped with only ordinary street boots, he said to me, "I will show you how to curve a ball from near the endline" and with consummate ease he screwed a free kick about 5 yards from the endline and it curved over the bar. I have yet to see a Gaelic footballer repeat this performance.'

Others followed Fitzgerald. From Paul Russell through to Seamus Moynihan. O'Keeffe did for St Brendan's in 1969 what Moynihan repeated in 1992. Won the Hogan Cup.

Like Moynihan he was called up to the county senior squad straight away. Thrown onto the Kerry panel with O'Connell, O'Dwyer, Culloty and Murphy.

'It was some experience. Before I knew it, I had two All-Ireland medals before I was nineteen. It was strange but exciting. I remember playing with Connell at midfield. I held the man in such high esteem that anytime I won possession, I gave him a short pass and let him do all the work. I wasn't playing my own game. That changed by the time '75 came around. It was a reversal. Suddenly, I was supposed to show leadership and example.'

1975 was when football's greatest rivalry was born. When Kerry were, in O'Keeffe's world, just 'young fellas having fun, enjoying the game, giving it a lash'.

His comments before the final bear this attitude out. 'We have the fitness and we have the speed,' he told *The Kerryman*. 'I expect our backs to be able to stay ahead of their forwards. We have the edge at midfield and I expect our forwards to pick off the scores. I'm confident we can win it.'

Johnno was 24 then. Brendan Lynch, at 26, was the only other man on the team with All-Ireland medals. Thirty-five-year-old Donie O'Sullivan was another medal winner in the substitutes. But it was O'Keeffe who really led the way, winning a Texaco Award at the end of the year.

'John O'Keeffe, of course, was superb – but we would have been surprised at anything less from him. He is a model footballer, sporting as he is skillful,' wrote Con Houlihan after the final.

'Not once in the game did he put a foot wrong. It was another brilliant exhibition of full-back play,' said John Barry of *The Kerryman*.

Not bad for a midfielder/centre-back. Never a comfortable full-back until he became the stop-gap in 1975 after the number three of ten years, Paudie O'Donoghue, retired. The stop-gap lasted eight years, all on the back of one appearance there as an Under 21.

'I remember being put back to mark Declan Barron in a Munster Under 21 final against Cork. I caught a few balls over his head but at the end of the game, he sold me a dummy and stuck it in the back of the net. I thought I had played my last game at full-back but it was only the start.'

Just as the Kerry versus Dublin saga was only beginning. Together they defined the platforms and flares generation. City versus country; Kennelly versus Hanahoe; Páidí versus Hickey; O'Dwyer versus Heffo. And O'Keeffe versus Keaveney.

'Those games are the ones I remember – the ones I recall. Every single game had its own special feature. When it really got tough in the second-half of those games, Dublin came out on top. 1977 was the all-action game. Up and down the field. It was rated a tremendous game in every aspect of Gaelic football. It was for Dublin and for neutrals – not for us.

'I remember my own performance that day. Things were going well until there was a ball with about ten minutes or less to play. I made a dive to intercept but set it up nicely for Tony Hanahoe who gave it to David Hickey.'

Bang. The Hill goes wild. Wilder when Bernard Brogan came from the oil rigs off Cherbourg and drilled another goal.

Kerry hit a roadblock, with an old full-back leading the charge. 'This football we play nowadays is a bastard game, a mixture of soccer and basketball. All that is involved is running and handpassing and it could easily be played by women,' said former selector, Joe Keohane.

'It enrages my full-back's soul to see the passing that goes on by defenders around the square these days. If it was my day, I know that would never have happened,' he added.

The new full-back said nothing. Got on with winning All-Irelands, ironically with Keohane back as a selector and O'Keeffe won five as a full-back, like Keohane.

Then he coached. Limerick, Clare and Kerry at various intervals. Tralee CBS all the time. Churning out All-Ireland winners like William Kirby, Pa Laide and Kieran Donaghy to sit with Charlie O'Sullivan, Paddy Kennedy, Joe Keohane, John Joe Sheehy, Joe Barrett, Jackie Ryan, Miko Doyle, Mick Morris and many more.

There are lists in the Sem, Dingle CBS, St Michael's of Listowel and Caherciveen CBS.

They, too, go on and on.

JÓM

Jack O'Shea

Jimmy Keaveney: 'He was blown out of it in the 1977 semi-final but came back to haunt Dublin. He was Kerry's answer to Brian Mullins and in 1978 he came of age. We had them that year, the Kerry defence were arguing among themselves but then we lost the plot. Jacko kicked a point, Johnny Egan goaled and everything changed. Jacko had arrived and we were gone.'

Paddy Cullen: 'Jack O'Shea's emergence was the biggest thing to happen to that Kerry team. He gave them something new. He was the engine of the team and drove Kerry on for the next ten years. His workrate was phenomenal and it summed up that Kerry team. There was a lot of graft there, not just skill.'

For Jack O'Shea the graft started in Wembley Stadium on 17 October 1976. Kerry and Dublin in the '70s always drew a crowd but only 13,000 passed through the Twin Towers that day for the annual Wembley Games final that pitted League and All-Ireland champions together.

'It was eerie,' says O'Shea, 'but great to play Wembley and to get to play the Dubs. I was nineteen and it was my chance to go in against the best. The Dubs were the players to measure up against.'

O'Shea was used to mixing with big boys. He moved to Dublin in June 1975 just as Kerry juggernauts were unleashed on an unsuspecting public.

Seamus MacGearailt had the minor team, O'Dwyer was rustling his Under 21s and seniors into action.

Micheál Ó Muircheartaigh was Jacko's new mentor, meeting him in Phibsboro a few days after he landed in Dublin to start an ANCO plumbing course and bringing him to St Patrick's Training College to train with the Kerry seniors based in the city.

John O'Keeffe, Paudie O'Mahoney, Pat McCarthy, Jackie Walsh and John Long all won All-Irelands that year while Jacko won a minor on the same day and an Under 21 with six of the senior team a few weeks later.

Life and football were great. Jacko had two All-Ireland medals within a few weeks and lived it up for the rest of the year and afterwards.

'The first drink I took was the night we won the 1975 minor All-Ireland and for a year I didn't concentrate too much on football,' he says.

He was still called up to the senior squad before the 1976 Munster final replay against Cork. He didn't make the cut for the All-Ireland semi-final or final but was on the periphery of the panel, playing in trial games and training with the team. He also drank with the seniors at the Grand Hotel in Malahide after the final defeat in 1976.

'I was enjoying myself at that time and didn't know the potential I had and didn't appreciate what needed to be done. I was trading on the honour of what happened the year before with the minors and Under 21s.

'I didn't drink more than average. I couldn't afford to, number one. It was a case that if you were having a few drinks, it was made out to be a lot worse than it was. The way people were talking you'd swear I was in the pub every night of the week. That wasn't the case but I was enjoying myself too much to be an inter-county footballer.

'If I was having one drink, the word was going around that I was having three or four. Everything was being doubled and trebled and the further the rumour went the more momentum it gathered.'

John O'Keeffe had seen Jacko at close quarters during training in St Pat's, saw his potential and was afraid he could throw it away. Jimmy Deenihan was the same and the two PE teachers tackled Jacko about his fitness and dedication to the game.

'They gave me a good lecture the night of the All-Ireland,' says O'Shea, 'along the lines that I had the talent but was going nowhere unless I put the effort in, that I could throw it all away. What they were saying to me stuck with me. I went away that night determined to make the team.'

O'Shea didn't have long to wait. He made his senior debut three weeks later against Meath in Navan, but two games against Dublin within the space of seven days held more significance. Dublin beat Kerry in Wembley by three points, then Kerry turned them over by five points in the league before a packed house in Austin Stack Park. It was their third meeting in a month and O'Shea was the star on the second and third days.

'Kerry were masters of the midfield battle with Jack O'Shea giving no less a player than Bernard Brogan the run around. The Caherciveen man certainly showed in this game that he has what it takes,' commented *The Kerryman* after the Wembley Games final.

'Jack O'Shea was Kerry's man-of-the match. What amazed most about him was his tremendous confidence. Most young lads would have frozen up at the thought of such a big assignment, but O'Shea took it all in his stride and that's why he rates as a player with a really great future,' was *The Kerryman* verdict on his display in the league game.

'Brian Mullins was the player I was trying to focus on from the word go,' says

O'Shea. 'I wanted to beat him. He wasn't physically much bigger than me but he was way stronger.

'I remember standing alongside him in that league game in Tralee. I was nineteen years of age, light and raw. I didn't have anything like the experience he had. It was an awful task but I played quite well that day. I caught the throw-in in both halves and both times kicked it over the bar. Mullins wasn't too happy about that. I was an upstart.

'The championship in '77 was different. I wasn't mature enough and there were a couple of occasions when he blew me out of it.'

Beating Mullins became the focus of O'Shea's obsession. He gave up drink for good in 1977 because it interfered with his game but trained harder again from 1978 onwards, and his athletic ability flourished.

As a teenager, O'Shea had finished fourth behind John Treacy in the Irish Schools Cross Country Championship. While Treacy was winning his first World Cross Country Championship in 1978, O'Shea's own athleticism was carrying him to his first All-Ireland.

'Football became a way of life for Jacko,' says Micheál Ó Muircheartaigh. 'He was the one player that if you weighed him in February when training would really start, then weigh him in September when they'd be in an All-Ireland, he'd have gone up two pounds. That was the sign of an athlete and Jacko was a great one.'

He had the strength too, without ever visiting a gym in his life. He went to the mountains instead, beagle hunting in Caherciveen.

'Whenever I got home, I'd be very anxious to get out onto the mountains. It was very good for my legs. That helped me handle Mullins and I knew I had the legs to get around him. I was always conscious that we had the football over Dublin. It was about getting the game going our way and getting stronger.'

Kerry did that with O'Shea riding shotgun, from 1978 onwards.

JÓM

Tim Kennelly

You could see that it hurt them, that it took them by surprise. The news came like a bullet and struck them from behind. The Horse was gone.

The morning of his funeral they gathered in the big reception of the Listowel Arms. The big reception with the marble floor and the windows with the view that sweeps over the Feale and onto the racecourse.

It was a sunny morning two weeks to Christmas and the night before, the town was bright with fairy lights; the shops were decorated with posters of The Horse; and every house in the parish draped the black and amber of Emmets some place where it could be seen.

That night too, Jimmy Deenihan and his old manager, Mick O'Dwyer, took a long walk through the crisp air of Listowel.

They talked about their days with The Horse and the fact that tomorrow they would bury the strongest man they'd ever seen kick a football. They knew that in the hours to follow the tributes would flood in and players would arrive from all over the country. They knew too that The Horse would think it all an unnecessary fuss.

After a while, O'Dwyer turned to Deenihan and simply said, 'Jesus, Tim Kennelly, he would think this would be worse than any wire to wire.'

You could see how it hurt because for the first time the players looked old. The first of their family was gone and little wisps of grey were beginning to flicker under the hats they wore.

It showed mostly on the faces of the Dubs. They had driven a long distance to get here – Tony Hanahoe, Jimmy Keaveney, Sean Doherty, Gay O'Driscoll, Paddy Cullen – along a road that usually only opened in late September and always led to racing and craic and celebration.

Ross Carr and Joe Kernan had travelled from the north and Ger Power picked them up at Farranfore airport. Matt and Richie Connor came too. So did Eugene McGee, whose tactics for the 1982 All-Ireland were written with military precision because Kennelly was centre-back for Kerry.

That morning in the hotel reception, the story was recalled how McGee, in spring of '82, decided that if Kerry and Offaly met again that season he would switch his toughest player, Richie, to centre-forward to curb Kennelly, man-of-the-match in 1981. Try and put the shackles on The Horse. Tim would have liked that one.

Facing page:
The Horse – Tim Kennelly in Listowel as he reflected on his time in green and gold.
(Shelagh Honan)

Some months before the yarns started to spill, Tim himself was in the same hotel, sitting in the little nook between the bar and reception, talking in his quiet way of football in particular and life in general.

He wouldn't mind throwing down his thoughts on paper one day, he said, maybe make a book out of them. He said he hoped he'd see the day when his son, Tadhg, would help Kerry win another All-Ireland and touched on his own time as a kid, when he made the short journey from home in Coolaclarig to play ball in Listowel and it seemed an awful big deal going from the country into the town.

He ran through his Kerry career. Memories of driving out to Bomber Liston's house, trying to rouse the big man for another evening of torture under Micko.

'Myself and Deenihan would go back to Ballybunion and we'd actually have to pull him out of the bed to go training. It was killing him. He'd be there, "Oh God. Oh no. Leave me alone." But we always got him into the car.'

He remembered those games in the late '70s that etched his reputation and the day in 1979 when he became the first child of Emmets to carry the Sam Maguire into Listowel.

There were times when he couldn't see it happening. 'After '76, there was no need to motivate us against the Dubs. Then in '77, I was so disappointed. I remember in the dressing room after I had tears in my eyes. I said to one of the lads, "Fuck it, we're never going to beat Dublin again."'

That winter morning, many of those Dubs who broke his heart 28 years before moved from the hotel to the graveyard to see their old friend laid to rest.

As Billy Keane, Tim's pal from town, walked through Listowel that morning, he bumped into a local outside Pat Whelan's shop on Market Street. 'The Horse is going to be buried in the new cemetery,' said Billy. 'Ah,' said the local. 'Sure, they'll all be dying to be buried there from now on, so.'

At the graveside, Stephen Stack, who Billy described as Tim's 'third son', recalled an image of Tim that had remained in his head.

'I was sixteen years of age and it was January. He was wintering well after an All-Ireland and he was carrying, as Mick O'Dwyer used to say, a small little bit of condition. I knew that, because it was unusual to see any man wearing two tracksuits and a black polythene sack turned over him and I saw it first hand at that stage the kind of punishment that the man was prepared to put his body through to achieve his sporting goals.'

He remembered, too, the occasion in 2003 when the Listowel Emmets organised a surprise bash for Kennelly. They were wondering who would act as MC for the evening when somebody suggested Tony Hanahoe, his old sparring partner from the Kerry/Dublin days.

A call was put to Tony. He said to give him an hour to sort the logistics and he'd get back to them. When Hanahoe called, he confirmed he'd be at the gig. It only turned out later that he'd cancelled a trip to the Melbourne Cup – that he'd already paid for – to speak about Tim in Listowel.

Jimmy Deenihan also addressed the huge crowd that turned up at the new graveyard. Those who have heard Deenihan speak in dressing rooms and in Dáil Éireann have never heard him orate with such controlled passion. He cast a gaze out into the sea of faces and recognised the men he and Kennelly had soldiered with.

'Could I say sincerely, I'm delighted that so many of our team turned up here today. There was a great bond between our team on the field of play. Maybe not off it that much because we were spread all over the county and the country but I must say, I felt that special bond there today outside the church and in the church last night. There was a special bond – something that people would not understand unless they were playing on that team. There were special understandings built up. Words hadn't to be said. People understood each other. It came just spontaneously to us, it was intuitive, it was within us.'

The week Tim passed away, Stephen Stack and himself shared their last conversation. That Sunday, the Emmets had beaten Finuge in the north Kerry semi-final.

'I asked him,' said Stack, "How are we going to beat Ballyduff in the final?" We spoke for about an hour and actually, I can feel him looking up at me now saying, "Stephen, say no more in case there's a few of 'em listening."'

Stack obliged, stood aside and helped lay The Horse to rest.

TJF

John Egan

There are two minutes left in the game. Always two minutes. John Egan goes back in time to that one moment in which he is always stuck. Two minutes left. He's in the corner of Croke Park, hands on his hips preparing his acceptance speech. In the distance, in one split second, a flurry moves towards the Hill goal and then everything suddenly explodes. The world changes. He feels sick.

Fast forward the clip a quarter of a century. Egan is in the Kingsley Hotel on Cork's Western Road. The place is packed with suits out for after-work drinks on a Friday evening but Egan is alone. A coffee pot and cup keep him company. He drinks it down before retreating to the lounge to talk football.

'1982,' he sighs, 'nobody remembers losers. Very few fellas will ask the question, "Who captained the team that lost the five-in-a-row?" They'd all know the fella that won the five-in-a-row. They don't remember the losing captain. That was me.'

John Egan is wrong, though. People remember alright. Seán Murphy's story about Pat 'Aeroplane' O'Shea is run by Egan. Aeroplane had *The All-Irelands Kerry Lost* as a working title for a book. He never got around to writing it but it would have been a big book. Before '82 they'd lost fifteen.

On hearing this, Egan smiles again. '1982,' he says, 'I was lucky to be captain but unlucky to be the man that captained Kerry to losing the five-in-a-row.'

That day would have crowned Egan's career in a Kerry jersey. He saw the five-in-a-row frenzy building all round him. The vinyl cut by Cork ballad group, Galleon, before the final.

'Five-in-a-row, five-in-a-row.

'Hard to believe we've won five-in-a-row.'

'Are you going to be the man to captain Kerry to the five-in-a-row?' everyone asked after Jimmy Deenihan's term as captain ended, following the National League final.

Egan didn't know. Ger Lynch was named Kerry captain the Tuesday night before Kerry opened their five-in-a-row campaign on 6 June against Clare in Ennis. Then Lynch gave the captaincy up – making the team was his priority for 1982 – and it went to the toss of a coin. Sneem wanted John Egan, St Mary's of

Facing page:
John Egan leaves the field in 1982 when he thought he should have been climbing the steps of the Hogan Stand to collect Sam Maguire.
(The Kerryman)

Caherciveen wanted Jack O'Shea.

So it began in Ennis. Five-in-a-row captain. Not bad for a lad from a footballing backwater called Tahilla, four miles outside Sneem. There was no underage football during Egan's early years but it still didn't stop him making the Kerry minors for two years and joining the senior team for their first game after the 1972 All-Ireland defeat. Egan was a young garda in Cobh then, had no car so hitching and bussing it to games in Killarney was the norm for a few years.

He was in awe as he entered the dressing room the first time for a league game against Kildare in Killarney. O'Connell and O'Dwyer weren't there but others made him feel uneasy, out of place. Pat Griffin, Liam Higgins and Mick Gleeson had All-Irelands. Egan had nothing.

'You felt people like that were superior to you. I looked around and said, "What the hell am I doing here?" I hadn't a fear, you don't when you're young but I didn't think I'd be playing with these fellas. It was half a new team and half an old team – it was very hard to fit in.

'My first big day was the League final against Roscommon in '74. It was an awful day in Croke Park and Roscommon were beating us off the pitch. They were three points ahead and time was up – I hadn't got three kicks of the ball all day.

'Mickey Ned got the ball and went to kick it over the bar. He slipped as he kicked, the ball came over and I put my fist to it and it went into the net. I made the headlines of the papers after that. I suppose I'd arrived as a Kerry player.'

Egan made headlines for another ten years. He enjoyed himself and you could tell his state of football health by the garda uniform he was wearing – he had a few in various sizes. The winter coat for when Kerry celebrated and drank hard; spring wear for when the real training was beginning; the summer suit for when O'Dwyer had Egan at his fighting weight.

'We laid off in the winter, had a few drinks. Micko would like us coming back with a few pounds on – it gave him something to work on. Then, he'd literally run us into the ground. Get the drink out of us. It was brutal from April onwards when he'd get down to the serious work. No one asked questions, you didn't question him, you just did it.'

The routine. The same every year. Egan found it harder as the weight was slower to shed with the years slipping by. 1978, 1979, 1980 and 1981. It was easier in 1982 because of the five-in-a-row.

The second he won the toss against Jack O'Shea, five-in-a-row fever gripped Sneem and Tahilla. The man who learned his football over the border as a boarder in Carrignavar Secondary School from Cork minor trainer, Brother McCarthy, was going to bring Sam to Sneem.

It was all sorted. Monday night Killarney, Tuesday night Tralee, Wednesday night Sneem. Marching bands, the podium in the square and late drinks. The bonfire material had even been collected. John Egan was going to captain Kerry to win the All-Ireland. Simple really.

Come final day, Egan reckons he was in the greatest shape of his life. It showed. Three points from play, fouled for a penalty when he was just about to pull the trigger for a goal that would have killed the game.

'It's a classic game for everybody apart from Kerry. It wasn't for us. It hurts and still does. We should never have lost that game.

'We were so well in control going into the last ten minutes and their points came from frees – you'd have to say that two of them were dubious calls. I had a funny feeling that the referee thought the game was petering out and when the goal went in, all hell broke loose.

'We definitely could have equalised but you don't blame anybody. There's no point reflecting on it. We could have been calmer. You don't like losing but the manner of the defeat was devastating. It was very hard to recover from it.

'It was hard to see another day for us. It's still hard to believe what happened and hard to take. I thought the position we were in and the way we played that we did not deserve to lose that day.'

Egan has seen the game re-run on TG4's *All-Ireland Gold*. Loves *All-Ireland Gold*, says 'it's fantastic that we're being remembered'. Hates 1982, though.

'When the goal went in, I had taken a few minutes out to prepare my speech. That's what I tell fellas, that I was up in the corner putting the few words together and clearing my throat.

'Jesus Christ, there's only one place in the championship and that's the place for winners. You don't get much sympathy if you lose.'

No sympathy, perhaps, but Egan conributed more than anyone that day in '82 and left a legacy of understated greatness.

JÓM

Jimmy Deenihan

What promised to be the best summer of the twentieth century begins for Kerry on 9 May 1982. Páirc Uí Chaoimh. League final. Cork come in hope, Kerry in confidence. Jimmy Deenihan is the most confident of all. Cocky almost.

Corner-back and captain, he lost Sam Maguire for a few days in New York a few months earlier when it was supposed to be en route to Pittsburg for a photocall with the Super Bowl and World Series Trophy won by the Steelers and Pirates respectively.

Someone pirated Sam but Deenihan got over it. Kerry were used to photocalls, there'd be plenty of time for them with Sam on the next world tour after the five-in-a-row.

'We won the league well. At that time the Kerry captaincy lasted for the championship and the league of the following year. That's me. 1981 championship captain and 1982 league captain. We win both.

'There's a strong sense among the players, Micko, supporters and everyone around the country that, barring accidents, we'll win the five-in-a-row.'

But accidents do happen.

A few pints on the way home from Cork, everyone enjoys the night, then the league cup is at home in Finuge. Never even got filled on the way home. Left in a corner. The league is just a stepping stone to something bigger.

Summer has started; best of the twentieth century.

Bring it on, says Deenihan. He knows training in Fitzgerald Stadium will get serious now. Wire to wire. Backs and forwards. It's what Deenihan loves. Loves getting stuck into Egan, loves getting stuck into anyone; Jimmy Barry-Murphy, Bobby Doyle, John McCarthy, Matt Connor, Brendan Lowry. He's a forward for Feale Rangers and Finuge but a Kerry back. A hard one.

'Jimmy Deenihan was tough. He'd always keep himself on the near side. He wouldn't hold on to the jersey – he'd hold on to the skin. You'd be got for holding on to a fella's jersey. You couldn't be got for holding on to a fella's skin,' says Charlie Nelligan.

In matches and in training. They're three weeks into championship training now, another night nearly over. There's a small crowd looking on, which will grow as the year grows.

'One more attack, lads,' says Micko. 'Kick it out, Charlie.'

Facing page:
Jimmy Deenihan in conversation with a constituent in John B. Keane's pub in Listowel.
(Shelagh Honan)

Egan and Deenihan are jostling for possession. Deenihan's mind is on the ball. Get the ball. Clear it. Finish off the session. Shower and go home.

But here it all ends. No ball, no clearance, no shower, no going home, just craaaaaaaaaaaaaaaaaak.

Deenihan is on the ground, can't crawl, can't even roll. It hurts really bad and it hurts more that his inter-county career is over. His five-in-a-row over. Micko and his last attack.

'Very simple,' says Deenihan. 'The tackle on John Egan – it wasn't even a tackle. A very innocuous incident. I was knocking a ball out of his hand, I put my hand in and, as I did, our legs got entangled. We twisted and I came down on my leg – John came down on top of me. The way we fell there was just a crack and I can tell you, it was some crack. It was heard all over the pitch by players, spectators, anyone who was in Fitzgerald Stadium.'

'It was a wet evening,' remembers John Egan. 'It was a freakish thing to happen. The ball came in on the ground and I went to collect it. It went straight through my hands and my legs and he stepped over the ball. He got an awful injury for what happened because there was no real contact with me whatsoever.'

Deenihan looks up. Egan is on his feet. Heads everywhere. Micko, Liam Higgins, Joe Keohane, physio Claire Edwards. All gather around. Summer is starting, yet this is the beginning of the end.

Shouts fill the background. 'Get a stretcher. Get back, give him some air, get some water, where's the sponge? There might be magic in it.' Seconds seem like minutes and then hours, before the ambulance arrives. Lying there amongst friends but lonely. Nearly too painful to think but thoughts keep flashing. It's over, the five-in-a-row is over.

The smell of pain; the smell of fear; the smell of disinfectant as he's finally carried away to Cork Regional Hospital. 50 miles to Cork, where the summer had started.

It's over now. Nurses and doctors say it. His consultant, Dr Freddie Moore, says the same. A mesanof fracture of the right ankle – in lay terms, an ankle broken in two places; torn ligaments too; a fractured tibia as well. Worst day of Jimmy Deenihan's life. 2 June 1982.

In the Regional in Wilton, Deenihan's football life flashed before him. Bryan MacMahon's Listowel and District School League – the rules allowed young Deenihan to cross the Feale River from his own school, Dreamlach NS, to play for Killclarin NS. Winning the 1965 final in Listowel Sportsfield. Meeting John B. Keane after the game, showing his medal to Billy, Conor and John Keane. Turning away Kerry minor selector, Dan Kiely, in 1968 and 1969 out of an inferiority complex of being a countryman. Finally answering Dan's call in 1970 and having a Kerry jersey on his back for the next twelve years. Senior debut on 29 October 1972 against Roscommmon in

Killarney. The glowing *Kerryman* reference: 'Deenihan showed tremendous dash in the left-corner-back position, having many fine clearances to his credit and covering with the effectiveness of a very seasoned campaigner.'

He's well seasoned by 1977 and ready for more success, or so he thought strolling along Ballybunion beach one evening with Pat Spillane, a fellow teacher at St Michael's, Listowel.

'We were going from the beach to the Castle Hotel and saw it in the paper that we had been dropped from the panel,' says Deenihan. 'Paudie O'Mahoney and Ger Power were also gone. None of us got any explanation and weren't told whether we'd be back again but after a bad league run we got back.'

Back to win more All-Irelands and National Leagues. But on 2 June 1982 there was no going back. Under the knife on 3 June; under the anaesthetic. You wake up and, for seconds, you forget you're injured; forget you're finished. Forget you won't be on the five-in-a-row team; forget you won't wear the number two again; forget you'll never smell your own sweat after an All-Ireland.

'For a while I thought I'd get back, I really did, even though I was told it would never happen. I did everything to get my leg right. I was running after ten weeks. It was crazy.

'I was running in pain but I was trying to push myself through that pain barrier. I was never going to make it but I had to try. Weight training, out on the beach at 6am every morning in Ballybunion. Anything.'

Seven days before the All-Ireland, Deenihan was togged out with the Kerry team again – training once more but not part of the first fifteen. While a final trial game was going on in Fitzgerald Stadium, Deenihan was joined by Sean Walsh, Pat Spillane and Mikey Sheehy – all carrying knocks – in a separate kick-around on the front pitch. He was the only one of the four not to play in the final.

'I would have preferred to have played in this All-Ireland than any other and that probably includes my captaincy,' he told *The Kerryman* the week of the game. 'This is the year when they're attempting to make history. I would love to be part of it.'

He wasn't – Jimmy Deenihan was finished. He never played for Kerry again, but it had a silver lining.

'If I hadn't broken my leg, I doubt that I would have gone into politics. I was only 30, but for the leg break I would have played in the '82 final and there would have been two or three more years in me. One door closed another opened. That's the way things happen.'

JÓM

Páidí Ó Sé

It's six o'clock the Monday before Christmas and Páidí isn't at his pub on Ard an Bhóthair like he said he'd be.

'Gone to Dingle getting decorations,' somebody says from behind the counter. 'Should be back in half an hour.'

Closer to seven, he ambles in carrying a bag of baubles and tinsel in one hand and a small cardboard box in the other. It's the box he has most interest in. 'Have a look inside,' he says to a small group. By now, four or five locals have wandered in but the bar is still half deserted, punters saving their money for the week ahead.

A little crowd gathers around him. Páidí roots through the box, like a magician poking into a top hat and with delight, he pulls out a sheaf of envelopes. Hey Presto! The box is filled with Christmas cards for each member of his Westmeath panel. A nice thought, one would think, but the sentiments expressed aren't supposed to be festive or friendly. He wants to get across that the road is long and the challenge is mighty.

Páidí has located an Irish verse, native to this part of west Kerry, that he had printed on the inside of the cards. He reads it aloud *as gaeilge* then gives it the English translation. The verse concerns a man who rowed around the Great Blasket through high wind and rough water. He needed perseverance to complete the journey. He needed to be strong and wilful and to believe in his task. This is what he wants to get through to his players in Westmeath.

He turns and says, 'What do you think?'

'Great poem. A nice touch.'

'Ah,' he says, 'a mighty verse alright. That'll get 'em going.'

Later that Christmas, he sends another gift to the team. A badge for each member of the panel with yet another inscription painted on. *'Ag builadh dair le dorna.'* Hammering an oak tree with a fist.

Páidí told them to wear the badge for the whole season and let the message seep into them. If a team came at them hard during the year, let their opponents feel like they're hammering their fist off a hard oak tree.

After finishing with his box of cards, he takes a seat away from the group at the bar and settles in to answer a few questions. There's a mythical tone to much of what he says. 'One of the gifts that God blessed me with was a great memory.

Facing page:
Páidí Ó Sé's island – his pub in Ventry where he's surrounded with images of the great and the good.
(John Kelly)

317

I really enjoyed the earlier part of my football career. Under 12. Under 14. In Ventry, playing at the bottom of the road, playing at the weekends, breaking the windows of the chapel and the priest giving out to me. They are my earliest memories. From once I could walk and from once I could think, I wanted to play for Kerry. And I just don't know what put that in my brain. Batt Garvey, God rest his soul, was a neighbour of mine. Played in 1946. Came from just a quarter of a mile back the road. He was a great influence on me. As was Mick Murphy and Tom Long as well. There's a certain amount of history around me.'

The mechanics of his brain are played out on his face. At times, he closes his eyes tight, wrinkling his forehead to coax an old image from some year to the front of his mind. Other questions he answers by staring into the distance, to the darkness of the bar room in front of him.

'I actually lived as a professional footballer. Did you ever hear that? It's true. I gave up the Gardaí because it was interfering with my football. Simple as that. Gave it up. Even though the Gardaí facilitated me in every way possible, I just felt it impeded on the football. So I lived and breathed and became surrounded in Kerry football for six or seven years. Nothing but nothing was going to get in the way. I had the full support of my mother and even when I got married in '84, I still won three medals after that.'

Páidí at home in his native place.
(John Kelly)

It's just over ten minutes since he's been on the stool and when most are now just warming up, shaking the cobwebs from the past, Páidí has his eye on the other side of the bar, where the craic is. A programme of Irish traditional music is playing on the television and he glances that way every now and then.

'Is that enough?' he wonders. 'Come on away over and we'll sit down with the rest of them. Turn that 'aul thing off.' There's a dictaphone running on the bar and every time he looks at it, he's visibly uncomfortable but, with difficulty, he's talked into a few minutes more.

'Two minutes so and we'll go over. Alright? Of course, I remember the first time I pulled on the jersey as well. It was '73. Unreal. I remember playing a couple of challenge matches around Christmas. We played Dublin, we played Clare, I was playing centre-forward and wing-forward and I did quite well. I was eighteen. Then I remember playing in Dunmanway. Kerry and Cork for the opening of a pitch.

'Joe Keohane was involved with the team and I was walking off the field with him. I said, "Mr Keohane, I hope you don't mind me saying this but I wouldn't mind at some stage in the future if I got an 'aul run at wing-back."

'That year we got to the National League final and I was a sub all the way up. In the league final, we were being beat by Roscommon going into the last five minutes and I was brought on to the 40. I got a point, John Egan got a goal and for the replay, I was selected wing-back. I'd a great game there and I didn't move out of that position. That was my jersey for the next nine years.'

Finally, the dictaphone is turned off, the batteries barely warm. He nestles in with the small group at the bar and immediately he's at home, relaxed and in good company.

The volume is quite low on the television and he breaks from the group to stand closer to hear two lively tunes. The third is a lonesome, slow air that he has no interest in.

He walks the few short steps back to the bar and says, 'Jesus boys, you wouldn't fire up a team for an All-Ireland semi-final with that kind of stuff. Imagine running onto Croke Park with that music on the brain.'

Almost immediately after he's sat down again, his mobile phone rings. The group falls silent and Páidí is talking aloud so all can hear. His son, Páidí Junior, across the road in the family home, is on the other line. It quickly becomes apparent he wants to buy a set of goalposts on the internet. 'Goalposts,' says Páidí. 'What kind of goalposts?' There's a pause for two seconds. 'Soccer goalposts,' he says with overplayed exasperation. He looks around the bar, throws his head back and gives a little wink. 'Soccer goalposts,' he says again, a little louder this time. 'Whaddya want those for? Soccer! You must be joking me.'

And the bar falls into a familiar laughter.

TJF

Ger Power

The end came softly. Ger Power opened his eyes one day in 1988, did the math and decided it just wasn't worth continuing. It wasn't one particular incident or event, just a series of circumstances. No point dragging it out, he thought.

He was golfing with some other senior players from Cork and Kerry back in Tralee and he noticed one or two were beginning to drag their legs around the fairways. This was the first time his attention was pricked.

He saw things differently after that. In the dressing room, a few more were complaining of aches and pains. He could see them suffering, railing against the inevitability of time and gravity. He sat beside them and wondered how he would get along when football was done with. Would his hips twinge in the mornings? Would his joints throb when the weather turned cold?

He had two good hands and two good legs. One day, he held the two hands in front of his face, stared at them and said it was time to get out. End game came in the sun of Páirc Uí Chaoimh. Bomber, Ogie, Páidí and himself sitting on the bench – old shotguns waiting for one final hunt.

'We faded away. It was the right time to go. You'd be looking around at lads with injuries and seeing the pain they were going through at that time. I decided it was right to call it a day. We'd played so much football, I just wanted to get out without doing any damage to myself and maybe the interest was going as well. Some of the players were leaving and new lads were coming in, so it was the right time to move on. At that stage, you might have felt you could do it and keep going but what was the point really?'

Over the years, he became intrigued with the workings of the muscles and joints – the nuts and bolts of the body. Hamstring trouble – a phantom ailment, according to Mick O'Dwyer, and the bane of his life as Kerry coach – dogged Power throughout his playing career. It stopped him lining out for the 1979 final when he was as fit as he ever was. A decade later, it put him thinking again.

When the boots were hung up, he set to finding out more about the problem and uncovered enough to make him realise he should never have suffered so much. He signed up to train professionally and every weekend for two full days, he travelled to Cork to complete a course in sports injury and massage. It didn't come as a surprise.

Power was always one of the fittest on the Kerry panel, one of O'Dwyer's

Facing page:
Ger Power followed his father Jackie into the All-Ireland enclosure – Jackie won two hurling medals with Limerick, Ger won seven football with the Kingdom.
(Shelagh Honan)

hares to push others on during extra training. Even now, when he's away golfing for a weekend, he still rooms with Mikey Sheehy, like he did in the Kerry days, and Power will be first to leave the bar and turn in early. He likes to look after himself.

In 2003, John O'Keeffe invited him to Australia as part of the Irish backroom team for the International Rules Series and the experience enthralled him.

'I was just helping out in Australia really but it was fascinating. We saw just about every possible injury in Gaelic football and trying to get the players back into the game as quick as possible was the challenge. Prevention and recovery are key now. We didn't have that attitude. In our day, after a game in Croke Park it was straight out the door and down to Mulligan's Pub in Poolbeg Street to Con Houlihan and the gang.'

Out in Australia he worked alongside Dr Con Murphy, a Corkman under whose care plenty of Kerry players were nursed back to fitness. They spoke of the old days and recalled Power's own time when he was a huge doubt, this time for the 1980 final when he was captain.

'I'd been in Cork the week before the All-Ireland final getting treatment from Con. During the International Rules he told me that back in 1980 he thought I mightn't play again after the treatment I was getting. But all I wanted to do back then was lead the team out. They eventually took me off at half-time. The injections for the hamstring were wearing off and there was no way I could play on.'

Ten years before, he led the minors all the way to the final during a period when Cork ruled the grade at provincial level. Getting to the final made more headlines in Kerry than it normally would. There was another reason too. For all that's spoken of the Under 21 victory of 1973, the minor campaign of 1970 pointed the way forward. Kerry won the senior All-Ireland that day and those that saw the minors draw with Galway knew there was fuel in the tank for years to come. They lost the replay by a point but the spine and experience for the golden years was beginning to build. Mickey 'Ned' O'Sullivan. Paudie O'Mahoney. John Egan. Paudie Lynch. Ger O'Keeffe and Power himself.

'We began to form a bond in the minors that year. You could sense that you were playing alongside some great potential. We beat Derry in the semi-final and there was a bit of confidence after that because Kerry hadn't done much at minor for years. I remember you could look around the field and see talent in every sector. That was the real beginning of the great Kerry team. The lads who played that season must have known we were going places.'

He was closing in on the legend of his father. Jackie Power had two All-Ireland medals with Limerick and a star of excellence stamped to his name. Work brought him to Kerry just ten days after Ger was born and even outside the hurling pockets of his new county, he was revered and appreciated. When Ger was growing up in Tralee, the kids of Ashe Street would pester him for a look at his old man's hurling medals. Every so often, a group would be quietly ushered inside the house for a glance and the gold nuggets would be revealed for a few seconds. It was enough to keep them going for weeks.

In the evenings when Jackie would come back after training Limerick, he'd bring with him a sliotar and a broken hurley which he'd mend and his son would give it new life. Ger played the game at underage level for Kerry but quit when he saw hurleys flying and heads disappearing.

Football became his outlet. He was sucked in by the noise and the sweat of the streets. He could never walk away from it. Too much passion bubbling away within him. Back in January 2003, it came back with a sizzle. A decade and a half since he played for Kerry but nothing had died away. Just after Páidí Ó Sé made his infamous 'roughest breed of animals' statement, Power was on Radio Kerry's *Terrace Talk* programme with Weeshie Fogarty.

Fogarty asked his guest's opinion of the affair and Power didn't hold back. 'I think Páidí Ó Sé is getting slightly carried away about his own importance,' said Power.

'Ogie Moran got a hard time after losing a Munster final and Mickey Ned was torn to shreds when Clare beat us in the Munster final in 1992. So Páidí would want to remember that we were beaten by Armagh [in 2002] and in my eyes, Armagh were handed that All-Ireland.'

No compromising. Not when it came to walking away in 1988 and not when it came to giving his opinion fifteen years later.

TJF

Ger Power, Páidí Ó Sé, and Eoin Liston before a training session.
(The Kerryman)

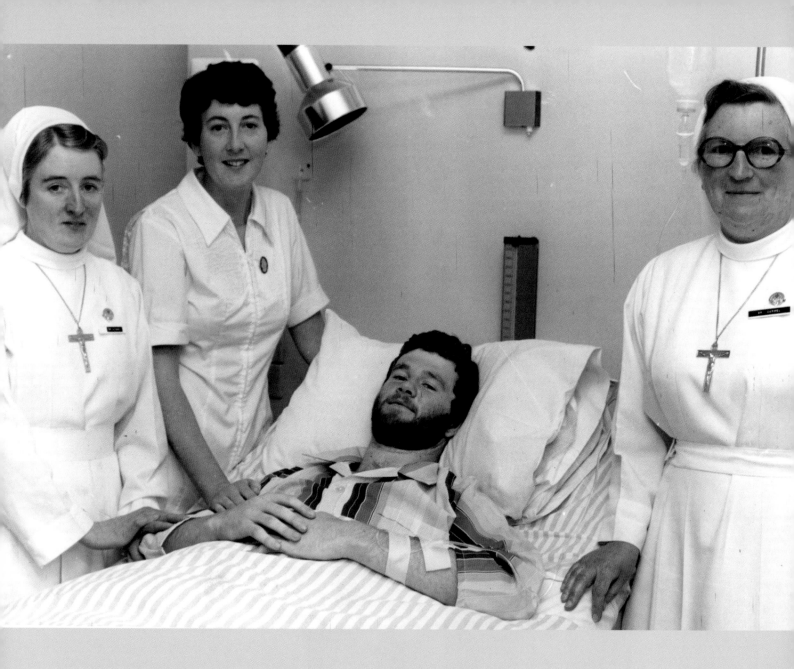

Eoin Liston

The morning of the 1980 All-Ireland final, Eoin Liston boarded a small aircraft in Farranfore and tried to make it to the game on time. His appendix had been removed two days earlier, so he was sidelined but had just managed to weasel his way out of hospital to be in Croke Park.

That Thursday, during a light training session in Killarney, Liston felt a sharp pain shoot down his side. Three days before the big one, he tried to put it to the back of his mind but it just wouldn't go away. On the trip back home, the agony increased and he ended up seeing a doctor who gave him 'a good dose of morphine'.

Then, the weekend began to diverge sharply from the script and events took on a life of their own. Friday morning, he was under the knife, his appendix ripped out. Hooked up to a drip when he woke and he couldn't believe it. After he got his bearings, he looked to secure early release from the sickbed, but the doctors wouldn't hear of it. There was a breakthrough in negotiations later that afternoon and he managed to talk his way into leaving hospital the morning of the game. Only thing was, he was cutting it tight to make Dublin.

Word spread of the fix Liston was in and a benefactor offered to ferry him up on his light aircraft. Halfway there, they hit a snag. Weather conditions dipped over the midlands. The plane was being bumped and rocked all over the sky. The pilot looked over at Liston with a grave face and said, 'Bomber, we're not going to make it.'

The Bomber, with his side still in bits, wasn't sure if the man meant they were going to miss the game or if they were about to crash-land in the bogs below.

'I was starting to brick it,' says the Bomber.

It took a few minutes but the pilot eventually gained control and managed to turn the plane around, back for the safety of Kerry. When they landed, the two didn't discuss their trauma, only filled the car with petrol and made a fast dash for Drumcondra. They made it as the Artane Boys Band was walking off the field.

It was Liston's first bump on the road because he came to the set-up a little later than the rest. He was introduced in 1978 – the missing piece of the puzzle, Grizzly Adams wearing number fourteen.

Micko had a personal hand in moulding him. He knew he needed more work than the rest. For a whole year Liston was on the fringe of the panel,

Facing page:
All-Ireland week and an angelic Eoin Liston is grounded in Tralee General Hospital after an appendix operation.
(The Kerryman)

making the cut for training and shedding a few pounds, but never being set free come match day.

O'Dwyer was still keeping a close eye, waiting for the right moment. At the same time Liston landed a job teaching science and biology in Waterville and a few of the panel wondered if O'Dwyer himself didn't have a hand in him getting the job.

'I was a lazy fella and Dwyer made it his business to get me in shape,' he says. 'Down in Waterville, he was like a father to me. Nothing would do him but to be out at something and he'd always rope me into coming along. Every day it was the same. Golf, badminton, football, snooker, darts, cards. Everything you could think of. If we weren't doing something, he wasn't happy. In the winter of '78 we started a keep-fit club. We'd do sessions in the local hall and finish off with a run on the road. There were times when 70 or 80 people would show up and it's still going on below. O'Dwyer knew what he was at, though. Another great move. Because it kept me moving through those months.'

All the work paid off and finally it came, the chance to stretch the legs on the fields of Ireland. It felt like a release to get some game time, because Liston had no form as a Kerry player. He didn't have an underage career to speak of and O'Dwyer only got wind of his existence through Ogie Moran, Liston's good friend. The manager was on the lookout for a strong target man and knew north Kerry was the best place to look for some brawn.

When he asked Ogie if he knew of anybody fitting the description, Ogie gave O'Dwyer directions to Liston's bar in Ballybunion.

It was there he found his man.

When he saw Liston, O'Dwyer's mind sped forward a few years. He knew that with the right approach, the big man would give his team natural penetration. This would lend width and depth to the attack out the field. The final piece, the unchiselled diamond.

Liston had exceptionally fast feet and was comfortable on the ball, something he picked up from his days playing soccer on the beach at home – it was also there he picked up his nickname of Bomber, after his buddies saw he shared the same lazy gait and penchant for goals as the German star, Gerd Muller, aka Der Bomber.

When time came to unleash Kerry's Bomber, the Dublin rivalry was in its pomp. It was the fourth instalment and both teams had intimate knowledge of the other. The previous year, 1977, the semi-final produced what was already labelled the game of the century. The Everest of the affair.

Supporters licked their chops in anticipation of the next chapter but for Kerry, 1978 had added significance, anyway. With two wins for Dublin and one for Kerry, a city victory could copperfasten their hold on the series. O'Dwyer's position as manager was becoming shaky but he didn't entertain thoughts of defeat. Before the game, he made it clear to Liston what was required. Hustle and bustle. Make the presence felt. Create havoc for the Dubs.

Kerry were slow to get out of the traps but Dublin didn't punish them and it was obvious the game wasn't going to reach the heights of the year before. Come half-time, Liston hadn't seen much action and had contributed nothing on the scoreboard. A few heads were turning in the stand, wondering what this giant from Beale had to offer.

'I was playing useless. Dublin really should have beaten us out the gate by half-time that day. John Egan got his goal, then Mikey got that famous chip. But I didn't think it was allowed. To tell you the truth, I went to the dressing room at the break thinking we were a point behind.'

When he came back out, it all fell into place. The ball followed him, he rose his arms and pulled down whoppers. He bagged 3-2 in 35 minutes and a legend was born. Kerry romped home, 5-11 to 0-9, and life had a dreamy quality.

It was 1982 before he knew what it was like to lose a championship game. 'I thought it was never going to stop. Then '82 hit like a brick. Psychologically, I think the pressure did get to us that year. We stopped playing. If you look back at the tape, there were good players who stopped playing, myself included. But if we'd have won that five-in-a-row, we'd never have come back and won three more. We'd all have been getting treatment for alcoholism. It affected a few of us. If we got the five we'd have gone berserk.'

In 1978, Liston was the final ace in the pack, the moon that brought the tide of success. 1975 wasn't a once-off. Potential was being fulfilled and the wrecking ball was gaining momentum.

TJF

Mick Spillane

Football final day, 1998. O'Connell Street is heaving with lily white and maroon shirts, all making their way towards Croke Park and breaking the journey in the bars along the way. For those looking for a ticket, the Gresham is the place to be. Inside, it's a sweaty affair, pints are supped and fingers crossed. Outside, a few more are trying to get lucky. Mick Spillane, with seven All-Ireland medals rattling about in his pocket, is among the masses.

He's without a ticket but wants to make the game to see his former mentor bring Kildare to national glory. He's scrounging and searching and keeping his eyes peeled for anybody to supply that precious ticket. He's just like any supporter who's travelled to Dublin without the currency that will allow them through the turnstiles of Croke Park. He's a nobody. He'd exhausted the usual routes to get that piece of paper. He'd written to the Kerry County Board. Asked them for a ticket. Just one. Explained it was for his own personal use. Told them he wanted to see Micko bring Sam to Kildare. And then he waited for a response. The Friday before the final he'd still heard nothing. So, he rang them up.

'Sorry Mick, no ticket.'

Seven All-Ireland medals. A career dedicated to his club and county but still no ticket from his own county board. No recognition.

Would other sons of Micko have been treated the same way? He wonders.

So that's why he finds himself standing outside the Gresham on All-Ireland Sunday 1998, waiting until a ticket is finally pressed into his palm. Maybe his benefactor recognises his face as the man who wore the number four jersey for Kerry during their golden years. Maybe he doesn't. Mick's not worried either way. Ticket secured, he finds a spot on the Hill and watches as Kildare and Micko are beaten by Galway.

The following Monday, the county board returned his letter along with the cheque he'd sent for that ticket. Today, he'll put the 1998 fiasco down to one of those bad football experiences. But he's kept the letter he sent to Tralee – just as a reminder. Looking back now, the incident has made him realise how things stand; a tidy cameo for his time in the green and gold.

Maybe it's the straw that broke the spine of Kerry's most decorated corner-back. Maybe that's why he's a recovered footballer.

He's sitting in The Fitzwilliam Lawn Tennis Club, surrounded by pictures

Facing page:
Mick Spillane, who made his senior debut in the 1978 All-Ireland final, is pictured between Dublin captain, Tony Hanahoe, and Kerry County Board secretary, Gerald McKenna, after Kerry's 5-11 to 0-9 win.
(The Kerryman)

of smiling club winners, all clad in their dainty tennis whites. He knows of only one other All-Ireland winner who has been a member of this exclusive south Dublin club and that's Jack Lynch, and reckons there's only one other Kerry member besides himself: Judge Hugh O'Flaherty.

These plush surroundings are a good hop from early morning Sunday treks down to Kerry with frost in the air and a draughty train for company.

Having moved to Dublin, there were requests for him to join up with one of the city teams. He resisted and stuck with Templenoe. After all, it was with his Templenoe clansmen on the Kenmare district team that he'd picked up a Kerry County Championship medal at the age of seventeen.

Old ways die hard, he says, and old friends are the best. No way would Spillane give up his time in the jersey of Templenoe.

Anyway, the craic was too good.

Saturday night games were the best. One of the brothers would ring during the week and they'd have the night planned out before any mention of who the opponents were.

'A pint in Waterville, maybe one in Castlecove and back to Sneem before closing time. And oh yeah, it's Waterville we're playing.'

Sunday games were a little trickier.

'I was living in Dalkey,' he says, 'which meant I'd have to leave home before eight o'clock on the Sunday morning for a game. I'd travel across the city and get the 8.45am train, so I was in Killarney by one o'clock. I'd have someone meet me at the station and bring me to the game.'

One particular Sunday morning, Templenoe were playing Dromid Pearses in a league match of little relevance. As usual, Spillane jumped off the train in Killarney into the waiting car and sat back for the bumpy journey over Macgillycuddy's Reeks.

'I grabbed a quick juice and sandwich in Fossa and we tore off to Dromid. Got to the field, played the game and one of the Dromid players was going back to Killarney so I got a spin in his Fiat Panda. The lads were going out for a few after-match pints so I said, "Good luck and I'll be home in Dublin before ye."'

With Spillane riding shotgun, the Panda nosed north towards Killarney but trouble struck at Ballyaghcasheen on the crest of the Reeks.

Tyre punctured. Out the passengers got and lifted the Panda on its side as the driver fixed the spare into place.

'I was saying to myself, "Jesus, I'll never make the train back." I had to get to Dublin. I had a wife and kids to go home to.'

Those were the days of late evenings to Heuston. He'd see other lads still in their gear, hopping out of cars and on to the train at Killarney and Rathmore. Spillane would wander from one carriage to the next for the craic and the gossip, and before the Silvermines came into view, he'd have all the day's club results. A travelling fraternity of Kerry footballers.

'Great times,' he says. 'Without a doubt.'

After the first great day, he could have given it all up and gone out at the top. Kerry appearances: one. All-Ireland medals: one. His debut came in 1978 in the All-Ireland final. Micko threw him in at the deep end and not a safety jacket in sight. He was to mark the elusive Bobby Doyle and the papers gave him no chance.

All-Ireland day came and the morning brought a head full of nerves. Brendan Lynch, former player and then team doctor, noticed Spillane in his high-strung state.

'He gave me a few brandies with a drop of port and said, "That'll sort you out." And to be fair, it did. I was ready for Bobby Doyle, or anyone else for that matter.'

Spillane's critics were proved wrong; he stayed with Doyle for the full game and kept the shackles on the danger man.

Years of commuting from Dublin to club and county games were to follow and, exiled in the city, he had to pound the Belfield grass with Micheál Ó Muircheartaigh as whistle man.

'Micheál was one of the best man managers I knew and he'd always have myself and Jacko in top shape. He'd have us doing 50 sit-ups some nights and when I was older he'd come over to me and whisper, "Mick, you're getting on a bit, sure, you only do 30." And then you'd want to do 70 to prove him wrong.'

Years after Kerry's name had been scratched onto Sam in 1978, Mick Spillane paid a visit to an old college library and its dusty stash of microfilm. He went back to look at newspaper reports during the week of the 1978 final.

'Before the match they said I wouldn't manage at all and, to be honest, I did all right. But the thing was, in the after-match reports, not one journalist turned around and gave me credit.'

It was to be like that until he walked away from the game with those seven medals jangling in his pocket. Mick was the quiet guy in the corner, the one who carried out his duties with zero fuss. He wasn't flamboyant with the foot or the tongue and so would never fill the column inches. And anyway, he had a brother who could keep the sports pages filled from September until Christmas.

'I would safely say I'm definitely the worst player to win seven All-Ireland medals.' He pauses. 'But I suppose there aren't a whole load more to compare me with.' And then he smiles.

TJF

Tom Spillane

Tom Spillane was two when his father died. Older brothers, Pat and Mick, were his father figures and that meant football.

He got it from his mother too. She was one of the Lynes from Clenagh in Killarney. Her brothers, Jackie, Denny and Fr Mikey, won All-Irelands. The Spillanes were destined for better. They all won All-Irelands on the same day and did it more than once too.

The father figures were first. Tom was thirteen in 1975 and in the Hogan Stand. Mick was eighteen and on the minor team. Pat was nineteen and on the senior team and he lifted Sam Maguire.

Pat was a superstar, Mick was quiet and Tom was still growing, finding his place.

That day in 1975 Tom climbed the wire on to the field just as Pat was told he would be collecting the cup instead of Mickey Ned.

Tom wasn't looking for Pat – instead he slumped to the ground and harvested clumps of Croke Park. Those clumps made it all the way back to Templenoe.

He had those pieces of Croke Park for many years and they inspired. He had pieces of Croke Park but Pat and Mick had more – so had his uncles. They were part of Croke Park.

Whether this was a help or hindrance to his football, Tom doesn't know. He thought about them all the time and it was pressure, constant pressure to emulate his family peers but Tom battled to block it out.

'I had to want it for myself, not just to emulate others. The fellas on the Kerry team were people I idolised, fellas that I got to write their autographs on my hand and swear afterwards I'd never rub it out. I did that. It was hero worship. John O'Keeffe was my real idol and suddenly, I found myself on the same team as him.'

It happened in 1981 when Tom played in the first round of the championship against Clare in Listowel. Nineteen years old and in the number nine jersey – playing midfield for Kerry alongside Jacko.

'I didn't have time to think about it. Sean Walsh was injured. I played a club match the night before in Tralee, so I had no idea what was coming. If they told me to carry the water bottles around I would have been delighted.'

Tom didn't play any other championship match that year. Closer to the water bottles than the team but still part of it.

Facing page:
Tom Spillane became an All-Ireland man like older brothers, Pat and Mick, and uncles, Fr Mikey, Denny and Jackie, before him.
(Shelagh Honan)

1982 was different. Man-of-the-match in the Munster final replay. Played well in the All-Ireland final and kicked three points, but the point Tom didn't kick still hangs in the air. Haunts him.

Seamus Darby's goal was scored and Tom had the ball in hand. He takes up commentary as he moves down along the Hogan Stand a quarter of a century ago.

'I remember,' he says, 'I won't be allowed forget. I was told by 25,000 people afterwards, "Why didn't you look up? There was somebody standing on the edge of the square." Bomber, was it? I don't know what I did, I went for a point or something and didn't score. That was it.'

Potential hero to zero. He slumped to the Croke Park ground for the second time. Tom Spillane was lucky though, he had time on his side. He was only twenty when the cynics barked he wasn't a forward. Micko must have listened because by 1984 he was a back. Above all, he was hungry.

'There was great appetite in '84. We got a slap in the face in '82 and another in '83 – we weren't going to get caught again. We put in an awful amount of work and that was really shown early in the season when there were two Kerry teams out, playing challenge games and opening pitches.

'I remember well, some time in May, when one team went to Corofin in Galway and another team went to Annascaul. The Annascaul game was at 3pm and the Corofin game was at 7pm where I played and made my debut at centre-back.

'Pat was playing in Annascaul. I remember coming home late and with the way RTÉ shut down late at night, the only station I could get was the BBC World Service. I was listening to the BBC at 3.30 in the morning as I drove up Moll's Gap, where you turn right for a short-cut down home.

'A car was crashed on top of a rock and who was coming out of it only Pat and a friend. They were after being in Annascaul all day and were pie-eyed. The match had gone well for Pat. It was ironic, I coming from as far away as Galway and they were only in Annascaul and I having to bring them home.'

Pat was celebrating. His right knee had been rebuilt. There were pints in Dan Foley's, Brosnan's, Kennedy's, the South Pole Inn and much of the way home.

It was Kerry's drink culture; when they drank there was no moderation, but Tom's answer was not to drink at all. He had no pints that night, he was afraid to. Afraid of Micko. Afraid drink might come between him and making the team.

'I remember Dwyer coming up to myself and Ger Lynch. He was scratching his nose and passing within two inches of you and looking for the smell. "Easy on the drink and the parties lads," he'd say. "What do you mean, I don't drink," I'd roar back.'

Ger Lynch backs this up. '"I hear ye're party boys," he'd say to myself and Tom. Tom got an award in Dublin one day and I went up with him. He was so committed that after the do, he went off to Micheál Ó Muircheartaigh's training in UCD with his brother Mick. I went drinking. The next time we gathered for a Kerry session, Dwyer put Tom through hell. He thought he was on the beer.'

Ger Lynch and Tom Spillane were great pals, coming on to the panel together in 1981 and, straight away, jetting to the other end of the world on a trip to Australia and because it was Tom's first time on an aeroplane, he even had to get a passport.

'This is all I ever wanted – playing for Kerry was my prayers answered. Going to Australia with them, I was going around the place starstruck. It was hard to believe I was part of this scene.

'It was great but the greatest day was probably 1984 when myself and Ger Lynch had a plan on All-Ireland day. We decided to stand very close to the Dubs we were marking before the game. I was on Tommy Conroy, Ger was on Barney Rock. There was no belting but the plot was to sing the National Anthem as loud as we could into their ears to put the fear of God into them. Neither of us were great singers but they must have thought we were wired to the moon.'

It was the same for Ireland in the Compromise Rules. The highlights for Tom weren't the dust-ups in Ireland or Down Under but a Gaelic football challenge against an Australasian selection in 1986.

A few years later, the All-Blacks Rugby team was touring Ireland and on the trip, outside-centre Bernie McCahill said one of the highlights of his sporting career was marking Tom Spillane in Gaelic football. Tom went shoulder to shoulder with Zin Zan Brooke the same day.

These are the small things he remembers.

JÓM

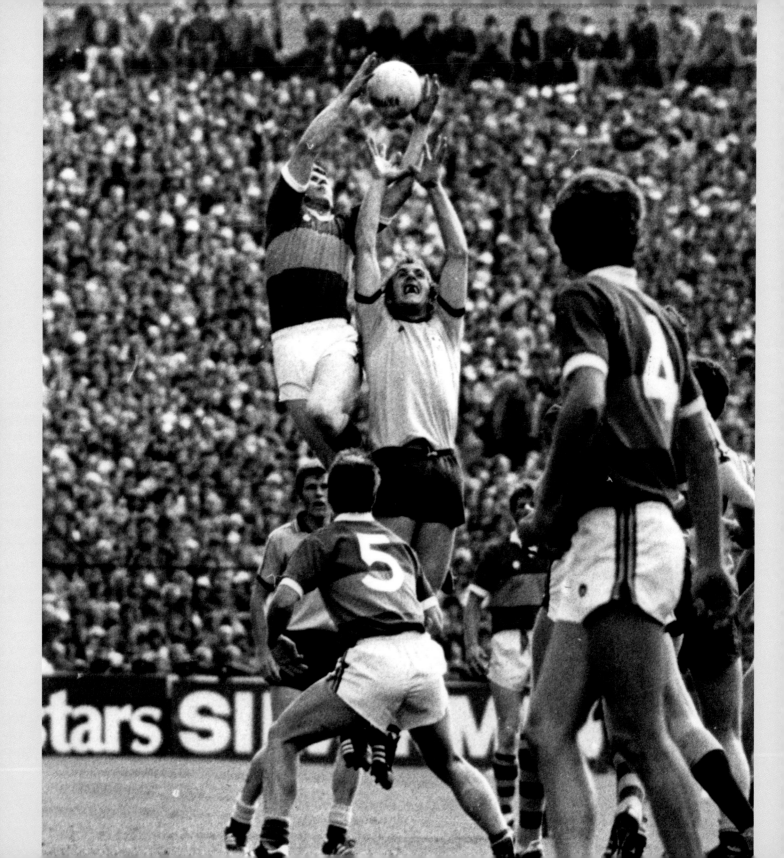

Sean Walsh

Six weeks before the Munster final of 1987, Sean Walsh was out on Tralee Golf course with Dr Arthur Spring.

Something about Sean's walk didn't seem right with the doctor. He was dragging his leg ever so slightly in a way that suggested there was a problem with his hip.

So, Dr Spring advised him to go see a specialist and investigate the matter further. Sean had an x-ray done and the look on the face of the specialist told him all he needed to know. Severe arthritis. He was 31.

In a way, Walsh sensed the news was in the post. For the previous three years his joints were worryingly stiff after games, his limbs heavy as lead. Turning sharply on hard ground was becoming impossible and the x-ray simply confirmed his fears.

Six weeks before the provincial final of 1987, he decided it wasn't worth any more torture. His body had been put through enough. It was time to pack it in. For the past decade, he had given himself to Micko and his methods and those were different times.

Every match day brought its own familiar routine. Final whistle. Shower. Change. Out for a few pints. Unlike today, there was no warm down, no ice bath and essentially, no recovery for the body. Something had to give.

In 2002, Walsh finally had his hip replaced. It's a procedure John O'Keeffe also underwent. Mike Sheehy still suffers the odd shot of pain in the knee, so does Pat Spillane and Tommy Doyle was plagued with achilles tendonitis.

It's the price tag that came with the lifestyle of a training addict.

Every Christmas now, the Tralee boys from the Golden Years will get together in town to sup a few pints and spin the odd yard. Inevitably, talk turns to Micko and those fierce, unyielding sessions of the past. At a certain point Ogie Moran will pipe up and proclaim that O'Dwyer's men trained on their own every winter just so they could train under O'Dwyer the following spring. Nobody wanted to go in cold at the start of the year. If Sam was secured, it was easy to spend a few months basking in the plaudits, lapping up the free flowing porter, but venture too far past the line and you ran the risk of coming in for O'Dwyer's special treatment.

An extra pound, an inch added to the gut? Micko would have that ran off in

Facing page:
Kevin Coleman's iconic image of Sean Walsh soaring above Brian Mullins for possession in the 1979 All-Ireland final.
(The Kerryman)

337

a couple of torturous sessions.

They laugh now at the code of silence they kept at the beginning.

It might be November in Tralee. Seanie is walking through town and he spots Mikey.

'Are you doing any bit on your own, Mike?'

'Nah … Yourself?'

'Not a tap.'

The reality was, Sheehy could be out on the sand of Banna running a few miles three times a week. Walsh could be nipping off at lunchtime to keep himself in shape. Ogie was right. Training to train.

After a while, things became more organised among the Tralee boys when John O'Keeffe arranged extra-curricular sessions on Banna Strand. The lads would march out there, eyes red and heads fuzzy, on Christmas Day or New Year's Day to play a game of soccer and click in a couple of miles just to get rid of the festive toxins. It made sense.

There was always competition and Micko stoked the atmosphere. Competition against yourself, against the man next to you.

'You were genuinely afraid of losing your place on the team,' says Walsh, 'and you'd do anything to keep your jersey.'

In 1978, Sheehy damaged his knee for the first time. A normal, every game knock. He continued to play and train at a ferocious pace and four years later, he had to be seen by a surgeon. He went under the knife and was warned not to run on it for at least a month but five days later, he was back out training with Kerry.

The most gifted forward in the country and he's pushing to keep his manager impressed. That was the attitude O'Dwyer instilled in his players. Living with a few niggling aches and pains was part of the deal.

'His [O'Dwyer's] training was fairly tough going,' Walsh says in his own, understated way. The night after night sessions have now seeped into folklore. Over 30 on the trot in 1975. 28 back-to-back in 1984. They were fuelled with a real intensity. Wire to wire in Fitzgerald Stadium at full pelt. Head to head with another man from one goal to the next, the tongue hanging out with a few dozen yards to go.

Winter training was the most monotonous. Constant laps. Seven clicks of O'Rahillys pitch was exactly a mile. O'Dwyer had it measured from an ESB pole on one side of the field to an upright on the other.

The year would kick off with a jaunty 40 laps. The next week, O'Dwyer would reduce it to 30, then twenty and fifteen, all the way down until the stamina had been worn in. O'Dwyer would time each run and compare it with the previous night.

All going well, the intensity raised a notch the first day of March and, throughout the season, it was maintained.

'If you weren't up to a certain standard by the middle of March, you knew you were going to be killed,' says Eoin Liston.

It didn't end there. After a successful Munster final, the players would head for the showers, breathing easily again. Into this steaming shower room, O'Dwyer would march. There would be a little congratulation but then, they knew, the bad news was coming. Four or five names would be called out. These were his 'Heavy Pets'. By the time the civvies were back on, it was obvious how little the Munster final meant.

The 'Heavy Pets' were back two nights later for special training. Punishment for a pint here or there, or a few pounds that still clung to the belly. Walsh, along with Liston and Sheehy, would often find his way into these sessions.

For the players, it was a long road. More often than not, the season craned its neck well into autumn and the same faces and legs were called upon. Players were pushing harder, digging deeper. Sacrificing.

'Towards the end, it was almost like flogging a dead horse,' says Walsh.

Without the training programmes and modern injury prevention methods, some were destined to leave the field with permanent battle wounds.

'There was very little stretching or warming up. I'm sure O'Dwyer might look back on it now and say he made some mistakes with the type of training but in reality nobody knew the long term effects of training hard back then. Those long term sessions are bound to take their toll over the years. We picked up a bit from the PE teachers in the team but that was it. Nothing scientific or anything like that.'

The hip still twists and turns the correct way. Those hard, long sessions are water under the bridge now but they were a ferry to success back then.

TJF

Ambrose O'Donovan

The dressing room in 1983 is an eerie scene that's still scratched into his memory. Twenty men, heads in hands, all silent and wondering if the end had come.

'I'll never forget the reaction in the dressing room at Páirc Uí Chaoimh after Tadhg Murphy's goal. It's something I wouldn't wish on any player. For the second time in less than a year, the team had been caught by a late goal. It's still the worst I've seen players take a beating.'

Ambrose O'Donovan had just edged into the senior panel. He was on the bench that Munster final Sunday, settling into the set-up when Murphy's goal hit like a bullet to the side. Even though he wasn't on the field, the loss hurt the Gneeviguilla man more than most.

In O'Donovan's part of the world, deep in the marrow of Sliabh Luachra, the River Blackwater is known as the great divide. It laps along the Kerry/Cork border, separating two football communities. And the Munster final defines summer happiness for those within earshot of the river's gush.

In the years that followed '83, after he solidified his place on the first fifteen, the Munster final was the bull's-eye for O'Donovan. He produced thunder and lightening.

There's a photograph from 1991, capturing him in the hot cloud of battle, which shows his pure, unbridled intensity for these games. He's in the air, rising towards the sky, arms stretched, veins rippling in his body, eyes fixed on the ball, teeth clinched tight.

Beside him is Cork's Shay Fahy, straining, inching, flapping for the ball. But O'Donovan is closer, he's jumping higher because he knows what it means and he wins the fight for possession. O'Donovan, simply, wants it more than Fahy. Come Munster final day, he wanted it more than anybody.

After the empty season of 1983, when centenary year finally rolled around, O'Donovan was named captain. It came as a surprise. Just turned 22, he hadn't started a game before that year's meeting with Cork – a thumb injury kept him out. Now, suddenly, he was midfield and the first man behind the band.

'Coming from the border area, it stirred me pulling on the Kerry jersey for that game. It was probably the most important day for me. There were nerves. It was frightening, absolutely frightening, just making the team. Being captain was the furthest thing from my mind.'

Facing page:
Ambrose O'Donovan home in triumph in 1984 with future GAA president Sean Kelly playing his part in the celebrations.
(The Kerryman)

The stakes were high that year with those late-goal nightmares still fresh in the mind. Darby's in 1982 prevented the five-in-a-row and Murphy's in 1983 halted the county winning nine back to back in Munster. Immortality was always just within touching distance. To attain it meant starting from scratch and putting together another big run over a number of years.

They began training in October of 1983, just after the All-Ireland final between Dublin and Galway. A full year before the prizes were given out. It was long range planning and Kerry were setting their sights on something huge.

'It was clear straight away that O'Dwyer wasn't taking any prisoners whatsoever. It was do or die. He was under pressure himself at the time because of '82 and '83. Now, O'Dwyer would always give a break to the club but in '84, every player's club took second place.'

They were building up reserves again on cold nights, pounding the sandy turf at Strand Road. Endless laps were clocked and O'Donovan still remembers those 28 aching, marathon sessions on the trot that April.

'It's one thing that really bugs me when people say, "You wouldn't last the training these days." Well, I'd like to know if the fellas today could stick the training we done. It was hard, hard training. Laps and laps with your tongue hanging out. There were mornings I wouldn't be able to stand up my legs ached so much. The wife could tell you that. I'd get out of bed and the legs would buckle.

'And you didn't question O'Dwyer. Never. Jimmy Deenihan came to training one night, maybe ten minutes late. We'd about two or three laps done. Still just warming up. Jimmy comes out onto the field and Micko is straight over. "We start training at a quarter to, Jimmy. Not at seven. See you tomorrow." And that was Deenihan, a senior player. Gone out the gate. Another night, Páidí [Ó'Sé] came in late after crashing his car on the way. Somehow, Micko got wind of it. So, Sé comes in and Micko just gives him one lap of the field. "We train at 6.45, Páidí." That would instil something in you. It didn't matter who you were.'

In O'Dwyer's world, every crime had a corresponding punishment. In 1985, the weekend before the Munster final, Annauscaul were due to play Lispole in the league. If Annauscaul lost, they were relegated to Division Three.

'O'Dwyer asked me not to play for Annascaul,' says Tommy Doyle. 'I said, "Mick I have to play." So I did and we won. I knew he'd get wind of it by the Sunday, so I rang him up on the Saturday night. "Mick, I played."

"I know well you played."

"Look, if you have to kick my arse over it, fair enough." He didn't drop me for the Munster final but I came in on the Tuesday night and I'll tell you one thing, I crawled off that pitch.'

In 1984, the regime led to September and Dublin but one week before the All-Ireland final, O'Donovan picked up a hip injury during training in Killarney. Doubts surrounded his fitness. He woke six days before the game and this time he definitely couldn't stand up. His hip was on fire.

That week was given over to therapy, twice each day with masseur Owen McCrohan at the Park Place Hotel in Killarney.

Saturday came and the treatment had worked. O'Donovan was fit and the last training session of that long year was light and easy in Killarney. They boarded the train at 2.10pm and a few hours later, they were at the Grand Hotel in Malahide.

With darkness cloaking north Dublin and the lights winking across the harbour, the team took a walk along the beach in Malahide. It was the ritual before the big game and O'Donovan was getting acquainted with it, one of O'Dwyer's little pre-match *piseoga*.

The manager moved through the group, offering nuggets of advice but never really mentioning the opposition. Instilling belief in his team. When the cold sting became too much, they made their way back to the hotel for the final team talk. Shuffling along in total darkness.

'There's one thing I'll never forget about that night,' says O'Donovan, 'When we were going in for our last talk, a fellow approached O'Dwyer in the foyer and says, "Micko, are ye going to win tomorrow?" O'Dwyer keeps walking, very serious, and says, "What do you think brought us up, boy?" I heard him say that and just thought to myself: lethal.'

The manager brought the mind games a step further. The team-talk was arranged for a small room in the hotel and when the players walked in, that week's headlines were plastered across the walls: 'Kerry Team Over The Hill', 'End Of The Line'. A psychological bullet years before the tactic became the norm in English soccer dressing rooms.

'Sometimes, you might actually feel you were in dread of him. I might take a cigarette for the winter but I'd never, ever, smoke in front of him. We'd be slow to take a drink in front of him, even after a match. You'd know well he'd run the shit out of you if he saw you with a pint.'

The feeling lingers. At functions these days, some of O'Dwyer's men are still reluctant to drink if he's in their company. It was the atmosphere he created. Respect rather than fear. Micko's way.

TJF

Tommy Doyle

At first they thought Micko might be up to his old tricks when he showed them the stopwatch. They reckoned he might be goading them, trying to wring the last ounce out of them as usual.

'4:12,' the stopwatch read. A few seconds above the magic number.

Micko had them running the measured mile at Strand Road again, in the field they knew as the Sandpit. Tommy Doyle had just clocked a serious time and Ger Lynch was right behind him. Had it been any man but Doyle, they'd have been sure Micko was grinding some angle.

Sometimes, he might add a few seconds to Pat Spillane's sprint times just for the reaction he'd get. Or he might pit Eoin Liston against Ger Power in a head-to-head if the Bomber wasn't pulling his weight.

With Doyle though, the players knew the outer reaches of his athletic ability and the look on Micko's face told them he wasn't ball-hopping this time. Doyle was pushing 30 years of age and he was within touching distance of the four-minute mile on a rough, sandy surface.

It was 1983 and all the stops had just been pulled out. After the heartache of the previous two years, the dust was let settle for a few months. By October, the players didn't know for sure what Mick O'Dwyer's plans were. Some believed he was about to retire as county manager, others reckoned he would stick around. They were still waiting for some sign when the call was put out.

'I was home late one night and Micko rang up. We were all curious to see what the story was because nobody had heard a word from him since July. "Are you around next Saturday?" he says to me. "I am."

"Will you be in Ballybunion at two o'clock?"

"I will." And I suppose to this day, if Dwyer called that squad together and told us to go up training on the top of Carrauntoohil, we'd do it.'

They made it out to Ballybunion that Saturday, a wet, windy, miserable October day and played a half hour soccer game before the weather had them retreating for a shower and lunch at the Red Cliff Hotel.

'Dwyer sat us down. "I've just watched the All-Ireland and if those fuckers in Dublin can win it with twelve men, I'd back us with fifteen." He really wanted us to have another big cut at it. He wanted to win the league, the Centenary Cup and the All-Ireland and we ended up doing that. After the talk, we had a big

345

beer-up and a big sing-song. Dwyer buying porter for us and that, in itself, told you he really wanted us onside.'

The following Tuesday, they were back training. The curtain was up and the show was back on the road.

'Nobody missed two nights in the whole season. There were no holds barred. No messing. There was a bit of freshness again. [Pat] Spillane was back for the league final after his knee problems, Johnno [Keeffe] was gone and [Seanie] Walsh was in full-back for the championship. Ambrose [O'Donovan] was midfield and we were flying.'

O'Donovan remembers that team meeting in Ballybunion as his introduction to the big stage. 'He [O'Dwyer] told a lot of home truths,' says O'Donovan. 'He said the team had under-achieved the two years before and we were the best county in Ireland. We could only beat ourselves.'

O'Dwyer had never gathered them for collective training as early but it didn't bother Doyle that much. He had massive reserves to call on. Before he made his name as a Kerry minor, Villanova, the Pennsylvania college of athletic excellence where Ronnie Delany and Eamonn Coghlan were schooled, had come knocking.

As a teenager, Doyle was a gold medalist at the All-Ireland Vocational Schools Championships in the mile event and word of his talents reached a Villanova scout. The American was recruiting talent in Ireland and phoned up Doyle at school in Tralee.

'Donie O'Sullivan was my English and history teacher at the Vocational School and he was a god. Simple as that. This was 1972 and he was still playing with Kerry. I was about seventeen and I'm told by another teacher the Villanova fella wants to see me, that he's going to come down from Dublin that evening. I said not to bother. I was going kicking ball with Donie after school. It's what we looked forward to. Catching those whizzing free kicks, 70 or 80 yards out the pitch.

'At that time, athletics was a different scene. We hadn't heard of spikes. I ran in green and gold socks and a pair of football boots.

'The first pair I got was in John Dowling's shop for £2.50. Myself and my brother called in. On the way out, he called us back. "Look at those." He was showing us a pair of boots inside the window. New World Cup boots. "Mick O'Connell wears those," he says. They had a price tag of £12 and all the way home to Annauscaul we're talking about those boots.

'Myself and Dowling often spoke about it after. This was when I'd be coming out of Fitzgerald Stadium with ten pairs of free boots around my neck. "Doyler, did you ever think you'd be getting those for free when I showed them to you long ago?" And when my son, Kevin, was born, right after the 1986 All-Ireland final, Dowling was the first man to the house. He had a pair of blue baby boots. "Doyler," he says, "I hope the boy plays for Strand Road some day."'

Days before that visit, Kerry had eaten away at Tyrone by playing from memory. Doyle was captain and the week before the game, his leg was plastered up. His achilles tendons were acting up again.

Other players were carrying knocks as well. Páidí Ó Sé and Sean Walsh. Jack O'Shea had woken up that morning with a huge temperature.

'I don't know how the man togged off,' says Doyle. 'Then Ambrose hurt his ankle very early in the game and I'm looking around at a load of players hobbling. The walking wounded. But we didn't panic. We got in at half-time and Micko was calm enough. Three points down. The Lucozade bottle might have been rattled off the table but that was about it.'

After the break, things immediately got worse. Paudge Quinn goaled for Tyrone, they led by six before Kevin McCabe stepped up to a penalty that could have put them out of sight. He fired it over the bar.

'Then Spillane caught fire. Sheehy as well. Not taking from Tyrone but there was complacency on our part. Tyrone were a Division three team that year and we would have been confident. Put it this way, if we were seven or eight points up with 25 minutes left, there was no way Tyrone were coming back at us.'

In the summer of 2007, he made it up to the twenty-fifth anniversary of Offaly's 1982 All-Ireland victory over Kerry. Seamus Darby invited him to the celebrations and he didn't have to think twice about the answer. The two have become close over the years. Darby stays with Doyle at his home in Ballincollig whenever he's in Cork. They golf and socialise together. Doyle made it to the midlands a few years back for the opening of Darby's new bar.

For years, Doyle backed away from answering the one question that has followed him around, but he finally let the guard down at the celebrations. Pulled a few of the Offaly boys in close and they discussed the famous incident in the dying stages of that game in 1982. They talked about it for real and openly.

Doyle's opinion stays in that little huddle though. Not for public consumption. A little corner of the Kerry story that remains coated in mystery.

TJF

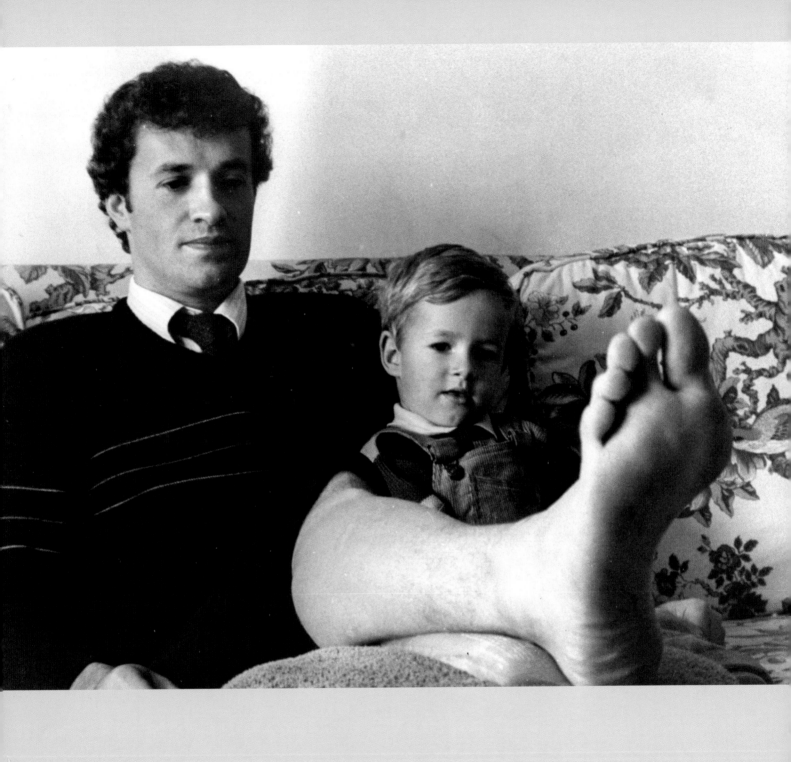

Mikey Sheehy

Awful. Terrible. Shanking frees all over the field. Nothing going right. 1987. Munster final replay.

To top it off, Mikey Sheehy is captain as well and now he's out there wilting in the Killarney sunshine, his head drooping like a sick rose.

A week before, he kept the life in Kerry. Netted with seconds on the clock and the fading corpse carried on breathing. For the replay, he couldn't buy a break but there was a simple answer – Ger Lynch's boots.

Towards the end of the drawn game, a Cork back stepped on Sheehy's boots and split them open. It was like splicing his heart, because these weren't any old shoes. These were the classic Adidas World Cup boots made from soft kangaroo leather; they were kneaded over the years to perfectly wrap around his feet.

And, as soon as the whistle blew his task was obvious. Find a replacement and fast. He scoured the county. Rang sports stores, asked favours from friends, called up players from other counties and still nothing. Not a sniff.

'Mikey, what's the big deal?' they'd tell him. 'They're just a pair of boots, boy. Who do you think you are, Cinderella?'

But they didn't understand and slowly, he was resigned to wearing his second pair, a firm, clunky model.

The evening before the replay, there was a light training session in Fitzgerald Stadium. He was changing into his surrogate pair when, in the clutter of the dressing floor, two boots caught his eye. He picked them up. An exact replica of his own lost treasures. Bingo!

He held them to the light and asked who owned these fine specimens of boots. Ger Lynch called back.

It was Lynch's spare set and he said he wouldn't be needing them, so Sheehy tried them on and they fit. He claimed them for Sunday's game and took them onto the field for a test run. They worked a treat.

That night, as he drove back to Tralee, he wanted to make sure Lynch's boots would definitely do the trick. Seeing as he was captain the next day, it wouldn't do to leave anything to chance.

So, when he reached home he parked his car, grabbed two balls and wandered down to Austin Stack Park. He kicked a few points, placed a few frees and the boots felt like the real deal. He smiled the smile of the content. The day

Facing page:
*Father and son –
Mikey Sheehy at home
with his son, Michael
Junior, after injury
ruled him out of the
1984 All-Ireland final.*
(The Kerryman)

349

was falling away and Sheehy was alone and happy and splitting the posts.

Around the same time, the Kerry players later heard, Larry Tompkins had climbed the boundary around Fitzgerald Stadium to kick a few practice frees of his own. He wasn't familiar with the Killarney ground and he, too, wouldn't leave anything to chance.

Sunday came and the Kerry captain led his side out. He kicked some more frees during the warm-up but slowly, it was dawning on him that something just didn't seem right. He had one or two shanks before it clicked. The grass had been cut since the previous day and the studs on Lynch's boots didn't suit. Sheehy was struggling to get under the ball. The parade was called and his head was a circus of confusion. 'Should I stay out here or break away and go get a pair of multi-studs?'

'I decided to continue in the parade,' he says, 'and this was such a silly, novice mistake. I thought to myself, "If fellows see me going back in just before the start of the game, how will it look? They'll think I'm gone mad." I should have sent one of the lads on the line in to get me another pair but I wasn't thinking.'

His first test came soon. A free kick 30 yards out. Slightly on the stand side. A handy one.

'I topped it. A brutal, brutal effort. And from then on, it got worse. I missed about five easy frees in the first half. In the dressing room at half-time, Ger Lynch looks over at me and says, "Get them fuckin' boots off you." He was the only one that knew about the set-up. I hadn't told anybody else.'

Sheehy asked to be taken off dead ball duty and Eoin Liston was handed the task of chief free-taker.

'The Bomber was kicking very well in training and he had this free, start of the second-half, about 21 yards out. You wouldn't mind having a cut at it. But this was the worst free I'd ever seen. It barely made the end line, just trickled over. And there was Micko roaring at me, "Sheehy. Jesus Christ. Why didn't you take it?"'

In their hearts, they sensed it after the game. The end. They gathered and crawled the pubs of Killarney and Tralee and looking back on it now it feels like a wake to him.

'I'd have hit the beer fairly hard on the Monday and Tuesday as well. I was shattered after what I'd done on Sunday. I was a disaster. I let everyone down. To be honest, in a way we were lucky to even get a replay. Injuries were starting to get the better of fellas by then and how many times can you go to the well? After the drawn match in Cork, we were winding down, thinking we did ok to get a draw and Micko comes tearing into the dressing room like a lunatic. He made a show of us that we got caught. We'd scored a goal and gone up a point really late and after that John Kerins took a quick kick and we hadn't even tried to block him taking it fast. They got a point from that to level. He [O'Dwyer] tore into Powerie [Ger Power] after for celebrating and swinging off the crossbar when we got the goal.'

Endgame came a week later. The tank was running on empty and Sheehy clocked up the most mileage.

From 1978 up to the '87 Munster final, he started and finished every championship game for Kerry bar one – the '84 All-Ireland final. A few years back, Micheál Ó Muircheartaigh collared him at a function and asked him who racked up the most minutes during the Golden Years. Sheehy genuinely didn't know it was himself.

'I missed '84 because of the knee. I'd worn it out. The doctor said it had more potholes than the road to Knocknagoshel. Deep down, I knew I wouldn't make the final but Micko gave me every chance and Jesus, I tried everything. Swimming in Banna, water from Lourdes. I was praying and I had the mother saying Novenas, but no good. But '84 was the start of the second phase. To come back and win the three-in-a-row was better than getting the five [in a row]. It showed the football and the desire was there. There's no way we'd have got the three [in a row] if we won in '82 and fellas can argue with me if they like. The same hunger wouldn't be there. Not a hope. We went on the beer for a month or two after '81. Can you imagine what we'd have been like if we won in '82? We'd have stayed at it for the year.'

TJF

Charlie Nelligan

Charlie Nelligan's first touch as a Kerry senior footballer was to pick the ball out of the net. Jimmy Keaveney's bullet went high to his left and into the roof of the rigging at the Canal End in 1976.

Nelligan later developed a theory about penalties into the Canal End – that most of them were missed. '95 per cent,' he says, 'because if you looked at the old Croke Park from the middle of the pitch, there was a mound on the penalty spot. It teed the ball up for the penalty taker, they were running uphill and most of them missed them high.'

Sadly, from Nelligan's perspective, Jimmy Keaveney was in the other five per cent. Didn't miss and so Nelligan had an ignominious beginning to a fifteen-year career between the sticks. It wasn't supposed to be like this.

His first time with the Kerry seniors was twelve months before. In 1975 Nelligan won a minor All-Ireland but after the game he went straight to the senior dressing room.

'I landed in the old timber dressing room under the old Cusack and Mickey Ned was standing up on a table roaring at the team. I wasn't prepared for it at all.

'I was even less prepared the following year. I never knew Paudie O'Mahoney was injured. There was a bit of a doubt about him beforehand and John O'Shea had a piece in *The Irish Press* saying, "Nelligan Ready To Go In". I thought it was bullshit. It was a total shock when I had to go in for Mahoney – and then picking Keaveney's ball out of the net. Awful.'

Nelligan got used to the feeling.

1982: 'The Darby goal – there's a lot of talk about did he or didn't he [push Tommy Doyle] and you won't get it from me whether he did or he didn't. I don't want to talk about it.'

He pauses for a few seconds, then comes the u-turn.

'One of those things,' he says of the goal, 'he just stuck it. It would have made a beautiful point. It was a daze to me. When the ball hit the net and I got up off the ground and was going back to pick up the ball, the spray from the net was hitting me on the head. It was an awful feeling altogether.

'I was in a such a daze that when I took the kickout, I placed the ball on the 14 yard line, not the 21. I didn't know where I was. It was a shit kickout and Gerry Carroll should have scored a point off it. I didn't open my mouth for three

Facing page:
*Charlie Nelligan,
in yellow, marching
behind his captain
Páidí Ó Sé in 1985.*
(Sportsfile)

353

weeks after. I've never watched the video of the game. I still have visions of it though.

'I was so close to getting it. I felt the breeze on my fingers as the ball flashed by. It was 2 inches – had I got a finger to it, the ball might have hit the bar. It was total devastation after the game. I remember a local publican came up to me. He put his arms around me and he was bawling his eyes out and thanking us for all the years. The tears were rolling down his face.'

He talks like a man who has replayed the moment over and over but 1982 might never have happened for Nelligan. He was 25 that year with four All-Ireland medals. The same year Ronnie Whelan made a name for himself winning a Division One League medal with Liverpool.

Nelligan thought of Whelan a lot back then. Whelan was Home Farm like himself and Nelligan could have gone across the channel like Whelan but chance kept him at home.

Shortly after seeing Mickey Ned up on the table in 1975, he enrolled in the College of Catering on Kevin Street to learn his baking trade. Soccer fanatic Shay Humphries, who was also in Kevin Street, dragged Nelligan on the number 16 bus out to Home Farm's ground at Whitehall on the old airport road. 'Training with us will keep your eye in for goalkeeping,' said Shay.

Nelligan loved Home Farm – loved the smaller dimensions of the pitch and the box that allowed keepers come way off their line to bark instructions, boss other players. He took that back to the GAA fields.

At Home Farm one thing led to another and from training with the reserves, he was soon on the League of Ireland team.

'The regular goalie broke his leg and I was at home one night. Next thing, I saw my mugshot on the television with the news that I'd be playing for Home Farm's first team. I got my chance and held onto my spot. Trevor Anderson was the goalkeeping coach there and he taught me a lot.

'When I was with the first team I went for a few trials and was picked on the Irish amateur squad that was bidding to qualify for the Moscow Olympics. The team was chosen the weekend Jack O'Shea got married and I was at the wedding. There was a breakdown with telephones because of some post and telegraphs strike so they couldn't contact me.

'What happened was, some asshole here in Kerry said I wasn't available. The FAI then got another goalkeeper and never asked me again. Another time I was supposed to go for a trial in England – it was all arranged but it clashed with a north Kerry League match so I played for the Desmonds instead of going. Ronnie Whelan went over around the same time.'

Ronnie Whelan and Charlie Nelligan went their separate ways. Ronnie made money from football; Nelligan's money came from baking bread.

In his college days, Nelligan held down a job to pay the rent. He juggled college, the job and football. On Fridays, after classes in Kevin Street, he'd catch a few hours' sleep and then begin the graveyard shift in a nearby bakery at 8 or 9pm. Finishing at 6am, he'd hop into his car and drive home to Kerry for training.

'I had to be in Killarney at 1pm. You *had* to be there. Dwyer demanded everyone be there for the Saturday session. In four years in Dublin, I missed two Saturdays – one when my son was being born, the other when my daughter was born.'

Professional soccer players seldom show such dedication. Charlie never questioned it though, being on the steps of the Hogan Stand most years made it all worthwhile.

'We used to go to a dance at home on New Year's Eve. When I got up the following morning the past was forgotten about. All-Irelands were put to bed with the old year. It was a new beginning and it wasn't about winning a second, third, sixth All-Ireland or whatever. It was about this All-Ireland.'

Nelligan's third last day in a Kerry jersey was in Killarney in 1991, against Cork in the Munster semi-final, with no medals at stake. Beforehand in a team meeting convened by manager Mickey 'Ned' O'Sullivan, Charlie produced a Cork jersey and tore it to shreds.

Come match day, it was like he was playing for Home Farm again. Out beyond the 21. Roaring. Dancing.

'1990 against Cork was humiliation – they totally demoralised us. Players didn't want to come out at half-time. In the second-half, we were praying for the final whistle. Billy Morgan totally and utterly destroyed us. That made the game in '91 the happiest day of my career. I knew I would never be beaten by Cork again.'

And unlike 1976, Nelligan didn't pick the ball out of his net that day.

JÓM

Denis 'Ogie' Moran

The week after the 1995 Munster final Páidí Ó Sé was driving to Kerry Under 21 training in Tralee. Páidí was over the team. To get the senior job he had to deliver an All-Ireland but on the journey to Austin Stack Park that night, he wondered whether the senior job was worth the hassle.

Páidí was listening to Radio Kerry's open season on Ogie Moran. The signal was poor as he made his way beyond Annascaul, so, to give the radio his full concentration, he pulled over in Gleann na nGealt.

He was shocked and confused at what he heard following Kerry's third successive championship defeat at the hands of Cork. Ó Sé was arguably the one man in the county who stood to benefit directly from the barrage of criticism over the airwaves but he couldn't believe what he was hearing.

Privately, Páidí had been critical of previous Kerry management regimes partly because he had been overlooked for the job himself but what he heard that evening, he reckoned, was a step too far.

For Ogie Moran, it was the worst of times.

Ogie remembers the good days, when people thought they'd never end. The eight All-Irelands; the North Kerry championships; All-Ireland seven-a-sides with Shannon Rangers; UCD; bringing Sam to Ballybunion.

It was 1978 and Beale's All-Ireland with Bomber's goals and his own captaincy.

'On the Wednesday, we paraded up the town with the cup and ended up in Liston's pub for the night,' Ogie recalls. 'The craic. I was only 22, very young but old enough to appreciate and take it in.'

Three days previously, Ogie stood in his centre-forward position with his back to the Canal goal. Stood helpless. Dublin were 0-6 to 0-1 ahead and he was wondering where Kerry's next score was coming from. He'd be remembered as the captain when Kerry lost to Dublin for the third year in a row, he thought.

'Dublin were buzzing and I said to myself, "Jesus, we're going to get slaughtered here today." I just didn't see a way back. Funny, it could have been the end of the team because O'Dwyer would have been slated. Then it just happened.'

Bomber's goals, like he was banging them in for fun on the Ballybunion sandhills; the convoy to Liston's when Ogie and Bomber were on their way to beating Bob Stack's local record of six All-Irelands. From then on, it was All-

Facing page:
Kerry's All-Ireland winning team from Centenary Year, with Ogie Moran pictured third from right on the back row.
(Sportsfile)

Irelands nearly every year, North Kerry finals most years for Liston and Moran and these district finals are the ones Ogie remembers.

'The first time Beale won a North Kerry final was in our time,' he says. '1977, I'll never forget it and afterwards we had some great years, winning seven. That first one was like an All-Ireland to us. We were playing a very good Ballylongford team in Ballylongford. They were the kingpins and we beat them. We celebrated that one.'

Rough days only came when Ogie succeeded Mickey 'Ned' O'Sullivan as Kerry manager in 1993. It was Ogie's law. Anything that could go wrong did, starting with his move to bring back Bomber.

'I started training on my own on Stephen's Day with a view to getting back into some shape,' says Liston. 'It was supposed to be just between Ogie and myself for a month or six weeks to see how I'd get on but the press got hold of it. Feck it, I was in an awful position because I had gone for a few runs and I said, Jesus, no way would I get back – not a hope, and next thing I had to be seen that I didn't just chuck it in.'

By the end of the summer, Bomber had a new punchline. He said he was sitting in jeans he hadn't worn in twelve years, but even a fit Eoin Liston wasn't enough.

Three successive defeats to Cork sealed his fate, with teammate of sixteen years through minor, Under 21 and senior teams, Pat Spillane, leading the charge. 'I'm not going to hedge it, I'm going to give it to Kerry tonight,' he said on *The Sunday Game* of 23 July 1995. 'Ogie Moran and his selectors stand indicted for many of the problems that surfaced today. They've been surfacing for the past three years. After three years, the jigsaw should be almost complete. They did some crazy things. The leading scorer in the National League, Dara Ó Cinnéide is back at wing-back. They had no midfield pairing. They've had three new captains over the last three matches.

'My mother at home probably had figured out that Kerry were in trouble at midfield. I think there's a long queue already gathering outside the Kerry County Board of potential candidates for another Kerry manager and hopefully a couple of new selectors.'

Anonymous callers to Radio Kerry echoed Spillane's words before Kerry County Board PRO, Eamon O'Sullivan, stuck his head above the parapet and called stop. 'The level of personal criticism of Ogie Moran on radio and television went way beyond the bounds of fair play,' he wrote in *The Kerryman*.

'Comments on national TV on Sunday night were both unnecessary and hurtful. Telling it as you see it is fine but at what price to Kerry football, Kerry teammates and, indeed, to Kerry followers in general?

'The comments on Sunday night seem to have given an open-season licence for a Monday morning programme on local radio. What made this programme very hard to take was that people who refused to give their names were allowed access to the airwaves,' he added.

Twelve years on, Dara Ó Cinnéide goes stronger. 'The treatment of Ogie was personal. It was horrible,' he says. 'The reaction after games was really nasty. I was directly involved because Ogie got slated for playing me wing-back.

'Six weeks before the Munster final, we had an injury crisis. Ok, I was top scorer for the League but I was still largely unproven as a senior inter-county player at that stage. I had played all my underage football at wing-back – it was only for the previous few years that I'd played in the forwards.

'He asked me how would I feel about playing wing-back and I was happy to be put there but in the end, it was used as a stick to beat Ogie with. The morning of the match, Paddy Bawn died and at his funeral people were saying, "Paddy Bawn, this legend of Kerry is gone, pity about the lads that are there now though." It was a horrible thing. I still remember Ogie in the dressing room after the game with his head in his hands. His kids were young, they were tugging his shirt, saying, "Come out of here."'

With that, Ogie Moran's three-year term as Kerry manager had come to an end with another defeat in Munster but the fruits of his work would only be seen two years later when the nucleus of his side won an All-Ireland medal.
The mid-'90s were bittersweet days for Moran – glad to answer the county's call but disappointed the way things spooled out.

His link to the big days went all the way back to 1962 when he was Kerry's All-Ireland mascot. The fascination continued six years later when his teacher at Gormanston College, Joe Lennon, brought the Sam Maguire to school the morning after he captained Down to beat Kerry. Seven more years on and the dream was brought to life – Moran was kicking the first point in an All-Ireland.

He was centre-forward on big Alan Larkin that day – but his only worry was what boots to wear. 'It was wet and I was deciding between rubber studs or screw-ins. Whatever Brendan Lynch did, I did. I turned to him and he was wearing the rubber studs. The early point really settled me. We won well. Pat Spillane lifted the cup and I'd made it.'

The carousel kept on for another twelve years. 'We didn't want those days to end,' says Ogie. 'We knew they had to. By 1986, it was wrapping-up. We were living on our wits. Meath in the semi-final, they had a lot of ball but we were winning games from habit then, with less possession. The Tyrone final was the same.

'You just hoped it would be the same the next day. You never walk away – you keep going until you don't get the call. It's the way we were. All of us.'

JÓM

Ger Lynch

Thanks to television, the summer of 1966 changed people. The tube in the corner with its rabbit's ears meant the World Cup to Ger Lynch. There was no escaping. He was eight years old that year. Impressionable. For the month of July, he was plonked in front of the television and it was the best seat in his house as he learned of Wembley, Ayresome Park, Anfield and Goodison. Eusebio, Beckenbaur and Riva.

The images bounced but Ger didn't mind – his grandstand seat was so close to the screen that he could touch it. Mick O'Connell had competition as soccer sucked young Ger in. Seduced him.

He knew the names of Alf Ramsey's wingless wonders as well as the Kerry team. And, because of England captain Bobby Moore, Ger was a happy hammer, a West Ham United fan.

Ger even took Bobby Moore out on to the Valentia football field behind his house. One minute he was like Jack 'Strawlegs' McCarthy or O'Connell soaring for the ball, the next he was playing it on the floor like Moore. Valentia's cosmopolitan culture allowed this. There was no Rule 27 on the island – people were used to garrison influences since the earliest days of the Valentia Cable Station, and not only was soccer played in Valentia, but rugby too.

Valentia's own Bob Graves paved the way for Mick Doyle, Moss Keane and Mick Galwey. Graves was Kerry's first rugby international and British and Irish Lion and Ger Lynch became Valentia's second international when he played in the Compromise Rules series against Australia. It was the icing on Ger's cake. He had All-Irelands and an All Star and he wore the Irish jersey in 1987. A neat bookend at the close of Kerry's golden years.

Sounds easy. Those three All-Irelands, the All Star and green *geansaí* came in four years, but the work was hard.

Hard being a tearaway wing-back like Paul Russell or Seán Murphy before him. Ger had the class of Russell or Murphy but it came much easier to them. Quicker too.

'At the end of the '70s I was called in for training sessions to make up the numbers. It was a great experience – it showed me what standard I had to aim for. I got on the panel before the '81 Munster final but the training was hell. I wasn't able for it. I was way off the pace required for that level of football.

Facing page:
Ger Lynch who emulated fellow Valentia Islanders, Jack 'Strawlegs' McCarthy, Mick O'Connell and Ger O'Driscoll in winning All-Irelands.
(John Kelly)

361

'The following winter I made my mind up that I was going to put in a huge effort to give me some chance of breaking onto the team. I did an awful lot of stamina work on my own, jogging across Cork City night after night. It was lonely and boring but had to be done.

'I remember going back to the first training session in '82. Dwyer was putting the new fellas through stamina work in the field next to the Fitzgerald Stadium. I left them for dead. Dwyer looked at me and I looked at him. He knew I had the work put in.'

It still wasn't enough. In 1982 Ger could have been Kerry captain – the five-in-a-row captain. South Kerry were county champions, Valentia were south Kerry champions and they had call on the captaincy.

Ger shied away from it in favour of nailing a place on the team and earned that jersey for the Munster final. Played well too in keeping Dave Barry in check, but the axe fell for the replay. Tommy Doyle was back – Ger still hadn't served his time.

1984 was different. He drove himself harder in training and was hard on his own pocket. Getting on the Kerry team came before work as a psychiatric nurse in Cork, even if it was left to himself to pick up the tab.

'You have to make up your own mind if you're going to do it, if you really want to make it. The sacrifices to make that Kerry team were huge. These were sacrifices of time, energy and money. The Sundays I was working that clashed with football games for Kerry meant I had to pay somebody to work my shift.

'Playing for Kerry cost money but I didn't give it a second thought. That's the way it was. I wouldn't ask for any favours from my Southern Health Board bosses in the hospital where I worked as a nurse. Why should I get special treatment when others were doing the same job as I was?'

Paying for the privilege of playing for Kerry was just another sacrifice.

Stay away and he could have been cast away – there were others in the queue behind him.

'I got my place in '84 and wasn't going to let go. The day you wouldn't travel to play with Kerry because of work was very dangerous. You could lose your place, training was competitive and the training matches were very intensive. They talk about the Clare hurlers in the '90s having brutally intense games in training. Kerry were doing that in the '70s and '80s. I'd spent enough time on the sideline from training with the team in the late '70s through to the time I came onto the panel in '81. After the disappointments of '82 and '83, I was going to do everything to make the team in '84.'

Ger's money was well spent. The island had three All-Ireland winners in Jack 'Strawlegs' McCarthy, Mick O'Connell and Ger O'Driscoll. Ger Lynch joined the club in '84. It's what pounding pavements across Cork City in the dead of night and spending every spare moment on the field behind his home were for.

For three years, he swept up along the Croke Park tram lines like an old outside-left, dodging the traffic as he went. It was similar to his journeys to Croke Park in those years. The luxury coach with Garda outriders wasn't for Ger, superstition kept him on the wings. Made him do his own thing.

'We were in the Grand Hotel before the '84 final and, by chance, a few of us decided to go to Croke Park by car. Myself, the three Spillanes and John Egan were all in one car. The others travelled by coach. After that day, I never came in by coach to Croke Park from Malahide.'

The journeys ended in 1987 when Cork beat Kerry in Killarney. The Golden Years over. Bomber said it was 'time for a new act' and in a sense, Ger was a relieved man.

'The Sunday after the Munster final, there was a regatta in Waterville and it was nearly my first Sunday off from football in six years. There was a freedom about it and that's what I was thinking of when I was driving back to Cork that evening.

'I took the Ring of Kerry road back and stopped at Spillane's Bar in Templenoe. Mrs Spillane was behind the counter and John B. Keane also happened to be there. I sat down with him and had a few pints. I really enjoyed them. I was free. The football with Kerry was great, great while it lasted but it was great that it was over too.'

He was back in the real world again. Back to the television and the exploits of West Ham United.

JÓM

Pat Spillane

How do you let go? Really. How do you walk away after seventeen years? After glory. Fame. After guts spilled and a soul bared? After Kerrymen and pressmen and seasoned observers studied your every move? After you've thrown coaching manuals out the window and re-invented the concept of position?

How do you turn your back to it after you were told your career was over, only to return and prove them wrong? In three more All-Ireland finals.

You begin thinking you can never slip away. You didn't when your teammate, your neighbour, your friend for Christ's sake, said you couldn't cut it anymore.

You had to stay put and prove him wrong too. Finish the game on your terms. And even then, you kept going for another eight years with your club. Lacing your boots 'til you were 44 years old.

Some said you were mad. What were you trying to prove, they asked. You heard that question many times during nothing games at strange places in the middle of winter.

You thought about what would happen when that void came. When football days were over.

You didn't play golf. Your knee saw to that. You put it through too much torture back in the day and now you wouldn't manage eighteen holes without tearing the life out of the stitched-up knee again.

So, how do you let go?

Well, that's easy. You don't. You never loosen the grip because you don't want to. You don't have to.

'This thing' as Spillane calls it – like a Mafia Don privately explaining away his day job – 'it never leaves you. Or I've never left it. I don't know.'

The big curtain call in 1991 was an end of sorts but mainly it was a transition, one he was prepared for.

When he ruptured his knee a decade earlier, days before the All-Ireland final, he was told to pack up and forget about football for good. After the doctors ripped his knee open, they told him nobody in Ireland had returned to sport after they damaged ligaments like he did.

Spillane became obsessive. For a full year, he scoured the country looking for a man to mend his knee but found none. So he went to Oxford, to a surgeon who, eventually, showed him the way back. But when Spillane could see the end

Facing page:
Pat Spillane makes one fan's day before the 1981 All-Ireland final against Offaly.
(The Kerryman)

line, a virus hit from nowhere. He lost 40 pounds in body weight. It looked like he faced another marathon away from the game and worst of all, this time he was cast aside from the Kerry team.

There was little communication with the players or manager – just the constant din of noise in his head goading him back to fitness.

Finally, when he could run properly again – over two years later – he obsessed once more and became 'one of the fittest men in the country'.

In 1990 when he was left out of the team, for a while he genuinely thought that was the end. Those were bleak times but the solitude and isolation of the knee injury in the '80s had taught him some lessons. Work hard. Graft. Get back and show them you were right, they were wrong. After a short while, that mechanism kicked in again.

'The more people criticised me and said I was finished, the more I was driven. That was the central thing to those two comebacks.'

The background to his exclusion in 1990 is simple. Mickey 'Ned' O'Sullivan had backed away from his role as Kerry selector after 1987 because he didn't agree with the road being travelled but in 1990 he was boss and had a new slate to make his own.

'Mick [O'Dwyer] was very loyal to players but I felt the time for blooding new men had arrived,' says Mickey Ned. 'That was a major factor in us going into the doldrums. We didn't keep the conveyor belt going. We slipped up. I said to Micko, "We have difficult decisions to make – we have to let lads go." Micko's attitude was, "Let the next man worry about that."'

The way things turned out, Mickey Ned was that man. His first week in charge, he told Spillane he was surplus to requirements but Spillane didn't listen. He trained hard on his own and clawed his way back.

'I was an extreme case in '90 and '91,' says Spillane. 'I would have crucified myself [to get back in the team] and I would have done it off my own bat. Running up hills with weights tied onto me and that sort of thing. It was great at the time but I was doing savage damage to myself.'

Even after the winter of 1990, when Spillane returned to the fold, Mickey Ned says there were conditions. 'I brought him in on the rule that he'd keep the mouth closed and would pass the ball. And it worked. I felt that was my greatest achievement in management, getting Pat to sing from a different hymn sheet. But dropping him before that was the hardest thing I ever had to do. I was a friend of his and I knew what football meant to him.'

It's the middle of the Easter school holidays and Spillane is travelling home from Bantry now, over the Caha Mountains with the blue ocean sparkling away to his left. He's just back from a trip to Florida where he picked up an NBA game between the Orlando Magic and the Memphis Grizzlies. 'My young lad is stone mad on basketball,' he says.

School is out for another week but in five days St Goban's, where he teaches in Bantry, play the Under 16 Vocational Schools Munster final and Spillane has been putting the final touches on preparations. It's his twenty-ninth consecutive year involved with the school team.

On the road into Kenmare, he tells a story from the year before, when he was in charge of the Templenoe Under 10s. Out of curiosity, he says, he decided he'd get his blood pressure monitored for a spell. Just some routine maintenance. The results came back regular and normal, save a single noticable blip.

'I had one savage high reading and that was between 6.40 and 7.40pm on a Friday during Under 10 training. They'd drive you cuckoo but you just can't leave it. Like, I was chairman of the club for seven years and it was fulfilling and satisfying and all that. I loved it. But one of the worst things you can do is stay too long. You need fresh blood. So, this year I took a complete step back from everything. Under 10s and all. Don't get me wrong, I'm available all the time and any team that needs training I'll do it at a moment's notice. I love being stuck in it.'

As it happens, it's a Friday – a lovely April evening, with the sun still high and the whiff of summer lapping somwehere in the lazy breeze. In the distance, Kenmare Bay is calm and flat.

Spillane looks at the clock in his car. It's edging close to 6.30pm. On he drives through the village, turning in for the pitch in Templenoe 'just to have a look at what's going on'.

A group of kids are hopping out of a car, a few more whizz around the field, lacing through a couple of footballs.

Spillane steps out now and surveys the scene. He puffs his cheeks and exhales. 'Jaaaaaysus,' he says. He can feel the heat and steam from the coalface again. At home. In Templenoe. Roped back in through some concealed, primeval pull that he doesn't fully understand.

'Can't leave it alone,' he mutters, slowly shaking his head. Not even if he wanted to.

TJF

After the Gold Rush

Connie Murphy

Connie Murphy had long hair. He rode a motorcycle to training. Liked loud music. Wore the odd leather jacket. He wasn't quite a rocker but he didn't exactly fit the profile of a Kerry footballer in the mid-'80s either.

He remembers the first time in the senior dressing room as a nineteen-year-old. A pitch opening in Glenbeigh and it wasn't just his edgy appearance that went against him. Making the team at this stage was like gatecrashing a royal wedding and plenty of others had a similar reception to Murphy's.

'They were all there,' recalls Murphy, Kerry's lone All Star from 1989 to 1995. 'Bomber, Ogie, Mikey, Jacko. I mean, they were huge men. Intimidating. And this was a very close knit thing. I won't say a clique but they had been together so long and they were just so in tune with themselves. Now, they were absolute gents but to let you into the team was a big ask.'

Murphy had been trying to make the jump to the senior team since 1985. It didn't really happen until the spring of 1988 and once he established himself, acceptance followed. Before that, it was clear who was top of the pile and in ways, the ladder had been pulled up after them.

'When you're going to a couple of trial games at the start, you mightn't be passed the ball when you should be or they'd be keeping themselves to themselves. You just had to realise it was part of the process. Any team that's been together for so many seasons would be the same.'

For years, Murphy's own season began and ended with Cork. He first played minor football for Kerry in 1983 and continued through the Under 21 system before cementing his place with the seniors. He could never have guessed back in '83 but it would take eight years to know what beating Cork felt like.

As the Kerry rollercoaster was reaching the peak of its ride, Cork were working hard stitching teams together. Building for the future, they won six Under 21 All-Ireland titles throughout the '80s.

In Kerry, all eyes remained on the senior team and as Mickey 'Ned' O'Sullivan said, the focus on the conveyor belt was dwindling.

The graduation of the likes of Teddy McCarthy and Niall Cahalane to Cork's senior team, coupled with the arrival of Shay Fahy and Larry Tompkins – wanderers from Kildare who had no respect for Munster's natural order – meant the mountain had transferred from underage to the top grade.

Previous pages:
Darragh Ó Sé was key to stalling Cork's dominance in Munster – he's pictured here, going highest of all in the 2002 championship clash against the Rebels (Sportsfile)

Facing page:
Connie Murphy was an All Star in the lost decade after 1986 when no All-Ireland came to Kerry. (Sportsfile)

It happened just as Connie Murphy finally nailed his place with the seniors. Everest was following him around.

'Cork were the Holy Grail for me. It goes to show where Kerry were at that stage. We had some bad years for sure, because we just weren't blooding players. Out of the minor and Under 21s that I played with, not too many would have made the breakthrough. Maybe myself and Kieran Culhane and not many more after that. The talent just wasn't brought through and the underage side of it died a bit because the focus was on the seniors. Now, it's hard to change a winning formula but we had some good players at minor and Under 21 but I don't think the work was being put in.'

The winning formula that had worked so well for Kerry over the previous decade was persevered with. Micko tugged and tweaked his starting fifteen in the mid-'80s, but rarely changed it. He was shuffling the deck but mainly using the same cards and change came only when it was forced.

Ambrose O'Donovan and Ger Lynch were drafted in to the first fifteen after John O'Keeffe and Paudie Lynch retired in 1983. But from 1984 to 1986 only four others – John Higgins, John Kennedy, Willie Maher and Timmy O'Dowd – started a Munster or All-Ireland final and none had an extended run in the senior set-up.

Still, the team bagged three All-Irelands in that period but the majority of players were always just one defeat away from retirement. After the loss to Cork in the replayed Munster final of 1987, players began to drop off. Holes appeared throughout the team and Micko had no choice but to introduce some new faces.

'A generation of footballers never got a look in to that team and when the transition did come, in hindsight, you'd say there weren't enough players just a few years older than me who would have got a good run at the end of the golden era. The likes of John Higgins, Mike McAulliffe, Timmy O'Dowd.'

While Kerry were busy persevering with the team that changed football through the '70s and '80s, Cork had found their feet. They took four Munster titles on the trot – something they'd never done before – as well as two All-Irelands in 1989 and 1990. In the space of four years, with Kerry's backbone beginning to wither, the pecking order had shifted.

Things were changing in Kerry too. Mick O'Dwyer exited in 1989 and made way for Mickey Ned. His philosophy of fresh faces and young blood was widely known by now and when he took the reins, he was eager for change. His involvement with the Under 21s put him in a prime position to view what was on offer over the coming years.

Once Mickey Ned took over, things moved fast and there was a sense among the senior players of the panel that anybody associated with the O'Dwyer regime was naturally disadvantaged.

Shortly after his appointment, a trial game took place in Castleisland. Pat Spillane scored 1-4. Mike McAulliffe scored 1-5. Both played well but neither was retained, though Spillane did, eventually, return.

'Mickey's attitude, I felt, was to wipe the slate clean,' says Murphy. 'Maybe he tried to bring the young fellas through that bit quickly and was trying to change things too soon.'

Senior players also recall a different attitude to training. Under O'Dwyer, backs and forwards sessions would have a sharp bite. The manager only took the whistle from his pocket if things were getting seriously out of control. Mickey Ned, on the other hand, was a strict referee. Senior players realised the manager may have been trying to protect the younger members of the panel but they also felt the intensity of championship should be reflected in training games – a sentiment O'Dwyer would have always expressed.

On the back of winning the All-Ireland Under 21 title earlier in the summer, Kerry's emerging side travelled to Páirc Uí Chaoimh for the 1990 Munster final. Cork devoured them, 2-23 to 1-11. Kerry were completely out of their depth. As Kerry fans escaped early from the scene, they were met with a Cork chorus: 'Lock the fuckers up and make them watch.'

For Murphy, it was one of the lowest ebbs but the following year, through contained aggression and hard work, the mountain was finally scaled. He remembers the day as one filled with expectation and a feeling that the corner might be turned.

The night before, a pivotal team meeting went ahead in Tralee. Micheál O'Muircheartaigh, who trained the Dublin-based players, attended and spoke. Then, Mickey Ned turned to some players who had never contributed to meetings in the past. Timmy Fleming and Maurice Fitzgerald stood up and talked before Charlie Nelligan turned around and famously ripped that Cork jersey to pieces. Those in the room still recall a real sense of anticipation when the meeting was over.

'We weren't supposed to have a hope. Cork were the All-Ireland champions but at the end of the first half, I looked around and I knew we'd played well. Even the crowd sensed it because they really cheered us off at half-time. They sensed the effort we were putting in.'

It was a false dawn though. After Kerry struggled past Limerick in the Munster final, Murphy carried an ankle injury into the semi-final against Down. Kerry came home empty handed. Worse followed when Clare beat them in the following year's Munster final and it was 1996 before Kerry would come again.

TJF

Stephen Stack

Speaking like a bluesman from the Mississippi Delta, Páidí Ó Sé promised to put the soul back into Kerry football. He did strange and wonderous things when he took over in '96. He began to use the jersey as a motivational tool again. He dabbled in propaganda and got on the radio and into the newspapers, pleading with the Kerry public to travel to the Munster final in Páirc Uí Chaoimh that year.

The province would be the target. The morning of the game, he pulled Dara Ó Cinnéide and Darragh Ó Sé into a church to say a prayer. The two lads swapped a bemused glance as they knelt down but they were happy to float along. Páidí was trading on passion and emotion and the vibes were seeping through.

Stephen Stack had been around the Kerry scene on and off for a decade and if soul is what it took, then soul it was.

By now, Cork's hold on Munster had strengthened again and Kerry's defeats of Cork in 1991 and 1992 were seen as blips on the screen. But Ó Sé looked at things differently. For the previous few years he had been keen, bordering on impatient, to manage the county and he wasn't going to let the chance pass him by. He had a core of young players breaking through and the previous year, he led them to the Under 21 title.

In 1996 Cork were going for a four-in-a-row in Munster though and in 1995, they believed they had left an All-Ireland behind them when they lost to Dublin in the semi-final. When the new season began, they were anxious to atone.

Things didn't look good from a Kerry perspective. Over the previous three years, they faded at crucial periods against Cork. 1994 was the most blatant example. Leading by five points with thirteen minutes left, they collapsed and Cork came away with a two-point win. 1995 wasn't much better. Kerry again took an early lead and considered themselves the better team over the entire game but they still couldn't put Cork away. The fitness and mental strength of the team was questioned and some players themselves began to believe that Cork had a psychological advantage.

In the spring of '96, Kerry played Cork in a league quarter-final and for once they didn't back away late in the game. They hung on for a draw and though Cork won by two in extra time, it was slowly sinking in that Cork weren't unbeatable. Dara Ó Cinnéide kicked nine points that day and for the first time, the focus was shifting from Maurice Fitzgerald.

Facing page:
Stephen Stack and Páidí Ó Sé celebrate after the 1997 All-Ireland win over Mayo.
(Sportsfile)

'I was 29 in 1996 and played through what was the biggest famine in Kerry football,' says Stack. 'You could see the team coming together in early '96 with the injection of the young crew. They were fierce enthusiastic. Mad for football. That's what always struck me. They'd be coming into training chomping at the bit and because of the underage success, they'd have brought some confidence in as well.'

After Ó Sé left the church that Munster final morning, he would have noticed the swell of Kerry support heading for the game. It was a young, eager crowd starved for success and quietly hopeful under a new vocal manager. The day was wet and miserable yet 10,000 more people showed up at Páirc Uí Chaoimh than had done the last time the two teams met there in the championship.

'The week before, I remember there was a huge determination among the players to end the Cork dominance in Munster. You could just feel that we weren't going to stand for being beaten by Cork. But the way we had been going up to that, there wouldn't have been the confidence to look ahead to an All-Ireland semi-final, even with the new players. We wouldn't even have considered being back at training after Cork.'

With one Munster title in nine years, brittle minds were understandable but all around things were changing. In the rain, the game began to unravel. It was Darragh Ó Sé's first Munster final start and his presence was vital.

Midfield was the ground on which Cork had recently prospered and for the previous three years, the Liam Honohan/Danny Culloty axis in midfield had controlled games for Cork. Ó Sé's introduction helped stem the tide.

But Kerry also got a break. A week before the game, Culloty injured his shoulder and couldn't play and come match day, Kerry were having the better of things at midfield. It pointed the way forward and more than any other player, Darragh Ó Sé's emergence helped break Cork.

Different snippets of that game stand out for different players. Seamus Moynihan remembers Killian Burns tearing up from corner-back with minutes remaining, scoring a huge point, then turning and jumping with a clenched fist.

For Dara Ó Cinnéide, it's the Kerry chant that rang around the terraces. 1996 was the year of the European Championships in England and the Kerry supporters borrowed a battlecry from the stands of Wembley. 'They were singing "Football's Coming Home" for us up in Cork and I'll never forget it,' says Ó Cinnéide. 'It was a turning point. It was the first time I saw Kerry supporters connecting with the team.'

Stephen Stack was away at the other end of the field, detached from the commotion at the opposite end when the breaking point came.

Kerry had a one-point lead with minutes left when they were given a free 60 yards out. Maurice Fitzgerald stepped up. Behind the Cork goal, a red flare was lit, defying Fitzgerald, goading him to even have a try at collapsing Cork.

'You could have blasted a fog horn into Maurice's ear that day he was so focused,' says Stack. 'Now, this was a long kick into the wind and you're wondering is he going to do it. I remember seeing it float over and that's when we knew we had it.'

Cork were crumbling. Niall Cahalane, a driving force, was taken off. Stephen O'Brien was run ragged. When Burns clipped over that late score it gave Kerry a three point win, 0-14 to 0-11.

Billy Morgan was the one who had plotted Kerry's demise in Munster and 1996 was just his third loss to Kerry during ten years in charge. In the dressing room after the game, though it was never said, the Cork players sensed the transition was coming. Morgan retired and was replaced that December by Larry Tompkins. He wouldn't terrorise Kerry from the sideline like he did on the field. The breakthrough had arrived. Páidí was back. Billy was gone.

'You have to give the management credit,' says Stack. 'There would have been huge pressure on the team but the management worked very hard at keeping that away from us. Páidí would never mention the old team, for example. He said we had to establish ourselves in our own right and there's no point in looking to the past. Not once can I remember him referring to that great team and that was quite deliberate. He felt it would intimidate us and there would be comparisons. He wanted us to achieve in our own right.'

They did and this time, Kerry were finally on their way.

TJF

Seamus Moynihan

The day after the breakthrough against Cork in '96, a group of players travelled back to Páidí Ó Sé's pub in Ventry for a good blowout. A few stayed going until the Tuesday night and somehow, a photograph of the players out on the beer was published in one of the Kerry papers later that week.

Around the county it was felt that the team had been celebrating for six or seven days and though they enjoyed winning Munster for the first time in five years, they didn't wallow in it.

They were tuned in again for training the following weekend with an All-Ireland semi-final to prepare for, but what happened in that game against Mayo gave weight to the theory that Kerry had basked too much in defeating Cork.

In reality, it wasn't that the team took too much satisfaction from winning Munster – they just weren't fully prepared for what came next. It was Seamus Moynihan's fifth Munster campaign and his first time reaching Croke Park in the championship.

Of all the games he's played – and he finished up just five short of Dan O'Keeffe's record of 66 championship appearances – he reckons Kerry learned more against Mayo in 1996 than in any other encounter.

'We didn't look beyond Munster and we found out an awful lot about ourselves against Mayo and in a way, losing that day was the best thing in the world because all of a sudden we knew what was ahead of us. We knew how hard we had to train if we were ever going to win anything.'

Páidí Ó Sé came into the dressing room after the Mayo game and clearly laid out what had to be done if Kerry were to seriously challenge.

'That Mayo game was a learning curve for Páidí as well. We were gauging ourselves off Cork and once we beat them we looked at nobody else. Páidí knew we needed to up the fitness and up the standards. The whole lot.'

The team was augmented slightly. A few new faces and a little nip and tuck. At the start of 1997, Moynihan was taken aside and told his long-term future was away from the middle of the field.

'He [Ó Sé] gave me the number five jersey and said, "This is yours from here on. Now get on with it."'

In his own image, Ó Sé set about building one of the country's strongest half-back lines. When he settled on a championship team for his second year in

Facing page:
Seamus Moynihan makes his way through the throng to collect Sam Maguire in 2000.
(Sportsfile)

charge, Moynihan, Liam O'Flaherty and Eamonn Breen formed the most solid sector on the field.

There were other changes too. Maurice Fitzgerald was moved closer to goal. The players that won the Under 21 title under Ó Sé in 1995 and again in 1996 were beginning to blossom and half of those that started in that 1995 victory would play a role in Kerry's senior victory in 1997.

'Going into '97, we knew there was a serious amount of work to do but the only good thing was there were some great players coming through. The likes of John Crowley and Barry O'Shea. And because Páidí had these guys at Under 21, it helped them gel with the experienced players like Sean Burke and Stephen Stack. The fitness picked up as well and what it all meant was you had very high intensity training. Basically, you had 30 guys in there shooting for jerseys.'

Once the season began, there was an almost immediate change in attitude. Cork were no longer the barometer of success and some of the older players became a driving force. Kerry targeted the League and wound up in Páirc Uí Chaoimh in early May for the final against Cork. It was a fit, hungry Kerry side with another point to prove. They ran out winners by five points and not only did that game reinforce the attitude that Kerry could rule Munster again, it was also the first time the county had won the League in thirteen years.

Clearly, the mental block against Cork was receding and crucially, Kerry were at last looking past the provincial stage.

'Players thought it was time to grow up and get into the real world in '97. There was an extra push – just in training and in attitude – and it was great to turn it around and win the league and the All-Ireland in the one year. It was a huge jump. We went from being eighth or ninth in the pecking order to becoming the best team in the country in the space of about twelve months.'

The turning point came early in the season. Kerry travelled to Kingscourt for a league game with Cavan missing a few players. Stephen Stack was out with a long-term injury, Mike and Liam Hassett were helping Laune Rangers with their All-Ireland club run and were spared the trip.

In Cavan, the field was mucky and the weather was atrocious. It was a game that could easily have faded away as a forgotten memory but Kerry showed qualities that Sunday which some didn't realise they had.

Cavan were emerging as the best team in Ulster and the game turned into a battle. Kerry played poorly but dug out a victory and afterwards, there was a feeling of achievement that came close to the satisfaction after the Cork victory the previous July.

Kerry didn't lose a game for the remainder of the year, challenge, league or championship and when Páidí Ó Sé reflects on the success of 1997, he always uses that Cavan game as the beginning of the story.

It was widely accepted among the players that Kerry weren't prepared for Croke Park when they arrived there in 1996 but it was a different story the following year.

'We looked at '96 as the introduction, the taster, but in 1997 we were becoming stronger mentally. Bit by bit. It was time to produce and there was a focus that wasn't there before,' says Moynihan.

Kerry played Cavan in the All-Ireland semi-final and the occassion to produce had arrived. Before half-time, Denis O'Dwyer received a knock and at the break he was concussed. As the players were sitting down at half-time, an ambulance was backing into the dressing room area to take O'Dwyer to hospital.

Kerry didn't flinch. There was concern for O'Dwyer but nobody lost their focus and Ó Sé was calm and controlled.

'Other years, something like that could have rattled us,' says Stephen Stack. 'But it didn't that year and that was important.'

'How important was it to get to an All-Ireland final that year?' wonders Seamus Moynihan. 'I'd say it was vital. After the performance the year before we had to step it up and we basically showed ourselves, more than anyone else, that we could do that.'

The fuse was lit. In Kerry, they sat back and waited to see what would happen.

TJF

Maurice Fitzgerald

Dara Ó Cinnéide: What [Maurice] did against Mayo in '97 was what he was doing in Fitzgerald Stadium for years and years in training.

Páidí Ó Sé: For whatever reason, Maurice was extremely uptight before that game. I didn't know going into it and it was only after that I found out. It might have been the physiotherapist that told me.

Dara Ó Cinnéide: There were a couple of years there when Maurice didn't deliver. At the time, people felt it was a case of [him] getting the game over and going to America [to play for the rest of the summer].

Seamus Moynihan: In '97 I never saw Maurice train as hard. It was the one year that, from the very minute we regrouped in October to the very last training session, Maurice was flying. His level of fitness that year was off the radar.

Kieran McCarthy: Back in 1995 Maurice, basically, asked me to come on board. I'd trained with him since we were kids and I trained him in 1991 with St Mary's. In '95 he'd plenty skill but he had nothing in the tank. Starting off, after four or five rounds of the field, you could hear him up the street. He was hurting.

Páidí Ó Sé: It was important to know Maurice's make up in that he suffered quite a lot with injury. Early on in his career he had his two groins done. You know, we had to be very careful with him. He found it very difficult to put heavy training sessions back to back.

Kieran McCarthy: I'll tell you the secret of '97 – I had a one-on-one relationship with Páidí Ó Sé. He'd ring me and ask how Maurice was getting on. I could say, 'Páidí, the best thing tonight would be if Maurice stayed at home and practiced the frees.' Páidí knew we'd do our bit.

Dara Ó Cinnéide: He did produce it in '96 but the team wasn't good enough to come up to his level. In '97 he had a team built around him. It was a case of 'get the ball to Maurice and let him do the rest'.

Kieran McCarthy: The Saturday before the Cavan game he was having an awful bad practice day. Everything was going to the corner flag. There were a few

Facing page:
Maurice Fitzgerald and Seamus Moynihan after the All-Ireland win of 2000 over Galway.
(Sportsfile)

383

curses thrown out and you could see he was frustrated. Another time, we finished a session and my legs were covered in blood. I gave all day getting the ball out of the briars. Maurice was there, 'Yeah, I know I'm useless. Get me out of here.'

Dara Ó Cinnéide: For a while, Anthony Gleeson – a very good player – would be put marking Maurice in training and Maurice would be on fire. He'd torture whoever was marking him. We'd be wondering why he couldn't do it against Cork's Mark O'Connor.

Kieran McCarthy: As regards training, there was no better man in the world. I remember we went to Portmagee, the Caherciveen field was closed. I looked out the window and Jesus Christ, the seagulls weren't even out this day. Gale force ten down in Portmagee, blowing in from the Atlantic. He wouldn't back away from it. The fitness was coming slowly. In December '96 we had the breakthrough. We trained in a place called the Brother's Field, up and over this hill seven times. At the start of the month we were doing a circuit in 31 minutes. Two days before Christmas, it was down to 22.

Seamus Moynihan: You'd be coming into training praying that you wouldn't be put on him. There was a guarantee he'd score three or four goals off you and maybe five or six points. It was a nightmare to mark him because he was just on fire. Left leg. Right leg. And then he'd sell you this dummy.

Mickey 'Ned' O'Sullivan: Even when I was over Kerry you became conscious of putting fellas on him [in training]. In the end, I had to rotate who was marking him because what Maurice could do in training could destroy a fella's confidence.

Kieran McCarthy: The Friday before the final the two of us sat down. We were sitting in the car with two nice ice cream cones. We went through every detail of what we'd gone through and what could happen. We knew he had the engine and the strength. Then we shook hands and I said, 'Go on away now and do it.'

Seamus Moynihan: Things just exploded for him against Mayo.

John Maughan: It was a horrible day for us. He beat us on his own. We lost Dermot Flanagan with an injury after about four or five minutes and Pat Holmes was put on Maurice for the game. Pat was an excellent man marker but as it turned out, it made no difference who was on him that day.

Dara Ó Cinnéide: The composure at half-time inside in the dressing room that day and the body language was something else. The serenity. He was a real man's man.

Páidí Ó Sé: Of course, you could see that Maurice was upset over it [Fitzgerald's accidental clash with Kerry's Billy O'Shea in the twenty-second minute]. But at half-time he just decided to keep going. That was Maurice's make up. The game was still there to be played.

Darragh Ó Sé: The air of authority he had in the dressing room was unreal. A great presence. A lot of people don't realise it but Maurice Fitzgerald was really mentally tough. He was very proud of his football.

Seamus Moynihan: It was as if he made up his mind [after the Billy O'Shea injury] and said 'I'm going to have to do something here.' And he did. He gave a tour de force.

Páidí Ó Sé: Probably his best play of the game came right at the end, his ninth point. When Mayo came back at us in the second half – and I still think they kicked some very, very bad wides – they had us on the rack. I couldn't relax at all. It was only at the end when Maurice kicked over this point from out on the sideline, 50 or 60 yards out. It was only then that I relaxed.

Junior Murphy: He came home and didn't say a thing about it [the performance]. You probably could have asked him on the Monday who he was marking and he wouldn't be able to tell you.

Kieran McCarthy: We ploughed on again. He broke a toe against Armagh in 2000 but we had to keep training for the replay. He'd put on a pair of runners and wade into the River Ferriter waist high, jogging. We had a boat, a small punt and I'd row out to Beiginish Island in it, towing Maurice. He'd be in the water, holding on to the back. We wanted to keep the fitness up and sure, salt water has a great curing process.

Dara Ó Cinnéide: Everyone I played with on the Kerry team in that era was a contemporary. Maurice was on a different level. For every one of us, he was a hero. The likes of Seamus Moynihan and Darragh Ó Sé, they're great, great players, but you didn't see them in the same light [as Maurice]. You saw them as teammates. With Maurice, there was this god-like status. He wasn't one of our peers. He was detached. He wouldn't join in any of the celebrations or anything. It was Mick O'Connell stuff.

TJF

Liam Hassett

When the final whistle went, suddenly there was just this massive swell of people out on the grass of Croke Park. In Liam Hassett's mind, it's like somebody clicked their fingers and his whole world changed in one second. He was swamped in an epic maul, half-beery and half-tearful.

It was eleven years since anybody with a green and gold jersey danced on the big stage and nobody was holding back now. Hassett was Under 21 captain when Kerry won the year before and he'd been there when they won it in 1995 too, but it felt nothing remotely like the release of emotion that was taking place all around him.

The first man to jump on his back was his brother Mike, ecstatic and roaring. He was left out of the team for the final even though he'd been captain himself for the Munster final and all that week, Mike's omission played on Liam's mind.

At the time, Liam was teaching in Dublin and Mike was teaching in Wicklow and their ritual was to meet in Kildare and drive home to training. They socialised together, roomed together. They were close.

The Tuesday before the final, Mike was called aside after training and told he wasn't going to be selected. He was coming back from injury but going well in training and he expected to start.

On the journey back to Kildare, in Mike's white one litre Corsa, he broke the news to his brother. When Liam thinks back now, he reckons it was the longest journey ever to get to Kildare.

Mike's omission also meant that Liam would captain Kerry on Sunday but that didn't seem important at the time and when Liam speaks openly about that year, he'll tell you the captaincy was more of a burden than anything.

So, just after the whistle went in Croke Park, with the two Hassetts clutched together on the field, Liam tells Mike he should be the one to go up and lift the Sam Maguire.

'Not a hope,' says Mike. Maybe if he'd played some part in the game, he says. Maybe then.

They're bobbing around in the mass of bodies out on the field, like two bottletops in the sea, and Liam is drifting over towards the stand, caught up in this huge wave. They all want him to climb the steps and lift the cup. *Show us for sure that football's coming home, that this isn't just one long sadistic dream*

Facing page:
Liam Hassett pictured during a traditional Bedouin evening in Saudia Arabia as part of the All Stars tour in 2001.
(Sportsfile)

387

where we wake up and Cork are stomping all over us again!

Eventually he gets to the presentation area but, still, he's looking down from the stand trying to put his eyes on his older brother and beckon him to come up. But he can't see him anywhere and he's too young and too inexperienced to force the situation. Time runs out so he clasps the Sam Maguire and hurls it over his head and life in Kerry returns to normal.

Since then, that day has been a strange memory. After he saw Ben and Jerry O'Connor jointly lift the Liam McCarthy Cup for Cork in 2004, it clicked with him. That's what he should have done.

'But I didn't have the nerve to do something like that back then,' he says. When the Kerry team returned home that Monday and the long, long celebration died down later that week, things got worse. Mike was told he wasn't going to get a medal. Nothing personal but only 21 medals were minted and because he didn't see any game time against Mayo, he didn't qualify. It was just like Eddie Dowling all those years ago.

Mike had captained Kerry to two cups that year and now this was the final straw. That winter, the two brothers sat down, talked about it and decided to quit Kerry football. No amount of persuading would bring them back.

They missed 1998 and all the talk of Micko meeting Páidí – master and pupil. They missed that shock defeat against Kildare in the semi-final and missed seeing Páidí's bewildered reaction afterwards.

On the train home, other players remember that Páidí barely opened his mouth. He just stared into the distance, as though he was replaying the game over and over in his head.

But in 1999, a Hassett peace deal was brokered. 'Sean W   a w   appointed county board chairman around that time and he approached   an said he'd like to have us back on the Kerry scene,' says Liam.

'Now, we weren't pissed off with Páidí or anything like that, we were pissed off with the county board and GAA headquarters in general so we listened to Sean and I turned to Mike and said, "Right, we'll see if we can't get you that medal." Páidí didn't seem to have a problem with us coming back and players knew I was standing by Mike. So we pushed on. Cork beat us th   year but 2000 was the big one. Mike got his medal.'

Unlike other years when a season was made in a private, team-only moment, the making of 2000, says Hassett, came in the prairies of Croke Park, in front of the whole nation.

Again, it was a mental thing. A realisation, he says, that Kerry could dig their claws into the earth, cling on and not let go. It was a feeling that Kerry weren't just about pretty football and trading on the name.

'There was a stage during the first semi-final against Armagh when they came hard at us. You could feel they were throwing everything they had but they just couldn't kill us off. The winning of that year was that moment against Armagh when we hung on to the game.'

It was a breathtaking encounter. After six minutes, Kerry led 1-3 to 0-0 and the day looked a breeze. But Armagh were already showing the way forward and the fight and the workrate they displayed for the last 64 minutes was a sign of things to come.

It took Maurice Fitzgerald, a bench player by now, to step up four minutes into injury time and sweetly strike over a point that would draw the game.

'We came home and nothing let up. Training was just as hard for the replay. Páidí as a manager was very tuned-in during 2000. He was good at analysing other teams and that year we looked at a lot of videos. He looked at Armagh and said we have to stop them building from the back, put pressure on their backline.

'That year we went behind in games and we were able to rescue it. There was nobody panicking. Players from that Under 21 team were that bit older, that bit more experienced and it showed. Then, you had Seamus on fire at full-back right throughout the year and Maurice on the sideline. Any time you see Maurice Fitzgerald on the subs bench you know you've a good panel of players.'

Four tough games in August and September to win the All-Ireland. A long journey. Liam was happy his brother was there to travel it beside him.

TJF

Darragh Ó Sé

In his *Sunday World* column of 30 July 1995, Pat Spillane noted that the four best midfielders in Kerry were on the terraces for the Munster final against Cork in Killarney. Timmy Fleming, Dermot Hanafin, Tom Spillane and Connie Murphy.

Darragh Ó Sé made the bench that day, coming on as a substitute near the end. He was on the field two minutes when he soared between Liam Honohan and Danny Culloty to field a high ball. It was the most spectacular catch of the day.

Kerry still went down badly though and the jury was well out on Darragh Ó Sé. One catch never made Kerry's summer and many football people still doubted his ability to make the top grade. But Pat Spillane was a believer.

'Darragh Ó Sé can still make it as a midfielder,' he told *Sunday World* readers after Kerry's third successive championship defeat to Cork. Ó Sé himself was the biggest believer.

He was always confident about his football ability. Cocky even. As an underage player with An Ghaeltacht, he looked on jealously as contemporary Dara Ó Cinnéide made teams before him. It always jarred.

Ó Sé badgered the selectors, talked himself up, looked for explanations as to why he was on the bench and Ó Cinnéide was playing.

Size came against him in those years. Hard to believe but Darragh Ó Sé was small in stature. Too small to mix it but it never stopped him jumping in with the big boys.

Then Darragh started to grow and moved to midfield. 'I was always in the backs growing up,' he says, 'but one day when I was playing a game for Dingle CBS, Liam Higgins put me in the middle. I never played anywhere else after that.'

His championship debut came with that cameo appearance in 1995 under Ogie Moran but in thirteen years since then, up to and including Pat O'Shea's reign, he's had more midfield partners than championship seasons. Noel O'Mahoney, Liam O'Flaherty, Seamus Moynihan, John O'Connell, Donal Daly, William Kirby, Johnny McGlynn, Noel Kennelly, Seamus Scanlan, Eoin Brosnan, Paddy Kelly, Kieran Donaghy, Tommy Griffin and Mícheál Quirke.

'At half-time against the Dubs [in the semi-final of 2007] Darragh was a big figure,' says Kerry manager, Pat O'Shea. 'He was after injuring the hip and I saw him coming off the table at half-time after getting an injection so he could come on later in the game. The first thing he did was go around to each player

*Facing page:
Darragh Ó Sé is congratulated by Kerry County Board chairman, Sean Walsh, after the 2007 Munster final win over Cork.
(Sportsfile)*

individually and speak to them. The only thing in his mind was, Kerry must win the second-half. We could have brought him on at half-time but we wanted to delay it as long as possible. As much as what he could do on the field, it was psychological. We felt it would be a setback for the Dubs just seeing him come on. That's the presence he has.

'He's an iconic figure, the spiritual leader in the dressing room. He sees himself as the leader of the young bunch of the Ó Sés and the manner in which they all hold Kerry football is phenomenal. Basically, Darragh sets the tone for how the younger Kerry players look at Kerry football.'

In the early days, the power of his personality helped knit the 1997 All-Ireland team together. 'To talk to him about football, you wouldn't think he cares,' says Dara Ó Cinnéide, 'but by laughing about football he was able to drag the likes of Eamonn Breen, Billy O'Shea, Stephen Stack and Liam O'Flaherty in with the younger generation to win that All-Ireland.'

Ó Sé's first All-Ireland was in 1982 when he was seven. He was up in the Hogan Stand with his father Micheál and brothers Feargal and Tomás. 'The noise,' he says, 'that's what I remember most. We were in the right-half-back position, looking out at Páidí in the second half and Pat Fitzgerald in the first. Offaly coming at us in waves near the end. Great to be there but a bad day.'

2004 was another bad day. Great for Kerry who won their thirty-third, but Ó Sé was on crutches and slightly peripheral to the whole thing even though Kerry wouldn't have made September without him.

'Earlier that year, I would say that I'd lost my appetite, I wasn't playing great football and wasn't happy with my game. But by the time the All-Ireland semi-final came around I felt good. Things were coming good for me.'

The week before that semi-final against Derry, Dara Ó Cinnéide talked to Ó Sé about his game. Got under his skin. Told him about coming too deep for the ball to get handy possession. It was what Armagh said in 2002, after he had more touches of the ball than any other player in the final.

Ó Sé said nothing to Ó Cinnéide in response, just went out and won the first high ball that came his way, burst forward and knocked over a point. He was on his way to having a great game until he went over on his ankle and his year was finished.

'I never got the *sásamh* from 2004,' he says. 'If I had played that All-Ireland I mightn't have stayed on. It made me realise to play on when I could. I have talked to lads who have finished. A lot of people. Páidí, Maurice Fitzgerald. The one thing you can't do is go back and play again. That's why I stayed.

'I wanted to win more medals. It wasn't to beat the northern teams. People say that, after 2002 and 2003 against Armagh and Tyrone, I stayed around to try and beat them. When Armagh beat us [in 2002] they were a better team, we played well enough in the first-half to get a draw but Armagh just choked the game. Same with Tyrone, they were better than us.

'There was never an issue with this Kerry team and northern opposition. Any team you are playing you want to beat. If we were playing Kilkenny in an All-Ireland football final it would be the same. Northern opposition? It was never an agenda with us.

'At the end of the day the most important thing is to come out with the medals. It's the medals on the table, it's winning the All-Ireland. Not who you beat in the final. That's all we want. Win Sam, win those medals.'

The north still sparked Ó Sé's greatest performance in a Kerry jersey. As Kerry stumbled to the All-Ireland quarter-final in 2006, Ó Sé was the one player to keep his play above the ordinary.

In the Hayfield Manor Hotel after the Munster final defeat to Cork, Ó Sé and Moynihan spoke louder than anyone else amid a mutinous atmosphere.

'Things hadn't been addressed,' says Kieran Donaghy. 'Fellas wanted to say things but it still hadn't been done. Those two men laid it on the line. They said we weren't representing the jersey, weren't representing the fellas who had gone before us who gave their hearts. They said Kerry were the best team in the country but we were playing shit. That was the turning point. It opened our eyes.'

After the loss to Cork, Kerry were deemed passé. The Armagh quarter-final proved they weren't. Darragh Ó Sé stood up. He hit hard, teed up six points for others, didn't look for handy balls.

'Every day you go out, you're facing something different,' he says. 'That was the case in the Armagh game, the Mayo final was different again. You can't hide anywhere but you definitely can't hide in midfield. The game is won and lost there. We won midfield against Armagh that day.'

Kerry won other battles that day too. Early in the game, a free was given against Marc Ó Sé. Kieran McGeeney came in, ripped the ball out of his hands and pushed him out of the way. Laid down his marker.

Then Darragh shot in with a shoulder on McGeeney. McGeeney came back for afters but was met by another hit from Ó Sé. They were like prize fighters in the ring but with the last hit, McGeeney took a few steps back.

JÓM

Dara Ó Cinnéide

Dara Ó Cinnéide went back training with the Kerry seniors under Jack O'Connor in early 2006. A thirteenth year with Kerry was his if he wanted it. Another All-Ireland as it turned out. But when it came around he had jumped from what he calls 'the cotton wool of inter-county football'.

Into the real world. Retirement. Marriage. Fatherhood. All in the same year that Kerry won their thirty-fourth. Ó Cinnéide was in the stands for the first time since 1993, supporting. Easy, he says.

'I had no problem quitting the county scene. I got football at a good time. It was still a sport. It's now gone over the top. Players who wouldn't have half the talent spouting off about living their life in a gym.

'These are guys who are soloing footballs out over the sideline, kicking sideline balls over the sideline. Come on, it's about football at the end of the day. I don't like the direction football is taking at the moment.

'The attitude of people gets me. People going on about what their diet is and how serious they are about football. They're almost giving the impression that it's a chore to play for their county.

'What used to piss me off was players, young fellas, telling you how to play the game – telling you the sacrifices they'd made. Telling you that there should be a government grant at the end of it. How they felt their image rights were being infringed upon and all that.

'You're playing for your county, like. There are kids out there who'd love to do it. Kids who can't get out of the bed in the morning who'd love to be there. That's not *grá mo chroí* stuff – it's a fact. I hated the attitude of these people who were giving the impression that it was a chore, that being a modern day inter-county footballer was tough and "I'm missing out on overtime here."'

Chasing a Kerry jersey was never a chore for Ó Cinnéide. Medals didn't bother him either because he says 'no matter what you win with Kerry and especially in Kerry, nobody cares. The fella down the road has eight; another has five.

'You don't think of it in terms of medals. You think of it in terms of "How long can I play for Kerry? How well can I play for Kerry?" You look back on it and say it was a privilege, you made lasting friendships, you saw the world, you're part of the jigsaw. No matter how badly you played you were part of the jigsaw. That was the privilege.'

Facing page:
*Dara Ó Cinnéide:
'You look back on
it and say it was a
privilege, you made
lasting friendships,
you saw the world,
you're part of the
jigsaw.'*
(Shelagh Honan)

No privilege was greater than captaining Kerry to number 33. Earlier, in that summer of 2004, Ó Cinnéide lifted the Munster cup but when he had a few celebratory drinks with the Ó Sé's in Páidí's pub in Ard an Bhóthair, the cup was left in the boot of the car. Munster was no big deal, but it was different with Sam.

Ó Cinnéide's 2004 boiled down to two big days in Croke Park. All-Ireland days. The first was a nightmare.

'It's the biggest disappointment in my life,' he says of An Ghaeltacht's All-Ireland club final defeat to Caltra from Galway. 'It seems almost trivial to say that a football disappointment is the biggest disappointment of your life, but it was.'

The Sunday before the club final Dara was working in Radió na Gaeltachta. The day's papers were on the ground in his office – he bent down to pick them up. As he did, he collapsed on the floor. The back injury he first picked up against Dublin in 2001 had flared up and he couldn't move. He played three days later but wasn't himself.

Fast-forward six months. Kerry stretching their legs in the Whitehall Colmcilles ground on the eve of the All-Ireland. Another nightmare.

'We were training and my back went again. I was holding my breath running – it was the only way I was comfortable. The core muscles were supporting everything. I remember saying it to Aoife Ní Mhuirí, the physio, and she said, "You're going to have to tell Jack [O'Connor]." I said. "Hold off, hold off." I wasn't being selfish, but I said, "We'll work on a need to know basis here."

'Ten o'clock Sunday morning, she told Jack that I was having serious trouble with my back. She got me strapped up and said I would probably do an hour. As it happened, bang on the hour, just after taking a free it started to go again, but thankfully we were out of sight at that stage.'

The last ten minutes flashed by in a second. Next thing Dara knew, he was lifting Sam. Seeing Gaeltacht faces in the crowd. Darragh Ó Sé on crutches. Thinking of St Patrick's Day, Armagh, Tyrone, Páidí.

'I thought Páidí was treated like shit, to be honest, by the county board. I said that to Sean Walsh [county board chairman]. In hindsight they would say it was time to move on and yes, it was time to move on – maybe in years to come Páidí will acknowledge that.

'It was horrible, though. It was badly handled in the papers. A lot of the old enemies came out of the woodwork. It was personal. People having a go at Páidí. Páidí, regardless of what people thought of him, he put the soul back into Kerry football.

'He always did what he thought was good for Kerry football. The next thing, he's being vilified. There were text polls on Radio Kerry – do you think

Páidí should stay or should he go? Horrible.'

Tyrone and Armagh?

'In 2003 we put up and shut up and we got on with it and won 2004. The only unfortunate thing is that we didn't get to meet Tyrone that year. The year we did get to meet them, they beat us again because they had come up another level again. I had fierce respect for Tyrone after 2005. I didn't respect them at all in 2003 because they were playing horrible stuff but in 2005, Tyrone beat us fair and square – there were no excuses.

'In 2002 and 2003, Tyrone and Armagh never felt we were giving them credit. I had no problem with Tyrone or Armagh. I felt they had a bit of a chip on their shoulder. I remember hearing a radio column on *Five Seven Live*, some fella from the north going on with "Take that Kerry".

'The one thing I hold against Tyrone, that I didn't like, is a few of them stayed down when they weren't injured. Kildare in '98 had a few lads like it. Big lads feigning injury.'

Dara's uncle, Seán Ó Cinnéide, never feigned anything. He was also his nephew's biggest supporter. When Kerry won in 2004 he was lying in a bed in St James' Hospital after surgery and up in the Hogan Stand Dara thought of Seán more than anyone else.

'In all the All-Irelands we won, I would never go to bed on the Sunday night. I would take it all in, not really drinking. At seven in the morning after 2004 I was having breakfast in the Burlington with Jack O'Connor. Liam Hassett was there too.

'Then I said to Jack, "I'm off." It wasn't to bed but to my uncle in hospital. He was dying but we didn't know it at the time. I was wrecked and when I got to St James', I just said, "Move over in the bed there a minute, Seán."

'He couldn't talk because part of his jaw had been removed. He was trying to talk to me but I told him I'd do the talking. Seán was my number one fan, all the way up along. He was devastated that he couldn't get to the final. But it was a lovely moment in the hospital the following day. He wasn't the type to get emotional, but he was half-emotional after the final. I said to him, "We'll have a special day of our own."'

It came on 30 June 2005. A dirty black day back west with the mist down. Micheál Ó Muircheartaigh had suggested it might be nice to climb the nearest peak to Ó Cinnéide's home with Sam. It happened to be Mount Brandon.

'The day you're going up, I'll go up with you,' said Seán Ó Cinnéide. He made it halfway, before turning back. So, they had their day and Dara took a picture of himself and Seán on his camera phone. He still has it.

'That's what I remember. Winning. The locals coming to An Bóthar pub on the Tuesday night. Mount Brandon. It's a holy shrine. It has huge spiritual connotations and that climb with Seán was important.'

JÓM

Colm Cooper

The warm glow of home. Two nights before his greatest moment so far, he rounded up a few nieces and nephews, left the open plains and familiar angles of the Ardshanavouley Estate and headed for Ross Castle. The air was warm and there was still some life left in the day.

They found a patch of grass in the shadow of the castle and kicked about until the sun was tucked behind the lake. It was late September 2004 and his young companions had zero interest in Sunday's final.

Cooper's head was clear and his body was ready but he'd sensed that all week. Whenever he knew the Dr Crokes field was silent and free, he would wander up there with his shorts and boots and run lap after lap, just to ease the mind. To make sure his brain understood that his body was doing ok.

Under Jack O'Connor, Kerry introduced Declan Coyle, a sports psychologist, to help with getting the players' minds right. Jack fed off the energy he got from Coyle but it wasn't rammed down the throats of the players – it was more or less there for whoever needed it.

Some took it on board wholesale. Others weren't that interested. Cooper himself fell somewhere in between. He took bits and pieces with him but for the past few years, he's set his own routine and he's known how to cope with the hype and the hyperbole. He's had to. Grow up quick or die trying is how it's been and he's flourished like a beanstalk.

Once, on a wet, miserable Killarney day with a black sky hanging above the mountains, Colm Cooper was thrown into the furnace with no more than a few positive words as preparation. One league start and one championship appearance is all he had by way of an introduction.

Just a few months before, he was playing in the East Kerry minor league but already it was caterpillar to butterfly time. Ireland played Spain in the World Cup that morning. Kerry played Cork in a Munster semi-final. Most kept their souls dry in the nearby bars. Those who did come to see his first game against Cork still couldn't have fathomed the ammunition he had, couldn't have seen he would soon score goals just to watch the netting billow.

Cooper was substituted before half-time in a terrible game that ended in a draw. Kerry lost the replay but after that, he lit the summer up, this copper strobe with magical feet.

Facing page:
*Colm Cooper
– Killarney's latest
Prince of Forwards.*
(Sportsfile)

He gave a series of Roy of the Rovers displays. You know the kind. We barely saw the player, just the whoosh lines he left behind as he swerved towards goal. It was comic strip class.

That chip against Fermanagh. The goal against Kildare after three minutes. Four points from play against Galway. The Gooch owned the qualifiers. Then he came of age – at nineteen – and pinged 1-5 against Cork in the All-Ireland semi-final. That year, he burst onto the radar like a bolt of new lightning and football's deft saviour. It was hallelujah stuff. Remember?

'In 2002, we played the best football since I've been with Kerry,' he says. 'Everything was going so rosy, the momentum was just building and there was no way I saw us losing to Armagh in the final.'

That was the only time he made such presumptions.

Back then, he was shielded from some of the commotion because he was so young. The week of the final, he turned up at Fitzgerald Stadium for a press night, got talking to a reporter and all of a sudden, there were a dozen dictaphones whirring in front of him.

There must have been a wince on the Gooch's face because Páidí sensed his unease, strolled up and told him to go stretch his legs. He'd field the questions and take the heat. Páidí was clever like that.

But after the Armagh game, there would be no more cocoons, only the cold sense of reality in October and November.

'It was a lonely place for a few weeks. Like, you're going into Christmas and it's still on your mind. Then you have the GAA shows at the end of the year, replaying games and you're watching them going "Oh Jesus, how did we leave it slip?" We had plenty chances.'

These few years he has known nothing but long seasons, coiled with intensity and a magnifying glass over his head and it feels as if he's been around since forever.

The evening after Cooper gave a masterclass in that final against Mayo in 2004, he found some time and space away from the party with Eoin Brosnan and Marc Ó Sé – each one a first time medalist that night. Marc told Eoin and Colm that he had been part of a strange conversation a few days previously. Somebody stopped him and asked would this be his second or third medal if Kerry won on Sunday. Marc couldn't believe it. The person who asked, he told the lads, reckoned he must be around for long enough to have bagged at least one by now.

Then Eoin said he was asked the same thing that very week and the Gooch, 21 years old now, said he knew exactly what they were saying. He'd been getting it as well.

The three of them laughed when they realised they weren't alone in being pegged for an ancient footballer.

When he remembers the aftermath of Mayo that year, he can sense the weightlessness of it all.

'To walk into the Burlington with the suit and the bag over the back was massive. Meeting the family. The parents, proud as punch. There was just great fun around at that time.'

For two years before that the road was blocked and the manner of Kerry's defeat in that infamous semi-final with Tyrone in 2003 had been claustrophobic.

'Half-time it was a case of "What's happening here?" It was like a train ramming into us. We weren't expecting it to be honest and it's hard to find that switch in the middle of a game to say, "Right, let's cop ourselves on." Because it wasn't there and we didn't react as well as we needed to. That day it was like we didn't have air to breathe.

'After that, there were a lot of questions asked in Kerry about certain players, managers, selectors. Maybe a few thought we wouldn't be back in a final for a long time.'

When he pebble-dashed the final with his magic in 2004, there was just no going back. Everything jumped a notch. The attention, the expectation. The Gooch effect.

After Kieran Donaghy arrived on the scene in 2006, in much the same way as Cooper had, it was welcome relief. For weeks he was hearing how his form had vanished, how his mojo had left him and even though he never really asked, he was told why.

Cooper dealt with it. In his own time, he went away and had a long think and reckoned with all the football he's been playing, well, he's entitled to some average games at some stage. The beanstalk had reached maturity.

Against Armagh in the quarter-final that year, Donaghy himself was taking the flack. The crowd was on his back, the goalkeeper was in his ear. When Donaghy spilled a high ball, the focus intensified. Cooper knew the drill.

'It would have been very easy for Kieran to crack. You could see he was questioning himself, so we just had a quiet word for a few seconds. At times, it feels weird that I'm the man giving the boost. Like, I still feel young but I suppose there isn't a load more left for me to see on a football field.'

So, he goes into the final and kicks 1-2. Anybody else on the field does that, anybody on the planet does that and they'll dip the guy in gold. But for the Gooch, they tell him it's a work-a-day haul. But it's the standard he's set himself.

It's the curse of brilliance.

TJF

Kieran Donaghy

He's stretched out on the bed with his shoes off and his suit on.

It's a good two hours since Declan O'Sullivan and Colm Cooper lifted Sam Maguire but it's only now that his belly is beginning to fill with butterflies. His heart is still pounding at full pelt and it feels like it could burst through his chest and splash onto the floor of Jury's at any minute. Wow. An All-Ireland medal. His first.

His head is spinning. There's a circus of thoughts going on in there and he needs to take twenty minutes to gather himself before he lets himself loose on the evening to come.

All that noise and celebration and those three pints of cool cider (his first drop of the stuff in six weeks) are all adding up and taking their toll.

He rolls over and turns on his phone. Beep. Beep. Beep. 67 text messages fly in before he shuts it off again and closes his eyes. Oh man. What a day! What a year!

Not once did he think it would go like this back before the Longford game in July. The nerves that day were the worst ever. His first game at full-forward, in the kamakaze position and all eyes on him.

In his mind, full-forward is the best of times and the worst of times. Catch some handy ones and you're sorted. Fumble one or two and they'll be baying for you. Nobody looks at who kicks it in, only who's inside jumping for possession. He knows how it works and before Longford, he's starting to second guess himself, which is nothing new, but it's getting so bad now that it's almost silly. What if he fucks up? Spills a few sitters? Rifles a few wide? What if Kerry actually lose to Longford and Kieran Donaghy is never heard of again?

The League had gone well. Very well, in fact. Midfield with Darragh and they were cleaning up. Jack O'Connor would pull them both aside every once in a while and show them the midfield stats. 80/20. 70/30. Gave them a pat on the back and said well done. Keep it going lads.

He had just settled into the centre and before Longford, Donaghy can't stop wondering if this whole full-forward thing is too much of a gamble. Maybe he should have just stayed out the field.

Even the early warm-up, half an hour before the match, didn't settle him like it should have done. The legs were heavy and the shoulders tense. The team headed for the dressing room and Donaghy began to count the minutes to throw in. The game can't start fast enough but just before they're about to run onto

Facing page:
Kieran Donaghy salutes his grandmother in the crowd after his goal in the 2006 All-Ireland final.
(Sportsfile)

403

the field, there's a knock at the door. Traffic is bad in town. Match delayed by fifteen minutes. He can't relax now. It's agony. He's pacing and wild. Moynihan tells him to calm down. Gooch throws him a glance.

'In the end, I thought there was something wrong with me. I thought I was after eating bad chicken or something so I went over to the doctor and said, "Doctor, doctor, you have to give me a shot or something, I'm sick from the food." He said, "What's wrong with you?" "My stomach is in bits." He said it was in my head and gave me a Motilium tablet.

'Then, when we got out I started to feel a bit more bouncy all right but the first two balls sailed over my head. The third one was coming in and I was saying, "I have to win this." If I dropped it, next thing fellas in the crowd would be saying, "Take that big long useless fucker out of full-forward." I know well that's what they'd be saying, 'cos, you know, I was the same on the terraces. If they were trying some new big fella out at full-forward and your season on the line, you'd have to see him winning ball. Otherwise he'd have to go.'

Donaghy begins to wade into the game. After 25 minutes, Kerry have tacked 3-4 on the scoreboard and his hands are on all but one score. He finds his breath and his afternoon is a breeze.

Longford settled him but after that, with Armagh just seven days away, the chorus started up again. Francie Bellew was waiting for him, they said. For a full week it was Francie this and Francie that but Donaghy wasn't nervous this time. He had it sorted in his head.

'My attitude was, I won't bate him but I won't let him bate me either.'

When it was over, he came back home to Tralee and felt the sun on his back. Summer was breaking and life was good. For a full fortnight, his uncle Brian Fitzgerald re-lived the Armagh game to him.

It was Brian's favourite. It cracked him up. Then, it cracked Kieran up that it cracked Brian up.

'Brian would be going up to Croke Park the past few years listening to [breaks into an Ulster accent] "How's about you, where's your Kerry football now?" And Brian walking out after the games with his tail between his legs and Tyrone and Armagh lads shouting after him. That's why it was Brian's favourite game of all time I'd say.

'We watched it back together the following Tuesday and the boys were outstanding. That old hoodoo thing was gone. It was my first time playing a northern team in the championship but I had still felt the pressure of the hoodoo thing. I wasn't worried about Francie Bellew, I wasn't worried about Armagh. I was worried about losing and them all coming out with this thing of a Kerry team with players like Seamo and Darragh and Mike Mac, Mahony and all these stalwarts and them saying

"Oh, they can't beat these northern sides."

'And it bothered me, like. It bothered me when I was a fan. I hated all those games when we lost to them. That was the only pressure going into the Armagh game. I couldn't live with fellas in Kerry going, "Ye couldn't get past them northern teams again." It was a real factor for me personally, in that I made sure I kept going 'til the end.'

Things just ballooned after that. The world changed. A leap and a goal against Armagh and the way people looked at football shifted once more. Catch it and kick it – just like the old days.

He repeated the trick in the final against Mayo, buried another goal and veered off to his right, pointing to his grandmother who was sitting by the sideline. It was her first time going to any game.

'The hips are bad by her, you see, so they brought her in on a wheelchair. For years and years she'd always say, "Get me a goal." That was her thing. Even when I was a Stacks minor, she'd say, "Get me an 'aul goal." And I wouldn't have a hope of getting any goal. Like, I was playing midfield. I'd say, "Ah, I'll try my best." Then I'd come back and she'd ask, "Did you get me a goal?" "Nah." That was the answer most of the time.'

He got her the goal when it mattered though. He did more than that. He lightened the mood of a whole county and changed the direction of the game.

It's all just sinking in when there's a knock on his hotel room door. Time to go and let the moment wash through him. His eyes are open and he wonders if it's really true, that he really has an All-Ireland medal.

'People say you pinch yourself after the first one. Too right you do. Because for me, a lot of fellas, say the Gooch or Seamo, when they were young they knew they were good enough to make the Kerry team. I never thought I'd make it. Never. It was even a surprise when I made the minors.'

He throws his shoes back on, opens the door, strides down the corridor to the elevator, a spring in his step, a medal in his pocket and the future in his hands.

TJF